Oriental Export Market Porcelain

Geoffrey A. Godden

Oriental Export Market Porcelain
and its influence on European Wares

GRANADA
London Toronto Sydney New York

Published by Granada Publishing 1979

Granada Publishing Limited
Frogmore, St Albans, Herts AL2 2NF
and
3 Upper James Street, London W1R 4BP
1221 Avenue of the Americas, New York, NY 10020, USA
117 York Street, Sydney, NSW 2000, Australia
100 Skyway Avenue, Toronto, Ontario, Canada M9W 3A6
110 Northpark Centre, 2193 Johannesburg,
South Africa
CML Centre, Queen & Wyndham, Auckland 1, New
Zealand

Copyright © 1979 by Geoffrey A. Godden

ISBN 0 246 11057 0

Printed and bound at
William Clowes & Sons Limited
Beccles and London

All rights reserved. No part of this publication may be
reproduced, stored in a retrieval system, or transmitted,
in any form or by any means, electronic, mechanical,
photocopying, recording or otherwise, without the prior
permission of the publisher.

Granada Publishing ®

Frontispiece A superb circular dish from the Lee service showing in the border the two extremes of the journey: the Pearl river below Whampoa and the London sky-line (see p. 16). Diameter $9\frac{7}{8}$ inches, *c.* 1730.   *Godden of Worthing Ltd*

Contents

	Acknowledgements	
	Preface	
1	The East India Company's porcelain trade	15
2	The 'Private Trade' imports	55
3	The *Earl of Elgin*, East Indiaman	89
4	The blue and white porcelains	111
5	The enamelled wares	165
6	The armorial, crested and initialled wares	195
7	The special designs and the figure and animal models	221
8	*Blanc de Chine*	257
9	The American market wares	281
10	The Japanese porcelains	301
11	The influence of Oriental wares on European porcelains	339
12	European decorated Oriental porcelains	363
	Selected Bibliography	376
	Index	382

Other books by Geoffrey A. Godden

Victorian Porcelain
Encyclopaedia of British Pottery and Porcelain Marks
Antique China and Glass under £5
An Illustrated Encyclopaedia of British Pottery and Porcelain
The Handbook of British Pottery and Porcelain Marks
Minton Pottery and Porcelain of the First Period
Caughley and Worcester Porcelains
Stevengraphs and Other Victorian Silk Pictures
Jewitt's Ceramic Art of Great Britain, 1800–1900
(Revised, edited and re-illustrated edition 1972)
The Illustrated Guide to Lowestoft Porcelain
The Illustrated Guide to Mason's Patent Ironstone China
The Illustrated Guide to Ridgway Porcelains
British Porcelain: an Illustrated Guide
British Pottery: an Illustrated Guide
Godden's Guide to English Porcelain

Acknowledgements

Very many people have given much valuable help to me in the preparation of this book over a number of years. In particular I am indebted to the Librarian and Keeper of the India Office Records in London and to the helpful staff there who have assisted me over so long a period in working my way through the mass of records relating to the English East India Company's trade to and from China from the seventeenth into the nineteenth century.

I list with gratitude other persons who have aided me in this project and apologise to anyone whom I may have inadvertently neglected to mention: J. C. Ayers, Keeper, Far Eastern Section, Victoria and Albert Museum, London; Theodore Beckhardt, New York; E. Bletcher, F. L. A.; Roger Bluett; R. J. Charleston; Committee of The English Ceramic Circle; A. J. H. du Boulay, Messrs Christies; A. F. Farrington; D. M. Forrest; John S. Godden; Leslie Godden; A. Green; Graham Hood, Director Colonial Williamsburg; David S. Howard; Mrs Jean Le Corbeiller, The Metropolitan Museum of Art, New York; R. E. Marston, F.L.A.; The Director, The National Maritime Museum; David Newbon; Miss Anne Pollen, Messrs Sotheby & Co.; The Keeper of Public Records, London; E. Clive Rouse; George Savage; Julian Thompson, Messrs Sotheby & Co.; Earle D. Vandekar; Christopher Weston, Messrs Phillips; Roderick Whitfield, Assistant Keeper, Dept. of Oriental Antiquities, British Museum; Geoffrey Wills.

The large selection of mainly hitherto unpublished illustrations is due to the generous co-operation of the following persons or concerns. To all these individuals – private owners, auctioneers, dealers, directors of museums and others – I am greatly indebted and trust that they will feel that they have contributed to a worthwhile book of lasting benefit to all collectors.

The Art Exchange, New York (T. Beckhardt)
Pls. 33–5, 73, 82, 84, 107, 125, 132, 138–9, 150, 159, 171, 210, 213–15, 219
Ashmolean Museum, Oxford
Pls. 120, 137
Blenheim Palace Coll.
Pl. 199
Bristol City Art Gallery
Pl. 20
Trustees of the British Museum
Pls. 10, 70, 117, 181, 190, 194
E. H. Chandler, Esq.
Pl. 146
Mr & Mrs Cheng Te K'un
Pl. 202
Messrs Christies, London
Pls. 83, 85, 109, 114–15, 123, 145, 151–2, 173, 180, 245, 287
D. Cowell, Brighton
Colour Plate 14; 2, 81
P. J. Donnelly, Esq.
Pls. 185, 191, 197, 200, 203–4
Geoffrey Godden Chinaman
Colour Plate 6; 257, 260, 265, 268, 274, 277–8, 285, 288, 289
Godden of Worthing Ltd
Colour Plates Frontispiece, 3, 7–11, 13, 15–20
Plates 1, 3, 7, 23, 26–7, 29–32, 36–44, 46–69, 74, 77–80, 88–95, 99, 101–2, 104–5, 110, 118–19, 122, 127–31, 133–4, 136, 142–4, 166, 175, 183–4, 187–9, 205, 212, 217–18, 221–6, 229, 236–8, 248, 251, 259, 261–3, 266, 269–73, 275–6, 280, 282, 290
India Office Records
Pls. 9, 230, 232
Messrs Liberty & Co., London
Pls. 71, 72, 182, 241–2, 244
H. L. Lloyd, Esq.
Pl. 45
Messrs Maple & Co., London
Pl. 100

David Newbon, London
Pl. 252
Peabody Museum of Salem, USA
Pl. 208
J. R. Peers, Esq.
Pl. 113
Messrs Phillips, London
Pls. 28, 235
Pottery Gazette
Pl. 243
Reeves Coll., Washington & Lee University, USA
Pls. 206–7, 209, 211
Herbert Schiffer Antiques Inc., USA
Pl. 216
Sotheby & Co., London
Pls. 12, 15–16, 25, 96–8, 103, 108, 112, 124, 126, 140, 155–7, 160, 162–5, 167–70, 172, 176–9, 192–3, 196, 198, 227, 231, 234, 239–40, 246–7, 250, 253, 255, 258, 264, 267, 283
Messrs Sotheby's, Belgravia, London
Pls. 111, 220
Messrs Sotheby Parke Bernet Inc., New York
Pl. 161
Earle D. Vandekar, London
Pls. 13, 86–7, 106, 154, 158, 174
Victoria and Albert Museum (Crown Copyright)
Pls. 4–6, 21–2, 121, 135, 141, 153, 186, 195, 233, 256, 279, 281, 284, 286
J. Waring, Brighton
Pl. 24

Some further private owners have asked that their names should not be listed and in such cases the general credit 'Private collection' is given in the caption.

I would like to thank Derek Gardiner and A. J. Whitcomb of Messrs Walter Gardiner, Photographers of Worthing, for so painstakingly posing and photographing the many illustrations credited to Geoffrey Godden Chinaman and to Messrs Godden of Worthing Ltd.

I am also indebted to my typists Miss Janet Belton, Mrs K. Gregory and Miss Rosemary Manley for interpreting my longhand notes in such a willing and accurate manner.

Preface

The porcelains discussed and illustrated in this book have been variously called 'Lowestoft', 'Chinese-Lowestoft', 'Oriental-Lowestoft', 'East India China', 'Export Porcelain', 'China Trade Porcelain'. The French terms 'Compagnie des Indes' or 'Chine de Commande' are also sometimes used, particularly on the Continent. Other names are applied to individual types or styles of decoration, for example 'Canton' or 'Nankin', but all these wares are basically Chinese porcelains made expressly for the European market, and also for North America. I employ the clear, self-explanatory term 'Chinese export market porcelain' to describe these varied and interesting wares, which in the contemporary records were referred to simply as 'china-ware'.

The Chinese export market porcelains destined for Great Britain were carried from China (often by way of India) mainly in the ships of the Honourable East India Company, stowed low in the holds to give the vessel stability, below the teas which comprised the bulk of the homeward cargo in the eighteenth century. The fact that these Chinese porcelains were shipped in vessels chartered to the East India Company, that these vessels traded also with India and with Indian goods and that they were subsequently sold by the East India Company at auction in London sometimes gave rise to the term 'India China' and this description is not so far wide of the mark, for early in the eighteenth century some of the Chinese and Japanese porcelain was trans-shipped in India, sometimes being carried home to England in vessels which had not visited either China or Japan.

The standard Chinese porcelain body was of the true, or hard-paste, variety and was that which the Europeans had striven to produce for hundreds of years. Without the ideal of the white and translucent Chinese porcelain which found its way into Europe from quite early times, it is possible that eighteenth- and even nineteenth-century European potters would have been content to produce traditional clay-coloured earthenwares rather than fine white porcelain.

Although previously the study of Oriental and British ceramics has been treated as two entirely separate subjects, there is close interplay. The story of eighteenth-century Chinese export market wares is firmly linked with British manufacturers, and Chinese wares are widely and quite thickly distributed throughout the British Isles. This interplay explains my own interest in the subject and the preparation of this book for, while I am known for my interest in English ceramics, it is true to say that I have in the course of business handled as much Chinese porcelain as I have English, if not more. The firm of which I am now a director has bought and sold some of the finest and most interesting examples of Chinese export market porcelains to be discovered in the present century, pieces that are now in famous collections and museums.

Also, while researching various aspects of British ceramics, I came across several hitherto unrecorded contemporary references to Chinese export market wares and, even when working on the site of the Caughley porcelain factory in the heart of the English countryside, I found many fragments of Chinese porcelains, for the Caughley management apparently traded in both Chinese porcelains and their own wares – which were to a great degree modelled on the fashionable Chinese styles of decoration and shape (see Chapter 11). The link between Chinese and British potters is even more remarkable when one considers that reputedly some British porcelain manufacturers included ground-up Chinese porcelain in their own mix, and that the Chinese potters themselves used British flint shipped to China on the very boats which brought the finished Chinese porcelain back to Britain.

One of the main objects of this book is to illustrate the very close connection between the Chinese and British porcelains made some fifteen thousand miles apart and to show the influence which the Chinese wares had on the growing British porcelain industry and on the market for which they both competed. I also hope to foster a greater general understanding of these eighteenth-century export market porcelains and of the Anglo-Chinese trade of the period.

Readers who believe themselves to be well-versed in this subject will find here several surprises, for much hitherto unpublished material has shed new light on Oriental wares, and the picture now painted differs in several respects from that given by other authorities. The story is told with the help of many quotations from the contemporary documents still available. This source material supports new, often startling statements that might otherwise be regarded as dogmatic but which can be seen to be well confirmed and authoritative.

While this work is, in the main, concerned with eighteenth-century Chinese porcelain it has been thought prudent to include a chapter on the Japanese wares for it is not generally understood that in the early years of the eighteenth century the two British East India Companies were importing nearly as much Japanese porcelain as Chinese. These Japanese porcelains are in general very little understood in Europe. For this reason the book is titled 'Oriental' rather than 'Chinese' Export Market Porcelains.

Geoffrey A. Godden
19 Crescent Road
Worthing
Sussex

IN MEMORY
of the many eighteenth-century
East Indiamen who lost their lives in bringing
Chinese porcelains and other wares to Europe

1 The East India Company's porcelain trade

A brief résumé

At the close of the eighteenth century there was in Europe more porcelain from China than from all the European factories combined.

In the middle of the eighteenth century the famous European porcelain factories at Meissen in Germany, Sèvres in France and Chelsea in England were principally concerned with producing prestige pieces often of an ornamental nature for the wealthy, rather than useful wares for the masses. The Chinese potters, on the other hand, were supplying vast quantities of useful wares for the humbler European homes – porcelains decorated in the main with underglaze blue designs rather than the enamelled wares favoured by the leading Continental manufacturers. For the 1749–50 season the British vessels brought home only 'useful sorts – not above one-tenth part of the coloured sort'.

The one great advantage enjoyed by the Chinese potters was prestige. Their forefathers had introduced translucent porcelain long before the Europeans succeeded in emulating it. For centuries travellers and others had keenly sought the Oriental porcelains which had achieved the international reputation that was to remain long after the Europeans' own porcelains were perfected. A certain wonderment was occasioned by all objects brought from the mysterious and largely unexplored East. The current taste was for all things Chinese. A writer in 1755 noted: '...almost everywhere all is Chinese...every chair in an apartment, the frames of glasses [mirrors] and tables must be Chinese; the walls covered with Chinese paper...'

The fine Chinese porcelain circular dish shown in the Frontispiece is a fitting commencement to my consideration of these Chinese export market porcelains. It is a single piece from a fine set of plates and dishes which my father purchased over thirty years ago and it represents one of my earliest

Colour Plate 1 A thinly potted and superbly painted Chinese porcelain saucer of the 1730–40 period, the centre, at least, very much in the Chinese taste. Diameter $4\frac{1}{2}$ inches.

Private collection

1A Detail of a border panel from the plate shown in the Frontispiece depicting a Chinese rendering of the London skyline.

memories of Chinese export porcelain. The panels (Plates 1A and B) in the border are highly appropriate to the main theme of this book, linking China with Great Britain.

Two identical panels show the River Thames, with the old London Bridge in the foreground and a Chinese painter's version of the London skyline copied from an early-eighteenth-century print – a mass of church spires and the dome of St Paul's standing high in contrast to the low-level dwellings. The remaining two opposite panels show the Pearl River below Canton, the destination of the vessel.

The order for this Chinese porcelain dinner-service and for an armorial tea-service which was made for the same Lee family at a period before 1734 would have been received by a representative of the Honourable East India Company in London, or by a captain of an East Indiaman, and carried on such a vessel from the River Thames to Canton (Kwangchow or Kuang-Chou in the Chinese language) on the Pearl River. As the decoration is entirely in overglaze enamels, this special subject relating to an individual order was perhaps painted by the enamellers who worked in Canton embellishing, at short notice, undecorated porcelains or 'blanks' made at Ching-tê Chên, the great inland centre for the manufacture of porcelain in China. However, Ching-tê Chên was by no means the only centre of porcelain manufacture in China; much was made at or near Tê-hua, in Fukien Province. Of these Fukien wares the white *Blanc de Chine* figures and related wares are the best known (see Chapter 8).

The Canton enamellers would have had available a coloured drawing (or engraved book-plate) of the Lee family's armorial bearings, crest and Latin motto and this, with the other relevant instructions, would have been given to the Chinese merchant at Canton by the ship's captain or by a 'Supra-cargo'. The term 'Supra-cargo' was used by the London East India Company from at least 1682. The East India Company vessels carried a team of Supra-cargoes, a chief and two or three assistants, some of whom enjoyed personal servants and many privileges. These Supra-cargoes were in effect responsible for the financial success of the voyage, selling to the best advantage the outward cargo of British exports and buying the right quantities of saleable Chinese merchandise at the lowest possible price. They were the Company's representatives on the vessel and could, and often did, give orders to the ship's captain who was merely responsible for getting his vessel to China and home again in the shortest possible time. In some early records the Supra-cargoes were termed 'Factors'.

The Supra-cargoes were not normally paid a fixed wage; their reward was reflected at first in the large amount of private trade in which they were permitted to engage, both on the outward and on the homeward voyage. They were also allowed, as an encouragement, a percentage of the total profit of the voyage. The directors of the East India Company in London appointed a Council of Supra-cargoes to sit at the Chinese port to control all their sales and purchases. These resident Supra-

1B   Detail of a border panel from the plate shown in the Frontispiece depicting the Chinese fortifications on the approaches to Whampoa and Canton   *Godden of Worthing Ltd*

cargoes often lived in luxury and had clerks and other staff to look after their daily requirements. Their diaries and journals often contained copies of the letters and reports sent home to London. Today these are of the utmost interest and have helped us to appreciate anew the conditions encountered in this Anglo-Chinese trade nearly three hundred years ago. I have retained the original spelling 'Supra-cargo', as used in the Company's records, but the modern spelling is 'supercargo'.

Once the Lee service was completed it would have been packed in chests and loaded aboard an available East Indiaman for the homeward journey (perhaps by way of India) to London, where it arrived some two or more years after the order was originally placed. Such a wait was, however, by no means unreasonable, for before the 1740s there were no English porcelain manufactories at all, and even in the early 1800s the English manufactories themselves sometimes required three or more years to fulfil a large order. In the early years the East India Company directors were not over-anxious about speed, their vessels being mainly engaged in trade with their stations in India, and we find records such as 'Resolved. That no ship be sent out for China this year to return directly to England.'

(Court Minute, 1 October 1702.)

However, the distance between Europe and China, in language and custom as well as in miles, did present problems. As demonstrated by many of the specimens reproduced in this book, the naive idea the Chinese had of European design and lettering left much to be desired, and the point must be made that some of the later wares were of purely commercial quality, made for a market the Chinese makers did not understand and held in little or no esteem. The lack of understanding between the Chinese manufacturers and their European customers resulted in many curious errors. Such errors today represent collector's jewels but they must have caused great anguish to the original owner who, having waited some two years for the delivery of a porcelain service painted with his coat of arms, found to his dismay that the porcelain bore an all-too-faithful copy of his original sketch, perhaps even with the words 'yellow', 'red' or 'blue' exactly copied where he had helpfully written the instructions on his drawing. On a less disastrous scale it may readily be assumed that the person, a Mr Bewicke, who in the 1740s ordered the armorial painted bowl shown in Plate 2, added to the original drawing the friendly note 'our coat of arms', which was faithfully copied on to the porcelain in a fair imitation of the owner's handwriting.

Many of the pieces made expressly for the European market are often more European than Oriental in feeling although a happy marriage of styles was frequently achieved. Other Chinese porcelains were very near the native taste and some of the thinly-potted porcelains termed 'egg-shell' can be superb, especially the tea-bowls and saucers which, even after some 250 years, are not notably rare in Europe today. The 'egg-shell' saucer illustrated in Colour Plate 1 displays little or no European influence, apart from the over-ornate border, and it is of exquisite quality.

2 A Chinese porcelain bowl of the 1740 period meticulously painted with a copy of the Bewicke arms together with the owner's written notation 'Our Coat of Arms' all too faithfully copied on to the porcelain. *D. Cowell, Brighton*

In general, the English East India Company's regular shipments consisted of purely utilitarian tablewares, mostly decorated in underglaze blue; in fact, some of the early imports were probably of earthenware or stoneware rather than of translucent porcelain. The contemporary records include very many early-eighteenth-century references to 'coarse cups', and one log, that of the *Oley*, gives an interesting reference to these: 'At three this afternoon rec'd on board nine tubbs of China earthenware cupps ordinary; being the first goods that were received on board we hoisted our colours and fired one gun according to the old custom. The nine tubbs is said to contain 12,135 cupps.' (Log dated 3 January 1707.)

The British trade in Chinese products (par-

The East India Company's porcelain trade

ticularly in china-ware or porcelain) started extremely slowly; it hardly existed before 1680 (although Chinese porcelains were by then well known and had been long emulated by British delft-ware potters), but it quickly gained momentum after 1710. The objects already illustrated and briefly discussed – the armorial porcelains and the fine quality pieces – were not in fact the imports of the English East India Company. They were certainly carried in its vessels but as the private venture of the captains, the officers and crew, or of the Company's agents the Supra-cargoes.

The Chinese porcelains imported into Great Britain fall into two main categories: (1) The Company's own imports; (2) The wares imported as Private Trade.

To understand the full story of the development of the vast Anglo-Chinese trade we must start here by clarifying the position – and names – of the various British trading companies.

The first of these, the London East India Company, received its Royal Charter on 31 December 1600, its full title being 'The Governor and Company of Merchants of London trading into the East Indies'. A new,[1] separate company received its charter in September 1698. This was called 'The English Company trading to the East Indies' or more informally the 'New Company' to distinguish it from the 'Old Company'. From 1698 the New Company was largely instrumental in opening up the trade in china-ware, both at the Chinese port of Chusan and at Canton (see p. 30).

The two rival companies reached outline agreement on amalgamation on 22 July 1702. The directors of the two companies now worked in some concert (references being made to their 'United Shipping' or the 'United Trade') until the official amalgamation in March 1709. The total combined capital was then calculated at £2,196,300. The new title was 'The United Company of Merchants of England trading to the East Indies', a cumbersome description subsequently shortened to the familiar 'Honourable East India Company'. Most references in this book, certainly those after 1709, relate to vessels and cargoes of this company, to which I have added the prefix 'English' to distinguish it from the similar companies of other European nations – French, Dutch, Swedish, Danish and Portuguese, to name the most important.

This book is concerned mainly with eighteenth-century and later Chinese (and Japanese) porcelains but some wares, now rare, pre-date this period. Chinese porcelains were arriving in Europe, and particularly in Portugal, early in the seventeenth century, if not before. In 1596 two London merchants, Richard Allot and Thomas Bromefield, set out on a voyage to Peking carrying a letter from Elizabeth I requesting that their English merchandise be exchanged for Chinese goods. Unfortunately they never reached China.

Some of the earliest Chinese porcelains to arrive in Holland were taken from captured Portuguese vessels; the *San Jago*'s cargo was auctioned in Holland in 1602, and some sixty tons of china-ware from the *Catarina* were sold in 1604. These early Portuguese trading vessels were called 'Carraca' and from this term the word 'Carrack' or 'Kraak' has been used to describe a class of broadly painted blue and white dishes and other wares mainly of the 1600–50 period. The earliest recorded oil-painting to show this type of Chinese blue and white porcelain is a banquet piece by Nicolaes Gillis dated 1611; three dishes filled with fruits and nuts are depicted. A typical Carrack ware dish is shown in Plate 3.

In 1614 the Dutch East India Company's ship *Gelderland* brought to Holland nearly 70,000 pieces

---

[1] For the purposes of this book we can overlook the separate Courteen association of the 1630s, especially as this was absorbed by the London Company in 1649.

3 A large circular dish broadly painted in a dark underglaze blue of the type known as 'Carrack ware' after the Portuguese trading vessels captured by the Dutch early in the seventeenth century and which carried this type of Chinese porcelain. Diameter 15 inches, c. 1610–20.   *Godden of Worthing Ltd*

The East India Company's porcelain trade

of Oriental porcelain, and soon the Dutch were sending drawings and models of special European shapes to be copied by Oriental potters, but from the middle of the seventeenth century the Dutch were mainly interested in Japanese wares imported into Europe by way of Formosa and their important trading-base at Batavia.

An English 'Factory', or trading-station, was established at Firando (Hirado) Japan in 1613, another at Taiwan (Formosa) in 1625, and in 1627 the original English Company had attempted to open trade with Canton by way of Macao, the island down-river from Canton, lying on the eastern side of the entrance to the Hsi Chiang River. The Portuguese, however, who already enjoyed trading rights there (dating from as far back as 1515), resisted the efforts of the British traders. Nevertheless, the London Company's records include reference to trade with Canton as early as April 1637. This was, however, on a very small scale, and it was not until Oliver Cromwell's Treaty of 1654 with King John IV of Portugal that free trading was opened to the ships of both countries to any port in the Indies, but even then the amount of china-ware brought home was extremely small and the supply spasmodic.

The early Oriental porcelains were, however, highly regarded in Europe. Some examples were richly mounted in silver or ormolu in Europe and the wares became a fashionable present between royalty or heads of state. The royal passion for Oriental porcelain helped considerably to increase its popularity, not only for use on the table, but for purely decorative purposes, as we can deduce from descriptions of Queen Mary II's seventeenth-century collection, most of which was housed at Hampton Court.

Although the Oriental porcelains were in great demand from about 1700 onwards, fifteen or so years earlier the directors of the London East India Company had shown little or no interest in this commodity. In the seventeenth century the Chinese goods that did reach England mainly came via the South Sea trading stations, and later from India. As early as June 1614 Captain Saris of the *Clove*, who had established the British trading station in Japan, wrote giving advice on the commercial aspects in the Southern Seas at that time. He noted:

I would not wish you to take in any pepper or china wares at Bantam, if you have time enough to recover Patanie and Syam by the begininge of February, for at those portes you shall meete the China Junckes, where you shall have greater trade, buy much cheaper, paye less custom and be in the way of the monsoone in the end of April to carry you for Japann afore the wind; from eather of which portes the voyage is usually made in 20 or 24 daies at most. Besides it is a temperatt place for your people, all things very plentiful and our nation resident in each place…

Having converted your [export] goods into silver, which disbursed in China silkes, Beniamine and spice for England, no doubt will make a proffitable voyage.

I quote this account of 1614 to make the point that although at that period there was no direct British trade with the Chinese mainland, Chinese junks were distributing their produce over a large area and the inter-trading between East and West was quite widespread.

The Anglo-Chinese trade was originally the concern of 'The Committee for Bantam and the South Sea Factories'. Bantam, in western Java, figures very early in the original English East India Company's trade with China, for Chinese junks were in the habit of bringing their goods for sale there and these articles certainly included porcelains. For example, in September 1615 John Jourdain reported home to London that the Company's vessel *James* had left Bantam on

1 February with china-ware, the prime cost of which he reported as:

Saucer dishes	nearly 2*d* each
possett dishes	4*d* each
small basins	1*s* 9*d* each
middle size basins	2*s* 6*d* each
large (or whole) basins	5*s* each

These are references to late Ming porcelains.

Bantam was the centre of British trade, just as Batavia was of the Dutch trade. In May 1617 the English 'Factory' at Bantam was required to send various porcelains to the King's treasurer at Isfahan in Persia, by way of a bribe to trade. These goods included: '200 dishes in sorts [sizes] to serve meat at table'. 'Their dishes here are like our English, broad and not deep and such ones he desireth. 100 small coffa dishes [coffee cups?].'

If we proceed forward some sixty years we see from the Company's Minute Book that Bantam still served as the British link with China: 'It is ordered that the secretary doe write to the Agent and Council at Bantam and therein enclose the several patterns of the colours of silks most desirable from China...' (17 November 1676.) Two points here are noteworthy: first, that the patterns were not sent from London straight to China. At that time there was no direct trade or shipping, only between London and Bantam and then between Bantam and China. Secondly, the directors' concern, at least in this order, was with fabrics, not with the importation of china-ware into England, and the auction sale records covering the imported goods confirm the almost total lack of china-ware at this pre-1690 period.

A Court Minute of 13 July 1677 appears to herald the commencement of a regular trade with China by way of Bantam. The relevant extract reads: '...we apprehend there will be a want of experienced persons to manage the Company's affairs in the said agency and for settling ye trade in China, which in short time may (through the blessing of God) prove very advantageous...'

From a subsequent Minute of 31 August 1677 we learn, however, that the Trade to China had begun slightly before this date:

...by the books [accounts] from Amoy we find that upon £5,000 cargo sent on the *Formosa* and *Advice* all the goods being then sold there was about 55 per cent gained, all charges paid except freight and factors salarys, besides the advantage of the goods bartered [this word is indistinct]...and upon ye whole debate we do offer it as our opinion, that the trade of Amoy be settled as being very hopeful for obtaining Japan and other goods at the best rates as well as for the vending of Europe and India goods...

The Court approved thereof...

It seems that the trading voyages of the *Formosa* and *Advice* in the early or mid-1670s pioneered the trade to China, and certainly from this period the original London East India Company took an increasing interest in it. It must be noted that, in the above quoted Minute, the chief concern was with the good profit gained on the export of goods *to* China, and that the port was Amoy.

The Company's Minute Book shows that the agents at Bantam ran their own vessels to and from China, and that the goods were then trans-shipped to India or sent home in other vessels trading between England and Bantam. For instance, under 7 November 1679, we find noted in the London records:

It is ordered that it be referred to the Committee for Bantam to consider of the best way and manner how the Company's trade in China and South Sea factories which is now carried on in a very chargeable manner by ships of their own may be managed by vessels to be freighted here and whether it will not be for the Company's interests to order the ship *Return* to be loaden with pepper and sent for England.

The East India Company's porcelain trade

And in a letter dated 26 November 1679, the directors in London wrote to their agent and Council in Bantam:

Upon a serious consideration of ye vast charge of ye shipping in Country ships [vessels not from Europe] we have resolved for ye future to manage ye trade from China and parts adjacent by freighted ship, which you may expect to be sent hence next year and therefore we do confirm unto you our order by ye *Caesar* to your sending home ye *Return* and also the *Tywan* and *Formosa* at their next return...

Hence we learn the names of the British vessels of the period that were engaged in the trade between Bantam and China, and we can also gauge when the company first began sending ships to China direct from London, some fifty years before the Dutch are believed to have sent their own vessels direct to China.

Two of the Bantam–China trading vessels mentioned by name in the November 1679 letter, the *Tywan* and the *Formosa*, were mentioned in a slightly earlier letter, from London to the President and Council at Surat (on the West coast of India) in a context which shows that the agents in Bantam were sending Chinese goods, including china-ware, to Europe via Surat, but that in this case they were not forwarded:

We note that you have disposed of several goods proper for Europe that came consigned to you from China on ye *Tywan* and *Formosa*, at very dispicable rates – as the thea [tea], china-ginger and china-ware – all of which would have yielded us great profit...and therefore we order you that henceforward you dispose of none of the said sorts of goods or any other proper for Europe – but that you send them to us by our shipping... (Letter dated 28 February 1679.)

Surat had been an important trading-post between Europe and China for many years, shared by the Dutch and the English, and probably by other nations. Volker in his excellently researched book *Porcelain and the Dutch East India Company... 1602–1682* quotes a letter of March 1618 from the Dutch company's agent at Surat reporting back to Amsterdam that the porcelains imported to Surat had not sold well 'because the Country everywhere is filled with it by the English'.

The Company's station or Factory at Tywan (Taiwan) or Formosa was closed in 1681. A large trade was also carried on with Tonquin (various spellings were employed, Tonqueens, etc) and much lacquer-ware was ordered from this source, also china-ware and pottery. In 1681 exactly the same instructions were sent to Tonquin (North Vietnam) as went to Amoy, 'cups of all kinds, sizes and colours and all sorts of small toyes...the more strange and novill the better' were requested, but the Supra-cargoes were warned off large beakers and jars which were then 'much out of esteeme'.

Not only did china-ware come from Tonquin, but some was purchased from the Chinese and Japanese trading junks at Batavia or from the merchants at this Dutch port. To underline the diversity of the Company's trading, it is worth mentioning that a single order concerning goods from Persia required not only Persian carpets but also a hundred chests of 'Earthenware of Carmania and Muskatt, made in imitation of china-ware of all sorts, the finest'. We cannot be sure whether these Near-Eastern earthenware copies were required because the Company still could not purchase enough of the true Chinese porcelain, or whether these copies were simply less expensive than the original.

The Company's agents at Bantam went in rotation to manage the trade at the Chinese port of Amoy and in Siam (the Company's Factory in Siam was closed in 1682), as is evidenced by a Court Minute of 24 October 1679. However, Bantam fell to the Dutch on 30 August 1682 in one of the many engagements which upset relations between the European nations engaged in Eastern trade, and the control of the English China trade was switched to Surat in October 1682, a decision taken, in fact, just before the fall of Bantam was known to the directors in London. Surat was not to remain long the centre of the English South Seas trade, for the directors had wind of the successful India–China trade being carried on by their Council at Fort St George, Madras. This great centre of trade had been established by the original English East India Company in 1643. In a letter of 13 February 1685 to the President and Council there, the directors in London sought to encourage and join them in this trade:

…We understand by Captain Harding that you have a profitable trade to China, which we do not grudge you but rather wish it may increase and that you may gain by all honest means as much as your selves can reasonably desire…

In all your trades to China and elsewhere we would have you – as becomes worthy publick spirited men such as we take you to be – to have as well a regard to the general good of the Company by increasing the trade and revenue at Fort St George, as the increase of your profits, and therefore we desire you that in such adventure you would admit to joyn with you not only such small stocks as our own servants have but likewise other inhabitants of our Fort and town – whether they be English, Portuguese or natives…and that place being become by such indulgence a mart for nations, it must consequently flourish and prosper exceedingly, that being the means to which God almighty of old promised to make Jerusalem great, viz. that it should be a mart for nations…

You have now a larger field to work in for the honour of the King, the good of your Country and the profit of this Company – that you know hath suffered so much of late years – than ever any of your Predecessors had, but if your minds be not as large as your Province the success will not answer our expectation. Narrow selfish souls are not frames for such work but we have reason to hope better of you…We have just now, and you have long since as we suppose, had intimation that the Emperor of China hath granted liberty to trade to the English and Dutch at Tywan [Formosa] and Amoy, so we hope you have effectively dispatched a small vessel with a proper cargo to Tywan on our account and would have you take care as soon as possibly you can to send another small vessel and right proper and fit persons to settle a factory at Amoy. We suppose two Factors and writers may be sufficient at first for Amoy…and that about £10,000 cargo.

It must be your great care to see that we pay freight neither out nor home for any more than our own goods or if you freight the vessel wholly for our account you must see that all Private goods whatsoever that go or return in any such freighter ship for our account do pay a full and just proportion of freight that we may be rather gainers than losers by such great indulgence to our servants…

An early reference to tea is made in this same letter of February 1685. Although the cultivation of tea in India was not to come for many years, we find here a reference to 'thea' (tea) shipped from India – at a time when its popularity in England was increasing after a slow start: 'In regard thea has grown to be a commodity here and we have occasion to make presents therein to our great friends at Court, we would have you send us yearly five or six canisters of the very best and freshest thea which will colour the water in which it is infused, a greenish complexion…'

The London Company certainly enjoyed friends at Court. Charles II had died on 2 February 1685, eleven days before this letter was written, and James II had succeeded to the throne, a state of affairs which seems to have met with the directors' approval, for they noted: 'The affairs of the Kingdom – blessed be God – continues on a very practical quiet posture as before, his Majestie is an adventurer in the Joynt Stock and is graciously pleased to vouchsafe us all possible encouragement in the carrying on of our Trade.'

The East India Company's porcelain trade

For the better 'carrying on of our Trade', the directors in the following letter transferred the affairs of China and the South Sea 'Factories' from Surat to Fort St George, Madras.

We have and doe appoint our Tonqueen, Atcheen, Amoy, Tywan and all other South Sea factories under the conduct and Government of our President and Council at Fort St George, because Surratt is more out of the way by the trouble of doubling the Cape of Zoilon.
We would have you forthwith settle a factory at Amoy if you find there is a leave given for a trade...
(To the President and Council at Fort St George, 16 March 1685.)

The high hopes which the directors in London shared regarding the China trade to be transacted through Fort St George got off to a bad start. Only twelve days after giving the President command over all the Company's South Sea Factories, they had cause to complain bitterly about goods which had just arrived via Madras:

We can now but briefly tell you that we are amazed at the prices you have invoiced to us, your own goods from Chyna, being 50 per cent as near as we can guess more than they will bring here...
The Rhubarb is not worth the freight, the thea generally trash...the thea cups dear at 1d apiece at the Fort – breakage considered...
We shall at more leizure think of proposing a method unto you wherein we may be saved from loss and you may be supported in all laudable attempts for the enlargement of trade...

This was followed-up in a letter dated 'London 14 January 1686':

We did in ours of March 28th and April 1st last express at large our just resentment touching ye China goods which you sent us on ye *Royal James*...we have since exposed ye china ware to sale which yielded but £1,053...and when ye buyers had paid for several lots upon view of them they found them crack'd and refused to take them away so that their money was to be returned to them...

There is evidence that the directors in London apparently had little or no idea of the ruling prices of Chinese china-ware, for the Court Minutes record:

It being represented unto ye Court that ye China goods brought home on ye *Royal James* are of a very mean quality and excessive dear. It is ordered that it be referred to Sir Jeremy Sambrooke, Mr Bowe, Mr Herne and Mr Sedgwick to examine whether ye agents and council at ye Fort had [directions or instructions? – this word is indistinct] for sending home such goods for ye Company's account and to inform themselves by Capt. Harding what he paid for ye Thea and other China goods by him brought and at what prices ye said goods might have been had in ye Country [China?] and to report the true state unto ye Court...
(Court Minutes of 25 March 1685.)

Captain Harding whose information was sought as to the cost of Chinese goods was Commander of the *Carolina* which sailed in the 1682–3 season to Batavia and Macao. It is strange that the Committee should need to ask Captain Harding the cost of his purchases and that the Company did not themselves have full records. This was probably because the *Carolina*'s china-ware comprised Private Trade (Chapter 2), not the Company's own purchases.

Two other Court Minutes relate to this chinaware imported on the *Royal James* from Fort St George, India. The first, dated 1 April 1685, reads: 'It is ordered that it be referred to Sir Samuel Dashwood and Mr Sedgwick to price the China goods brought home on ye *Royal James* which are appointed to be exposed to sale ye 14th instant.' A week later it was reported: 'The Court now appointed the China bowls and dishes to be put up at the [reserve] prices following, viz. 12*d* a piece the largest bowl, 8*d* the middle sort and 1*d* a piece the small ones.' These last ones were referred to as cups in the catalogue.

These wares were put up at auction in large lots such as:

1 chest, 10 bundles china bowls at 12*d*
4 tubs thea cups at 1*d*

On 13 and 15 April 1685 forty-one chests of bowls, 244 bundles and 107 tubs of cups were sold. As we have seen, however, the buyers refused some of the goods – which were, apparently, sold in unexamined chests, bundles or tubs – when the contents were found to be cracked.

These 1685 imports from Fort St George certainly seem to have proved troublesome but they represent the first goods shipped home by way of Madras. Contemporary letters and minutes show the lack of understanding in London of the Chinese market and prices and also the mundane types of china-ware then being imported, at a period before the trade in these wares was firmly established.

Surprisingly, we learn that as late as 1690 Chinese goods in general were not saleable in London. The directors in a letter of 3 October 1690 informed Fort St George:

China goods of all sorts are in a very low esteem here, we sell them cheaper than ever we did in times of peace. That trade hath been much overlaid of late and must be declined for a while to recover its reputation. Lacquered ware of Tonqueen and China are great druggs and so is thea, except it be superfine and comes in pots, tubs or chests that give it no ill scent of the oyl or any other matter. The custom upon thea here is alone five shillings a pound, whereas a mean sort of thea will not sell for above two shillings and six pence per pound.

In a slightly earlier letter dated February 1689, addressed to the Company's agents at Fort St George, the London directors stopped the purchase of china-ware on their account: 'The china bowles you sent us by the *Beaufort* and other china wares, were all too dear, buy no more such commodities for us...'

Luckily fashion, or the market, quickly changed and in January 1694 the directors in London requested that the *Dorothy* destined for the Chinese port of Amoy bring home 'China ware of all the variety that can be got in the Country, both fine and coarse.'

The position regarding other Chinese produce also improved, particularly regarding tea which was to become the main concern of the China-trade, and the real reason for sending the numerous East Indiamen to China throughout the eighteenth century.

However, statements to the effect that by the end of the seventeenth century large importations of porcelains from the Far East were coming into the country and that the East India Company had about fifty ships engaged in the trade are misleading in the extreme. Five ships a year bringing china-ware into Britain in the seventeenth century would be an exaggeration. In some years, even in the eighteenth century, none was sent, and some vessels carried relatively little china.

As late as June 1705, the London East India Company Minutes listed only eight vessels destined for all the Company's various trading stations:

Resolved that the following ships be sent out this year, viz. –

Coast and Bay [India]	2
Surat	1
Borneo	2
Bencoolen [the centre of the pepper trade]	1
China	1
Mocha	1

The single vessel sent to China was the *Oley* which took an outward cargo worth £25,000, but the required cargo to be brought home from China puts the china-ware trade into perspective. It was to comprise:

60 tons Singlo tea
20 tons Imperial tea
20 tons Bohea tea
20 tons copper
15 tons Quicksilver and Vermillion
15 tons Wrought silks
15 tons Raw Silk
10 tons China-ware
 3 tons China cloth
 2 tons Rubarb and China root
(Court Minutes, 12 September 1705.)

That is, a hundred tons of light-weight tea and thirty tons of silk to ten tons of comparatively heavy china-ware. In 1705 the New Company instructed its Supra-cargoes not to bring china-ware, 'the market being hard overloaden with it...' In June 1709 the Court of Directors of the now united Company still could not decide whether to send one or two ships to China in the following season:

Resolved, for China, one or two ships...and for the better ascertaining whether one or two ships – Ordered, that it be referred to the Committee of Warehouses to examine the goods brought home on the *Stringer* [1706–1709 voyage to Batavia and Chusan] with relation to their prime cost and what they will in likelihood yield here as also what profit was made on the outward-bound cargo, to the end this Court may be better able to judge what direction to give therein.

The directors chose the *Rochester* of 330 tons burthen as their China-trade vessel for the season 1710–11. However, the report on the profitability of the *Stringer*'s voyage must have been favourable, for in September 1709 we find minuted: 'Report from the Committee of Correspondence dated the 15th instant being read representing it to the Court as their opinion that a ship of about two hundred tons be taken up to be sent to China and thence to Mocha.'

The trade in china-ware was undoubtedly increasing, as was the demand for it, although in 1715 no British vessel was sent to China since the market was 'overglutted' with tea.

We can understand that the early Chinese porcelains caused wonderment and that the East India Company sale catalogues of such wares offered early in the eighteenth century printed conditions which seem quite remarkable today:

CHINA WARE
...to be taken with all faults, as cracked, snip'd or rub'd edges and none to be refused except visibly broken below the rims: no ringing to be allowed, nor any allowance to be made on any lots, on pretence of not answering the sample, difference of figures, or painting or any inequality or disproportion of bowls or plates, cups or saucers, or any other goods that match together, each lot to be taken more or less...

The Company was obviously taking advantage of its monopoly in the trade and of the saleability of Oriental porcelains. The goods sold even included lots of 'broken China ware' and teapots with odd covers, as '16 painted teapots, over-handles, 4 sorts, mostly odd covers' and lots obviously unbalanced in their make-up, such as '780 chocolate cups blue and white, 2 sorts, 600 ditto saucers' (Sale, March 1704). It also seems that the buyers were content to purchase some goods almost blind, relying perhaps on a sample and the printed catalogue description, and receiving an unexamined case of china, as is shown by the following complaint minuted in the Court records: 'This Court being made acquainted that in the delivery of several chests of china ware it appears the contents thereof have not exactly answered the number of pieces mentioned in the book of Sales...'   (17 November 1699)

It is remarkable that the prestige remained even when European porcelains approached perfection and when the general quality and novelty of these Chinese export market wares declined.

It is also remarkable that the English East India Company should have been content to order year after year much the same selection of unexciting tablewares (objects often ordered by the ton) '25 to 30 tons of china ware – the ordinary sort, viz. Dishes, plates and bowls.' (Order relating to the *Sidney* in 1702.) Or 'Eight hundred chests useful china ware, of which bowls, dishes and plates of all sizes as many as you can get.' (Order relating to three Canton bound ships in 1722.) Even in the 1740s the Supra-cargoes were instructed to bring home only 'useful and cheap' china-ware for the Company.

The main Chinese ports used by the British and other European vessels were Amoy, Chusan and Canton. The latter was to become the main and in fact the only port at which the Europeans were permitted to trade, but it came into prominence only in the eighteenth century. We will therefore discuss first the earlier trade at Amoy and Chusan.

Amoy was the port favoured by the original London Company; its trade with Amoy dates from 1684. This was on a quite small scale, being largely hampered by the Dutch, who had traded there from at least 1662. Nevertheless some British 'Country' vessels from Bantam and India did call at Amoy on their trading voyages in the seventeenth century, before the main trade had been established.

The importance of Amoy as the main English trading port at the beginning of the eighteenth century cannot be over-emphasised, although most collectors think only of Canton in relation to the shipment of china-wares. The great importance of Amoy in the last quarter of the seventeenth century was that here the British could purchase goods imported from Japan without having to rely on the Dutch. The available ships' logs record several references to the supply, or temporary dearth, of Japanese goods. The 1685 log of the *China Merchant* records:

> On the 29th July [1685], God be praised we arrived safe here, and anchored close by the Town...On the 6th August we took a house and carried a few goods of several sorts ashore. The rent we pay is very considerable being 80 Tales [about £27] per month.
>
> The goods now to be brought in Town is Alum, some sugar which is very dear, Pelongs, Gelongs, Pounches, Sattins, Velvets – which is held up at a high rate. Copper none to be had but ships from Japan are expected in a months time...

This report of the mid-1680s does not mention china-ware but, by the 1690s, this commodity does figure in the list of investments ordered by the Court of Directors in London. They instructed the Supra-cargoes of the *Dorothy* (bound for Amoy) in January 1694, to purchase:

> China ware of all the variety that can be got in the Country both fine and coarse, particular a quantity of fine teapots, blew and white, purple and white, red and white, a grate to be made before the spout within side.
>
> Lacquere ware the finest that can be made...Fans of all the variety the country affords...Hands skreens for ladys...
>
> Tea fine and good quality, all well packed in Tutenage [a zinc-like metal] as close as can be and then wrapt round in leaves of the country and then put into tubs...Bring the tea in no small pots, in sweet-wood chests not in any pots till well assured that they are cleared from all scents, especially from the smells of the sodering oyl.

I have included this reference to the careful packing of tea to show not only that it was proving troublesome, but also to show that the 'pots' mentioned in the many contemporary references to tea were metal (Tutenage) containers – not ceramic teapots, as some authorities seem to suggest.

Moving forward to complete our picture of Amoy in the eighteenth century, we find that the log of the *Montague*, which arrived at Amoy on 20 June 1704, gives some further information on the trade at this port. The point is made that the British traders packed their own wares, for on 21 October the entry includes '...employed at ye Factory in providing of chests for china ware' and later 'began to pack ye china ware at ye factory [headquarters]'. More important, this log includes a reference to the purchase of Japanese goods at Amoy. On 3 November the following strangely worded entry occurs: 'Came in a junk from Japan...our China Merchant for our ship went out and meet her and brought her cargoe.'

Within a few days 112 chests of china-ware were loaded aboard the *Montague*. Further evidence of the Japanese trade at this Chinese port appears in the log under 17 November 1704: 'Came in a Japan junk loaded with Japan ware and copper.' Two more arrived the next day and one on the next. The extent of the *Montague*'s cargo of china-ware is reflected in a note of 28 November 1704: 'Hearing of a new Hoppo coming, shifted all our chinaware aboard containing from ye first to last 171 chests [112 had previously been loaded] on ye Companys account. Likewise cleared the factory of all things that pay custom...'

Unfortunately we have no record of the contents of these chests loaded at Amoy, apart from one case which was in fact not loaded. The log explains the situation: 'This afternoon a Sampan coming with a china ware chest a longside ye ship, one fell overboard and sunk, containing 234 cups fine'.

The logs of several English Company vessels trading to the port of Amoy underline the point that much trade was there carried on with Japan; entries occur, such as 'expect the Japan Fleet'. Much of the Japanese porcelain and lacquer-work shipped to Europe would have arrived in European ships from the Chinese port of Amoy, for the English Companies had no direct contact with Japan at that time (see Chapter 10). Amoy was also the port from which most of the white *Blanc de Chine* porcelain was shipped (see p. 258). The English trade at Amoy must have been very great in the closing years of the seventeenth century for in 1697 the British Customs claimed duty of no less than £5,254 7s 0d on imported porcelain from the East, representing twelve and a half per cent of the total value and, at the time this was loaded, in 1695 or 1696, the port of Canton was not used by the British who mainly traded from Amoy, sometimes using India as an intermediary off-loading point. Several vessels reported at Amoy were in fact 'Country ships', or India-trade vessels. In May 1689 the *Morning Star* and the *Princess of Denmark* left Fort St George for Amoy, arriving back in India in March 1690. Unfortunately there is no record of their cargo but if china-ware was included this would no doubt have been trans-shipped at Madras on to a vessel bound for London.

After about 1710 few British vessels traded at Amoy, the Chinese seeking to confine European traders to Canton. A Supra-cargo's report of May 1727 reports that the silk weavers had left 'since the English left going to Amoy' before 1721, and a letter dated 15 June 1728 repeats that the English Company had quitted Amoy and Chusan. However, some later attempts were made to trade at Amoy, for example the *Houghton* called during her 1734–5 voyage. The Supra-cargoes, however, had to order the vessel to Canton after a stay of six weeks at Amoy for apparently the trade had declined and no stocks were available for purchase. The Supra-cargoes recorded: '...went to see a merchant who had sent to Chinchew for samples of silks and china, as to his samples of china could not pick out a chest proper for us.'

The port of Amoy, however, remained in other

respects a thriving one. As Captain Phillip Worth of the *Houghton* noted in his log in August 1735: 'From the 3rd to ye 16th there has gone into Amoy from foreign voyages fifteen junks, viz. from Batavia, Siam, Cambodia, Manelia and other places.'

The last British vessel which called at Amoy, as far as I have been able to trace, was the *Hardwicke*. On 1 August 1744, the log of the East Indiaman records: 'At 9 a.m. the Supra-cargoes went on shore, we saluted them with 9 guns, we have but little prospect of doing anything at this place.' This belief was confirmed by the log entry three days later: 'The Mandarines will not let us trade here nor go into their inner harbour but upon condition we would send all our guns and sails on shore, which we would not comply with. They promise us, however, some water and provisions.'

As a consequence the *Hardwicke* sailed for Canton, where it traded successfully. The Chinese port of Amoy does not reappear in the history of the Chinese export market porcelains. However, reproductions of early Chinese porcelains are at present made on the Island of Quemoy (Kinnen), situated just outside Amoy harbour. A first-hand account in *Arts of Asia* (vol. 2, no. 4, July/August 1972) reports that local clays are used in the production of these modern porcelains.

Apart from Amoy and Canton, British vessels also traded at Chusan, nearly a thousand miles north of Canton and the nearest of the Chinese–European trading ports to Japan. Herman Moll's map of c. 1710 marks expressly a 'British Factory' at Chusan and one at Amoy but there is no such notation against Canton. The Chusan trade appears to date from 1700. The log of the East Indiaman, *Rooke*, which was in Amoy harbour during the period July to December 1700, recorded under the date 24 August that the *Eaton* passed with 'Mr Ketchpooll, Mr Loyde and several others to settle a factory at Luzon [Chusan], alias Limpoo'.

It was the New English Company which sought to establish a trading Factory at Chusan. The records relating to the events of November 1699 make interesting reading:

The Court having chosen Mr Allen Catchpole to be their President in China had obtained a commission from the King to constitute Mr Catchpole...to be the King's Minister or Consul for the English nation...[officially the first British Ambassador to China was Lord Macartney in 1793, but he was treated rather as a vassal and it was not until 1861 that a British Residential Mission was established in Peking]...we have directed Captain Phillips, Commander of the ship *Eaton*, in whom you take passage, to sail first to Borneo and from thence to proceed to Limpo, alias Liampo, in the northern parts of China, also we direct you to settle, if it be possible or at some convenient Port for trade thereabouts where you can be permitted by the Government and it is most likely to introduce you directly into the Trade of the City of Nankin...Let the Government there know you expect another ship and that you have orders to continue to trade with them if you are favourably and kindly used...

We have been greatly encouraged to this northern settlement from the hopes we entertain of opening a way into the Japan trade and of finding a considerable vent for our woolen manufacture.

The Court appoint the limits of the Presidency to be the whole Empire of China and the adjacent Islands.

Fine words, but in fact the 'King's Minister or Consul' arrived at Chusan somewhat belatedly on 11 October 1700, to find the *Trumball*, the *Macclesfield* and a 'Country' ship from Bombay – the *Bombay Merchant* – already there and loading. On 28 January 1701 the President and Council of Supra-cargoes at Chusan reported that they had contracted for 'two parcels of china-ware to the amount of 9,000 tales' (£3,000).

In the meantime the directors in London, assuming that the Chusan trade had been successfully opened, wrote to President Catchpole: '...we intend to send you three or four ships next year, resolving to drive the trade to the utmost...' They also added an amusing comment on changing fashions at home: 'take notice that rich silks are in no demand, nor any embroideries, nor any dark colours, for all the female sex, even our old women are become youthful'.

If the directors back in London were resolved to drive the trade at Chusan to the utmost, their man on the spot was not so happy.

On 1 February 1702 he wrote home: 'The monopoly and tyranny of the Mandarines of this place is so great that we cannot believe it your Honours interest to continue at it, nor do we intend the next shipping shall have product here unless your Honours have made provision for an Ambassador or otherwise for better terms or that the Mandarines unexpectedly alter their tempers.'

Also, a Supra-cargo of the Old Company, writing back from the Port of Amoy, commented on the New Company's recently established Factory at Chusan that 'all the customs and duties are much higher than at Amoy'.

Nevertheless, the Company continued to trade at Chusan, having by 1703 apparently softened the attitude of the Chinese officials – with numerous presents. In a letter of 10 February 1703 the Council at Chusan wrote back to London:

> For presents you will do well to send annually two repeating clocks, four striking watches and twelve common brass clocks of 50s each. Guns and pistols they are pretty well cloyed with, but glass lanthorns we have been much baited for.
> The annual assortment may also include two dozen prospective painted sticks and two dozen eight inches long without joints. Silver-hilted rapiers we have been obliged to buy of all the ship companies at excessive rates [these would have been the ship crews' Private Trade goods], of these therefore send about one dozen – the blades to be very clean and gilt about half way down, also small pictures in gilt-frames glazed, of curious beautiful women.
> We are extremely plagued for curiosities of birds and dogs etc. Mr Dolben we heard paid the measure [port fee] of the ship with one great Irish dog.

Returning to the opening of the New English Company's trade at Chusan, we find that the *Trumball*, which left the Thames in October 1699 (after an earlier very successful voyage bringing home china-ware), arrived at Chusan on 28 July 1700. The captain of the *Trumball* was well received at Chusan, as he noted in the log: 'This morning [29 July 1700] I went ashore to ye General with my linguist and was nobly treated.'

On this voyage of the *Trumball* little china was carried. The log records only 'bundles of coarse china cups', but then this vessel was not sailing home to England; instead she sailed on 2 February 1701 for Batavia, to return to Chusan where she lay between 26 August and 25 November 1701. From the Court Minutes we learn that in March 1705 Captain Duffield of the *Trumball* was awarded £100 'commission of what he transacted at Chusan before the Company's Factory arrived there'.

Mr Catchpole and his party returned to Chusan in subsequent seasons (in December 1704 the directors in London appointed him as President of the Factory at Borneo). Sometimes, however, the President arrived at Chusan after the arrival of the Company's vessels. The log of the *Liampo* records that she arrived on 19 July 1702 to find the *Sarah* already there and on 1 August 1702 the captain recorded: 'We lay here in expectation every day of Mr President Catchpole with three ships, so that we hold back all manner of business till he shall arrive.' This party arrived on 6 August 1702. Chusan was apparently a busy international port, for the captain of the *Liampo* reported 'a great many junks from Siam, Batavia and elsewhere'. The directors of the New Company in London do not seem to have differentiated to any great extent between the Chinese trading ports of Amoy, Canton and Chusan. In December 1702 they gave orders to dispatch four vessels to China. One, the *Sidney* was sent to Canton; two, the *Montague* and *Stretham* were ordered to Amoy and one, the *Northumberland*, was sent to Chusan. Fortunately in all cases the basic orders for purchases in China were recorded and they are largely similar for all three ports. The *Northumberland* carried treasure to the value of £16,000 to be laid out on:

100 Tons of Copper, if procurable, if not more Tutenage
100 Tons Tutenage
  7 Pecull of Quicksilver
 20 Pecull of Virmillion
 10 Tons ordinary china ware
To lay out the surplus in gold.

For all four vessels the china-ware requirements were expressed in tons, underlining the commercial quality of the goods required. This is bluntly clear in the orders concerning the *Sidney*, destined for Canton: '25 to 30 Tons of China ware – The ordinary sort, viz. Dishes, plates and bowls'.

Few English East India vessels called at Chusan after the 1709–12 voyage of the *Rochester*. This vessel stopped briefly at Amoy, moving north to Chusan on 24 August 1710. The instructions given to this vessel's Supra-cargoes by the Court of Directors in London indicate that the port of call was of little importance as long as the required goods could be purchased at a cheap price. The original instructions read:

Resolved that the *Rochester* be consigned to Chusan.

That liberty be granted to the *Rochester*'s Supra-cargoes if they judge it most for the Company's service to proceed to Tinghoy on the main, five hours sail from Chusan and which is a good port and from whence all the goods are brought to Chusan and that if the Supra-cargoes have an invitation and find they don't run any hazard they may go to Lingpo.

That the Supra-cargoes may be permitted, if there be time for it to call in for forty-eight hours at Amoy, so as they don't put the ship under the power of the Chinese there, to bespeak tea and get China ware if to be bought, cheap and of the sorts directed.

The china-ware ordered at Amoy was to be delivered to the *Rochester* at Chusan.

Instructions to the Company's Supra-cargoes in November 1721 noted that the Company had quitted Chusan and Amoy, but a Supra-cargo's report to London, written in January 1737, mentions Chusan (and Lingpo) 'where all the great junks load and unload', also that the china-ware was 'made but 20 days journey away', but no merchants with knowledge of European requirements and customs were available at Chusan so that trade there was not possible.

Isolated attempts were made to re-establish trade at Chusan, but the Chinese were obviously intent on confining the Europeans to Canton. In the mid-1750s, some few European vessels were at Chusan but found that having a Factory at Lingpo, while the vessels were unable to get further than Chusan, necessitated much transportation between these two places. In December 1755 the *Earl of Holderness* loaded twelve whole and eighty-six half-chests of china-ware at Chusan, but this was the captain's Private Trade. In November 1756 the *Griffin* loaded seventy-two half-chests for the Company's account. By 1757 the various duties had been doubled, apparently in an effort to dissuade the Europeans from using this port. A Supra-cargo's report of 11 October 1757 indicates that as far as the porcelains were concerned little was available at Chusan: 'We have examined all the China Ware upon the place, and that article very scarce and what there is the most part of it very indifferent, that we shall be obliged to pack half chests instead of whole ones finding it impossible to make out a proper assortment for our whole quantity ordered in our list of investments.' In fact, the total packed was seven whole chests and eighty-seven half chests.

A further report from the Supra-cargoes, dated 2 December 1757, notes that the Chinese officials enquired 'what can be the reason of any of our ships coming to Lingpo in preference to Canton which is the proper Port for the European trade and where all our goods are to be acquired so easily. As Lingpo is solely for vessels which come from Japan and Corea. He thinks it also unreasonable for us to expect to have liberty to trade where we please when we permit the Chinese junks to go only to Batavia and Bornio...' This point was denied by the English in their reply, but still the Chinese insisted that if the Company's vessels came next year, in 1758, the duties would be raised yet again. A general letter of 24 June 1760 from the Supra-cargoes to all captains stated: 'The trade at Lingpo is positively forbid by his Imperial Majesty'; the captains were required to sail their vessels to Canton. The European trade at the ports of Amoy and Chusan (Lingpo) was now finally stopped, and the Europeans confined to the Port of Canton.

It was not until the 1699–1701 voyage of the New English Company's first China-trade vessel, the *Macclesfield*, that successful trading at Canton was firmly established after several earlier incidents. The *Macclesfield*'s 'rich and full cargoe' comprised in part china-ware costing over £380 (1,147·46 tales), 100,000 fans, 300 nests of six tea-tables, each inlaid with Mother of Pearl, a massive quantity of woven and raw silks, tea and other commodities.

This voyage of the *Macclesfield* is of great interest, marking as it does the commencement of a regular trade to and from Canton, a trade that was concerned with the profitable *export* of British wares to China, as much as with the import of Chinese wares. That the *Macclesfield* did successfully trade at Canton was a happy chance, and the Supra-cargoes' instructions left the port of call reasonably open, for if a trade could not be settled with the Mandarins at Canton 'you must then seek further northwards, either at Amoy or any other place where you can meet with encouragement'. The Supra-cargoes did not exactly meet with encouragement at Canton but they persisted in their endeavours to trade there, whereas they could easily have moved on to the then more usual European trading port of Amoy.

The following brief summary illustrates the financing of the voyage and some of the highlights, although it must be remembered that the details concern the 'New' upstart English Company, not the well-established original London Company. The Journal accounts, still preserved in the India Office Records at the Foreign and Commonwealth Office in London, start under the date 23 February 1698:

INVOICE of sundry goods and merchandizes and money loaden on board ye *Macklesfield* [sic] Gally, Capt. John Hurle, Commander: Bound for China or India and consigned to Mr Robert Douglas and his successors being on Acct. of ye Honoble. English Company and ye persons under mentioned, viz.

The Honoble. English Company	£25,036 0s 3d
Capt. John Hurle	£400
Edward Carleton and Company	£500
Joseph Daberon	£100
Nicholas Pickering	£100
William Strong	£1,000
John Biggs	£500
William Harding	£100
Nathaniel Johnstone	£300
Edward Harvey	£250
and Mr Robert Douglas	£3,800
Amounting in ye whole to	£32,086 0s 3d

Robert Douglas was chief Supra-cargo, having as

his assistants William Strong, John Biggs and Edward Harvey, each of whom had a share of the investment. Robert Douglas wrote the Journal from which the following quotations are taken. The investment comprised fifty-five bales of cloth, in various colours, to a value, or cost, of £2,541 10s 6d. Other fabrics were valued at £2,030 0s 9d. Twenty-seven chests of silver valued at £2,613 9s 3d and sixteen chests of coin – pieces of eight – being 64,000 at 5s or £16,000 were also included.

Also carried out to China was a consignment of English glassware, surprisingly including glass teapots and teacups and saucers, also mirrors of various sizes (perhaps for over-painting and for re-export back to Europe as Chinese mirror-paintings). Pistols and other firearms were purchased, as were sword-blades. A large number of spectacles were packed; clocks and watches were carried for sale, for barter, or to serve as gifts. Other articles listed in this Journal were most probably for the Supra-cargoes' use in their duties; items such as scales and stationery come into this category. English glassware and sword-blades were apparently a standard item of export to China at this period.

The *Macclesfield* sailed on 2 March 1699. By 16 May she was off the Cape of Good Hope and on 27 August she was anchored at Macao, the island off the Pearl River where the Portuguese had their trading-post. Here the Portuguese at first suspected that the *Macclesfield* was a British privateer – British vessels had been plundering Portuguese boats off the Chinese coast in the seventeenth century, before the official Company trade had become established. It may be that some pre-eighteenth-century Chinese porcelain found its way to Europe as the result of piracy.

During September 1699 the Supra-cargo's Journal reported some progress in trade while they were still anchored off Macao awaiting permission to sail up-river to the Whampoa (Huang-pu) anchorage below Canton. On 1 September Robert Douglas reported: 'The Hoppo's secretary sent me word that there were several great merchants come down from Canton who designed to be on board next morning.' At this period letters were received from Canton, from the French agent named as M. Bonae (the first French vessel had arrived at Canton only the previous year, 1698), from a Jesuit Father, Padre Bassett, and from the captain of a French ship, each congratulating the *Macclesfield* on her arrival and warning the captain and Supra-cargo of the Chinese behaviour and tricks. However, the formalities slowly proceeded; on 9 September the vessel was measured to determine the correct payment of dues (see p. 97). The Mandarins sent presents of fresh food aboard and were in turn rewarded with gifts from the outward cargo. On 15 September Robert Douglas and his assistants travelled up-river to Canton to make arrangements for the sale of their own goods and for purchase of the homeward cargo.

After their return to the *Macclesfield*, still anchored off Macao Island, and as a consequence of further 'gifts' (to use a polite term), the vessel was permitted to proceed up-river to Whampoa on 7 October 1699. Here they found only three other non-Chinese vessels, the *Loyalle Captaine*, a 'Country' ship from Fort St George, Madras, one French vessel and a 'Moor' ship from Surat. This lack of European shipping was in sharp contrast to the gathering of vessels reported in ships' logs in the eighteenth century but the trade steadily progressed from this date. The presence at Whampoa of the India-trade vessel *Loyalle Captaine* from Madras indicates the existence in the seventeenth century of the trade between Indian ports and the Chinese coast (see p. 81). In the eighteenth century the number of these 'Coast' or 'Country' boats was considerable. One brief entry – 'Hoppoes engaged clearing Junks for Batavia' – reminds us that the export trade from Canton (and Amoy) was by no means restricted to Europe and India. The Dutch shipped their china-ware to Europe from Batavia – wares brought there by the Chinese trading junks.

The trans-shipment of China-trade goods at various ports is evidenced by the logs of many vessels. We can for convenience single out one example of this little known fact. It concerns the voyage of the *Seaford*, under Captain Martin Gardiner, which left the Thames on 31 October 1700. This East Indiaman arrived at Batavia on 16 June 1701 on passage to Canton where she arrived on 24 July. She does not appear to have met with the difficulties encountered there by earlier vessels, for the holds were reported full of silk, china-ware, copper and other commodities, and further supplies had to be refused before she sailed from Whampoa below Canton on 4 January 1702. The *Seaford* did not, however, take her cargo directly to England, but sailed for Batavia where she arrived on 1 February 1702, finding there eighteen Dutch vessels.

Five days after arrival at Batavia the log records: 'came onboard a Country boat [engaged in the Indian trade] to take in our goods, put onboard him silk, chinaware and gallingall.' On 11 February we find entered: 'Discharged ye Country boat having taken all our goods out, filled up and caulked ye after hatch, stored 7 large and 1 small chest of china ware between decks.' But further off-loading was still to take place, for the log records under 14 February 1702: 'Put 10 great and 6 small chests of ye Companys china ware on board a brigantine bound for Banjar.' And on the following day: 'At 2 this morning put ye rest of ye Company's chinaware, which was 11 small chests and 26 bags of Gallingall...which was left out of ye hold...on board ye brigantine for Banjar.'

Having loaded fresh ballast the *Seaford* left Batavia on 20 February 1702 and arrived back in the Thames in September. This example of the trans-shipment of Chinese goods demonstrates that the trade with China was somewhat larger than British records lead us to believe, that the respective fields of operation of the two separate British East India Companies were greater than was realised, and that they were by no means restricted to the direct China–England trade.

Returning to the voyage of the *Macclesfield*, we find that the Supra-cargoes quickly established themselves at Canton, for they reported on 9 October 1699: 'This evening we removed from our Merchants home to our own Hong [Factory], which was by ye water side...' However, the amount of Chinese goods available for purchase at Canton was then extremely limited. Robert Douglas reported on 19 October: 'This day I went about to several places to see china ware and some Nankeen silks, all very dear...' A week later in a letter to the Court of Directors in London, he reported:
'...China ware there is none yet in ye Place that is worth ye buying but there is some expected in a month...if ye china ware comes as is expected and if merchant performes his contract I hope to saile by ye 20th of December...'

The china-ware apparently did not arrive in a month as promised, at least not in quantity, for on 4 December Robert Douglas noted:

...China ware of which there is no quantity in ye place at present, and such as there is, [is] likewise very dear, so if there were not a necessity upon us to buy some for Kentledge, we should hardly meddle with any, for ye French Ship, the Surat [-bound ship] and ye Coast ship [for Fort St George, Madras] have sailed with theirs to a very dear rate, [they?] buy all that comes to hand good or bad.

Note that the Supra-cargo of this pioneer English ship at Canton in 1699 would 'hardly meddle' with porcelain, if he had not need of it as kentledge to floor the holds to give stability to the ship on its homeward voyage. Meddle with it he did, for he then reports receiving a small selection packed in five tubs, comprising:

200 dishes costing 20 Tales [approx. £7]
 78 sets of small jars and flower-pots,
   5 in each set, costing 11 tales [approx. £4]
 74 nests of small blue and white covered bowls
440 small red and green bowls and dishes [saucers]

On 6 December 1699 the Supra-cargo and his assistants William Strong and John Biggs went again 'in search of china-ware but agreed about none they held, everything too dear and ye French we found upon ye same errand which occassioned so great a strife'. Three days later these British agents had made up their minds and we find reported: 'This day agreed for several parcels of china ware at ye Great Shopp in Hun Quins Street, which is to be sent in two days hence.'

On 12 December these goods purchased at 'ye Great Shopp' were received and listed in the Journal. They comprised nine tubs holding 9,440 teacups and dishes (saucers); 4,820 chocolate cups and dishes (saucers); 20 footed cups; 49 small dishes; 2 pairs of blue and white small beakers; 989 small bowls and dishes (saucers). When the contents of the tubs are listed separately fuller descriptions were given. The prices are the approximate eighteenth-century sterling equivalent of the Chinese cost.

2,230 tea-cups, buff colour without	[£16]
1,010 ditto red and green paint	[£7 10s]
940 ditto buff colour	[£7]
1,000 ditto ash colour without	[£7]
329 Buff colour bowls	[£2 15s]
395 Buff dishes	[£2 15s]
215 ditto bowls	[£2 15s]
2 pairs blue and white beakers	[2s]
20 choca cups with a foot	[2s]
1,000 Buff coloured tea-cups and saucers	[£7]
870 chocolate cups and saucers blue and white	[£8]
3,260 Buff coloured tea-cups and saucers	[£24]
1,870 chocolate cups and saucers	[£17]
2,080 ditto much blue pattern	[£19]

This, together with other early records of the 1690–1710 period, reflects the great interest in drinking-vessels – bowls, beakers and thousands of cups and saucers – tea, coffee and chocolate cups. Very few teapots are listed and practically none of the now-standard tea equipment. The contemporary early-eighteenth-century oil painting (Plate 4) to be seen in the Silver Galleries at the Victoria and Albert Museum in London helps us to see that the other objects in use on European tables – the sugar bowl, the cream or milk jug, the tea-caddy, the waste bowl, the spoon-tray and the large pot (on stand with oil burner below) were very often silver. This picture also shows the different manner of holding and drinking from the standard form of handleless tea-bowl. These tea-bowls were normally referred to as 'cups' in the records of the time, although coffee cups had handles and chocolate cups often had two handles. Later chapters deal in more detail with the standard imports of the period and the introduction of new forms in Chinese export market porcelain.

We learn from the Supra-cargoes' accounts that the china-ware was packed in sago and that sago also filled the larger hollow pieces. On 30 December 1699 we find the note 'Bought 3 parcells of sago for filling up ye china ware', and after this there appear numerous references to filling the ware and the packed chests with sago and on occasions with rice. While on the face of it the use of sago or rice as filling and packing amid the china-ware appears to save space, much of this must have been in an unsaleable state on arrival in Europe. In one instance a captain reported in his log: 'One of the

The East India Company's porcelain trade

4 An oil painting of the 1740 period showing a family at tea, drinking from Chinese porcelain handleless tea-bowls. The other tea equipment, including the spoontray, is of silver.
Victoria and Albert Museum (Crown Copyright)

chests of china-ware with sago happened to burst, upon which was obliged to new stow the china-ware, find the sago musty and full of cockroaches'. This was before the vessel had started her long voyage home to Europe. Nevertheless, the British continued this practice. We find an American reporting in the 1790s '...the English to save room have it packed in sago, instead of straw, it would be well to examine whether the practice would not be advantageous.' Other packing materials such as powdered kaolin may have been used but the official records do not mention this.

Two early references to sago serve also to scotch the belief that the Oriental red unglazed teapot of the type much copied in Europe was packed in with the tea as a kind of bonus. On 13 March 1700 the purchase of such pots was listed:

> 458 Red teapotts, Tales 29·77 [approx. £10]
> 30 plates
> Sago to fill up ye chest.
> 520 Red tea potts, Tales 33·8 [approx. £11 or 5d (about 2 new pence) each]
> Sago to fill up do.

The small-sized unglazed reddish pots were the local speciality of Yi-hsing in Kiangsu. Chinese examples were widely copied in Europe – in Germany by Böttger at Meissen, in Holland by Arij de Milde, and in England principally by the Elers brothers, who were later to deal in Chinese porcelains purchased at the East India Company sales in London. A typical Yi-hsing teapot is shown in Plate 5. Most are very small in size, seemingly for a single cup of tea.

As I have previously explained, the main port with which the British traded was Amoy, or 'Emoy' to use the old spelling. This point is underlined in a letter sent back to the directors in London. Robert Douglas at Canton reported in January 1700:

> ...china ware is but scarce and what is procurable not extraordinary and were it not that we are under a necessity to take some for helping to ballast our ship, I should not have adventured upon much because of ye great quantity that I am advised goes from Emoy and as for bespeaking any better it is not to be effected under six months at least and not without an extraordinary price and also money advanced because ye place where it is made is some thirty days journey from hence...

The term 'ballast' here used by the Supra-cargo would seem to be an inaccurate one. The ships' logs, written up by the captains or ships' officers, do not speak of china-ware as ballast although, being heavy, it was loaded low in the holds, directly above the true ballast, to give the vessels stability. Further evidence on this point is given on p. 102.

Here we see not only that large quantities of china were being shipped from Amoy but also that all the purchases made from the several china-ware shops in Canton would have been of stock patterns. It was not possible to order special pieces because their vessel would have departed before the goods were available at Canton some six months later. It appears that the later practice of porcelain painters in Canton decorating ready-made blanks to special order had not then been established, possibly because the number of Europeans trading at Canton did not at this time warrant it. However, fans were made in Canton (some 100,000 being purchased for the *Macclesfield* alone) and the fan-painters may perhaps have started the porcelain enamelling establishments to cater for the special and urgent orders of visiting Europeans.

We also discover from this 1699–1700 Supra-cargo's Journal that goods were shipped from Amoy to Canton. On 13 February 1700, Robert Douglas reported:

> This evening having advice that there was several sorts of goods come from Emoy by ye last Junk proper for us, I and my assistants went to the Hong where they were landed to see them...

The East India Company's porcelain trade

5 A small unglazed Chinese red stoneware teapot of the type made at Yi-hsing and widely copied in Europe, *c.* 1700.
Victoria and Albert Museum (Crown Copyright)

We see some Emoy lackred work and some china ware and some Nankeen and Emoy fans but very dear...

The following extract from the Supra-cargo's Journal, one of several that relate to requests for presents (or bribes) to Chinese officials, is typical. Under 2 February 1700 we find: 'This being ye last day of ye Chinese year several of ye Hoppos' under officers and others came for their fees and box money, just as in England.'

Robert Douglas's Journal, recording in detail the day-by-day events in Canton in 1700, ceases on 17 June of that year after more than eight months spent in protracted dealings with Chinese merchants and officials. After reading of the many troubles one wonders that the Company sent other vessels to trade at Canton. Double dealings and intrigue are recorded on page after page of the Journal and, sad to say, the outward cargo of British goods did not sell well. Six months after the vessel's arrival we find entries such as: 'This day [4 April 1700] treated about our glasses, pistolls and swords blades in exchange for fanns – but could not agree.' Moreover, when goods were sold the Chinese merchants, on various pretexts, withheld payment. I can only assume that trade at Canton was continued and built up because the Chinese goods brought home to London sold to such advantage.

The *Macclesfield* Journal ends suddenly while the vessel was still at Whampoa and the Supra-cargoes were at Canton, but we see from the entries that the ship's business was being completed and the vessel was nearly ready to start the return journey. In fact we can trace part of the homeward voyage because logs of some other vessels contain – as was the practice – references to East Indiamen met with in the various ports. In this case the log of the *Trumball* in the port of Chusan in the July 1700–February 1701 period records that the *Macclesfield* entered the port at four o'clock in the afternoon of 6 August 1700, seven weeks after the Journal entries ceased at Canton. This news is somewhat unexpected, for Chusan lies almost a thousand miles to the north of Canton, in the opposite direction to the *Macclesfield*'s homeward course. We may surmise that the Supra-cargo decided to try another Chinese port so as to sell her remaining cargo of British goods or to fill her holds with Chinese merchandise which was not available at Canton. Or perhaps urgent repairs were necessary before she could start on the long journey to England, as the vessel had been greatly delayed at Canton and had 'lost her voyage', that is, missed the season's monsoons and had to wait a further year for the right winds to take her south, away from China. The log of the *Trumball* also records the death of Mr Strong: 'This day [9 September 1700] Mr Strong, Supra-cargo of ye *Macclesfield* gally dyed after a long sickness and was interred.'

The same log shows that the *Macclesfield* left Chusan on 26 December 1700 on her homeward passage; the log of the *Neptune* reports her at Batavia on 1 February 1701, and she was certainly back in London by March 1703, when a past-tense reference occurs in the Court Minutes.

It would be out of place to quote lengthy lists of the *Macclesfield*'s 1699–1700 cargo of china in this introductory chapter. Relevant facts from this highly interesting Journal will be found in later chapters.

It is worth turning for a moment from our account of porcelain to record some of the other homeward cargo, for as we have noted china-ware was considered of little consequence at that time. On 3 November 1699 Robert Douglas wrote in his Journal: 'This day I see several musters of Lackered ware and since there was no right Jappan procurable [the Japanese lacquered ware was generally preferred to that of the Chinese], I by ye

The East India Company's porcelain trade

advice of my assistants ordered tea tables according to directions from England, inlaid with Mother of Pearle...' Later he reports: 'The Musters of Lackered tea tables ordered to be made six in a sett, largest $23\frac{1}{2}$ inches long, smallest 14 inches long.' On 20 December 1699 thirty sets of these tables were delivered, that is 180 items, costing a total of thirty tales, or ten pounds. Ten days later a further ninety sets were delivered.

The East India Company vessels also brought home thousands upon thousands of Chinese fans. From Robert Douglas's notes it appears that many were made locally in Canton. On 21 November 1699 he recorded:

This day desired our Merchant to send for some of ye best fann makers that we might give directions for making some fanns...we made an agreement for 80,000...three quarters [of them] to be on white paper, a quarter on coloured and all to be well painted with figures upon one side and flowers upon the other; the side sticks to be lackered black and inlaid with Mother of Pearl, for 30 Tales [£10] per mille.

Two days later a further 10,000 fans were ordered.

The various European vessels were required to anchor off the island of Whampoa some twelve miles down-river from Canton, and the goods were ferried to and fro. Even today ocean ships cannot proceed to Canton, but still need to anchor at Whampoa. In the early eighteenth century Canton was already a thriving trading centre. In 1703 Captain Hamilton observed: 'There is no day in the year but shows 5,000 sail of trading junks...lying before the city.' In these junks goods from different parts of China were gathered together and shipped to other ports and countries.

The principal trade was carried out directly with Chinese merchants, especially when particular goods were required. The cargoes were at first very mixed. The diary of Edward Barlow records that the *Fleet*, which left Whampoa in February 1703, carried:

205 chests of China and Japan ware, 507 chests of copper, 122 chests of quicksilver, 416 tubs and baskets of sugar candy, 2 chests of fans, 23 chests of china lack, 2 tubs of oil for lacquering, 70 chests of screens, 60 large jars of ginger and a great deal more loose China and Japan earthenware.

The East India Company vessels early in the eighteenth century were in the nature of general trading vessels, not then carrying, as they did later, tea, silks and china-ware direct to Europe.

However, a few ships were sailing direct to Chinese ports and bringing home china-ware, and soon the quantities reached large proportions. In the 1719–21 season the *Carnavon*'s cargo included 326,210 pieces of china, and more than a million items may have been sold that season: the March 1722 sale alone included 639,451 pieces.

In this year, 1722, a Supra-cargo in Canton wrote home to the directors in London lamenting the high cost of renting the waterfront Hong or Factory. This early-eighteenth-century complaint is evidence that the Canton trade was steadily increasing:

Hired half the Hong that was formerly the French Factory at 500 Tales rent, by great interest we also obtained half of the adjoining Hong at the same rent. The number of shipping that have lately visited this port, have caused the owners of houses conveniently situated to ask incredible rates.
(Report dated 3 August 1722.)

It has been stated by other writers that the Emperor K'ang Hsi banned all foreign trade (except that with Japan) between 1718 and 1722, but if this was the case, the prohibition appears to have had remarkably little effect on the import of Chinese porcelains by the English East India Company, as the records and the previous quotations readily show; the ban was evidently only partial. However, at home the trade was not as rosy as some would have us believe. On 28 September 1722, the Court Minutes record:

The Court of Directors having considered the state of their Trade to all parts of the East Indies particularly that to China, formerly a profitable branch, but now by the Ostenders interfering, greatly decayed – together with other hardships the Company lately have and still do labour under, have unanimously resolved that it be represented to the General Court as their opinion that for the future the half yearly annuity and dividend warrants be four per cent. This was agreed by the General Court.

In the previous year three of the leading china-ware buyers could not pay more than £542 to meet a bill of some £3,000 and they desired that their goods be resold in the next sale. In 1724 only one vessel, the *Macclesfield*, was sent out to China and in 1730 no china-ware was ordered on the Company's account.

As late as 1736 the number of European vessels trading with China was relatively small; in that season only four English vessels, two French, one Danish and one Swedish arrived at Canton. The British Government had for over thirty years imposed a tax on imported porcelains. An Act of 1704 imposed a twelve and a half per cent tax on all porcelain commonly called China-ware or Japan-ware imported from the East Indies, Persia, China and other parts within the limits of the Charters granted to the East India Companies. The value was to be fixed at the prices at which the porcelains were sold at auction.

The imported Chinese and Japanese porcelains sold at auction in London were arranged in large wholesale lots intended for the dealers – 'chinamen' – and merchants. Typical lots comprised '800 blue and white cups and 800 ditto saucers' or '1895 blue and white bowls'. A Court Minute of 22 February 1710 shows both the large number of items of the Company's china-ware included in their sales and the relatively small selection of objects, in this case all useful table-wares. The instructions relate to the goods to be included in the next sale, to be held in April 1710.

Ordered that 180,000 cups and saucers, being two thirds of what remains in the warehouse be put up to sale.
Also 27,000 plates being all that remain.
Also 26,000 bowls and dishes being half the quantity of what is in the warehouse.
Also 4,000 teapots being all that remains.
Also 45,000 coarse cups being all that are in the warehouse.
And 26,000 cream-coloured tea cups being two-thirds of what are in the warehouse.

As previously explained, these goods were divided up into large wholesale lots; the various trade buyers distributed the porcelains up and down the country, having first sub-divided the large lots and made up sets, when required, from the individual pieces. It is not generally appreciated that the goods brought back to London and sold at auction were often re-shipped to other countries. The few remaining records show that tens of thousands of pieces of Chinese or Japanese porcelain were shipped to Ireland; other shipments went to the North American colonies, to Jamaica, Madeira, Italy, Germany and, rather surprisingly, very large quantities went to Holland, although the Dutch had their own East India Company shipping Oriental porcelains home to Holland. A Court Minute of October 1699 records the desire of some foreign buyers to preview a forthcoming London sale: 'The Court being made acquainted that severall foreigners were desirous to see the Company's goods per the *Martha* and *Nassau*, now making ready for sale, before the printing of the books [the Catalogues], in regard their occasion require a sudden departure for Holland…' The *Nassau* carried much china-ware on her successful voyage from China.

While the selection of goods just quoted as being available in the Company's warehouse in February 1710 was extremely utilitarian, the Company at this period must have appreciated that the new shapes or designs would be saleable and that objects geared to European requirements were better than the almost random purchase of china-ware made by the Chinese for their own general export markets. A brief Court Minute dated 31 March 1710 shows that at least by this period the Committee of Correspondence had ordered special designs to be made as patterns to be sent to China: 'Ordered...that the Committee of Warehouses be desired to examine the bill given in by Mr Joshua Bagshaw for wood patterns for china ware, and for patterns for fans, provided by direction of the Committee for Correspondence and sent by the Supra-cargoes of the *Stringer*...' Unfortunately we can learn nothing about these wooden patterns except that Joshua Bagshaw was paid £23 for them on 13 April 1710.

From this point onward the shipment of Chinese porcelains into England increased and the selection of basic forms and especially of special designs became more ambitious; metal, salt-glazed stoneware and glass models were also sent out as samples. Many aspects of these new patterns are discussed in subsequent chapters and in this outline there is no need to cover in detail the period 1720–70, when the trade was firmly established. The presence of British porcelain factories after 1750 did little to stem the flood of Chinese porcelains coming into Britain for Oriental useful wares could still undersell the native products. Even the London Livery Companies purchased Chinese porcelain instead of patronising the local porcelain factories at Bow or Chelsea. The relative cheapness of the imported Chinese porcelain is probably best illustrated by Plate 6, a tankard ordered by an Aberdeen bank. When a Scottish bank sends across the world for its goods there must be a sound reason!

In the 1770s the selection of the general cargo of china-ware was dictated by the directors in London, acting, one assumes, on the result of the sales of the previous season's shipment and on reports from their agents and the trade buyers. We find, for example, the Council of Supra-cargoes in Canton writing back to London, reporting that the new orders had arrived too late to influence that season's shipment as the goods were ordered in advance and were already packed:

We beg leave to observe that the contract for china ware we annually make the preceding season for the ships of the ensuing one, having been found by long experience to have been the only method of procuring that article of a superior quality – has impeded our complying more than partially with the orders transmitted to us by the *Ceres* relative to that investment...

We have paid very particular attention to the china ware ordered for the ensuing season, for which we have contracted two months ago in doing which we have paid the most minute regard to the list of investment which in every particular we have taken for our guide and we hope the execution will answer our wishes and the Honourable Courts expectations.
(Letter dated Canton, 20 November 1774.)

This order is of the greatest interest, because the wording includes 'been found by long experience' and because it reflects the instructions sent out from London to the Council of Supra-cargoes in Canton. The order appears in the Supra-cargoes' records under the date 21 September 1774. The quoted currency is in most cases given in mess, i.e. a tenth part of a tale, or about eight pence (approximately three new pence), so that the 24,000 pairs of cups and saucers in the first line cost less than two new pence each.

Contracted with Exchin for the following China ware...to be made of the very best China Ware and free of all cracks and flaws to be delivered in July next...

Coloured

24,000 pairs cups and saucers 2 patterns at			042
16,000 pairs breakfast do.	,,	,,	052
8,000 pairs ½ pint do.	,,	,,	090
4,000 chocolate cups with handles	,,	,,	160
1,200 teapots	,,	,,	130
2,000 sugar boxes and covers	,,	,,	100
4,000 milk pots	,,	,,	070
4,000 coffee cups with handles	,,	,,	026
800 custard cups	,,	,,	050
400 sets patty pans, 3 to a set	,,	,,	200
120 pairs sauce boats	,,	,,	120
200 Quart mugs	,,	,,	110
200 Pint do.	,,	,,	090
200 ½ pint do.	,,	,,	070
200 ¼ pint do.	,,	,,	050
1,600 Water plates flat	,,	,,	036
400 do. deep	,,	,,	039
8,000 plates	,,	,,	080
1,600 soup plates	,,	,,	090
8,000 Pint basons	,,	,,	035
8,000 ½ pint do.	,,	,,	055
200 1 Gallon bowls	,,	,,	330
800 3 Quart bowls	,,	,,	270
1,600 2 Quart do.	,,	,,	130
2,400 3 pint do.	,,	,,	100
3,200 1 Quart do.	,,	,,	080
40 breakfast sets, viz. Teapot, sugar-box, cover and plate, slop bason, milk pot, 12 cups and saucers	,,	,,	Tale 1·200 [7s 6d or 37½p]
160 teasets, viz. 1 middle size teapot and 1 larger, 1 slop bason and plate, 1 sugar box and cover, 1 milk pot and stand, 1 tea cannister, 12 cups and saucers, 12 coffee cups with handles	,,	,,	Tale 1·800 [12s or 60p]
40 table [dinner] sets Oblong and Octagon			
2 tureens, covers and dishes			
4 smaller do.			
8 octagon salad dishes			
2 do., deep and square shape			
4 sauce boats and stands			
2 18 inch dishes			
2 2nd size			
2 3rd size			
4 4th size			
4 5th size			
4 6th size			
72 plates octagon			
36 soup do.			
24 Water plates, ½ deep, ½ flat			
24 Water plates, a size between the water plates and the plates	,,	,,	Tale 30 [£10]

The blue and white porcelains ordered at the same time comprised exactly the same objects but in greater numbers, often twice as much blue and white porcelain as enamelled: 187,600 individual items (or pairs) of blue and white porcelains, plus the services, as against 101,120 enamelled items, or pairs. These figures total 288,720 (plus the services) ordered by the English East India Company in one season. This china-ware was divided between the four ships then at Whampoa, each carrying approximately £1,500 worth, packed in sago.

The order for the following season, 1776, follows exactly the same pattern; the same range of goods

The East India Company's porcelain trade

6   A Chinese porcelain mug painted with scenic panel and inscribed 'The Commercial Banking Company of Aberdeen'. 5¾ inches high, c. 1790.

Victoria and Albert Museum (Crown Copyright)

was ordered, but in even greater quantities; 168,000 blue and white cups and saucers against 96,000 in 1775; 2,100 pairs of sauceboats against 1,200 and 35,000 dinner plates instead of 20,000 in the previous year.

These orders are remarkable in several respects, particularly as the Supra-cargoes wrote to the directors that they had 'paid the most minute regard to the list of investments which in every particular we have taken for our guide...'. Yet in the whole 1774 order of over 100,000 enamelled specimens only two (unspecified) patterns were ordered, and in the vast mass of blue and white only four patterns were requested. If we accept 'patterns' as meaning painted designs, not shapes, and I think this is reasonable as items such as bowls and pattypans normally come in only one basic shape, then the ordered china-ware was of a more utilitarian nature than one would suppose from the items still available. The small number of patterns may reflect the Chinese mass-production methods or be due to the need to reduce the cost as much as possible, hence long runs of a few designs.

The selection of objects, too, is in all cases basic tablewares, not ornamental vases and similar decorative objects. The Supra-cargoes, acting for the directors in London, appear to have been over-concerned with the purchase of low-cost objects – 3,200 one-quart bowls, but only 200 more costly (about 2s 6d or 12½p) gallon bowls. The fact that they were satisfied with only two enamelled patterns and four blue and white designs would have simplified manufacture for the Chinese and consequently would have kept the price down.

With two comparable lists of identical objects ordered at the same time, one set in enamelled designs, the other painted in underglaze blue, one can illustrate the point that there was little difference in price between the two modes of decoration; some objects were even the same price and a few were more expensive in blue and white than in overglaze enamels. I give below some examples; again, the prices are in mess (or a tenth of a tale), about three new pence.

	Coloured	Blue and White
Coffee cups with handles	026	025
Custard cups	050	050
Gallon bowls	330	300
3-Pint bowls	100	110
1-Quart bowls	080	080
Water plates, flat	036	030

The four sizes of mugs were all more expensive in underglaze blue than in enamel. This may surprise many readers, but the cost of raw materials, of forming the object and of transport – and the profit margin for the Chinese – would have been the same, whatever the decoration. Also, the underglaze blue designs were often more ornate and required more work than some of the later enamelled repetitive patterns which could be of a simple nature. Also, as the underglaze decoration was added at inland Ching-tê Chên, any loss in transit to Canton would have been complete, whereas the enamelled pieces at this period were sent in the undecorated state to be enamelled at Canton.

These lists of china-ware for the 1775 season also illustrate the fact that much of the tableware was still being ordered individually, not in complete sets. Taking, for example, the blue and white assortment: only eighty teasets were ordered, but individually 48,000 cups and saucers, 1,200 teapots, 2,000 covered sugar-bowls and 4,000 milk-pots were required. In dinner wares we again have only eighty complete services but 20,000 dinner plates and 4,000 soup plates. The plates were most probably sold on their own, not made up into sets in England, for no tureens or dishes were separately ordered.

The fact that only tablewares were ordered for 1775, and of only six stock patterns, underlines the point that the East India Company's bulk imports were standard utilitarian wares. These must have enjoyed a ready market, but we have to look elsewhere for the source of the decorative objects and of the finely painted examples made to special order with the owners' armorial bearings, initials or other individual designs (see Chapters 2 and 6).

The home-coming vessels of the East India Company, were normally 'topped-up' after they had crossed the second bar on their voyage down-river from Whampoa to the open sea. The two bars were the cause of much trouble to European vessels which often ran aground upon them, hence the practice of loading the last of the cargo after the vessels were safely across. These late loadings included a box of 'musters', samples of the articles and patterns comprising the main cargo. Also, being loaded last, these samples were easily unloaded when the vessel arrived back in England and the samples were available many days before the china-ware at the bottom of the hold was unloaded.

A letter written by the Council of Supra-cargoes in Canton explained the new system of compiling these 'musters'.

As the sending of a muster for each of the 192 articles of china ware packed for the *Grosvenor* and other ships might occasion some confusion at home in the sorting them and would be attended with great expense to the china ware merchants, we have judged it more expedient to send only the different patterns painted on a dish of the 3rd size and a complete assortment of musters of one pattern painted and gilt and one pattern blue and white which we hope will be sufficient to show the size and shape of each article as well as the painting...
(Canton, 1 November 1775.)

This amendment to the standard practice of sending a sample of each article suggests strongly that this 1775 shipment was larger and more complex than those previously sent, hence the need to simplify the system and paint the different designs on one dish. Yet, when we study the list (p. 44) we are struck by the small range of objects ordered.

The Council of Supra-cargoes at Canton appears to have had exact details of the cargo carried in the vessels of each Company (excepting the 'Country' vessels plying between China and India) and precise particulars of both imports and exports are recorded in their diaries. In regard to china-ware it is of interest to tabulate the basic details concerning the china-ware shipped from Canton in the 1777–8 season.

China-ware carried by European East India Company vessels

No. of vessels	Country	Tons china-ware
8	Britain	348
4	Holland	111
6	France	100
2	Sweden	99
2	Denmark	39

The total weight of china-ware was approximately 800 tons. To this must be added the china-ware carried in the Portuguese and Spanish vessels which normally remained at Macao, their Chinese goods being purchased there or sent down from Canton. We must also add to this total the china-ware carried in the many English 'Country' (India-trade) vessels trading at Canton. In this 1777–8 season there were eight such 'Country' ships, the same number as was engaged on the full voyage home to England (see p. 82).

The English Company's china-ware shipment of 348 tons in the 1777–8 season was all purchased from the one Chinese merchant, Exchin and, as stated, comprised only two different enamelled patterns and four designs painted in underglaze blue. These goods were divided nearly equally between the eight vessels available, each carrying for the Company's account seventy-six whole chests and a hundred half-chests of china-ware (plus the variable 'Private Trade'). The stated value (cost price) of china carried by each of these English East Indiamen was approximately £1,560. Of course, in different years the number of each country's ships varied as did the proportion of cargo carried, but English vessels always outnumbered those of any other nation.

At about this period the demand for the normal range of Chinese porcelains seems to have slackened, and we find the Council of Supra-cargoes at Canton writing to the directors in London regarding their earlier letter of instruction:

As the orders this year received from the Honble. Court give us reason to suppose that China ware is not now an article in so high demand as some seasons past we have come to the resolution not to make any contract for the ensuing year as the quantity we have remaining will...be sufficient to load eight ships and in case we should want a small quantity it will be much better to purchase a few chests than be encumbered with a large quantity by engaging before hand for it...
(Canton, 21 January 1779.)

Hence in 1779–80 the English Company did not ship home any new china, only stock left over from the previous season and ordered in 1777–8. They do not appear to have been over-concerned with new patterns or shapes – only, as noted previously, with stock lines.

However, an unusual circumstance arose in the 1781–2 season which does point to the fact that new patterns were required, and perhaps that each yearly order was for new or different patterns. The situation is explained in a letter from the Council of Supra-cargoes to the directors in London: 'As the season is far advanced and the arrival of our instructions uncertain, we thought it necessary to contract with Exchin for 1,200 chests of china-ware, the quantity contracted for last season – the Patterns to be new.' (Letter dated 9 October 1781.) While new designs were stipulated it can be assumed that the assortment of purely useful wares, as well as the quantity, was to be the same as that previously ordered.

In another letter from the directors in London to the Supra-cargoes in Canton we gather that all was not well with the china shipments:

We think it necessary to repeat, we continue to sustain very heavy losses by the china ware being much false packed, that is to say the goods have come of a variety of Patterns, where they should all have been alike particularly in Table and other sets – In some cases there have been so many patterns and so very different from each other that they could not possibly been put up to Sale in Sets but have been obliged to be sold as odd pieces.

We seldom open a parcel of sets especially Table and tea, but we find several articles different from the pattern.

Trade in London was poor. Joseph Lygo, the manager of the Derby factory's retail establishment in London, reported back in October 1788 to William Duesbury in Derby: 'In the India House sale this week I am informed out of more than eighteen hundred lots there was not five-hundred sold' and trade was 'very dead'. This was at a period when more and more good, decorative, English porcelain and inexpensive earthenwares including the serviceable creamwares were coming on to the market and when the high rate of duty charged on the imported wares was beginning to outweigh the old advantage – the cheapness of the Chinese porcelain. The import duty in the early 1790s was very nearly fifty per cent, and was soon to be more than doubled.

This high rate of duty, however, was scarcely to affect the Company, for in December 1791 the Court of Directors decided to abandon their bulk import of china-ware.

So that this heavy, water-resisting commodity should continue to be used as 'flooring' for the cases of tea, the Private Trade venture of the ships' officers and crew was further encouraged, but on certain conditions. The position was regulated in a resolution made on Wednesday 7 December 1791:

Resolved that the Commanders and officers of the Company's ships be prohibited from shipping any china-ware whatever as Private Trade except the same be packed in half-chests and made use of as flooring for the Company's teas and that a clause be inserted to this effect in the Court's Instructions to the Commanders, also that this regulation be communicated to the Supra-cargoes with orders as far as is in their power to see it put into execution that in case any private trade china-ware shall in future be brought home in any packages except half-chests or stowed otherwise than as flooring for the Company's teas the Proprietors of such china-ware shall be charged whole freight for the same. The owners of the ship be credited for the Freight thereof in the same manner as for the Company's cargo...

However, with communications as they were the Company could not stop in a day, a week, or even in a year, the importation of china-ware on their own account. The orders had to be carried to Canton on that season's boats and the vessels there loading and on their way home would have carried the normal china-ware cargo ordered by the directors in 1790. In May 1792 there were still the usual references to china-ware sales: 'Resolved that 1818 lots of china ware more or less, be declared for Tuesday the 24th July next and that no more china ware be sold until September sale next, except as may be uncleared or in Private Trade.'

The directors' decision to discontinue the purchase of china-ware certainly had its effect on the

Company's china-ware merchant, Exchin. This is told in the following report written by the Select Committee of Supra-cargoes at Canton in their letter home to the Court of Directors. The letter is dated Canton, 14 May 1795.

We have lately had an application from Exchin our late china ware merchant to afford him some relief from the loss and inconvenience he has sustained by the discontinuance of that article in the Honble. Company's investment.

It appears by the Honble. Courts Instructions on that Head that the Select Committee were directed to send home no more china ware than they had existing engagements for and accordingly it was discontinued in the year 1792, there being then no existing contracts.

The plea urged by Exchin is, that although no contract was made at the close of the season 1791, the then President of the Select Committee had encouraged him to make a quantity under the presumption that it would be wanted, but as no china-ware was ordered that year, it has been upon his Hands ever since, till this time that his losses and misfortunes have compelled him to have recourse to the Honble. Company for relief. The amount of the china-ware is about 60,000 Tales [some £20,000]…

It is pleasing to record that this Chinese merchant continued in business for many years. An American report of 1809 relates: 'Exchin…has much business…does not pack so well [as old Synchong] and china ware not generally so good…has considerable business', but from the Supra-Cargoes' letter we note that the English East India Company's direct interest in Chinese porcelain ceased in 1792. However, owing to the considerable stocks of china-ware aboard home-coming vessels and in the Company's warehouses, it was seemingly not until January 1795 that the trade buyers of Chinese porcelain awoke to the fact that fresh supplies were not available. A Minute dated 4 February 1795 reads simply: 'A letter from the buyers of china ware dated the 28th ultimo being read expressing their hope that the trade in that article may be continued by the Company. Ordered that the said letter be referred to the consideration of the Committee of Warehouses.' This Committee's deliberations were recorded on 13 March 1795:

The Committee of Warehouses in a report dated the 11th instant, now read stating that the reasons urged by the dealers in china ware in their memorial are not sufficiently forcible to induce the Committee to recommend to the Court to depart from their former resolutions as to the non-importation of china ware; and with regard to the china ware now on hand, application be made to the Lords Commissioners of the Treasury praying that the period for allowing the drawback on the sum may be extended for two years from the expiration of the usual period.

Resolved that this Court approve the said report.

This Minute shows not only that stocks of the Company's china-ware were still available but also that the export trade from London was important, for the 'drawback' was the repayment of import duties on wares reshipped out of the country. The normal period permitted for the claiming of 'drawback' was three years from importation. As this period was running out, now that only old stock was being included in the sales, the dealers and the Company sought (and gained) Government sanction for the period to be extended for a further two years, giving a five-year period during which import duty could be reclaimed on re-exported Chinese porcelain.

In April 1795 the Minutes of the Court of Directors surprisingly record the fact (or opinion) that heavy water-proof china-ware was not now required to floor the all-important teas. This information stems from a request to the Company from the dealer (and later porcelain manufacturer), Miles Mason. On 8 April the Minutes recorded: 'The Committee of Shipping in a report dated the 7th instant now read stating that they have taken into consideration a letter from Mr Miles Mason requesting to know on behalf of the dealers in china ware upon what terms of freight the Company will permit their officers in the Company's service…to import china ware.' The Committee's negative reply to this was agreed by the full Court and so finally ended the commercial importation of Chinese porcelains by the Honourable English East India Company. The directors opted out of the market at a convenient time, for a new act of 1799 increased the rate of duty to over a hundred per cent, to £109 8s 6d per hundred pounds. This is increased to about 118 per cent when the Company's charges are added to the duty.

The market for Chinese export market porcelains was now supplied solely by the private venture of the ships' officers and crews for, notwithstanding the directors' refusal of April 1795, the Private Trade continued, but before discussing this Private Trade in detail in the following chapter I shall touch on the international aspect of Chinese export market porcelains.

Various authorities have tended to divide Chinese export market porcelains into several national types, referring to patterns or shapes as having been made for the Dutch, French or American markets. I believe that this division is largely imaginary and that Chinese porcelains are, in the main, international. No one nation held a monopolistic position with Chinese manufacturers and merchants. While the agents or Supra-cargoes of any one company may have brought to Canton a new European shape or design to be copied, the Chinese were the last to recognise any form of copyright, and the new design was henceforth available to the buyers of all nations. For example, the tureen shape shown in Plate 7 is believed to have been copied from a standard English form introduced in Wedgwood's cream-coloured earthenware, yet Chinese tureens of this shape – popular in the 1785–1800 period – are to be found bearing decorations indicating production for many different markets. The single East India Company (probably the English) which introduced this shape to the Chinese potters certainly did not enjoy any special privileges in its subsequent use.

Decorative patterns introduced for one country were found to be saleable, with little or no modification, in another. My own family firm, situated on the south coast of England, purchased locally a magnificent, large Chinese service bearing the American eagle and emblem in all its splendour, and of such size that it is difficult to see how such an American-oriented porcelain service could be brought to, and sold in, Great Britain. Parts of this service are now in most of the largest American collections. It is doubtful if the present owners, or the museum curators, realise that these American eagle-decorated pieces were in Britain for some 150 years before they reached American shores. It is also not unusual to find, in the British Isles, Chinese export porcelain bearing the supporters of the Arms of the City of New York, the central position being adapted to display a neutral emblem or the initial of a private European owner. It can be assumed that an order for the complete New York Arms was placed by an American captain or Supra-cargo, but very soon the design was adapted to become a general one for sale to all buyers. There can have been few British buyers who realised that their own initial was accompanied by the supporters to the New York Arms.

A considerable quantity of so-called Dutch market Chinese porcelain has been found in Britain, including pieces bearing the emblem of the Dutch East India Company, as seen on the dated 1728 teapot shown in Colour Plate 2. This design is taken from, and no doubt commemorates, the introduction in 1728 of the Dutch East India

Colour Plate 2 A rare small Chinese porcelain teapot, the enamelled decoration taken from the Dutch East India Company's new coinage of 1728. 4½ inches high, *c.* 1730.
Private collection

7 A finely enamelled Chinese armorial soup-tureen of the 1790s, showing a European form widely popular at the time. Various styles of decoration were applied to it. 9¼ inches high.
Godden of Worthing Ltd

The East India Company's porcelain trade

Company's own coinage. This is not to be taken as the exact date of manufacture of this teapot, although it would date from shortly after this. Records show the importation into England of Dutch-style goods. For example, in 1704 the English Company's vessel *Union* brought home goods including '70 Dutch men, sitting, 2 sorts' and '2 Dutch families' (see p. 276). We know, too, that the English Company purchased Chinese and Japanese goods at the Dutch station at Batavia. Moreover, some English East Indiamen sailed to Dutch ports before returning to the Thames, and much Oriental porcelain landed in London was re-exported to Holland and other countries. Porcelains bearing French inscriptions, such as the covered cups and stands shown in Plate 8, are to be found outside France, and Chinese porcelains made for the Persian market are by no means rare in Europe.

In time of war particularly – and there were many such times in the eighteenth century – East Indiamen of different nations were taken as prizes, and their cargoes landed and sold in foreign countries. In July 1783, for example, the following advertisement appeared in the *Norfolk Chronicle*:

> WILLIAM BELOE, CHINAMAN
> MARKET PLACE, NORWICH
> Has just received from the India Company's sale a large and regular assortment of useful and ornamental china…He has also a large parcel of useful china from Commodore Johnstone's Prize Goods taken from the Dutch…

In December 1797 the cargoes of three Dutch vessels were sold in London (see p. 214), and in 1790 the English Company had even agreed to purchase the cargoes of two Swedish East Indiamen then in Portsmouth harbour.

For one reason or another eighteenth-century Chinese (and Japanese) porcelains were widely spread throughout Europe and, to some extent, North America and while this book is concerned primarily with articles shipped to Great Britain, these wares have their counterparts in other countries and the information here given should be of interest to collectors in any country.

The various periods of Chinese porcelain discussed in the following pages are given below. These periods are related to the Chinese Emperors of the Ch'ing dynasty:

Shun Chih	1644–1661
K'ang Hsi	1662–1722
Yung Chêng	1723–1735
Ch'ien Lung	1736–1795
Chia Ch'ing	1796–1820
Tao Kuang	1821–1850
Hsien Fêng	1851–1861
T'ung Chih	1862–1873
Kuang Hsu	1874–1908
Hsüan T'ung	1909–1912

8 A Chinese porcelain covered handleless cup and stand painted in underglaze blue with a French inscription. French market. Cup 4¼ inches high, c. 1750. *Private collection*

2 The 'Private Trade' imports

We have seen in the previous chapter that the main bulk of the East India Companies' shipments of china-ware comprised standard tablewares decorated with a relatively small number of designs. They were porcelains that could be sold universally.

We have, therefore, to account for the large quantities of porcelains bearing special designs, particularly the personalised wares decorated with armorial bearings, crests or initials. Such wares, and a host of the more interesting designs, were not as a general rule imported by the various East India Companies, but were brought home as part of the Private Trade of Supra-cargoes, ships' officers and crews. Personal trading was permitted and even encouraged, at least by the English East India Company, and the profits served the ships' officers and crews as the main reward for the lengthy voyage with its very real dangers.

Private Trade imports from the East arrived in London long before the English Company had succeeded in opening its own trade with China. On 9 February 1615, a special committee met to consider the trading of Captain John Saris who had returned from Japan on the *Clove* in September 1614: '...taxinge him greatlie for the same and houldinge him worthie to bee made an example for haveinge straied soe farre beyond his commission...' Captain Saris then explained that others before him had brought home Private Trade goods, in one case double the quantity that they now objected to with him. After a lengthy debate the committee permitted Saris to keep his own trade venture as well as his normal wages, but left open the question of payment for the freight. It is doubtful if this 1614 Private Trade from Japan included porcelain, but certainly later private imports included very considerable quantities.

The extent of this Private Trade has not hitherto been realised, but it is true to say that over three-quarters of the Chinese export market porcelain now in national and private collections (or in fact illustrated in this book) is Private Trade porcelain rather than china-ware purchased by the East India Company.

I consider that Private Trade preceded the Company's imports of china-ware and that the saleability and profitability of such private ventures prompted the directors to join in. This is especially true when they started to send ships direct to China from London, since these vessels needed the heavy waterproof china as flooring for the teas. The direct European trade stemmed from the 'Country' vessels trading between Bantam, India and China, and in October 1686 the London directors wrote to their station at Fort St George, Madras:

…we give you leave for the future, if you like the proposition to send us any entire cargo of chyna goods proper for Europe marketts…at the first cost in Chyna…

If any gain arise by such chyna goods here, 20 per cent of the profit thereof shall be ours in consideration of our running the hazard of the sea, general charges of the Company and disbursement aforehand of our money in India. The rest of the gain…shall be yours and immediately returned you in Dollars by the first boat after the sale of such Chyna goods here…

In a further letter written in April 1687 the privileges were further extended: 'It is hereby ordered that the same liberty is and shall be granted to all persons here in England to direct their correspondents in India to load for their respective accounts what Chyna goods they shall think fitt on the terms following, viz. 20 per cent of their nett produce at the Company's sale.'

Not content with 20 per cent free of risk the Company in London resolved to enter the trade themselves. In a letter to Fort St George, dated 28 September 1687, we see the marriage of the two modes of importation, the Company's own imports and the Private Trading of its agents and employees. The letter read in effect: '…as the Court intend to carry on the China and Tonquin trade direct from England under their own management, they prohibit Madras on any pretence whatever from trading to those places on the Company's account but permit them to trade thither on their own private account…'

In another letter (dated 15 February 1689) the directors in London instructed their President at Fort St George not to send any dear Chinese porcelain on their account but permitted it to be sent as Private Trade – on which they could extract their percentage, without running any risk of investing their own cash. The letter reads: 'The china bowles you sent us by the *Beaufort* and other china wares, were all too dear, buy no more such commodities for us, but you may send, if you will, china goods for your own account upon the Indulgences we have granted to others.'

Private Trade was sometimes the cause of much trouble to the East India Companies. As early as 1609 the Dutch East India Company wrote to their Governor-General in the East Indies: '…as the agents in our service have been frequently buying the best and finest china-ware on their own account in contravention of the agreement sworn before departure, you are now expressly ordered to forbid, prevent and put a stop to all such Private Trade and buying up of goods'.

Nearly a hundred years later, when the English Company was striving to commence regular trade at Canton, the Supra-cargoes complained of the adverse effects of the crews' Private Trading. The vessel concerned was the New English Company's vessel, *Macclesfield* (her adventures have already been told at some length on p. 33). On 13 December 1699, her Chief Supra-cargo Robert Douglas noted in his Journal: 'This morning Mr Strong, Mr Biggs and I went…about some china ware and at one

The Private Trade Imports

shop we found some of our own people's marks upon some goods that we were in terms about for the Company and at another place we found they had outbid us for a parcel of goods that I had actually agreed for...'

The Supra-cargoes issued instructions to the ship's captain, that 'his officers and seamen... forbear buying till they receive orders in writing, according as it was agreed by ye Court of Directors'.

The reason for this concern about the private purchases of the ship's crew was the great dearth of china-ware at Canton, a state of affairs evidenced by entries in the Supra-cargo's Journal:

> This day [29 December 1699] Mr Strange, Mr Biggs and I went all about ye city to every china-ware shop of any note to find some more but see none that was good so that we returned without any.
>
> Mr Biggs went all about ye city to look for some more china ware to make up our remaining parcell but could find none but some coarse cups [entry dated 28 January 1700].

Moving forward ninety years we find that the superior quality of the goods purchased as Private Trade was causing concern to the Company's directors in London. A letter of May 1790 from London to the Supra-cargoes in Canton states:

> ...if you had been led to believe...that the Private Trade china-ware is in general inferior to that of the Company's you have shewn yourselves possessed but of little knowledge, as the fact is notoriously the reverse...we have an opportunity of knowing this by actual comparisons as both sorts go through the same channel of our sales and even the selling prices would prove the fact, if we had no other way of judging.

Having quoted references to Private Trade dated 1609, 1699 and 1790, we can retrace our steps and consider in more detail this important aspect of the porcelain trade, remembering that from 1791 onwards, when the English East India Company ceased to order china-ware on its own account, *all* such imports would have comprised Private Trade.

The early records are unfortunately scanty; we find in the Company records such instructions as: 'It is ordered that a tubb of china belonging to Mr James Woodhouse brought home on ye *London* be delivered to him free of "freight"' (14 September 1670), but there are no details of the exact contents of the tubs. However, these simple records are evidence that Private Trade china-ware was entering the country at an early date, before the Company itself was concerned with its importation.

In 1682 the original Company laid down regulations for Private Trading to ensure that it benefited from the proceeds. On 21 June 1682 permission to trade was granted to 'the Company's factors and all Commanders, officers and seamen employed in the Company's service...provided the said goods and merchandise be duly registered in a book appointed to be kept for that purpose and that a certificate thereof be transmitted to the Company from their agent or Chief [Supra-cargo]...and that the same be brought into ye Company's warehouse in London and not sent home upon ye Company's tonage and that permission money be paid...'

The amount of 'permission money' was laid down in a Court Minute of 30 September 1682: 'All sorts of puslin [sic] and earthenware, china-ware and all other goods and merchandises not prohibited by the Company – 6 per cent by Englishmen and 8 per cent by strangers for Permission, according to their value to be adjudged by the Court of Committee or such as they shall appoint thereunto and also the same Freight that shall be paid by the Company.'

The amount of goods to be allowed, the 'Indulgencies', were also laid down. In December 1683 we find recorded a list of 'New Indulgencies' on the following scale:

Colour Plate 3 Finely painted early-eighteenth-century Chinese blue and white porcelains. The quality of the painting is suggestive of Private Trade imports rather than the bulk purchases of the various East India Companies. Diameter of plate 8¼ inches, c. 1740–50.   *Godden of Worthing Ltd*

For every 100 tons the ship –
- Commander   £200
- Chief Mate   £60
- Second Mate   £40
- Third Mate   £30
- Fourth Mate   £20
- Junior Officers   £15
- Midshipmen   £10
- Other seamen, a total of £15 each.

The 'permitted goods' that could be purchased as Private Trade included 'all sorts of china-wares, all sorts of lackered wares'. A similar order of 1694 lists also as permitted goods 'china images and pictures, cabinets, screens, sugar-candy, Persian carpets and diamonds'.

Although permission was granted to the ships' officers, the Company records include many references to china-ware to be delivered direct to private individuals, for example:

It is ordered that it be referred to the Committee of Private Trade to give direction for delivering to Mrs Priscila Haddock eleven tubs of china ware brought home on the *Princess of Denmark*, she paying freight and other charges due thereon…
(Court Minute, 10 November 1691.)

It is ordered that the goods brought home on the *Princess Anne of Denmark* [on her 1689 voyage to Madras and China] belonging to Mrs Haddock be viewed by the Committee of Private Trade, who calling Mr Rousby to their assistance are desired to value the same and upon payment of the Permission due thereon to cause them to deliver to her as desired.

It will be observed that the Company had a special Committee for Private Trade, and a very hard-working committee too, for the records abound with directions to this Committee, which met regularly twice a week to value or deliver items to private persons: 'The Committee of Private Trade are desired to give direction for delivering of a parcel of china ware brought home on the *Benjamin*, for Sir Robert Howard.' (Court Minute, 13 April 1694.)

For the bulk of the Private Trade the standard practice was to sell it by auction; it was 'put up at the Company's candle'. In the early days there seems to have been a choice, for in September 1696 we find minuted: 'It is ordered that it be referred unto the Committee of Private Trade and warehouses to value the Permission goods brought home on the *Armenian Merchant*, belonging unto Mr Obediah Sedgwick, or any other person, that is unwilling to have them put up at the Company's candle and upon paying the Permission money and other charges the said goods be delivered unto them.'

This seems to have been an exception; most of the imports – apart from presents – were sold by auction. Digressing for a moment, it is interesting to read that the Commander of this vessel, Captain Newman 'brought home a large quantity of Private Trade goods on his own account, far exceeding the three per cent allowed in Charterparty', he desiring 'to have the same free of permission aledging that the greatest part was stowed under the pallating and took no part of ye ships tonnage.' Alas, he was still charged the standard 6 per cent Permission.

Some consignments of china-ware imported into Britain in the seventeenth century were goods purchased on speculation in the East by the ship-owners. However, as the Company enjoyed the monopoly of this trade the goods had to be sold to it, or at least sold at its auction sales and 'Permission' paid. As an example of this practice I quote the relevant passages from the Court Minute concerning the vessel *Sarah*.

It is ordered that it be referred to the Governor Sir Jeremy Sambrooke and Mr Eyles to meet with the owners and proprietors of the goods brought home on the ship *Sarah* from China and to treat, agree and conclude with them on such terms and conditions as they shall think fit, touching the landing, housing, making sale and paying permission of such goods as they shall judge best for the mutual satisfaction of the Adventurers of the general joynt stock [the Company] and the proprietors of the said cargo...The Governor now acquainted the Court that the Committee thereunto appointed had agreed with the Proprietors of the *Sarah* the ten per cent permission ...and that the owners are to advance moneys for the Customs and [the goods] to be brought into the Company's warehouse and sold at their candle. (Minute dated 30 September 1696.)

The matter was shortly concluded, for on 9 October 1696 a Minute records: 'A writing of agreement between the Governor and Company on the one part and Sir Joseph Herne, Sir Stephen Evance and Sir James Houblon on behalf of themselves and the rest of the Proprietors of the goods and merchandise lately imported on the ship *Sarah* from China ...was now read and approved of...'

China-ware from the *Sarah* was sold on 8 December 1696, and comprised 99,550 articles. These privately imported goods from the *Sarah* constitute the first recorded *large* auction sale of china-ware to be held by the Company. The cargo was a very mixed one and was apparently very profitable – a pair of lacquered *escritoires* or desks fetched £296, nearly three times the estimated value, or reserve price, of £100. This successful private venture may have suggested to the directors that they should import china-ware as part of the Company's own trade, so taking the full profit rather than the mere 10 per cent Permission.

The fact that such privately imported goods (and also the later Private Trade of the ships' officers and crews) was in the main sold at the Company's auction sales enables us to discover at least some of the items brought to England from China some 250 years ago, for many of these auction sale records are still available. The practice of selling by auction was required under the Royal Charter, presumably so that the correct market value could be gauged for customs duty. It also permitted the Company to add its own percentage for Permission and other charges.

In general, the Company's bulk purchases comprised tablewares, and these were offered at auction in large lots, for example: '1,500 blue and white cups at 4*d*' or '720 ribbed bowles at 8*d*', but when, in the auction records, we find in one lot a small number of mixed wares such as: '2 teapots, 1 Image, 4 blew bowls', we may reasonably deduce that these goods were Private Trade purchases, and brought home by the officers and crew. In the years for which we have records of the detailed purchase orders given to the Supra-cargoes by the Court of Directors, we can with reasonable safety assume that the multitude of objects not mentioned in the directors' orders represent the private venture of the ships' officers and crews.

Private Trade was by no means confined to Oriental porcelains; much lacquered furniture was brought to Europe in this way, as well as tea, silks, fans, rhubarb, ginger, and other Oriental products. Private Trade was often a two-fold investment, persons being permitted to take out to China bullion (normally silver pieces of eight) with which to purchase gold in China, so that precious stones could be bought in India on the return journey for ultimate sale in London. This trade is shown by many Court Minutes granting permission to export bullion. One such request from William Bowridge, the chief Supra-cargo on the *Fleet*, is reflected in the following note: 'It is ordered that Mr Bowridge be permitted to ship on board the *Fleet* to the value of £4,000 in forreign bullion, to be invested in gold at Amoy, wherein to be purchased Diamonds, Bezoar stones in India...he paying into the Treasury after the rate of 2 per cent freight on the same.' The Company seems to have wanted its cut from everything.

The Private Trade Imports

Since Private Trade was a two-way venture much English merchandise was exported to China, including glassware, clocks and mirrors. In October 1693 the Company fixed the freight charge on outward-bound Private Trade at £11 6s 0d per ton. The china-ware brought home to England by the ships' officers and crews could itself be varied: 'The Committee of Private-Trade reported to the Court that having essayed to view the goods brought home on the *Trumball* belonging to Mr Power and Mr Maidstone they find they consist each chest of such variety and sorts of goods as that they cannot possibly be viewed in the place where they now are…' (Court Minutes, 4 August 1699.)

While the bulk of the china (137,132 items) from the *Trumball* was sold in July 1699 in large quantities, and probably comprised the Company's purchases, many lots were made up of small mixed selections which were almost certainly Private Trade goods. These small lots included, for example:

Lot 11	1 pair beakers
	1 pair flower pots
	3 large jars, red
	1 do. blew
	1 do. cream colour
	2 do. blew and white
	23 butter pots with ears and covers
	6 small beakers, red
	8 do. bottles
	3 small bottles
	2 sugar pots with covers
	22 small beakers
	1 red coarse plate
Lot 14	8 wrought flower-pots
	1 square do. painted
	2 long necked bottles
	4 do. as if cracked all over
	1 beaker do.
	[These would be the well known Craquelure wares which were deliberately crazed all over with surface cracks]
	10 bottles
	4 large butter pots
	5 wrought do.
	1 do. olive, blew and white

The goods brought home from Amoy on the *Nassau* at the same period, including figures and animal models, were even more varied and interesting. We learn that some at least of these goods comprised the Supra-cargoes' Private Trade: 'It is ordered that the goods brought home by Mr Hillier and Mr Brewster, Supra-cargoes of the *Nassau*, for their private accounts be valued by the Committee of Private Trade and sold at the Company's candle, except such part only as are designed by them for presents, which are to be delivered to them on the usual terms…' (Minute, 13 October 1699.)

It is interesting to see that items designated as gifts were excluded from the Company's sales (and the available records) on payment of a small fee. These two Supra-cargoes from the *Nassau* were paid some £5,000 for commission and Private Trade goods.

From the *Nassau*'s Amoy shipment of over 242,000 articles of china-ware, I have selected the following sample lots which I consider were Private Trade, belonging either to the Supra-cargoes, or to the ship's officers:

	Valued at	
32 large lyons, gilded	7s each	⎫
6 middle-size do.	5s	⎬ Sold at 1s 7d
56 small women painted	2s	⎬ 'advance' on
37 children do. large	4s	⎬ each piece
Several small images	6d	⎭

Colour Plate 4 A fine Chinese covered bowl decorated with typical semi-translucent *famille verte* overglaze colours. 8½ inches high, c. 1740. *Private collection*

(This manner of selling, by the 'advance' over the stated value or reserve, was quite normal at the Company's sales.)

45 Tartarian women	2s	
21 do. painted	2s	
10 large Sancta Marias	4s	Sold at 1s 2d
9 small do.	2s	'advance' on
8 large lyons, painted	5s	each piece
38 cocks, painted and white	2s	
40 images, very small	6d	

I believe it can be assumed that where no mention of colour is made, the figure was undecorated or white *Blanc de Chine*. This point is reasonably clear from the first two items in this lot: '45 Tartarian women; 21 do. painted.' The subject of Fukien porcelain is treated more fully in Chapter 8.

Many lots from the *Nassau* relate to tablewares. Of the smaller mixed lots, which I believe were Private Trade selections, we find, for example:

64 blew and white bowls	2s	Sold at 6d
81 do.	2s	'advance' on
433 coffee cups	3d	each item
82 red teapots	2s	
10 brown bowls and plates	2s	Sold at 3s 7d
10 bowles	2s 6d	'advance' on
3 teapots	4s	each item
3 Jarrs and 2 beakers	1s 6d	
100 chocolate cups		

The variety of different shapes and styles of decoration included in shipments late in the seventeenth century is shown by selecting from the *Nassau*'s Amoy cargo sold in London in November 1699 some of the most ordinary of ceramic objects – saucers. The prices given are the sale-room valuation or reserve price.

798 saucers, fine flowered	10d
570 fine saucers, 18 squares	10d
1,081 fine painted saucers	8d
225 yellow saucers – painted	8d
1,085 saucers, square painted	8d
542 fine waved saucers	8d
152 fine painted ribbed saucers	8d
267 purled saucers	8d
298 saucers, blue and white	8d
243 saucers, large blue	8d
169 white small painted saucers	6d
50 saucers, brown painted	6d
930 flowered saucers	6d
107 saucers waved blue and white	6d
900 saucers, fine ribbed, blew	6d
560 saucers, fine scollopted	6d
361 saucers, whey coloured	4d
389 saucers, olive coloured	4d
716 saucers, fine brown	4d
1,470 saucers, cream coloured	4d
1,148 codlin coloured saucers	4d
166 blew scollopted saucers	4d
85 fine purled saucers	4d
42 saucers, flowered	4d
1,865 brown saucers	3d
12 coarse saucers	3d

Not all these saucers would have been for teacups, especially not the larger ones, for we find an interesting triple entry:

17 saucers large	8d
189 do. not so large	8d
186 do. for tea	4d

The cups in the same sale included chocolate cups, coffee cups, covered cups and teacups – large and small.

While the *Nassau*'s cargo from Amoy was being sold the up-and-coming New Company was establishing a settlement at Chusan, one of the main purposes of which was to purchase Japanese products (see p. 30). The vessel carrying the new President to Chusan had some £3,500 worth of silver pieces of eight for the Private Trade purchases of the ship's officers and the owners. Often

the ship's owners – normally a partnership of two or three wealthy investors – traded on their own account, and we can perhaps assume that some at least of the captain's purchases were on behalf of the owners of the ship.

By the end of the seventeenth century, the Company was beginning to simplify its Private Trade accounting by charging a set percentage to cover a number of small charges: 'It is ordered that for the future the Accountant General do charge $\frac{1}{2}$ per cent on the produce of the goods sold at the Company's candle for the account of any private person in lieu of lighterage, wharfage, cartage, warehouse room and charges on the sale etc.' (Court Minute, 8 December 1699.)

This percentage seems unduly modest, so modest that I rechecked my notes with the original record before quoting it, but the position may not have been so simple in practice, and by 1706 the percentage for china-ware was a full 4 per cent 'in lieu of petty charges'. In 1701 Edward Barlow, a somewhat mournful writer, recorded his expenses in the following manner:

…all our goods being put into the East India Company's warehouse along with their own goods, they were not to come into our possession any more unless we would buy them again of the Company…and the Company…had 10 per cent of all goods that they demanded as their due on all goods from China…and then there was $6\frac{1}{2}$ per cent the Company allowed for discount [for prompt payment by the buyers] and then all other charges upon them as – waterage, wharfage, portage, cartage, warehouse room and more – as entering in the Customs House, and fees paid and to the East India House for bonds stamped, sealed and any clerks fees, so that by the accounts made up most people that served the Company found themselves great losers by goods they brought as freight.

This account is quoted from *Barlow's Journal of his Life at Sea in King's ships, East and West Indiamen and other merchantmen from 1659 to 1703* (London, 1934). It is obvious, however, that Edward Barlow was painting too black a picture – as he was prone to do – for if he had been correct in stating that persons bringing home Private Trade goods were 'great losers' there would be no more story to tell. As you will see, the eighteenth-century shipments abound with Private Trade, which proved profitable to all.

One entry in the Court Minutes of 1701 shows that Private Trade was not the sole prerogative of the captain and officers, but that the lower ranks dabbled in it – as far as Permission or their pocket would permit: 'On reading the petition of John Portusum, Gunner of the *Armenian Merchant*, it is ordered that it be referred to the Committee of Private Trade to cause the goods therein mentioned viz., one chest of china ware, a tub of tea and a small lackered box, to be delivered him on the usuall terms.'

While the amount of goods brought home on the private account of the ordinary seamen must have been quite small, the Private Trade of the captains often ran into thousands of pounds: 'The Committee of the warehouse are desired to consider the desires of Captain Merry [of the *Fleet*] for delivering him a parcell of fans and china ware brought for his account at the late sale and if they see fit to direct the cashire to take Captain Merry's note for £2,661 8s 3d being the amount of the said fans and china ware…' (Court Minutes, 14 May 1701.)

This entry shows again the strange practice of the owners of Private Trade goods buying them back at the Company's sales. Captain Merry could not, however, have bought back all his goods, for the Company records show that over £5,000 was paid to him 'on account of goods sold at the late sale'.

Apparently the china-ware was often stowed

The Private Trade Imports

loose in the East Indiamen and in the following Minute of 20 August 1701 we learn again of the goods belonging to the officers and crew:

Mr Brewster, the Second supra-cargo of the *Dorrill* now presented himself to the Court, acquainting them that there was a considerable parcel of china ware stored loose in the bread room part of which is belonging to the Company and the rest to the Captain and officers and that of the other china ware on board packed in chests there might happen very great damage in case the chests were put into the Hogs with their bottoms upwards. It is thereupon ordered that Mr Roe and Mr Ball do take care that the chests be sent down and such trusty servants as they can confide in do look after the packing up all the china ware in the bread room and that it be sent up under distinct marks to the end those who claim any part thereof may have their share ascertained.

The reference to distinct marks on the packages to distinguish personal Private Trade goods is of significance, especially in connection with the sales held in 1706 (see p. 70). The *Dorrill* which brought home the above-mentioned loose china sailed for Batavia and Amoy in August 1699 and returned in August 1701.

In 1702 the Company amended slightly the amount of Private Trade, and the captains were permitted to bring home goods to the value of £300 per hundred tons tonnage of the vessel. The three Supra-cargoes normally accredited to each vessel received a percentage of the total sum realised on the cargo. This percentage was usually 5 per cent, shared between them, and – importantly – they were permitted to invest their commission in goods on their own account. The Supra-cargoes were also at this time permitted to carry out £1,200 for their personal trading. This money was normally taken out in the form of silver pieces of eight, the international currency of the period, often purchased in Holland. The Company's silver bullion or 'treasure' sent with each trading vessel was also drawn upon by the Supra-cargoes and ships' officers to finance their own Private Trade goods. A Court Minute of 31 December 1703 illustrates this point:

Ordered that Captain Harrison have a declaration that he has paid four thousand four hundred ounces of silver into the Company and therefore is to have out of the bullion loaden on the *Kent* four thousand four hundred ounces being the quantity allowed him by the indulgence as Commander.
That Captain Harrison have a further declaration that he has paid into the Company six hundred pounds and is therefore to have two thousand ounces of the bullion on board as supra-cargo.

The *Kent* under Captain Harrison sailed to Canton. The above Minute also shows, with many other records, that sometimes, especially before 1710, the ship's captain also served as one of the Supra-cargoes.

I have already stated that Private Trade goods had to be offered at the East India Company's auction sales, but that exemption was granted to goods brought in expressly as gifts. However, the Company still required their standard charges. One of many requests for the delivery of such gifts is given below. It is interesting because the china-ware is recorded as being packed in aniseed instead of sago.

The Court being moved that Captain Richards may have some parcels of china ware delivered him, which were brought only for presents, and the list of the particulars being read, amounting to Tale 304 as per invoice, including some anniseeds wherein the same was packed, ordered that the Committee of warehouses be desired to value the said china-ware...and to deliver them unto him, he paying to the Company the money due thereupon for custom and other charges and duties.
(Court Minutes, 29 January 1703.)

We can perhaps assume that such presents, especially those from a wealthy ship's captain, were rather special. In the case just quoted the china-ware presents cost in China just over a hundred pounds.

The extent of the Private Trade at this period can be gauged from goods brought home from Amoy in the *Dashwood*. On 12 March 1703, the Court of Directors 'Resolved that none of the china ware by the *Northumberland* and *Dashwood* to be put up at the next sale, except only the Private Trade.' It seems, therefore, that the china-ware credited to these two vessels and sold in March 1703 comprised not the Company's cargo but only the Private Trade goods of the crew. But when we examine the list of such goods we find not only the small mixed lots that I have hitherto regarded as private imports but a mass of other china-ware in very large quantities. One of the Supra-cargoes, and the ship's captain, Marmaduke Rawdon, had, before the sale, taken delivery of some of their goods – presumably the presents. The Court Minutes record on 19 February 1703: 'On reading the Petition of Abraham Wilmer, junior, it is ordered that the Committee of Private Trade be desired to value four small cases of china ware claimed by him. As also three small chests of china ware, one of Jappan earthenware and two China goods, claimed by Captain Rawdon and to deliver the same to them, they paying the freight, customs and other duties chargeable thereupon.'

Private Trade imports were a real form of trade and profit for the ships' captains and officers. One request to the Court of Directors is particularly interesting as it relates to the china-ware imported by a deceased captain, his widow requesting that the goods be delivered to Henry Tombes. This person was one of the chief 'chinamen' or china-ware dealers in London. His name continually appears in the available sale records as a steady buyer of the most expensive lots. One can assume that Tombes and similar dealers of the period financed some of the captains' Private Trade investment, requesting the captains to order and bring home especially saleable wares of individual designs of the type not catered for in the Company's standard imports. In the 1730s Henry Tombes was to stand security for Thomas Oaker, the senior porter at the Private Trade warehouse. The required security was £500. All the Company's servants were so secured by third parties – even the Supra-cargoes and ships' captains. Apart from ensuring the honesty and continued service of the various employees, the Company must have enjoyed the use of a sizeable amount of security money, unless only signed guarantees were required.

The china-ware credited to the *Northumberland* and the *Dashwood* in the sale of March/April 1703 amounted to 571,832 items – all apparently Private Trade goods. Obviously I can pick out and list only a very small proportion of these lots, and I will confine my attention to those items brought home on the *Dashwood* from the Chinese port of Amoy, and to those lots purchased by the ship's captain, Marmaduke Rawdon. He was probably buying back his own goods, this being the only way that he could retain them and have them available for resale at a further profit. The first price given is the official valuation, reserve, or starting-price. This, in all probability, would include an element of profit over the original cost and subsequent charges (see p. 261). The selling price is also given, often expressed as the 'advance' over the valuation or reserve; this 'advance' is per piece.

1,370 Chocolate cups	4d	Sold at 3d advance
370 Custard cups	3d	
620 Coffee cups	2d	
380 Dishes	1s	Sold at 2s 3d each
46 Painted men	2s 6d	Sold at 2s 5d advance
26 Sancta Marias [see p. 261]	5s	
144 Parrots	2s	Sold at 5s 3d each

645 Basons	6d	Sold at 1s 5d each	
120 Bowls, 96 dishes	1s 6d	Sold at 3s 8d	
380 Painted tea cups	4d	Sold at 1¼d advance	
1,830 do.	3d		
1,177 Saucers	—		
231 Patch boxes	1½d		
720 do.	1d		
46 Salvers	4d		
9 Salts	3d	Sold at 1d advance	
24 Mugs	4d		
27 do.	6d		
36 Bird pots	1d		
17 Wall flower-pots	3d		
16 Images	1s 6d		
4 Sucking bottles	2s		
14 Ink stands	6d		
13 Sand boxes	—		
50 Jarrs	4d	Sold at 1¼d advance	
110 Rowl waggons[1]	—		
43 Bottles	2d		
468 Essence bottles	1d		
35 Rowl waggons	—		
137 Jarrs and waggons	—		
250 Spoons	—		
310 Red chocolate cups	8d		
498 do.	6d	Sold at 1s 1d advance	
150 do.	—		
120 do.	4d		
36 Bowls and plates	1s 2d		
200 Bowls and 220 plates	8d	Sold at 1s 3d advance	
7 Incence pots	2s		
7 Pulpits and padries [See p. 272]	1s 6d		
6 Sugar boxes	8d		
47 Lyons	3d		
9 Cruits	2d	Sold at 2½d advance	
162 Mugs	3d		
90 Pipes	2d		
655 Essence bottles	½d		

(Plus hundreds of cups and saucers)

[1] Rowl waggons: the English version of the Dutch *Rolwagen*, French *Rouleau*, a standard shape of vase.

2 Japanese basons	£3	Sold at £2 4s advance	
4 Punch bowls	£2		
492 Rose water bottles	8d	Sold for 11d each	
208 Painted bowls	8d	Sold for 4s 2d each	
1,050 Patch boxes	1d	Sold for 2¼d each	
560 Chocolate cups	6d	Sold for 9d each	
476 Rose water bottles	8d	Sold at 5d advance	
180 Painted bottles	10d		
12 Large painted bowls	7s	Sold at 16s 6d each	
1,786 Beasts	1d	Sold at 2¼d each	
134 Lyons	2s	Sold at 3s 11d each	
5 Cocks	—		
9 Lyons in their dens	—		

Apart from these sample lots purchased, or re-purchased, by Captain Marmaduke Rawdon, we find many other lots sold to, or 'bought-in', by the Supra-cargoes. For example, Abraham Wilmer (see p. 66) purchased:

	2 Images	2s 6d	at 6d advance per piece	
	274 Belly mugs	6d		
	40 Can [or straight-sided] mugs	1s		
	22 do.	6d		
also	156 Wrestlers	4d		
	277 Men	3d		
	500 Dogs	2d		
	364 Dogs and lyons	1d	Sold at 1d advance	
	160 Rabbits	2d		
	36 do.	½d		
	276 Buffeloues	1d		
	510 Horses	—		
	1,070 Essence bottles	—		

These two sample lots suggest that many of the items in this sale brought home by the *Dashwood* from Amoy were of white Fukien porcelain of the *Blanc de Chine* type (see p. 258). Other wares were undoubtedly of Japanese origin, and some were so described in the original records.

The goods were not all sold to the ships' officers and Supra-cargoes; large quantities were purchased by the leading 'chinamen' of the time, London china dealers such as Henry Tombes. I will quote just three of the lots purchased by this one dealer:

21 Teapots	2s 6d
18 Painted mugs	1s
79 Teacups	4d
91 Saucers	—
18 Chocolate cups	4d
2 Sugar boxes	1s 6d
8 Coffee cups	2d
9 Saucers	—
8 Rose water bottles	—
6 Jarrs	1s
4 Pulpits and padries	1s
2 Men on monsters	2s 6d
2 Men on horses	2s
30 Men on antelopes	1s 6d
11 Soldiers	4d
36 Men leading horses	1½d
10 Men on birds	3d
40 Men on pedestalls	4d
123 Men	3d
10 Men and birds	3d
11 Images	1s 6d
2 Painted cocks	4d
8 Cranes with candle-sticks	1s
14 Dolphins	—
88 Birds	1d
46 Lyons	3d

This one lot was sold at 6d advance, per piece. Another lot on a more utilitarian level comprised:

114 Teacups	5d
380 do.	4d
389 Saucers	—
420 Teacups	—
378 Saucers	—
680 Teacups	—
380 Saucers	—

sold at 1½d advance. Among larger objects such as vases Henry Tombes bought:

50 Jarrs	3s
8 do.	—
19 do.	2s
4 do.	—
30 Beakers	2s
12 do.	1s 6d
48 Sucking bottles	3s

sold as one lot at 1s 1d advance over the stated valuation or starting price.

I have shown a representative section of the 571,832 items of Private Trade goods sold at the Company's 'candle' in 1703, and have demonstrated that the private venture of the ships' officers and of the Supra-cargoes was both varied and on a large commercial scale.

The quantity of china-ware included in this auction might seem too large for a Private Trade sale but the resolution of the Court of Directors suggests that it was Private Trade, as do facts recorded in the Court Minutes. For instance, on 9 April 1703 the chief mate of the *Dashwood* reported that he had bought-in at the sale some of his own venture: 'On reading the Petition of Humphrey Foss, chief mate of the *Dashwood* setting forth that part of his adventure in china ware, he was forced to order to be bought for his own account and praying that the same may be delivered him...'

Even a humble gunner from the vessel purchased china-ware as Private Trade and in the following record two relevant sale dates are mentioned, including that of March 1703: 'On reading a report from the Committee of Accounts of the 20th December last, ordered that the several parcells of china ware etc. therein mentioned amounting to £201 16s 10d belonging to Edward Smith, late gunner of the *Dashwood* and sold at the Company's Sale in March 1703, and September 1703 be delivered to his widow, she paying only £21 16s 7d into the Company's Treasury for the reason mentioned in the said report.' (Court Minute, 2

The Private Trade Imports

February 1708.)

This former gunner's Private Trade china was sold for over £200, and a later Minute mentions one lot of 221 items being valued at £4 19s 10d so we can deduce that the gunner's investment represented a large number of items.

The quantity of Captain Rawdon's Private Trade in china-ware can be gauged from the following petition recorded in the Court Minutes of 7 May 1703: 'Captain Rawdon moving the Court that he might be allowed to take out of the warehouse several parcels of goods which as he alledges were brought home on his own account and bought partly by himself and partly by other persons, by his orders amounting to £3,960, on the gross-sale and the customs and other duties and charges payable thereon might be deducted out of the produce of the other goods belonging to him, which were sold at the Company's candle.'

Most of the china-ware brought home as Private Trade goods in the eighteenth century was of Chinese origin, but some was Japanese (see Chapter 10), especially on those vessels that traded to Amoy. Some of these Japanese wares may have been earthenware rather than porcelain – if we can take literally original statements such as: 'Ordered that a cannister of Bohea tea, an escritoire, and a chest of Jappan earthenware being part of the Private Trade by the *Liampo* belonging to Captain Monck and brought by him, be delivered him...' (Court Minute, 18 May 1705).

The same Minute also shows that various members of the ship's company shared in the trade to a considerable extent, for half a ton of china is no small amount. The relevant order reads: 'Ordered that no freight be charged to Mr Ellwood, Surgeon of the *Liampo* for half a ton of chinaware by the said ship, belonging to the said Ellwood.'

In our consideration of Private Trade goods it is relevant to examine again the instructions given by the directors in London to the Supra-cargoes going to China to purchase china-ware on their behalf. The emphasis had for years been on useful wares 'the ordinary sort – dishes, plates and bowles', but in 1705 and 1706 the instructions were more detailed and precise. The instructions given to the Supra-cargoes of the *Oley* bound for Canton read: 'China ware, ten tons to consist of the ordinary cups and table plates and no other sort whatsoever.' (Letter dated 28 November 1705.) The Supra-cargoes of the *Stringer* bound to Chusan were instructed: '...china ware, we are vastly overstocked with all, however, it being Kentlege commodity and the ship must have a weight in her bottom to make her sail worthy, therefore buy twenty tons to be chiefly plates, trencher plates and others, and some small dishes – they will stow-close but buy no large pieces as Jars, beakers, images etc., nor any such china ware as is not heavy enough for Kentlege.'

The directors were playing right into the hands of the ships' officers and their Private Trade investment, but the Company extracted its percentage from this.

By this period the amount of Private Trade was increasing, and the situation was obviously getting out of hand. On 19 April 1706 explicit instructions were laid down:

Ordered, that the method to be observed for the future in making up the accounts of private goods claimed by any person, be as follows –

That Mr Wilmer and Mr White do certify to ye accountants the Customs due on such goods.

That Mr Granger and Mr Major do in like manner certify the freight due thereon.

That Mr Sargeant and Mr Fletcher do enter into a book for that purpose all accounts of Private Trade Goods...

That 2 per cent be charged on all Private Trade Goods in lieu of petty charges thereon, except China and lacquered ware on which 4 per cent is to be charged...

April 1706 was a most important month for our consideration of Private Trade goods sold at auction, for the Court Minutes again clearly state that in the forthcoming sales of the Old and New Companies' goods no china-ware would be included, but that 'all the Private Trade' goods would be offered. Of the series of April 1706 sales the one held on 16 April is of special interest, including as it did many lots of mixed china-ware. Here we have the recorded fact that none of the Companies' goods were included, and against the list of goods we find sets of initials showing the ownership of the various groupings. No doubt such initials are of the same nature as the 'distinct marks' mentioned in the Court Minute of 20 August 1701 (p. 65). One such marked page is shown in Plate 9 and, with such firm evidence, we can linger and list some of the Private Trade goods sold in the spring of 1706 (goods purchased in China in 1704 or 1705).

Apart from the goods included in the list (Plate 9), we find credited to the *Kent* from Canton lots such as the following, against the initials 'E.H.E.C.':

160 Teapots	1s 6d	Sold at 5s each
77 Bowls	3s	
96 Dishes	–	
2 Painted bowls	2s	Sold at 1s 1d advance
34 do. dishes	–	
20 Japanese plates	2s 6d	
13 Painted plates	1s 6d	
9 Jars with caudle cup covers	15s	Sold at £1 5s 8d each
6 Beakers with sielabub-pot covers	–	
224 Bowls	1s 6d	Sold at 6d advance
234 Dishes	–	
40 Bowls with panels	2s	
45 Dishes	–	
11 Longnecked bottles, red and gold	10s	Sold at 11s advance
3 Brown hubblebubbles	6s	
1 do. shipped [chipped]	5s	

55 Painted plates	1s 6d	Sold at 9¼d advance
270 do. scolloped	–	
428 Chocolate cups with handles	6d	
9 Dishes with blue and gold rims	2s 6d	

The initials E.H. conveniently fit the captain, Edward Harrison, but unfortunately one of the Supra-cargoes, Edward Harris, shared his initials. However, this sale record also includes lots listed against the initials 'E.H.T.P.', so the sale may have included goods from both the captain and the Supra-cargo. The second section credited to 'E.H.T.P.' comprised:

190 Teapots	1s 6d	Sold for 4s 1d each
89 do.	–	
7 Sugar dishes and covers	1s	Sold at 2s 2d advance
2 Bowls	–	
4 Patch boxes	–	
86 Bowles and dishes	2s 6d	Sold at 11d advance
15 Jars and covers	6s	
4 do. broken covers	5s	
2 do. no covers	4s	
14 beakers	6s	

Some of these goods could have been of Japanese origin, although the contemporary sale-records do not mention the word. However, when the Company's own china-ware imports on the *Kent* and the *Sidney* were sold later in the year the Court Minutes confirm my contention: 'Ordered that 273 chests and parcels of China ware and Jappan ware by the *Kent* and *Sidney* be put up to Sale.' (18 September 1706.)

The amount of Private Trade continued to increase and we find in 1707 a move to establish a special warehouse for such wares: 'Ordered that it be refered to the Committee of Private Trade to consider of the motion now made for putting all Private Trade goods in a warehouse apart and report their opinion thereupon.' The Committee acted quickly; four days later they recorded:

The Private Trade Imports

9 The original return of Chinese and Japanese porcelains sold by the English India Company on 16 April 1706, with the initials or 'distinct-marks' of the owners of these Private Trade imports.
India Office Records, London

The trade began to be better regulated with the appointment of a Surveyor of Private Trade who had to 'repair on board all the Company's returned ships' and ensure that all such Private Trade goods were speedily removed to the appointed warehouse – before they could be sold or delivered on the sly to avoid Customs duty and the Company's dues. Other abuses were obviously worrying the directors, apart from the smuggling of goods: extra money was being taken out to finance the profitable purchase of merchandise in Canton. In January 1711 the following was minuted:

Reported by the Committee appointed to inspect the bylaws and to make enquiry into the observation and execution of item...
The Committee having taken into their consideration the great importation of Private Trade and upon examination finding that several persons who here had lycence to carry out several small sumes, the least not under £700 and the greatest not exceeding £1,300, in Private Trade have brought home goods which have sold at the candle, for 3, 7 or 8 thousand pounds and for £16,000 to near £19,000.

The directors' claims were certainly based on fact, as is shown by minuted requests for payments such as: 'Request of Captain Robert Hudson being read, praying to have one thousand pounds advanced him on account of several goods by him brought home on the *Loyal Bliss*, which sold for £4,942 11s 9d.' (Court Minute, 12 December 1711.) The request was granted but, as was usual, only half was in cash, the remainder being in the Company's bonds.

It is fortunate that we have available the list of goods, including the china-ware articles, which the Court of Directors wished the Supra-cargoes of the *Loyal Bliss* to purchase and bring home. This list underlines the utilitarian nature of the Company's imports, all of it being useful tablewares, with no mention of decorative objects such as vases, or

'Ordered that a warehouse or warehouses be appointed on purpose and apart, for holding the Private Trade goods that shall be imported on the Company's ships...'

even large bowls. In fact, a postscript gives permission to buy Japanese wares of the 'above sorts, or pretty near them but buy none that are large pieces, such as Jars, beakers or great dishes or bowles'. The required goods were:

    300 Nests [sets] flat dishes, 7 in a nest
  4,000 Boats, three in a nest
  4,000 [Tea] cannisters
40,000 Handled chocolates
12,000 Milk pots
  6,000 Teapots
20,000 Plates, half to be blue and white
  8,000 Dishes
  2,000 Nests scollop shells, six in a nest
110,000 Cups and saucers various
  8,000 Slop basons
    400 Dishes, five in a nest
  2,000 Sugar pots, two in a nest
  4,000 Deep square small dishes.

This 1712 selection was repeated in ship after ship for year after year with remarkably few alterations. However, from 1718 each vessel carried a mere 45,000 cups and saucers instead of the previous 110,000. We may wonder how the market absorbed such quantities of tablewares, and why the English Company's directors were not more venturesome in their orders, leaving much of the profit readily available to the Private Trade buyers.

In 1715 various frauds in the Private Trade warehouse had been reported to the directors. This resulted in further efforts to control the trade, and on 21 September 1715 we find: 'Resolved that the Court of Directors be desired to consider of the most effectual method to prevent Private Trade...' and on 4 November 1715 firm action was taken against the Supra-cargoes and their writers: 'The Court taking into consideration the great clamours that have of late arisen by reason of the Private Trade brought home from the East Indies, by persons entertained in the Company's service.

Resolved that none of the said supra-cargoes or writers be permitted to carry out or bring home any bullion goods or merchandizes in Private Trade.' The trouble may have arisen over the activities of the Supra-cargoes of the *Hester*. Certainly a new resolution recorded on 20 December 1715 affected especially these persons: 'Resolved that the Company do pay the several supra-cargoes of the *Hester* the prime cost of all the goods by them respectively brought home in Private Trade and allow them thirty per cent thereon...' The directors probably thought a mere thirty per cent profit would be a form of punishment and serve as a discouragement to others. If this is so, the profitability of the Private Trade venture is underlined.

At this time, late in 1715, the Court of Directors was seriously reviewing the situation regarding Private Trade. This is well surmised from the following lengthy Minute:

At a General Court of the United Company of Merchants of England trading to the East Indies, holden at the East India House on Wednesday the 19th of October, 1715 at 11 in the Forenoon.
Present
Sir Robert Child, Knt., and Alderman, Chairman, with most of the Directors and a very large appearance of the Generallity.
The Transactions of last General Court of 21st September last being read, the Chairman laid before the Court a representation of the Court of Directors, which was twice read, and is as follows, viz:
State of the Case of Private Trade goods imported in the Company's ships from the East Indies.
July 22nd, 1702.
Upon the first union of the two Companies, their Court of Managers apprehended it absolutely necessary to settle an indulgence for the Commanders, officers and mariners of the shipping, to be by them employed, before they proceeded to take them up, and to that end, they examined the Indulgences, which had been at severall seasons from time to time granted by the Old Company.

The Private Trade Imports

They also found the New Company had tollerated, or at least connived at their Captains bringing home any sorts of goods, and on easier terms than were allowed by the Old Company.

The said Indulgence was settled, printed and published [on 8 October 1702] for the generall notice of all concerned, which yet subsists in force. By that Indulgence they allowed the Commanders, officers and mariners, to carry out in foreign bullion or goods to trade withall, viz:

For every one hundred tons the ship should be let for, wherein such officers served –

The Commander had liberty to carry out to the value of	£300
The chief mate	£60
The second mate	£40
The third mate and purser, each	£20
All other officers as surgeon, boatswain, gunner, carpenter, steward, quartermaster, each	£15
The midshipmen, each	£10

Every other seaman might carry but to the value of £10 in the whole.

...On the Produce of these Goods the Company were to receive only the five per cent, settled by Act of Parliament...

The Charterpartyes of the ship had proper covenants therein inserted forbidding the carrying out or bringing home of any adventure [bullion] uninvested, they did at length on weighing all circumstances determine and order – on September 25th, 1706 – That fifteen per cent on the Gross sale be laid on all unindulged goods, besides the five per cent chargeable by Act of Parliament, and this to be a rule for the future also...

Noted, besides the said fifteen and five per cent, the Court always charged two per cent for warehouse room, sale and other disbursements on all Private Trade... [here follow details regarding muslins, some types of which were prohibited]

...On November 10th, 1709, the General Court in the tenth By-Law laid down rules touching the examining marking and shipping the Private Trade to be licenced by the Court of Directors. These have been observed ever since.

In their eleventh By-Law they directed a clause to be put into the Ships' Charterpartyes, obliging the Commanders and owners to forfeit all the goods brought home in Private Trade, that shall be received on board without registering, this hath been ever since inserted accordingly.

...and although by the said By-Law it doth seem as if the Owners of ships might be thereby allowed to be concerned, yet such care hath been taken, that a Proviso is added to the clause, that it shall not extend to any owner or owners of such ships, nor any other Persons who are not intitled to the Company's Indulgence.

On December 9th, 1713, the Court of Directors finding one ship from China had brought home a very large quantity of tea in Private Trade, they thereupon directed a clause to be put into all Captains' instructions for the future, to the purport following, which hath been ever since observed, viz:

That the ships bound for China, may bring home on the Captains and officers account half their three per cent tonnage in tea and no more, and in consideration thereof that they pay fifteen per cent to the Company for the same, besides the five per cent charged by Act of Parliament, and the two per cent for charges, excepting thereout the two hundred weight for every hundred ton allowed by the Indulgence and that if the Captain and officers exceed the said tonnage the surplus be forfeited to the Company...

This being a true state of the rise, progress, regulations and restrictions of the Private Trade goods imported in the Companyes ships from the East Indies the Court of Directors do unanimously declare that they can't offer any further regulation for preventing the excesses of Private Trade, unless by a total Prohibition, and whether that will be for the real interest of the Company must be left to the consideration of the General Court.

Then the General Court debated the severall particulars contained in the said representations and having considered the objections made thereto, together with the answers to those objections, and also the reasons which were given, why the Court of Directors could offer no further regulations for preventing the excesses of Private Trade, except by totally prohibiting of Private Trade.

A motion was made to put the following question, viz:

That this General Court do approve of the Regulations which have been made by the Court of Directors, for preventing the growth of Private Trade and that they be desired to continue their care therein.

And the said question being put, after twice reading over was agreed unto.

Then a motion was made adjourning the Court and carryed in the affirmative, and the Court adjourned accordingly.

At the next Court, held two days later on 21 October 1715, the matter was again raised and it was resolved: 'That a Committee be appointed to consider of all such further regulations, as they shall at any time think necessary, or proper, for the more effectuall preventing the growth of Private Trade, and the prejudice, that may accrue to the Company thereby, and report their opinion to this Court from time to time.'

This new Committee was called the 'Committee for Preventing the Growth of Private Trade', but the Private Trade had survived a grave risk of prohibition and it was to continue unabated throughout the century.

The Private Trade of the ships' officers and crews continued openly, being permitted by the Company, which continued to charge 'Permission' fees and other charges. To quote one further example, Captain John Gordon of the *Montague* on her 1719–1721 voyage to Canton brought home 850 chests of tea, 168 chests of china-ware and 261½ bundles of china-ware. These goods included: '17 Large dishes – gold and colours, 151 Plates, 100 Blew and white bowls, 4 Sets of blue and white dishes', also candied oranges, crimson velvet, a jar of ginger, embroidery and a screen.

The *Montague* sailed for Canton with two other of the Company's East Indiamen, the *Carnavon* and the *Sarum*. The Supra-cargoes of each vessel were given the following order for their china-ware purchases on behalf of the Company:

For each vessel – chinaware, with the copper and tootenague sufficient to stiffen the ship – of the sorts and quantitys according to the following Directions –

   300 Nests flat dishes – seven in a nest
10,000 Boats
 4,000 Cannisters
40,000 Handled chocolate cups
12,000 Milk pots
 6,000 Teapots
20,000 Plates and dishes
 3,000 Nests scollopt shells, three in a nest
45,000 Cups and saucers
 2,000 Nests bowls, four in a nest
10,000 Slop basons
   400 Nests dishes, five in a nest
 4,000 Small dishes or patty pans
50,000 Coffee cups

Yet when we refer to the catalogue of these cargoes when exposed to sale in March 1722 we find not only wares answering the above descriptions but also:

2,820 Blue and white Porringers
1,236 Painted   do.
  270 China tyles
    2 Blue and white soup-dishes
   13 Black and gold candlesticks
    3 Japan jars, 2 beakers
    2 Blue and white flower-pots
    7 Blue and white muggs
   11 Painted knife handles
   11 Blue and white   do.
    9 Blue and white baskets
    9 Painted   do.
    6 Blue and white castors
    2 Blue and gold   do.
    3 Painted   do.
   11 Blue and white fruit dishes
    4 Blue and white salts
    4 Painted   do.
   28 Blue and white coffee pots
    4 Large blue and white garden pots
    4 Smaller   do.
    4 Painted   do.

The Private Trade Imports

6 Painted bottles
6 Painted candlesticks
2 Large painted mugs
2 Smaller do.
5 Smaller do.
2 Blue and white cisterns
3 Painted do.
133 Blue and white chamberpots
190 Painted do.
2 Blue and white crewits

These items represent Private Trade imports, as they are not featured in the Court of Directors' precise orders to their Supra-cargoes.

By the early 1720s the 1715 restriction on the Private Trade of the Supra-cargoes and their writers had been at least partly lifted, although no doubt the trade was now more closely regulated and had become the concern of the special 'Committee for Preventing the Growth of Private Trade'. Officially the Supra-cargoes' scale of remuneration was set out clearly and recorded in the Court Minutes. The 'China Council', the team of Supra-cargoes working together at Canton in the 1723–4 season, were given the following amounts and agreed on 31 October 1722:

That in lieu of Commission to be allowed The China Council...they be allowed the following sums –
That Mr William Fazakerly be allowed £2,500
That Mr Richard Norton be allowed £1,500
That Mr Edmond Godfrey be allowed £1,500
That Mr Thomas Atkyns be allowed £1,500
That Mr Thomas Carter be allowed £1,500
That Mr Thomas Dade be allowed £1,000
That Mr Devereux Bacon be allowed £700
That Mr Samuel Skinner be allowed £500
[Supra-cargoes in other years were given a set percentage of the yield of the homeward cargo after its sale by auction; this was normally 5 per cent to be shared amongst three Supra-cargoes on a single vessel.]

That the said eight persons be allowed to carry out in foreign silver to be invested in Gold [in China] and sent to Fort St George to be invested in Diamonds or paid to the Companys cash there or remitted by Bills or else joyned with the Companys Cargoes to be returned to England as they severally shall choose –
Mr Fazakerly to the amount of £1,500
Mr Norton to the amount of £900
Mr Godfrey to the amount of £900
Mr Atkyns to the amount of £900
Mr Carter to the amount of £600
Mr Dade to the amount of £600
Mr Bacon to the amount of £500
Mr Skinner to the amount of £500
That they also be allowed to carry out as a separate adventure to be paid out in China and the produce returned to England on the Company's shipping and on their usual terms.
Mr Fazakerly to the amount of £200
Mr Norton to the amount of £150
Mr Godfrey to the amount of £150
Mr Atkyns to the amount of £150
Mr Carter to the amount of £130
Mr Dade to the amount of £130
Mr Bacon to the amount of £100
Mr Skinner to the amount of £100

It should be noted that these amounts were renewable from year to year. The Court Minutes include numerous requests from Supra-cargoes to export goods and money to China, and to have their Chinese purchases included in the Company's sales.

While the Company sought to regulate Private Trade imports, the Customs also had an interest in seeing that such imports went through the official channels, and that duty was paid. Various letters passed between the Customs and the Company concerning Private Trade, and I quote, as typical examples, three entries from the Court Minutes of 1723:

Letter from Charles Carkesse, Esq., secretary to the Commissioners of the Customs, dated January 9th, 1723, being read and signifying that several parcels of goods in Private Trade had lately been sold to Lawrence Lane, desiring a stop may be put to the delivery of the said goods and that some of the Directors will meet them. (Court Minute of 11 January 1723.)

The result of this meeting is recorded later in the same Minute:

Sir Matthew Decker acquainted the Court that Mr Lydell and himself had attended the Commissioners of the Customs and discoursed [with] them on the reference of the last Court upon the complaint relating to the sale of goods in Private Trade and had agreed that for the future before the sale of any goods in Private Trade timely notice should be given thereof that the same be fairly exposed to the view of the buyers and sold to the highest bidder in the same manner as the Company's goods are.

This suggests that Private Trade goods had not always been fully exposed for sale to the highest bidder and that the owners sought to buy back their own goods (for later resale) at a cheap rate perhaps by having them included at the end of a sale without publicity.

Other requests from the Customs were of a more regular kind, but like the following example they serve to show that the smuggling ashore of Private Trade goods – to avoid both Customs duties and the Company's charges – was not unknown. 'Letter from Charles Carkesse, Esq., Secretary to the Commissioners of His Majesties Custom, dated 13th June, 1723, was read desiring this Court will order Hoys to be sent down to the ships lately returned to bring away the goods in Private Trade to prevent their being run.' (Court Minute, 19 June 1723.) Nor could ships' officers bring home duty-free china-ware claimed to have been used aboard ship, as the following Minute of 29 July 1724 suggests: '...The Court being acquainted that the *Shoreham* now in the river will be cleared as is supposed on Saturday next – the Custom House officers at present on board her, that Captain Mayne had on board some two casks of arrack...that he had also some plates and other china ware stores and necessaryes which be made use of in India and the voyage home, and a motion being made thereupon that he may have the same delivered to him on his paying the duty's as if the same were in his Majesties Warehouse...' Obviously some Private Trade slipped through the net and escaped the watchful eyes of the Customs officers and of the Company's 'waiters' and other servants. We in turn regret this, for such goods were not recorded, and did not feature in the Company's sales. However, the amount that was correctly declared was very considerable and, in fact, by the 1730s the quantity appears to have swamped the market. In October 1731 the trade buyers petitioned the Court of Directors, seeking: 'Longer time to clear (and pay for) the china ware in Private Trade brought by them at the last sale.'

As a consequence the directors ordered: '...that the buyers of china ware sold in March sale last [1731] in Private Trade be allowed to the 29th January next [1732] to clear the same – with discount – and that the secretary signifys to the several captains that in case they do not clear it by that time shall be at liberty to sue them.' (Court Minute, 27 October 1731.)

In this year, 1731, there is an early reference to china-ware decorated with armorial bearings: 'Ordered that the china ware with Coats of Arms etc. and some white goods for presents be put up to sale on Tuesday the 23rd instance, and that notice thereof be given accordingly.' (Court Minute, 12 November 1731.)

Armorial porcelains are discussed in Chapter 6, but it is interesting to see that such personal goods, presumably specially ordered and bearing the Arms of one person or family, were submitted to public auction. There are several similar records relating to the sale by auction of Private Goods, even in the

The Private Trade Imports

following case, where goods were in transit and were later to be re-exported: 'Ordered that the warehousekeeper of Private Trade do prepare some china ware, such and other small things belonging to General Diemar, which were brought home on the China ship to be put up at the same time with other Private Trade at this sale, as soon as conveniently may be, in order that the same may be sent abroad to him.' (Court Minutes, 11 July 1733.)

At this period the amount of china-ware imported as Private Trade was obviously getting out of hand; not only were dealers requesting that sales be postponed but the amount of Private Trade must have affected the sale of the Company's own imports in an already glutted market. The Court of Directors took action on 12 September 1733 requiring the Committee of Warehouses to consider 'some expedient to prevent the extravagant importation of china ware in Private Trade'. The results were minuted on 10 October 1733:

On reading a report from the committee of warehouses and shipping dated the 5th instant – Resolved that the Commanders and Officers of each ship from China be allowed to bring home china ware to the value of £2,500 at the gross sale at the candle.

That the value of £300 be allowed among the supracargoes of each ship from China to be delivered in proportion to their respective priviledges.

And that no ship do bring any china ware but from China directly.

And also that on all china ware brought in contrary to these resolutions 15 per cent on the gross value at the candle shall be paid over and above all duties now payable for the same.

Ships' officers were now permitted to bring in at the standard rates a mere £2,500 worth of china-ware. The prohibition on the purchase of porcelain from non-Chinese ports indicates that such wares had previously come from other sources – mainly India (see p. 81).

Sadly, the records of Private Trade imports are very few after the end of the period covered by the available sale-records – that is, after 1722 – and at the earlier period the fashion for special designs, armorial or otherwise, had not been firmly established, so that there is an unfortunate lack of information concerning these particular Private Trade imports.

One such dated bowl is shown in Plate 14, and several others are recorded which include the name of the vessel. Many other bowls bear paintings of unnamed ships. These appear to be painted to a standard pattern. Standard views of unnamed vessels occur also on teawares and on mugs. The national flags vary according to the buyer.

Apart from the Private Trade imports of Supracargoes, and of the officers and crew of East India Company trading vessels, some china-ware was also brought home by men-of-war. An account of the Duke of Bedford, dated 31 May 1753, conveniently makes this point and lists the various payments incurred:

His Grace the Duke of Bedford, on account of two boxes of china out of the *Rainbow*, man-of-war.
Expended at the Customs House with china dishes –

To Mr Gibbs	5s
Warehouse keeper	1s
Weighers and wharfage	1s
Agency and attendance	5s
Porterage	3s 6d
Expenses	8d
	16s 2d

In the middle of the eighteenth century Private Trade continued unabated; in fact, some returning East Indiamen brought no china-ware on the Company's account, only Private Trade. In 1759 we find that the *Pitt* was such a vessel, for the Supracargoes sold the captain a supply of porcelain. 'In order to expedite the despatch of Captain Wilson [Commander of the *Pitt*] we agreed to make over to him 10 whole and 90 half-chests of china ware, cost tales 1,459 [£489] which he informs us will be sufficient to floor the ship so that we shall not send any on board for account of the Company.'

The point here was that the main flooring of china had to be put aboard before it became possible to load the main cargo of light-weight tea, and no delay could be permitted, as the ship had to sail in the monsoon season – or lose a year's passage. In 1771 the *Cruttenden* carried home 116 chests of Private Trade china, but none for the Company's account.

The extant Company records concerning Private Trade goods in the middle of the eighteenth century are few. This is partly remedied by catalogues of sales held in London by Mr Christie. These records are still preserved by the present directors of Christie, Manson & Woods Ltd, but unfortunately the goods sold in these public auctions did not include special orders, for any wares made for china-dealers or for private persons (such as the armorial porcelains) were delivered before the standard objects were offered to the general public. A sale held by Mr Christie in November 1767 was advertised as being 'The Private Trade of a Gentleman, lately returned from India'. Sample lots included:

A fine rich imaged three-gallon bowl
A set of imaged jars and beakers
A pair of rich imaged octagon jars and covers
A tea and coffee equipage of imag'd china, 43 pieces
A fine three-gallon bowl, curiously painted with horses, etc

The description 'Imaged' was a contemporary one for figure-painted wares.

The extent of these mid-eighteenth-century imports of Private Trade porcelains from Canton can be gauged from the following entry in the Court Minutes of 31 July 1765:

On reading a memorial of Mr James Wood, chief mate of the late ship *Harcourt* representing that since the china ware brought home by him on his Private Adventure has been in the Company's warehouse there is a deficiency therein of 5,406 pieces and praying that as the memorialist saw his said china ware packed up in Canton himself and that the packages were whole when delivered out of the ship in the River Thames, an enquiry may be made into the cause of such deficiency and such relief granted him as the Court shall deem just...

These 5,406 pieces were merely those 'lost' in the Company's London warehouse, representing but part of the Private 'Adventure' of the *Harcourt*'s mate, not the Captain's larger allowance.

Porcelains, as we know, were but part of the imports. In the 1770s, when the English East India Company's own Chinese imports were restricted to tea, silks and china-ware, Private Trade accounted for an interesting assortment of other goods. We find, for example, Captain John Lennox of the *Anson* shipping home on his own account: '11 boxes china, 4 tubs of china, 2 boxes ornaments, 2 boxes clay images, 2 boxes painted glass, 1 roll of tea-boards, 4 boxes lacquerware, 3 boxes sweetmeats, 3 boxes paper, 1 cask soy, 15 chests cassia, 450 bundles of mats and 340 bundles as well as 90 chests of tea.'

Apart from china-ware correctly imported – declared imports on which Customs duty and the Company's percentage had been paid – there were wares smuggled into Britain to avoid the paying of these dues. Obviously, little is known about this aspect of Private Trade; we only know about some of the seized landings, which must have represented a very small proportion of the whole, the successful landings being no doubt sold in the southern counties of England without comment.

In 1764 one seized consignment offered for sale by

The Private Trade Imports

the Customs included 3,000 plates and 300 dishes from one East Indiaman. These goods must have been undeclared Private Trade of the officers or crew. In 1768 a general six-day sale of contraband was held at the Customs House, two days being devoted to the sale of seized china-ware. These were mostly standard objects: '7,000 cups and saucers, 3,000 basins, 2,800 plates, 600 dishes and similar goods.'

China-ware was also smuggled into Britain from the Continent, mainly Holland. This could have been legally imported into Holland in Dutch vessels, sold in the normal way of trade and then shipped over to England in the many small boats that plied their trade between the two countries in time of peace. Other smuggled goods may originally have been legally imported into London but exported again, so qualifying for repayment of the high duty, only to be landed again at a small port along the coast where, with luck, they escaped the unwelcome attention of the Customs.

Apart from smuggled Chinese goods and those shipped by the East India Company, much of the Chinese export market porcelain illustrated in this book must have been ordered by, or through, the numerous 'chinamen' who practised their trade in London and other cities and towns. Much of the porcelain painted with the owner's initials, crest or armorial bearings was probably first ordered from the major china-dealers of the period, who probably held a stock of 'pattern plates' from which the would-be purchaser could choose the general style or border pattern to enclose his personal arms. Such sample plates (Plate 121) were each painted with a segment of a standard border, which had a number to aid identification. These plates are clearly of a post-1791 period in style and so do not relate to the Company's own trade. Other pieces bore similarly divided borders of differing patterns, but without reference numbers; these pieces could also relate to the 'musters' mentioned on p. 46. Armorial, crested and initialled porcelains are discussed in Chapter 6.

In 1791 the directors of the East India Company regularised the trade carried out on behalf of a third party, although commissions had no doubt been accepted and executed for many years before this – probably for the whole of the eighteenth century. The new regulation stated:

Resolved that all the Company's servants in China under the select Committee be allowed the privilege of transacting business by commission for private persons and that the particular person to whom the consignment shall be made shall be entitled to half the commission on such consignments and that the remaining half shall be appropriated to a Fund for all the Companies servants...to be divided into shares, giving a double share to every person above the degree of waiter.
(Court Minutes, 2 March 1791.)

The Private Trade imports continued in the early and mid-1790s, probably on an increased scale now that the Company had stopped its own imports and now that it actively encouraged the imports of private china-ware in order to gain heavy 'flooring' for the teas (see p. 48). Apart from the flooring, one authority – Northcote Parkinson in his *Trade in the Eastern Seas 1793–1813* (Cambridge, 1937) – states:

...besides this thirty tons or more of chinaware and his [the Captain's] original allowance, there was the dunnage. Dunnage was the packing put in to protect the cargo from injury...The Crockery was used, in fact, as dunnage although it was not given that name...as the sale of dunnage was highly profitable it sometimes happened that the crevices to be filled were rather large. In some ships the cargo threatened to become merely incidental...

This dunnage, or palleting, can be traced back into the previous century. The instructions given to the Supra-cargoes of the *Amity* in December 1696 read: 'We would have you in the first place take care that the ships palleting be filled up as tight as possible with coarse useful chinaware…' but in an afterthought the directors in effect warned the Supra-cargoes against trespassing on the captain's 'priviledge' in such matters: '…if Captain Heath should claim the priviledge thereof…we would not have you insist.'

The reasons for the Company's ceasing to import porcelains in 1791 – the high rates of duty and the growth and advance of British porcelain and pottery manufactories – were also applicable to some degree to the Private Trade imports. To overcome these difficulties the ships' captains and others engaged in this trade may have concentrated on special commissions for the supply of armorial or initialled wares and for the purchase of the more unusual objects, neglecting to a large degree the standard wares formerly imported by the Company. This may explain why Exchin, the Company's former china-ware merchant at Canton (see p. 49), was so anxious to sell to the Company at almost any discount the wares he had ordered before the cessation of trade, and which were now left on his hands. The Supra-cargoes reported back to the directors in London (letter dated 14 May 1795, see p. 49): 'The amount of the china ware is about 60,000 Tales [£20,000] which he is willing to let us have at an abatement of 15 per cent on the old prices…he will nevertheless be glad to accept whatever price they [the directors] may think proper to allow him.'

It would therefore seem that the Private Trade buyers did not offer an outlet for these regular wares of the type formerly imported by the Company, otherwise Exchin would not have been so anxious to sell cheaply to the Company.

Select as I believe Private Trade was, the import of china-ware was doubtless much affected by the Act of 1799 which increased the Customs duty to over a hundred per cent (see p. 50). This was a special war-rate, but in times of war the Private Traders would have to bear the whole loss of their venture should the vessel be taken or destroyed by the enemy. In the early 1800s the trade gradually declined although it by no means ceased. The English East India Company's Charter lapsed in 1813, ending its invaluable monopoly in the trade; in 1834 it finally withdrew from competition with private firms, which started to trade to the East once the Company's Charter came to an end. Henceforth all china-ware imports were of a private nature, or the concern of new shipping firms, and we have few details of such trade, except the basic figures of imports for 1800–1810 as given in William Milburn's *Oriental Commerce* (London, 1813).

1800–1801	£268,701
1801–1802	£312,081
1802–1803	£469,713
1803–1804	£366,208
1804–1805	£352,778
1805–1806	£331,070
1806–1807	£267,507
1807–1808	£238,122
1808–1809	£476,621
1809–1810	£353,418

The china-ware was entirely Private Trade.

In June 1853 the method of charging duty on china-ware was changed from £10 per cent *ad valorem* to 10s [50p] per hundredweight. The Customs returns as published in the *Annual Statement of Trade of the United Kingdom* gives the following figures for the weight of declared china-ware imported from China between 1855 and 1900. I have selected returns for five-year intervals, the figures represent hundredweights of 112 lb, twenty to the ton.

The Private Trade Imports

Year		
1855	474	(against 2,862 from France)
1860	710	
1865	1,492	
1870	1,055	
1875	3,462	
1880	4,594	
1885	931	
1890	1,020	
1895	980	(against 14,613 from Japan)
1900	1,538	

William Milburn, writing in or before 1813, gave in *Oriental Commerce* the four main types of export from China; he was referring to all products, but the divisions as recorded by a contemporary authority are of great interest to our understanding of the trade in china-ware. These categories were:

I. That carried on with Great Britain; this includes the imports and exports on account of the East India Company and the Private Trade of the Commanders and officers of their ships.

II. That carried on with the British settlements in India, in ships commonly called Country ships, the property of European residents, merchants or natives of the different Presidencies.

III. That carried on with the other European powers, who, previous to the war which commenced in 1793, had factories at Canton, but which are at present abandoned –

France	Denmark	Portugal	Spain
Holland	Ostend	Sweden	Leghorn

IV. That carried on in their own Junks or vessels to the Coasts of Siam, Cochin China, Tonquin, Japan, the numerous islands to the Eastward and to Batavia.

I have already discussed at length the trade to Britain – first on the Company's account, and then the Private Trade aspect, but I have hardly touched upon William Milburn's second category, the trade between China and India.

This is largely an unknown quantity, but it can reasonably be considered as Private Trade, and some at least of the goods sent to India were transhipped to Europe. In fact, before the 1680s the whole of the Company's China trade was carried in 'Country' vessels.

Early in 1687, when Fort St George, Madras, was for a short period (see p. 25) the centre for the China trade, the directors in London were almost begging for private persons and traders to send goods home to be sold at their sale – on payment of a commission. In a letter of 22 March 1687 to the President and Council at Fort St George, the directors wrote:

We have said before that we would contrive the liberty for private persons to consigne china-goods to the Company for ye space of three years but it is very likely after some tryal we may make ye liberty perpetual and it is likely ye persons there which may think the terms proposed hard, not knowing what the Company's general charge amounts to may upon tryal find such an advantage by ye justness and speed in making them returns and ye benifit of selling at the Company's candle find their account come out as profitable by consigning their goods to ye Company at 20 per cent commission and general charges as they could do by sending the same goods to any private person paying only 5 per cent.

In a letter of 20 April 1687 the directors further sought to widen Private Trade by permitting persons in England to order Chinese goods by way of India or, more exactly, via Fort St George: 'On further consideration thereof it is hereby ordered and declared that the same liberty is and shall be granted to all persons here in England to direct their correspondents in India to load for their respective accounts what china goods they shall think fitt on the terms following – 20 per cent of the nett produce at the Company's sale...' and in informing the Council at Fort St George in a letter dated 28 September 1687 that the directors in London were henceforth going to manage the china trade direct from London, they at the same time permitted the Council in India to trade on their own account with China.

The later Indian trade is largely an unknown quantity precisely because it was mainly a private venture not controlled by the directors in London and not featured in their records. It was, however, considerable. I mentioned in Chapter 1 that in the 1777–8 season eight 'Country' ships from India were at Canton, the same number as the Company's vessels from England. In terms of ships, if not of cargo, the India-trade ships equalled the Canton – London vessels, or the combined fleet from France and Sweden, in this particular year.

While the English Supra-cargoes often write of trouble arising from the India-trade vessels and misbehaviour on the part of their crews, they do not report on their cargoes. The agents of the English Company stated: '…we have in no instance any control or authority over the Commanders of the Country ships…' (letter of 23 September 1781).

From the late seventeenth century the Indian settlements caused concern to the directors in London over their habit of forwarding the Company's vessels to China when these ships had been sent officially only on the England–India voyage. On 8 March 1698 the directors in London wrote: 'The Court censure Bombay for sending the *Dorrill* to China and express a strong dislike to Europe ships being sent on these Country voyages…it was evident those voyages [referring to past ones] were undertaken to serve private purposes…'

In the Chinese ports the 'Country' vessels were a source of opposition to the English Supra-cargoes, and their buying must have forced up the price of articles in limited supply and lowered the price realised for goods sent out to China. In January 1700 Captain Hurle of the *Wentworth* reported back to London: 'The ship *Loyal Merchant*, Captain Armiger from Madras arrived here thirty days after us fully laden with merchandize, which have bartered and brought their full ship in a readiness to sail. The reason for their quick dispatch I impute to their dealings with several principal merchants in this city.'

The captains of the 'Country' ships, acting largely on their own initiative, seem to have been more forceful traders than the agents of the English Company. They no doubt turned their vessels round rapidly just as, later in the century, the newly-arrived American captains were able to do, acting mainly as private traders rather than as a unit of a large concern centred many thousands of miles away. The Indian-based vessels were also probably instrumental in distributing Chinese porcelains to many islands in the Eastern seas, although Chinese vessels were also involved in this trade.

Direct records are scarce in the extreme for the reasons stated, but we do have a second-hand report that in 1701 one vessel carried over 37,000 items of china-ware to the Indian port of Surat. This trading centre was much concerned with the supply of Chinese or Japanese porcelains. As early as 1618 the Dutch had cause to complain of their own trade here, for: '…of porcelain not much has been sold, because the country everywhere is filled with it by the English'. (Letter dated March 1618, quoted by T. Volker, *Porcelain and the Dutch East India Company 1602–82*, 1954.) Such china-ware would at this date probably have been Private Trade ventures of the 'Country' ships.

One of the few original accounts known to us relates to a blue and white crested service made for Charles Peers. This set was shipped in November 1731, not straight home to London but to Madras. The preliminaries read:

Canton, the 19th November, 1731
Invoice of two chests of China ware laden aboard the ship *Canton Merchant*, Captain Timothy Tullie, Commander, bound to the Port Madrass and consigned to Nicholas Morris Merchant there, on account and risque

The Private Trade Imports

10   A Chinese plate painted in underglaze blue, part of a crested service consigned to Charles Peers in November 1731.
British Museum

of Charles Peers, Esq., being marked as per Margin...' (see p. 195).

The *Canton Merchant* was one of four 'Country' ships then lying at Whampoa, below Canton. In passing, we may note that this 1731 dinner-service, made to special order and comprising four fine circular dishes in different sizes, a hundred dinner plates, sixty soup, four bowls, twelve sauceboats and salts, and six soup dishes, cost in China only the equivalent of £13 6s 8d. A plate from this service is shown in Plate 10; this specimen is now in the British Museum. Further details of the two Peers services are given in Chapter 6.

Not all the India–China trade was a private venture; the vessels were controlled by the various governors appointed to the Indian trading settlements and the ships carried on a staple trade exporting Indian products to China and importing Chinese goods. The directors in London sent money to India to finance this trade. In the London records there are entries such as: '£90,000 to be sent to Madras for the China ships whereof £60,000 to be invested in gold.' (Court Minute, 30 August 1732.) And in 1733, when the directors had declined to send any of their own chartered vessels to China, they did request that one of the Madras-bound vessels be sent. Whether as Private Trade or regular imports for the Company, the flow of Chinese goods into India continued through the eighteenth century, and at least some of these goods were forwarded to London.

The fact that in the early 1730s the dealer Henry Tombes stood security to a factor in Bombay, to the considerable amount of £1,000, may be significant, indicating an important dealer's interest in traders operating in India.

The preliminary pages of a Christie sale-catalogue of November 1767 probably gave the source of the goods offered correctly when they stated: 'The Private Trade of a Gentleman, lately returned from India' (p. 78), although the term 'India' was very loosely used, or misused, in the eighteenth century, and there are countless examples of Chinese porcelains being described in England as 'India china ware'. This common error no doubt arose from the fact that so much porcelain reached England (and probably other European countries) by way of India in vessels of the East India Company. This trade was considerable but we have little firm knowledge of it. An interesting paper by Basil Gray entitled 'The Export of Chinese Porcelain to India' is printed in the *Transactions of the Oriental Ceramic Society* (1964–5) but in general this deals with the pre-1700 imports and the wares shipped to India for local use, not for re-export to Europe.

In the next chapter, I shall show how the purchases in China were shipped home to Europe, and a little of the conditions then experienced on the round voyage. But first it is essential to summarise the main classes of Private Trade in Oriental export market porcelains.

A. The commemorative wares made for the ships' officers and crews, for their own use or for their families and friends. The ships' bowls were good examples of this class (see Plates 14, 153 and 161).

B. The special designs made for, or to the order of, friends. The mug, a detail of which is shown in Plate 11, falls into this category, and one imagines that a ship's captain or Supra-cargo had spent many a merry evening at this Gravesend inn partaking of its hospitality and the 'clean & well md. beds', while his vessel was anchored off shore taking on supplies.

We are on firmer ground in illustrating in this section the bowl shown in Plate 12. The bowl bears a panel which is inscribed: 'The Gift of a Commander of an Indiaman, a small but grateful testimony in Respect to Lord Rodney's merit and

The Private Trade Imports

11 A detail from a Chinese porcelain mug inscribed 'John Johnson. Queen's Hd. Gravesend. N.B. Clean & well md Beds, neat post chaises, a coach to Chatham and a Boat to London every Tide', *c.* 1790.   *Private collection*

services.' Obviously this is a rare piece and here, as in several other cases, the good drawing is because the Chinese decorators at Canton were supplied with a European print to copy. The scene is the action between Admirals Rodney and de Grasse in the West Indies on 12 April 1782, taken from an engraving by Robert Dodd. The bowl was probably painted about 1785, allowing time for the print to be engraved, published, and sent out to China.

The wares of classes 'A' and 'B' were presumably imported as presents and are not featured in any available records.

C. The special designs made to the order of private persons or traders. Orders placed with the ships' captains or Supra-cargoes on which they were paid a commission. The armorial, crested and initialled wares are mainly of this type.

D. The porcelains specially ordered by the leading china-dealers of the period. Small orders in particular would have been placed with Supra-cargoes or ships' captains rather than with the Company for, apart from the lower freight charges on Private Trade goods, the directors do not appear to have been interested in special orders. Special designs, such as the one shown in Plate 13, would have been of this Class D, the result of orders placed by the London china-dealers with their contact-man. Thousands of such special designs or shapes could be cited here and most probably much of the armorial ware falls into this category, the original order being given to a china-dealer and subcontracted to an East India Captain.

E. It is probable that the Private Trade venture of the ships' officers and crews included a percentage of more ordinary china, objects that could be purchased at the several shops in Canton that catered for European traders. Again, designs and shapes may have been of an unusual nature, for if a merchant had available, say, six special vases, these would have been snapped up by Private Trade buyers but they would not have interested the Supra-cargoes acting for the Company. As we have seen, the Company's requirements had mainly been ordered the previous season and their orders were quite precise as to what should be purchased.

In many cases it is now difficult to determine in which class individual pieces of Chinese export market porcelain should be placed. For example, was the punch-bowl shown in Plate 13 ordered by Mr H. Jones of Gravesend himself as an advertisement, or was it perhaps given to this 'man–midwife' as a gift from a grateful new father – a ship's captain or officer? Is it of Class B, C or D? It hardly matters. I list the several basic types only to show the various means by which they could have been ordered.

The Private Trade Imports

12 A superbly decorated presentation Chinese porcelain punch-bowl bearing the inscription 'The Gift of a Commander of an Indiaman, a small but grateful testimony of Respect to Lord Rodney's merit and Services'. The main subject depicts the engagement of 12 April 1782. Diameter 15½ inches.
Sotheby & Co., London

13 A detail from a Chinese porcelain punch-bowl, obviously a Private Trade order, not part of the Company's bulk purchases, c. 1785. *Earle D. Vandekar, London*

3 The *Earl of Elgin*, East Indiaman

The following chapters are devoted to china-wares of various types, but before considering these in detail, we should have some understanding of life aboard the East Indiamen, and at Canton. The manner and difficulties of getting Chinese porcelain to England can conveniently be gauged by following the adventures of one vessel on a single voyage in the mid-1760s. The Chinese porcelain punch-bowl shown in Plate 14 depicts an English East India Company vessel, the *Earl of Elgin*, rounding the Cape of Good Hope in August 1764 on passage to China. While several ships' captains ordered porcelains painted with representations of their vessels, this example is particularly interesting as a panel on the side gives the name of the ship, the position and the date.

This information permits us to trace the log of the voyage, a document preserved in the India Office Records in London, and to extract from this log the more notable features of the journey to China and back home to London.

The vessel was a three-decker of 687 tons, built on the River Thames by the large ship-building firm of Perry; she was launched in 1760. The Perry yard at Blackwall was one of the most important in the country. Here were constructed numerous naval vessels and East Indiamen, and the Company's Arms were proudly displayed over the gate. In the nineteenth century the site of the Perry yard was taken over to make way for the new East India Docks.

The *Earl of Elgin* was managed by a consortium of owners under Charles Foulis and was on charter to the Honourable East India Company. In the eighteenth century the Company did not own the many East Indiamen which traded on its behalf; each was chartered. The first voyage of the *Earl of Elgin* was to India between May 1761 and April 1763 but we are concerned more with the second voyage, to China between May 1764 and June 1766.

14 A Chinese porcelain punch-bowl decorated in Canton with two views of the *Earl of Elgin* East Indiaman off the Cape of Good Hope in August 1764. Diameter 10¼ inches.
Private collection

This adventure, and other voyages to the East, commenced in East India House, at a sitting of the Court of Directors, at which the following instructions were given:

Ordered – that the following publication be signed by the Secretary and fixed up at the Royal Exchange and this House, viz.

The Court of Directors of the United Company of Merchants of England trading to the East Indies do hereby give notice that they are ready to receive proposals at any time on or before Wednesday the 6th July next from any person on what terms and conditions they are willing to let their ship to this Company for this ensuing season, each proposal being made by two of the owners and Captain in writing expressing therein the names of the Owners…(Court Minute, 22 June 1763.)

A Minute of 6 July 1763 records: 'The tenders of the following twenty-eight ships each of the burthen of 499 tons were now open'd and read each being proposed to let to freight to the Company for a voyage to the East Indies at £33 (for Coarse goods) and £36 per ton (for fine goods), and the outward-bound freight, passengers and diet of soldiers and military Gentlemen on the same terms as last year.'

The owners were obviously acting as a body, each submitting an identical quotation – one later slightly reduced. The *Earl of Elgin* was included in the list of twenty-eight tendered vessels, but when nineteen were selected on 29 July our vessel was not included. That the *Earl of Elgin* did sail to China, as depicted on this bowl, is due to the misfortune of one of the selected vessels. For on 12 January 1764 the Court Minutes record: 'The Chairman informed the Court that advices had been received from Deal of the ship *Earl of Holderness*, Captain Robert Brooke bound for Bencoolen and China having grounded for several hours on the 10th instant, in her passage to the Downs and afterwards floating, was run ashore the next day near Deal, which would inevitably be attended with the loss of the ship.'

As a consequence the Committee of Shipping were ordered to find a replacement vessel and on 19 January 1764 it was: 'Resolved...that the ship *Earl of Elgin*, Captain Arthur Evans, tendered the 6th July last be taken up for a voyage to Bencoolen and China in the room of the *Earl of Holderness*, upon the same terms as the other ship of the season...' However, the Minutes for 27 January 1764 read: 'Resolved that Mr Thomas Cooke be approved as fitly qualified to command the ship *Earl of Elgin* in the room of Captain Arthur Evans who hath resigned...whereupon Captain Cooke [he was a mere third-mate in 1761] was called into Court and took the oath against trading to or from India without the Company's license.'

In effect this meant that the captain and his officers had to seek permission for any goods they wished to export as Private Trade, or for any money or bullion they wished to take with them to purchase goods in China on their own account. Captain Cooke lost little time in requesting permission. On 9 February 1764 the Court Minutes report:

> On reading the request of Captain Thomas Cooke for liberty to carry on the ship *Earl of Elgin* 80 tons of Flints in lieu of ballast for sale in China also other requests of Captain Cooke...for liberty to carry out the particulars therein mentioned on their indulgencies in Private Trade.
>
> Ordered that the above requests be referred to the Committee to regulate and allow as they think proper.

He was permitted to ship to China the flint stones, as the ship's log records both the loading and unloading of this material. I will have occasion to return to the subject of flints later (see p. 100).

We do not have a list of the captain's other Private Trade goods exported to China but we do have details of those carried by Captain William Baker of the *Cruttenden* in 1768. Probably this was a reasonably standard assortment although the value given was very high – £10,980. It was made up in the following manner:

	Valued at
15 chests of clocks and jewellery	£5,000
20 Hogsheads Ginseng	£3,000
250 boxes tin plates	£800
7 chests of glass ware	£500
6 chests of cutlery	£500
24 tons Lead	£360
15 casks smalts [cobalt blue perhaps for the Chinese blue and white porcelains]	£300
Cloth cuttings	£150
10 chests glass lanthorns	£100
6 chests window glass	£100
Brass wire	£70
40 faggots steel	£60
2 tons iron hoops	£40

In addition there was a special unpriced entry relating to: '100 tons Flints in lieu of Ballast and for sale in China.'

Although the vessel was officially registered at a mere 499 tons, as were all the others tendered (see p. 90), her crew was large. On this voyage to China it comprised the following personnel, to which I have added in brackets the *monthly* wages, which were standard to all East Indiamen of the period.

The 'Commander' – Thomas Cooke	[£10]
(who enjoyed the services of:	
A personal cook	[£3]
A personal steward and	[£1 10s]
Two personal servants)	[£1 10s]
Chief Mate	[£5]
Chief Mate's servant	[£1 10s]
2nd Mate	[£4]
2nd Mate's servant	[£1 10s]
3rd Mate	[£3]
4th Mate	[£2]
5th Mate	[£1 10s]
6th Mate	[£1 3s]
Purser	[£2]
Surgeon	[£3]
Surgeon's Mate	[£1 10s]
4 Quarter-masters	[£1 8s]
Boatswain	[£2 15s]
Boatswain's 1st Mate	[£1 8s]
Boatswain's 2nd Mate	[£1 8s]
Gunner	[£2 15s]
Gunner's Mate	[£1 8s]
Carpenter	[£3 10s]
Carpenter's 1st Mate	[£2 10s]
Carpenter's 2nd Mate	[£2]
Caulker	[£3]
Caulker's Mate	[£2]
Sailmaker	[£2]
Cooper	[£2 10s]
Cooper's Mate	[£2]
Armourer	[£1 10s]
Ship's Cook	[£1 10s]
Ship's Steward	[£1 10s]
Butcher	[£1 3s]
Poulterer	[£1 3s]
Barber	[£1 3s]
Baker	[£1 3s]
Tailor	[£1 3s]
Coxsman	[£1 8s]
5 Midshipmen	[£1 3s]
57 Seamen (of whom 12 died on the voyage and 11 'run' or deserted the ship at various ports. Twenty extra seamen were taken on at Batavia. Most of the seamen received £1 3s per month, but some, presumably the youngest, received only 18s.)	

Apart from this considerable crew, the *Earl of Elgin* had on board eighty-one soldiers for the Company's station at Bencoolen (now spelt Bangkakulu), on the west coast of Sumatra. There were also various passengers for the same destination, each passenger paying the captain £30 to cover 'dieting at his table'. It will be observed, from the crew-list and from the picture of the ship (Plate 14), that the East Indiamen were well armed.

The *Earl of Elgin* was lying at, or by, the Company's wharf at Blackwall (London) from 3 February until 12 March 1764, taking on stores and in general preparing the ship for the lengthy voyage. The amount of stores is of some interest but unfortunately we cannot gather a complete picture since the log contains numerous unhelpful, brief, entries relating to 'sundry stores'. However, we learn that the stabilising ballast comprised eighty tons of kentledge (normally in the form of iron bars) and at least eighty tons of lead. This lead acted as ballast and as a very saleable commodity in China. It was apparently smuggled out occasionally by the crew, for the log records: 'Scavenger to Rummage our coal-hole for lead on information...Company's officers completed rummaging the ship but found nothing.' The reference to the coal-hole reminds us that in the age of sail coal was taken aboard, presumably for the cooking stoves, for one would doubt the wisdom of having open coal fires aboard a wooden vessel.

The *Earl of Elgin* also loaded 138 water casks and at least twenty tons of water. This was fetched from the Thames but above Chelsea, as the water downstream was 'brackish'. On 19 March 1764 the log records the loading of 'thirty butts small beer and fifty-two hogsheads strong do.' There was also wine and beer on account of the captain. Of solid provision the log records the loading of twenty-nine live hogs (which enjoyed thirty-one bales of hay), eighty-two puncheons of beef, forty-five hogsheads of port, nine barrels of suet and lard, also much flour and 'stock fish' – dried fish, normally cod.

On 3 March 1764 the log records: 'Received on board our oil and vinegar and variety of other small stores and cabin furniture, likewise 40 tons of Flint on account of the Captain.' On 19 and 20 March two further loads, each of forty tons of flint, were loaded, making a total of 120 tons. Some of this may have been the Private Trade of the first-officer as the captain sought permission to ship only eighty tons of flint.

Apart from the lead and flint, the outward cargo comprised 831 bars and ten faggots of steel, hundreds of rabbit skins – a quite regular export – and over two hundred bales of British cloth: the export of a quota of cloth was compulsory. In addition, fifty fathoms of timber were loaded. The small-arms, guns, shot and powder, and other stores were also taken aboard as were of course the sails, canvas, rope, etc. As early as December 1702 a detailed victualling list had been drawn up by the directors for vessels bound for the East. This basic list comprised:

Ale, strong beer or cider in bottle or cask	5 tons
Strong beer in casks	5 tons
Small beer	40 tons
Wine in cask or bottles	5 tons [36 dozen bottles to the ton]
Beef, Pork, bacon, sewitt [suet] and tongues	15 tons
Brandy or English spirit	250 gallons
Bread	30,000 [loaves]
Butter	30 firkins
Cheese	50 cwt
Flour	70 cwt
Fruit	15 cwt
Lyme juice	100 gallons
Fish	7,000 [bundles]
Red and white Herrings and Salmon	5 barrels
Mustard seed	10 bushels
Oatmeal	50 bushels
Sweet oil and lamp oil	300 gallons
Sauces of all sorts	5 cases
Oats, barley and bran	200 bushels
Peas	150 bushels
Salt	40 bushels
Vinegar	6 hogsheads
Sugar and spice	1,000 lb
Drugs	2 chests, value £50
Billet wood	25,000
Coals	7 caldrons
Candles	50 dozen
Tobacco	1,000 lb
Tobacco pipes	100 lb
Water, not less than	40 tons

One may gather from this impressive list that the journey was long and arduous.

Having loaded part of the stores, such as those just listed, the *Earl of Elgin* sailed down the

Thames to Gravesend on 12 March 1764. She remained there for over a month taking on further stores and the outward cargo. The log contains many entries such as 'Received on board sundry of the Honble. Company's goods and Private Trade'. On 20 April the Pilot came aboard the *Earl of Elgin* at Gravesend but the journey was by no means started, for on the 22nd and 23rd they were anchored at the Downs off the east coast of Kent, taking on more supplies. On 23 April passengers were taken on board from Deal and the journey for China started in earnest, the captain having previously taken his leave of the Court.

By August 1764 they were off the Cape of Good Hope (as depicted in Plate 14), having sailed down the Atlantic, and were turning eastwards into the Indian Ocean. By the end of August 1764 the ship was surprisingly far south near the Islands of Amsterdam and St Paul's, near Latitude 38, midway between the Cape of Good Hope and Australia. One can reflect that if this ship had remained on its course instead of striking north for China her captain, Thomas Cooke, would have discovered Australia before his near-namesake.

By October 1764, having been some six months at sea with a large crew (over two hundred, including the soldiers and passengers), it is not surprising that the water was running low. Off the coast of Sumatra the captain had cause to note: 'We are now so weak and our people falling sick every day and at short allowance of water...and unless we have a fair wind in two or three days shall be obliged to bear away for Manna for water and refreshments.' (11 October 1764.) On the following day a similar log entry records: 'Soldiers were very sickly and falling down dayly and a scarcity of water on board.' Owing to this lack of water they anchored off Manna (Sumatra) to replenish their supplies – with disastrous results – for in sending the ship's boat ashore for fresh water the chief mate, four seamen and a passenger were lost when the boats were swamped in the surf.

The *Earl of Elgin* eventually reached Bencoolen on 4 December 1764, and after saluting the fort with nine guns the East India Company soldiers were sent ashore. The next day the passengers likewise left the vessel, which remained at Bencoolen until 3 February 1765. During this time the Company's goods were delivered, the ship underwent various repairs and more cargo was loaded. This comprised a great quantity of pepper (over 3,000 bags), six casks and five chests of cloves, twenty-four chests and two boxes of camphor, seventeen chests of spice and a chest of Rupees. The pepper was normally sold in Canton, not brought home to Britain.

Having left Bencoolen they were off the extremes of the Java coast within three days but on 9 February they were again short of provisions; the log reads: 'A.M. called a consultation of my officers and finding the people very sickley and weak resolved to touch at Batavia for refreshments before we proceeded to the eastward.' The next entry reads: 'At half past 5 p.m. came into Batavia Road. Saluted the Dutch Commander with 11 guns but they did not return it. Found riding here the *Duke of Gloucester* and the *Duke of Richmond* [these were sister ships of the *Earl of Elgin* and they were also on passage for China]...found likewise riding here a Country ship called the *Bombay Merchant* from Bombay [this vessel 'oversett' on 14 February with much loss of life] and the *Elizabeth* from Bencoolen, with several sail of Dutch ships and China junks.' (Log entry, 10 February 1765.)

The East Indiaman remained at Batavia for nearly three months, taking on provisions and repairing the vessel, 'Caulker finished with ships sides and poop' (26 March 1765). She had in fact, like several other vessels, 'lost her passage' – missed the prevailing winds – and was unable to reach her destination in the prescribed season.

The *Earl of Elgin*, East Indiaman

15 A general view of the shipping at anchor off Whampoa Island, down-stream from Canton. China-ware and other goods were ferried down to European vessels which were being overhauled and revictualled.   *Sotheby & Co., London*

On 24 June 1765, just over fourteen months after leaving Gravesend, the *Earl of Elgin* was approaching China. On this day the log relates: 'At 4 p.m. got Pilot on board to carry the ship to Macao,' some eighty miles below Canton. From here on the various foreign vessels were very much under the strict eye and regulations of the Chinese.

Three days later they completed the trip up-river to arrive at the international (neutral in time of war) anchorage off Whampoa Island: '...at 5 p.m. ...dropped further up with the tide of flood, saluted His Majesties Frigate *Argo*, with 13 guns, she returned do. The Honble Company's ship *Admiral Pocock* saluted us with 9 guns which we returned and a Swedish ship with do. which we likewise returned. At $\frac{1}{2}$ past 7 came to...in Whampoa Road in $\frac{1}{4}$ less 6 fathom...'

The oil painting reproduced as Plate 15 shows

shipping anchored off Whampoa Island but at a rather later date.
In 1769 William Hickey noted:

Whampoa is pleasantly situated, having two islands close to the ships, one called Danes Island, upon which each ship erects what is called a Bankshall [or Banks Hall as some logs state], being a lightly constructed wooden building from sixty to one hundred feet in length into which the upper masts, yards, spars, sails, rigging and stores are deposited, and, previous to being re-embarked, are all repaired and put into order. The other is called French Island...

One log of 1737 records the size of the *London*'s Bankshall as seventy feet long and thirty-four feet broad. The Island was apparently infested with white ants, and the stores had to be lifted two feet off the ground; nevertheless the ship's tackle was stored and repaired here, the food was cooked here and the meat was salted for the return journey. These Bankshalls acted as the ship's depot and each crew constructed and later dismantled its own special building.

Having reported the safe arrival of the ship to the Council of Supra-cargoes at Canton and having delivered the invoices and bills of lading for the outward cargo brought from London, the Supra-cargoes in their turn would have given Captain Cooke a letter containing the following standard instructions:

Sir,
We are directed by the Court of Directors to acquaint you with the following orders –
That you, your officers or ship's company are not to run any goods, on pretence of saving the Customs of this Port, and that they shall expect satisfaction for any embarrassment in their affairs a breach of this order may occasion.
That neither you, nor your officers are to go a shooting on any pretence whatsoever and that you give positive orders to your officers to keep your ship's company within the bounds of sobriety and decency, so as not to give offence to the Chinese Government.
That you take care that all goods delivered out of, or received into your ship are duly entered in the Boatswain's book, for which purpose, when your homeward bound loading is compleated you are to deliver it to us. That your own and ship's company's private trade be registered with us, before your departure, in which quantity, quality, mark and number and value of every parcel are to be particularly mentioned and to whom they belong and we hereby give you notice as well for your own information as for that of your officers and ship's company that all goods not so registered shall be forfeited.
That you are on no account to load any goods belonging to yourself, your officers or ship's company in the boats that carry the Company's goods to and from Canton.
That you do not load or suffer to be loaden on board your ship any Camphire or Musk, lest the scent spoil the tea and no more Arrack than is necessary for stores, and that to be stowed in such manner as not to prejudice the teas.
That the fine teas are to be stowed in the after part of the ship between decks, abaft the well in the hold – to the bulkhead of the breadroom and a bulkhead must be made at the after part of the well and battened down to prevent any steam damaging the tea.
The privilege of the flag has been nearly lost by bringing up goods and silver in the Pinnace with the Flag flying – you are therefore to give strict orders that the flag is never to be hoisted on board the Pinnace, except for the service of the Company or when you come up, or go down yourself and then nothing is to be put into the Boat. At all other times you are to direct the boats without the flag to call at the Hoppo houses and that your people behave properly.
Danes Island was some years past appointed by the Chinese Government for the English seamen to walk and divert themselves upon; and French Island for the French – to prevent any quarrels between the two nations. You are hereby ordered not to suffer your people on any occasion to go to French Island.
We hereby give you notice that the Company's orders

The *Earl of Elgin*, East Indiaman

are – that we fix a day after which no private trade must be sent on board your ship, of which we shall acquaint you further.

If you have occasion to borrow money of the Company at this Port, according to the Charter party agreement, you are to make the demand in writing before you leave Canton and not to draw bills on us, while on board your ship at Whampoa, or going down the river – made payable to Compradores etc. as we hereby declare to you, that such bills will not be paid by us.

On 19 July 1765 the log of the *Earl of Elgin* records in simple terms an important ceremony: 'This day the Hoppo measured the ship, she being from the centre of the foremast to the centre of the mizon mast 80 covids and 4 punto's [approximately ninety-five feet or about the length of three London buses] and upon the gun deck at the mainmast 24 covids [approximately twenty-eight feet] broad. Saluted the Mandarine on his coming and goings with 9 guns.'

I give below an account of a similar measuring conducted eighteen years earlier. Here the narrative is fuller, being a diary entry rather than the bare bones of a log:

…On August 1st, the Captain, Supra-cargoes, the Interpreter and Company's agent, came again on board, to attend the Mandarine, who was appointed by the Chongtou, or Vice-roy of the province to measure our ship. He soon after arrived. We saluted him with 9 guns. He brought a numerous retinue with him. There was a great deal of magnificence and grandeur in his Sampans or boats, but no less in his person and habit. He was attended by several inferior Mandarines, and these last had each their Attendants. On his approaching our vessel, a band of musick played all the time…On entering the quarter-deck, the Mandarine saluted the Captain with a great deal of complaisance, and the inferior Mandarines, with bended knee, did the same. The Chinese Interpreter and Mr Flint, the Company's agent, stood by to explain what passed. The Chief Mandarine was seated on a grand-chair, which was brought on board, and placed on the quarter-deck for him, while the inferior Mandarines measured the ship, which took about an hour. At his departure there was a great deal of ceremony, in cringing, bowing and firing cannon.

The object of the measuring was to determine the rating and the charge to be levied on the vessel; this was normally 1950 tales or £650 for a 'First Rate' European trading ship.

These two accounts do not mention that presents were exchanged and that the Mandarins customarily gave each ship two bullocks, eight jars of wine and eight bags of flour. Notwithstanding the exchange of presents and the compliments that must have flowed from one side to the other, I must in fairness to the Chinese (who were often accused of trickery) record that the British captains were not slow to make the most of the fact that the Chinese measured the vessels between the mizen and main or fore-mast for the purpose of charging their fees. One log candidly records: 'We got the foremast as far aft as we could, and the mizen-mast forward before the ship was measured.'

The anchorage at Whampoa was the meeting place of the European maritime powers. William Hickey on the *Plassey* at Whampoa in August 1769 noted: 'Found at anchor five English ships, four Swedes, six French, four Danes and three Dutch, all the foreigners being of immense burthen of from twelve to fifteen hundred tons.' The large size of the non-British vessels is noteworthy, for before 1772 the British East India Company vessels were usually of relatively small size, being listed in the Company records at 499 tons, to avoid the necessity of carrying a chaplain – who was required for each vessel over 500 tons. In practice, however, it seems that the vessels exceeded the stated tonnage and certainly they were of different capacity. After about 1777 the size increased and the vessels sometimes ran to over 800 tons; some in the 1790s were of 1,200 tons.

Colour Plate 5 A Chinese mug of rare squat form with spreading base and finely enamelled in the *famille rose* pattern. 5¾ inches high, *c.* 1750. *Private collection*

In contrast the earlier vessels were quite small; the log of the *Rochester* during her 1709–12 voyage records in some detail the size of the vessel; she was of only 310 tons and measured 85′ 6″ long by 28′ 6″ wide. The hold was 12′ 4″ deep and there was clearance of 6′ 1″ between decks. Other British vessels were slightly larger; for example the *Princess Royal* in 1737 was given as 100′ long, with a beam of 32′ 6″. The depth of the hold was 14′ but there was a clearance of only 5′ 4″ between decks.

After the *Earl of Elgin* with Captain Thomas Cooke had arrived at the Whampoa anchorage in late June 1765 the ship's log records the arrival of numerous other European vessels. Such details help us to gauge the immense European trade in Chinese porcelains, teas and other commodities. These entries for 1765 read:

11 July	'…arrived here a Danish ship from Europe.'
14 July	'…arrived here the *Talbot*, Captain Dethick and the *York*, Captain Lascalles, both from Bombay.'
23 July	'…Came to an anchor here the *Salisbury*, Captain Wyche, from St Helena.'
26 July	'…Came to an anchor here the *Dutton*, Captain Rice, also a French ship.'
27 July	'…Came to anchor here the *Ankerwyke*, Captain Ross, from England.'
28 July	'…Came to an anchor here the *Essex*, Captain Read, from England.'
30 July	'…arrived here the *Cecil*, Captain Brown from Bombay.'
6 August	'…Arrived a Dutch ship from Batavia.'
26 August	'…in the morning came to an anchor here the *Thames*, Captain Haggis, from Bencoolen.'
27 August	'…Came to an anchor here a Dutch ship.'
29 August	'…Came in and anchored here the *Grosvenor*, Captain Saunders from Bencoolen, anchored here also a Dutch ship.'
21 September	'…Anchored here the *Royal Captain*, Captain Tanner and *Horsenden*, Captain Marter, both from Madras.'
24 September	'…anchored here a Dutch ship.'
29 September	'…arrived a Sweed [Swedish] ship and two French ditto.'
12 October	'…anchored here the *Tilbury*, Captain Mainwaring.'

To complete the record of the European vessels anchored at Whampoa during 1765 it should be stated that there were also the earlier arrivals: His Majesty's ship *Argo*, and the *Earl of Elgin*'s sister ships, the *Duke of Gloucester*, the *Duke of Richmond* and the *Pocock*. The log of the *Duke of Gloucester* records the arrival on 27 June of a 'large Sweed' [Swedish ship] named the *Finland*, on 29 June the arrival of the British ship *Chesterfield* and on 3 July the arrival of a Dutch vessel. Otherwise her log entries duplicate, as regards the arrival of other ships, those quoted from the *Earl of Elgin*, with the exception of a Swedish ship logged on 24 August. The totals taken from the logs are: seventeen British vessels, four Dutch, four French, three Swedish and one Danish.

The months of July to September represented the season when the European vessels normally arrived to take advantage of the prevailing winds. These same vessels endeavoured to be ready to depart in November, December or January, again to take advantage of the helpful winds of the north-east monsoon, to sail southwards into the Indian Ocean.

On 25 July 1765 the first log entry relating to

contact with the Chinese mainland was noted, after the ship had been at anchor at Whampoa for very nearly a month. This entry reads: 'Dispatched a chop to Canton with private trade.' (A 'chop' in this context was a form of licensed lighter, by which the cargo was transferred to and from Canton.) From this date on, almost daily entries record the passage of cargo to and from Canton. Sample log entries read:

'Dispatched a chop to Canton with goods belonging to the Honble Company.'
'Loaded boats with private trade belonging to Captain.'
'Dispatched two Chops to Canton with Private Trade.'
'Dispatched one chop with Private Trade to Canton.'
'Dispatched two boats for Canton with Honble Company's pepper and Bales.'
'Dispatched two boats with the Honble Company's goods for Canton, viz. one with Lead and the other with the remainder of the Bales and pepper.'

It should be recorded here that the ship's captain and the Supra-cargoes spent their time at Canton, leaving the vessel down-river at Whampoa in the charge of the First Mate.

On 7 September 1765, over two months after arrival, the cargo had nearly been cleared, and on this day the following entry was logged: 'Loaded two boats with Flints for Canton', and the same entry was repeated on 11 September. These would be the 120 tons of flints loaded at Gravesend in March 1764, and while it is well known that the flints which abound on the south coast of England and on parts of the east coast were transported to the English pottery centres, it is surprising to find that the East India Company vessels took them to China, where they presumably formed a part of the Chinese porcelain or its covering glaze or were used in the flux for the colours.

The *Earl of Elgin*'s cargo of English flints was not an isolated or freak shipment; her sister ship, the *Duke of Richmond*, on passage to Canton at the same period, loaded a hundred tons of flints representing the captain's Private Trade, so that one can deduce that it was a profitable cargo. In fact the flints were sold in Canton for about £10 a ton. In 1787 over a thousand tons of British flints were sent to Canton and the trade continued into the nineteenth century, having started in the 1690s.

It was at Canton that all business was conducted, and here the various East India Companies had their Factories. Various contemporary accounts give an interesting picture of Canton and of life there as experienced by the visiting Europeans. Canton, or rather a restricted section of it, was the only part of China where a European was allowed to set foot at this period.

In August 1769 William Hickey, on board the *Plassey*, noted in his memoirs:

We arrived at Canton about noon. The view of the city…is strikingly grand, and at the same time picturesque…The scene upon the water is as busy a one as the Thames below London Bridge, with the difference, that instead of our square-rigged vessels of different dimensions, you there have junks…

About half a mile above the city suburbs in going from Whampoa, is a wharf, or embankment, regularly built of brick and mortar, extending more than half a mile in length, upon which wharf stands the different factories or places of residence of the Supra-cargoes, each factory having the flag of its nation on a lofty ensign staff before it. At the time I was in China they stood in the following order: First the Dutch, then the French, the English, the Swedes, and last the Danes. Each of these factories, besides admirable banquetting or public rooms for eating, etc, has attached to them sets of chambers, varying in size according to the establishment. The English being far more numerous than any other nation trading with China their range of buildings is much the most extensive. Each Supra-cargo has four handsome rooms; the public apartments are in front, looking to the river; the others go inland to the depth of two or three hundred feet

The *Earl of Elgin*, East Indiaman

16 A finely painted Chinese porcelain punch-bowl showing the various European 'Hongs' or 'Factories' on the waterfront at Canton. Diameter 14¼ inches, c. 1785.   *Sotheby & Co., London*

in broad courts having the sets of rooms on each side, every set having a distinct and separate entrance with a small garden, and every sort of convenience. Besides the factories which belong to the East India Companies there are also others, the property of Chinese, who let them to European and country captains of ships, merchants and strangers, whom business brings to Canton...

Some very fine Chinese porcelain punch-bowls exist showing these European Factories or stores-cum-residences (Plate 16). One finds rather more frequently paintings on canvas or paper of these Factories. These were popular pictures right into the nineteenth century and one can often date quite accurately the period of the picture by the changing water-front scene. Carl L. Crossman's book *The China Trade* (1972) gives helpful information on these buildings or 'Hongs'.

These imposing Factories date from 1751, or later, for it was only at this period that it was resolved to hire them for a term of years, rather than annually as had previously been the practice.

The various Company officers, in particular the all-important Supra-cargoes, lived extremely well in their 'Factories'. William Hickey's 1769 account continues:

...The number of Supra-cargoes employed by the English East India Company in the year 1769 was twelve...Upon our landing, Captain Waddell immediately conducted Mr McClintock and me to Mr Revell, the chief Supra-cargo, who after an exchange of compliments, took us to a handsome set of rooms, consisting of two spacious bed-chambers, with pleasant rooms adjoining each, two large sitting rooms and one for eating – the whole neatly furnished and having a complete small library…He also observed that, as it was customary for gentlemen to breakfast in their own chambers, every requisite would be amply supplied by the factory steward. He further informed us that all the Supra-cargoes, and any guests that honoured them with their company daily dined together in the great hall at two o'clock…we sat down, in number about thirty, to a capital dinner consisting of fish, flesh and fowl all of the best, with a variety of well dressed made dishes, being served up in two courses, followed by a superb dessert, the wine, claret, madeira and hock, all excellent, and made as cold as ice…After sitting near three hours at table, the company separated…

At seven in the evening we returned to the hall and drank coffee and tea, after which some went to cards, some to billiards, whilst others walked up and down, or sat chatting on a terrace which projected from the hall and went several feet over the river, being supported by large piles; the situation was cool and refreshing. At ten supper was announced, from which every person retired when he thought proper to his bed. McClintock and I had Chinese servants appointed to wait upon us, who we found in attendance at our rooms with candles, slippers and all the etceteras of the night.

Small wonder that in December 1769 William Hickey was able to record, 'thus I left Canton where I had spent four months very happily, having been received with hospitality and kindness that nothing could exceed'.

However, for the sailors and tradesmen busily preparing the vessel, anchored down-river at Whampoa, for the return voyage, life was far from luxurious, and several lives were lost. The *Earl of Elgin*'s log on 15 September 1765 records: '…In the morning departed this life, Thos. Dandy, carpenter and also James Rout, his mate. In the afternoon sent both the deceased corps. to French Island to be interred.' Others simply fell from the ship and were drowned. These losses were by no means unusual; each ship seems to have had its share of accidents and illness, as a study of the logs and crew-lists shows. Seven days later life at home was remembered: 'This being the anniversary of their Majesties [George III and Queen Charlotte] Coronation, at the one of the clock fired 21 guns.'

At this point, having unloaded all the incoming cargo including the flint stones, Captain Thomas Cooke then commenced reloading for the homeward journey – starting with the ballast. Some writers have stated that the china itself acted as the ballast, but this does not appear to be the full story, for the log records: 'Loaded with rough ballast and shingle ditto.' Later there is the entry: '…employed clearing Hold and levelling the Ballast to receive the china ware.' (23 September 1765.)

The china-ware was loaded above the ballast, as 'flooring', before the chests of tea were added; this standard method of stowing was employed to give stability to the vessel with the ballast and heavy china-ware deep in the hold, below the light-weight tea, the main cargo, and the silks. These wooden vessels were leaky, and while the sea water would not harm the ballast and china, it would ruin the tea and silks, had these been loaded low in the hold.

The choice of the amount of china-ware carried for the account of the English East India Company was largely left to individual captains. Captain Cooke might have written to the Council of Supra-cargoes at Canton a letter on the following prescribed lines:
Sirs,

As you are pleased to leave it at the option of the Commander of the respective ships, what quantity of china ware you shall send towards the flooring of each ship, I think it necessary to acquaint you that if you'll please to order ninety half-chests on account of the Honble Company, on board the *Earl of Elgin*, the rest will be completed in the Private Trade.
         I am
           Sirs,
               Your most obedt. humble servant

The text of this letter recorded in a Supra-cargo's diary has been changed only respecting the name of the ship and the number of cases, as the relevant request respecting our vessel is not available. At this period in the 1760s and 1770s half-chests seem to have been the normal container-size, although some whole chests are recorded.

According to one log entry the standard chest of china-ware measured 3·4 long by 2·4 wide and from 1·10 to 1·5 deep. These measurements were presumably in feet and inches although the log entry of the *Lyall* under the date 1 October 1722 does not make this clear. It is the only instance of recorded measurements that I have traced and it shows the chests to be relatively shallow, rather similar to a large suitcase. This basic shape is confirmed by contemporary Chinese paintings. Later in the century, as we know, most of the china-ware was loaded in "half-chests". Some china was apparently carried loose in the holds, a fact shown by the unloading entries in some logs: 'Packers employed packing the loose china' or 'employed in the hold packing of china and delivering part of ye Honble Company's china'.

On 27 September the ship's company 'employed chiefly as days past, received on board on the account of the Honourable Company 90 half-chests chinaware'. The log for the next day records: 'Quartermaster and Midshipmen stowing the china'. Still more ballast was taken on board, for on 30 September the officers 'Received on board two sampan loads of shingle ballast, weighed each at 16 tons.' The next day this new ballast was levelled 'for receiving the Private China', and on 4 October 'Received on board one chop of china ware belonging to Captain and officers'. The next day the crew were 'employed stowing the china'. It is suggested that this Private Trade included the punch-bowl shown in Plate 14, depicting the vessel on her outward voyage. Probably soon after the ship's arrival in June a sketch was taken or forwarded to Canton where the order was placed, the bowl being specially decorated by one of the many china-painters employed at Canton and packed with other, similar Private-Trade orders, for delivery to the vessel some three months later. William Hickey relates how he went out to see the different Canton manufacturers including the porcelain enamellers: '...We were shown the different processes used in finishing the china ware. In one long gallery we found upwards of a hundred persons at work in sketching or finishing the various ornaments upon each particular piece of ware, some parts being executed by men of very advanced age and others by children even so young as six or seven years...'

A French account of 1797 (quoted by M. Beurdeley in his *Porcelain of the East India Companies*) relates to the decoration of special orders by the enamellers at Canton: 'If you want to have pieces copied from European designs [shapes] they must go to Ching-tê Chên [see pp. 111–12], but in that case you have to wait...for the next voyage. For sailors who cannot afford to wait, white pieces can be bought [in Canton] and painted on the spot. The painting is applied over the glaze and fired on in the kiln. Afterwards it stands out in slight relief...'

Having loaded the ship with ballast and heavy china-ware 'flooring', the ship could now be safely heeled (or tilted over) without risk of capsizing. This heeling was done on 6 October and on many subsequent days the now exposed parts were cleaned and retarred.

At about this time the Supra-cargoes at the Factory at Canton would have issued to the captain of the *Earl of Elgin* a further set of standard instructions:

Sir,

We are directed by the Court of Directors to acquaint you with the following orders, which they expect will be as strictly complied with.

That you stock your ship with as much salt provisions as you may want for your voyage home, not to be under the necessity of applying for any from the Governor and Council at St Helena.

That if you or your officers shall neglect or refuse to deliver to us before your departure from Canton, full, true and perfect registration of your own and their Private Trade according to the Covenants in Charter Party, or shall break bulk or dispose of any tea, or other article of your own and their Private Trade, in your return homeward, that the offenders will experience the severest resentment, not only by an irrevocable dismission from the Company's service but suits of Law will be instituted against them, for recovery of the Penalties they will render themselves liable to by such unlawful practices.

And we are further to acquaint you that the Court of Directors positively direct and order that you do not ship or cause to be shipped any tea without giving to us sufficient previous notice thereof, that we may obtain a Chop [licence] in the Company's name for that purpose. And you are to deliver to us a complete register signed by you in our presence of the entire exports in Private Trade of Tea of yourself and officers on board ship.

And we are order'd to demand of you to inform us, in the most certain and precise manner of the actual quantity of Gun Powder on board your ship, for the homeward bound voyage, and are order'd to caution you against any needless expense of this article during your stay in China, that you may not be obliged to depart from hence without less quantity than thirty-five barrels of serviceable Powder and we are to acquaint you that the Court of Directors are positively determin'd to avail themselves in the most ample manner of the Penalties you shall render the Owners and yourself liable to, by the infraction of the Charter Party Covenants in this instance.

We are,
Sir,
Your humble servants

The warning about selling or smuggling Private Trade to escape Customs and other dues was very necessary, but apparently not always heeded.

William Hickey relates how on his homeward voyage from Canton the captain received a cheque for £12,024, drawn on a London bank, for sixty-eight chests of tea sold from aboard his vessel as they were sailing home in the English Channel. The other officers received £800 for their Private Trade tea. The directors in London wrote to the Supra-cargoes in Canton: 'Our sales having been lately much affected by the great quantity of tea smuggled, particularly from our own ships which we are informed has sometimes been to the amount of three or four hundred chests each ship...we strictly require you to give us every information that may enable us to bring the offenders to punishment.' (Letter dated 4 December 1777 and repeated in several others.)

The Supra-cargoes endeavoured to have recorded every item loaded aboard each vessel. One assumes that such loading records would have been checked when the goods were unloaded in London, but there must have been remunerative abuse of the Private Trade privileges, notwithstanding all efforts to suppress smuggling (see also p. 78). By 1782 the East India Company had caused an Act of Parliament to be passed prohibiting 'the clandestine unshipping from and receiving goods at sea, on board vessels employed in the Company's service'.

Having floored the ship with cases, or rather half-cases, of china-ware, the main cargo of tea was loaded – some four months after arrival of the vessel at Whampoa. Again the ship's log shows the progress: 'Received on board on account of the Honble Company 250 chests, Bohea [black] tea.' (23 October 1765.)

Two days later the crew had 'completed our first height of Bohea tea, fore and aft'. During the next month, 2,398 whole chests and 1,329 half or small chests of tea were loaded. In the main this was of the popular Bohea variety and each chest contained nearly 350 lb. Other types were Congou,

Nankeen and Singlo (green). The chests of tea were apparently not of the proportions of modern tea-chests for the log of the *Monmouth* records under the date 20 October 1729: 'The green-tea chests are 2 foot in length and 18 inches in breadth and depth.' They were apparently sealed with paper, for the same log records: 'When we received ye chests of tea on board most of ye Papers was torn off and in a bad condition being slip't off when it rained.' The Supra-cargoes' journals abound with details of the purchase of tea, of protracted bargaining, of shortages, of differing qualities and of the difficulties caused by the various nations, the French, Danes, Dutch and Swedes, all endeavouring to procure teas to fill their respective vessels.

Tea was of course the main cargo and the chief reason for the voyage. If tea had not been the highly saleable commodity it was, it is doubtful if European vessels would have traded with China – the one source of tea – at least, not in the large numbers that they did. Consequently, if it had not been for tea, we would not have had the china-ware. In the second half of the eighteenth century the East India vessels brought home from China as official cargo only tea, silks and china-ware, listed here in the order of their importance to the English East India Company. Other goods were shipped home as Private Trade.

Tea was certainly profitable, as is partly evidenced by the scale of smuggling, for the price in Canton was approximately one shilling and sixpence per pound for Bohea tea, and this could fetch over twenty shillings a pound in London, although the price fluctuated considerably. Clearly, however, even after all the charges had been paid, the Company could afford the wastage occasioned by bad packing or stowing, or the ruses employed by the Chinese to pass off bad tea for good, or the practice of filling some of the tea-chests with bricks and other rubbish – practices complained of in the directors' letters to the Supra-cargoes in Canton.

The collector of English porcelain will readily see the importance of tea by looking at his porcelain collection, for unless he collects purely decorative objects, such as figures or groups, some two-thirds or more of his pieces will comprise teawares.

Throughout November preparations were in hand for the voyage home of the *Earl of Elgin*. The log records items such as: 'steward at shed [bankshall, see p. 96] overhauling the provisions'; 'killed 50 hogs at the shed for salting'; 'sent our powder to Powder Island to dry'; '573 bags rice for ship's use', until on 11 December 1765 the *Earl of Elgin* weighed anchor and dropped down-river below the shipping to a fresh anchorage, below the second bar. In passing down, she 'saluted the shipping with 9 guns and at noon the Purser came on board with the Company's Packet from Canton.' This must have been the final letters, bills and reports from the East India Company resident officers for delivery in London. The water-butts had of course been filled, but the water at the anchorage at Whampoa was not wholesome and fresh water had to be fetched from above Canton. On 21 December the vessel cleared the Pearl River on the start of an uneventful trip home to London.

Like most East India Company vessels the *Earl of Elgin* called at St Helena on her return voyage. Apart from delivering Chinese goods such as tea, and often small quantities of china-ware, the East Indiaman could, if need be, replenish with fresh water and food. However, the main purpose of this call was to pick up dispatches from London and also to enquire if there was war and, if so, with whom – for the vessel had been out of direct contact with the European political situation for two or more years.

Some seven months after leaving China the *Earl of Elgin* was back in the Thames at Blackwall. Here

Colour Plate 6 A superbly potted thin, light-weight porcelain teabowl delicately enamelled with a Chinese interior scene. In its modest way this is a ceramic masterpiece. 1½ inches high, c. 1740–50.

Geoffrey Godden Chinaman, reference collection

the unloading of the Private Trade and the Company's cargo took a full month, and the last log entry for this voyage was entered on 24 July 1766: 'Employed delivering the remains of the Honble Company's goods and private trade, officers [of the Company] came on board and cleared the ship.'

On 30 July Captain Cooke reported to the Court of Directors, delivering his ship's papers, after which £2,000 was paid to the owners of the *Earl of Elgin* on account of freight and demurrage. On 6 August a further £1,200 was paid and, after a special request, payment of £9,000 was made on 5 August. Over £12,000 was thus paid well before any of the cargo was sold. A further £4,000 was paid on the order of the Committee of Private Trade on 16 January 1767.

I have not been able to trace positively the sales at which the *Earl of Elgin*'s china-ware was sold, but it was most probably sold in February 1767. The relevant Court Minute reads: 'Resolved that the 1,371 lots of china ware be put up to sale on Wednesday the 18th February next... and that on account of the said china ware be printed with the following declaration, viz. – That this Court will sell no more china ware till September sale 1767, except what may be uncleared and in Private Trade.' (2 January 1767.)

The 1,371 lots must have consisted of a vast amount of china for typical single wholesale lots could exceed a thousand objects. The declaration that no more would be sold until September underlines the Company's standard practice of selling only in the spring and autumn, except for the smaller selections bought in as Private Trade. Three sales of Private Trade china-ware were held after the *Earl of Elgin*'s arrival home, and any or all of these could have included china-ware from this vessel. The sale dates were 29 September 1766, 24 February 1767 and 14 July 1767.

While we do not have precise details of the china-ware brought home on the *Earl of Elgin* we can reasonably conclude that the Company's cargo comprised much the same assortment as that carried in other vessels of the same period, for the Supra-cargoes were in the habit of buying in bulk and dividing the purchases between the available vessels for their journey home to England. As we know, the wares bought for the Company's account were usually standard designs that could be sold to any buyer at the London auction sales. Even in the 1760s the vast majority of such china was decorated only in underglaze blue (see Chapter 4).

The *Earl of Elgin*'s cargo of the Company's china was probably very similar to that recorded as carried by the *Neptune* in the 1761–2 season. This comprised:

3,356 octagonal blue and white soup plates [costing approximately to the nearest pound, £48]
2,190 breakfast cups and saucers, blue and white [£25]
4,204 blue and white chocolate cups and saucers [£83]
1,799 blue and white cups and saucers [£27]
70 blue and white table [dinner] services @ £4 [£280]
80 water plates, 2 sizes [£1]
532 handled cups blue and white [no saucers] [£3]
400 cups and saucers [£4]
180 blue and white cups and saucers [£1]
1,980 cups and saucers enamelled [£18]
333 enamelled bowls [£78]
120 half-pint sneakers, coloured and gold [£1]
90 enamelled teasets [£60]
150 do. [£60]

A lengthy list of a season's china-ware ordered from one Chinese merchant in 1768 is given on p. 133, while later orders are listed on p. 44. These lists show well the standard nature of the Company's

imports of Chinese ceramics. Porcelains of the standard types are discussed in Chapters 4 and 5, but it must be conceded that *some* special pieces – such as the wares bearing the Arms of the different City Companies and Guilds, and services made for noblemen – were probably ordered direct from the East India Company, if not from ships' captains, and these special orders would not have been included in the basic orders or in the auction sales.

As I have suggested in Chapter 2, it is reasonable to assume that the captains' and officers' Private Trade generally comprised the better-class individual and personal wares, for the amount of Private Trade was restricted in weight. Many lightweight objects would therefore be a better proposition than, for example, the relatively heavy and standard blue-painted dishes that the Company shipped in bulk.

A year after the vessel's arrival home the eleven Supra-cargoes who were collectively responsible for the trade of the twelve China Trade vessels in the 1764–6 seasons were paid their commissions – amounting to no less than £20,530 – the Supra-cargoes of the *Earl of Elgin* having previously delivered to the directors the detailed accounts, comprising their journal, ledger, packing book, diary and details of the Factory expenses during their stay in Canton.

The last entry that I have traced relating to this voyage of the *Earl of Elgin* seems to refer to the final payment to the ship's owners, a payment made after all the cargo had been sold: 'Report of the Committee of Private Trade being read, ordered that warrant for £4,292 4s 9d, be made out to the owners of the *Earl of Elgin*.' (Court Minute, 11 May 1768.) If we add this to the £16,200 paid to the owners earlier, we can deduce that it was a very profitable voyage.

In 1767 and 1768 the *Earl of Elgin* traded with India. In October 1769 she started preparing for a further trip to Canton by way of Madras and Batavia. While at Batavia on 16 January 1771 Captain Thomas Cooke died, having been captain for just under seven years and, as in so many cases, not living to enjoy the fruits of his Private Trade ventures. However, the Company granted the widows of its captains a pension of £30, raised to £40 in December 1771. On this, his last, voyage the cargo was mostly tea, the porcelain comprising ninety-eight half-chests and eight whole chests for the Company's account, and eighty-two half-chests of china-ware on the ship's Private Trade account. The proportion of this Private Trade is noteworthy, there being, on this occasion, relatively little difference between the quantity shipped on account of the East India Company and that shipped by the officers on their own account. At the same period the *Duke of Richmond* carried more Private Trade china than Company china, 110 chests as against 70. It should be noted that these East Indiamen were normally permitted to undertake only four voyages to China (later this was increased to six), and on her return from China in 1773 the *Earl of Elgin* was taken out of service, as these journeys were deemed to play havoc with the ships of the period.

It is noteworthy that during the second China war in the middle of the nineteenth century, the real Earl of Elgin was in command of the European forces that bombarded and took Canton in the enforcement of British Treaty rights. Also, the 8th Earl of Elgin was the British Ambassador-Extraordinary in China.

Other aspects of the Company's shipping, trade and vessels, of a rather later date, are given in C. Northcote Parkinson's *Trade in the Eastern Seas 1793–1813*.

We have seen in these first three introductory chapters how the China trade was established in the seventeenth century, and how it was carried out in the eighteenth century. We have also learnt of the importance of the Private Trade goods, how the articles were purchased and brought home to Europe, and also a little of life at Canton. We can now proceed to discuss the several basic types of Chinese (and Japanese) porcelain, which preceded and later served as a model for European wares.

Colour Plate 7 A magnificent large tea (or punch) pot decorated with a rich version of the formal floral designs which were so popular on Chinese export market porcelains in the 1770s. Capacity five and a half pints. 9½ inches high.

Godden of Worthing Ltd

4 The blue and white porcelains

The porcelains known as 'blue and white' were decorated solely with cobalt applied to the raw porcelain before glazing. These blue and white Oriental porcelains far outnumber all other types and were made from the fourteenth century throughout the whole period covered by this book.

Blue and white porcelains from whatever source, Oriental or European, are properly referred to as being decorated in 'underglaze blue' because as I have stated above, the pigment – oxide of cobalt – was applied under the glaze. The term 'inglaze' would, however, be more apt for in practice the cobalt fused with the covering glaze and in most cases arose through it to the surface so that the blue on a glazed and fired example is *in* glaze, rather than under it. This fact is illustrated in the photograph (Plate 17) of a broken piece of eighteenth-century Chinese blue and white porcelain. So well does the cobalt flow into the glaze that it is even possible to apply it over the glaze, and in fact some designs which are called 'underglaze blue' could have had the pigment applied over the glaze.

It can, however, be taken for granted that all pieces bearing the whole design in underglaze blue were decorated at the place of manufacture, not at Canton, where much of the overglaze enamel painting was added to prepared blanks to the special order of European buyers and there re-fired at a relatively low temperature. Most Chinese porcelain – probably over ninety per cent – was made at Ching-tê Chên, far inland in the Province of Kiangsi. In many respects this centre must have been like our own ceramic district of Stoke-on-Trent in the eighteenth century – comprising a host of small manufactories as well as the Imperial Kilns, all rather remotely situated from the main centres of trade, causing troublesome transportation problems. Water-transport was the salvation of both centres, for by this means the finished wares

17 A cross-section of a broken Chinese plate decorated in blue under the glaze but, as can be seen, the blue rises into the added glaze.

were distributed to the ports, and hence to diverse markets.

Although Europeans were banned from inland China there was fortunately an important exception to this rule. This exception was the Jesuit priests and to one of these, Father d'Entrecolles, we are indebted for a contemporary early-eighteenth-century word-picture of Ching-tê Chên. This information was conveyed back to France in two letters – one written in 1712 the other ten years later. Father d'Entrecolles' account of the method of manufacturing porcelain was widely published throughout Europe by means of Du Halde's comprehensive work the English translation of which, *A Description of the Empire of China*, appeared in 1738. This book contains a wealth of information – all that was known of China and its industries at the time, and in the section on ceramics Du Halde draws extensively on the two letters written by Father d'Entrecolles. Other, later works are based on the same prime source. I quote below from a similar account first published in England in 1788. The 1788 review is almost identical with the original letters of 1712 and 1722, a fact that shows how little the Europeans' knowledge of China had increased in the eighteenth century. It could hardly have been otherwise for the country was, for all practical purposes, completely closed.

This account is from a translation of Abbé Grosier's French text, a two-volume work entitled *A General Description of China*. It gives the now standard description of Ching-tê Chên in the eighteenth century:

This village [it was so termed only because it was unwalled], in which are collected the best workmen in porcelain, is as populous as the largest cities of China. It is reckoned to contain a million of inhabitants...it extends a league and a half along the banks of a beautiful river...the people complain that the buildings are too crowded and that the long streets which they form are too narrow...

This village...is an asylum for a great number of poor families, who could not subsist anywhere else. Children and invalids find employment here, and even the blind gain a livelihood by pounding colours...

Ching-tê Chên contains about five hundred furnaces for making porcelain...the flames and clouds of smoke which rise from them in different places, show even at a distance the extent and size of this celebrated village; to those who approach it by night it has the appearance of a large city on fire...

The fuller text given in the second volume gives details of the raw materials, the forming of the wares, their decoration and firing. This information must have been of great value to Europeans who were struggling to master the mysteries of porcelain manufacture. The accounts by Father d'Entrecolles are quoted, in part at least, in most books on Chinese porcelain, particularly in Soames Jenyns's *Later Chinese Porcelain* (London, 1951 and later editions). William Burton's *Porcelain, a sketch of its nature, art and manufacture* (London, 1906) contains a very full English translation and Edward Dillon in his *Porcelain* (London, 1904) makes interesting comments on the original French account.

The blue and white porcelains

Almost all the Chinese porcelain discussed in this book was made in the inland centre of Ching-tê Chên. Here also all the pieces decorated in underglaze blue were formed and completed although, when we turn to discuss enamelled ware in the next chapter, we will find that some of this was decorated at Canton where overglaze enamel colours were added to Ching-tê Chên blanks.

As with other Chinese ceramics, export wares are related to far earlier types; Chinese blue and white porcelains in fact date from the fourteenth century. The full history of the rare early blue and white porcelains is clearly explained in Sir Harry Garner's excellent *Oriental Blue and White* (London, 1954, third edition 1970), a work with which all students of Chinese wares will already be familiar.

Father d'Entrecolles in his letter of 1 September 1712 remarked that most Chinese porcelains to be seen in Europe were blue and white: 'In Europe people hardly see anything else but a vivid blue on a white ground, though I believe that our merchants have also imported some of the other kinds...' In this instance Father d'Entrecolles was rather overstating the case, for contemporary records – the London sale catalogues and the Supra-cargoes' journals – show clearly that quantities of enamelled Chinese (and Japanese) porcelains were imported into England before 1712 (see Chapter 5). Nevertheless the *majority* of the imported porcelains were decorated in underglaze blue.

These Chinese blue and white porcelains vary enormously in quality, ranging from well-painted attractive designs, such as that shown in Colour Plate 3, to crudely painted designs on thickly potted utilitarian objects such as the water-bottle shown in Plate 68.

In the year 1699 Robert Douglas, the Supra-cargo of the *Macclesfield*, was purchasing his 'china-ware' in Canton and recording the purchases in his Journal (see p. 33). Of the articles mentioned as blue and white there were the following classes, to which I have added the sterling cost to the nearest pound:

1,168 small blue and white bowls, upright sides	[£8]
1,149 ditto, bell mouthed of 4 or 5 sorts	[£8]
910 teacups, blue and white	[£3]
240 large blue and white dishes, 2 sorts	[£18]
78 large deep dishes	[£6]
199 dishes and 90 do. bowls, blue and white	[£7]
46 nests of small bowls blue and white, 5 in each nest	[£2]
23 small do. 3 to each nest	[£1]
870 teacups and perings [saucers] blue and white	[£7]
4,400 fine blue and white cups	[£26]
1,252 plates blue and white	[£13]

There are many other articles – such as vases and beakers – listed without details of the decoration. Many of these were probably decorated in underglaze blue. The series of catalogues covering the sales in London of the cargoes of the various East Indiamen give a good idea of the types of porcelain brought home to England.

These sale records include both the Company's official imports and a large amount of Private Trade goods. The Company's china-ware is, in part at least, shown by the buying instructions given each year to the departing Supra-cargoes. Typical orders include wording such as 'we would have you provide china ware as far as twenty tons in useful sorts, which stow-close' (1704); 'Ten tons china ware to be mostly brim-plates, and a good part of them blue and the rest tea cups and saucers because they stow close' (1709); and '800 chests useful china ware, of which bowls, dishes and plates of all sizes – as many as you can get...' (1722.)

The East India Company sale which commenced on 6 March 1705 included as the cargo of a single vessel 15,979 blue and white porcelain plates. Today we may see little remarkable in such a plate, but if

18 Detail showing part of the reverse of a typical Chinese plate. The glaze has been turned away from the edge of the foot before firing.

we consider the contemporary circumstances such utilitarian articles command new respect, and we can understand why they were brought to Europe from the other side of the world.

Quite apart from the novelty of all things Chinese and the fashion for such Oriental wares, we must remember that no other white translucent table porcelain was generally available in Europe in the early 1700s. Most English families ate from pewter plates or from wooden trenchers. British earthenwares were still clay- or brick-coloured. The white salt-glazed or cream-colour bodies had not yet been introduced. Both on the Continent and in Britain there were various types of tin-glaze earthenware of the Delft type but these wares were far from practical, the covering white glaze easily chipping away from the clay body in normal day-to-day use. This earthenware proved most unsuitable for all important teawares and for most tablewares. From the housewife's point of view the Oriental porcelain plate, with its pleasant, thin feel and its durable covering glaze, was a godsend, and the vast numbers that were shipped into Britain and other European countries must have been eagerly snapped up. They were a useful novelty. There was a vast untapped market, and there was no competition.

The sale records show that the standard Oriental blue and white plates were valued by the Company at a shilling each in 1705, but that they fetched at auction between eleven pence and two shillings. However, the cost in the Chinese ports must have been about half the Company's valuation of a shilling, and even less in inland Ching-tê Chên.

It is of interest to consider for a moment a single Chinese plate, one of tens of thousands imported into Britain and other countries. Having mined, transported, refined and prepared the ingredients, a standard plastic porcelain body was available to the thrower. It is remarkable how standard this Chinese porcelain was, considering the many small potteries at Ching-tê Chên. Over a period of more than fifty years one cannot detect any difference in the basic porcelain. The standard plate, without any moulded decoration, was spun out on the potter's wheel which was very low on the ground by European standards, the potter having to sit with his legs outstretched horizontally working the wheel. Once formed, the plate was removed from the wheel and left to harden. With the later English porcelains the plate would then have been fired, before the blue was added. A covering glaze would then have been applied and the whole fired again. Apparently, however, the Chinese potter painted the cobalt design directly on to the unfired body – which must have been very fragile – and he dipped the decorated, still unfired plate in the glaze. This decorated and glazed plate was subsequently returned to the wheel or lathe after drying, so that the glaze could be trimmed away from the foot to prevent the glaze affixing one plate to another, or to the saggar, during the firing. This glaze-trimmed foot is characteristic of Oriental plates, tea-bowls,

The blue and white porcelains

teapots and other footed wares. A detail is shown in Plate 18. This illustrates a typical Chinese-style countersunk foot-ring mainly found on dinner-plates.

The plate, or other object, was then ready to receive its first firing. Eighteenth-century reports relate how the wares were piled on boards and carried at the run through the crowded streets to be fired in a different part of Ching-tê Chên. No wonder the Chinese preferred the single firing process, rather than the European double firing. The firing, in wood-stoked kilns, was necessary to vitrify the body and glaze, for without this the body is opaque and porous, the blue appears black and the glaze opaque and matt, in fact similar to chalk.

A plate requiring enamel decoration would need at least one further firing (at a lower temperature) to fix and mature the enamels, but for the standard blue and white plate the single firing was all that was required.

This simple plate shows centuries of experience on the part of the Chinese potters. The hard-paste or true porcelain was pure, showing little or no blemish or staining. It was translucent and would 'ring' like a bell. It shape was true with very rarely any evidence of sagging or distortion. The foot did not need to be ground level although fired in the range 1,350°C to 1,450°C. The covering glaze was clear, thinly and relatively evenly applied, without tears or gatherings near the foot. The blue was good in colour and static: it did not run or bleed into the glaze. Although the standard eighteenth-century export market wares are not works of art, these inexpensive, humble utilitarian wares approach technical perfection and must have been the despair of British manufacturers some fifty years later when they were trying to rival the imported Chinese blue and white porcelains (see Chapter 11).

While Chinese porcelain was generally 'hard-paste' and translucent there are exceptions to this

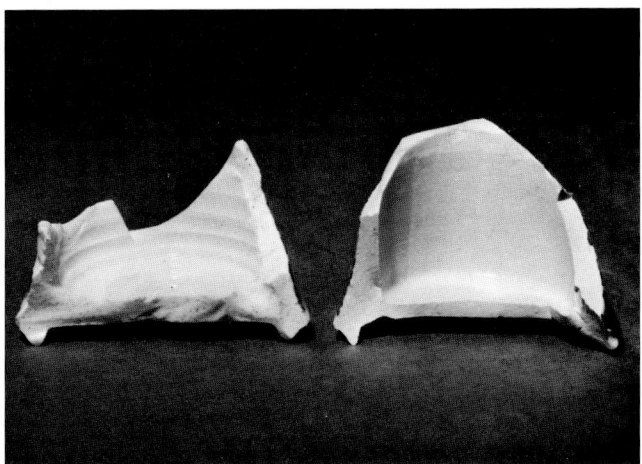

19 Two fragments of eighteenth-century Chinese porcelain vases; the one on the left shows the standard hard-paste body with vitrified appearance. The example on the right appears much softer and granular.

rule. Most of the robust export market china lacks the translucency that we expect of it, but this is generally due to the thickness of the body and Chinese porcelain more than 5 mm thick is often opaque. There is a class of porcelain known as 'soft-paste' used in the eighteenth century for the manufacture of mainly small objects. Of these, the late W. B. Honey in his *Guide to the Later Chinese Porcelain* wrote:

The most important of the porcelains with a body of abnormal composition are those generally known as 'Steatitic' or 'Soapstone porcelain' often misleadingly called 'soft-paste'...Two varieties were made; both are, as a rule, opaque. In one Hua Shih[1] (slippery-stone, soap-stone) replaced the Kaolin in the body: these pieces were very light in weight and of a fine grain. The other merely received a coating of Hua Shih and this method was apparently used for the larger specimens...The soft-looking glaze sometimes contains lead...

Here W. B. Honey like other writers was largely

[1] This appears as Hoa-Che in the 1788 English translation of the Abbé Grosier's work.

following the contemporary accounts of Father d'Entrecolles (1712 and 1722) and his later translators, but even if this represents a true picture of the variety then being made, one wonders if it is true of the later so-called soft-paste porcelains which came from China.

This query arises from the discovery of a so-called soft-paste fragment of a well-known type of export market vase, one of a set or garniture of the 1770 period. This fragment is shown in Plate 19 with a normal hard-paste fragment from a similar vase of approximately the same period (both pieces came from the site of the Caughley porcelain factory in Shropshire where *many* examples of Oriental porcelain were found, see Chapter 11). It will be readily seen that one example, that on the right, is granular or chalk-like. You may also observe the slight nick easily made by a file. The other, hard-paste, example is of a compact body with a glass-like fracture. A file will not easily cut this true porcelain fragment.

I asked the British Ceramic Research Association to test the two fragments to discover if they were of two different basic types of body. The Spectrometric Semi-Quantitative Analysis suggested that there were no major differences, although the amount of magnesia (0·1 and 0·05) may have some slight bearing on the amount of soapstone present. However, the conclusion reached was that these two bodies – one hard, the other relatively soft, appear chemically similar, but a small difference in the sodium oxide content suggests a higher level of fluxing in the hard example. Basic characteristics of an underfired ceramic body are the loss of translucency and the chalkiness of the unvitrified components, and here these points are present in the apparently soft-paste Chinese fragments. These visual characteristics may be more significant than the analysis, and this fragment and similar complete examples may simply be underfired specimens of the standard (or slightly varied) hard-paste mix. It is also true that such species are covered with a crazed glaze, another characteristic of underfiring. Margaret Medley, on p. 259 of *The Chinese Potter* (Oxford, 1976), discusses this interesting class. My Plate 285 illustrates a mid-eighteenth-century vase of this porcelain.

A contemporary account of the painting process is included in Chu Yen's *Description of Pottery* published in about 1774, based in part on observations made by T'ang Ying between 1743 and the date of publication. Dr Stephen W. Bushell's translation entitled *Description of Chinese Pottery and Porcelain* (Oxford, 1910) relates:

The different kinds of round ware painted in blue are each numbered by hundreds and thousands and if the painted decorations be not exactly alike, the service will be neither regular nor uniform. For this reason the men who sketch the outlines know how to design, not how to paint the colours, while those who fill in the colours are taught colouring not designing, by which means the hand becomes skilful in the one art-work and the mind is not distracted. The delineators and painters although distinct occupy the same house to secure uniformity in their work.

By the beginning of the eighteenth century the Chinese potters were quite used to making shapes and patterns to suit the European market. The Portuguese and Dutch had been trading in these wares for many years, although in the eighteenth century the English East India Company enjoyed the major part of the European market. In general it can be stated that the blue and white porcelains were of standard patterns as special orders were nearly always carried out in enamelled porcelains. There were, however, exceptions; in many cases these would have been Private Trade purchases.

The earliest recorded example of blue and white with a special British design is the jardinière bearing the armorial bearings of Lovelace impaling

The blue and white porcelains

20 A fine jardinière painted in underglaze blue bearing the armorial bearings of Sir Henry Johnson who was married in 1693, c. 1693–7. *City Art Gallery, Bristol*

21. A superb Chinese porcelain charger painted in underglaze blue with a European figure subject copied from a French print, c. 1720.
Victoria and Albert Museum (Crown Copyright)

The blue and white porcelains

Johnson. This jardinière, in the Bristol City Art Gallery, is shown in Plate 20. The order for the design can be dated to the period 1693–7 by the armorial bearings, but its delivery in England could have been delayed to 1699.

Other early blue and white porcelains of a special nature are shown in Plates 8, 21 and 22. These pieces were again almost certainly Private Trade imports and the designs may have been originally placed by one of the Dutch or French Supra-cargoes or ships' captains, for the dish especially displays Continental influence. Indeed several of these early designs have been traced to French prints.

The basic types of Chinese blue and white porcelain imported in the first quarter of the eighteenth century can be gauged from the instructions given to the Supra-cargoes and from Company sale catalogues. These show, as we might expect, that most of the porcelains were tablewares and, even at this date, tea wares. Such teawares were not auctioned as complete services but rather as groups of the different components, for example:

1,080 blue and white tea cups and saucers
1,120 large blue and white tea cups
  195 teapots, blue and white, 2 sorts

The teacups were most probably what we would call tea-bowls (originally Chinese wine-cups) because they lack the now conventional handles. The contemporary coffee cups were often, but not always, handled. Then as now, they were taller and narrower than a teacup or bowl.

Saucers were sometimes called 'dishes' in the contemporary accounts but it is not generally realised that cups did not always have saucers. The orders for the 1700–1 shipment record: '…coffee, tea and chocolate cups sell best without saucers, therefore buy up fewer saucers.'

The early chocolate cups were apparently used without saucers, being placed upon, or handed round on, a salver. In the 1700–5 period the Supra-cargoes were told to: 'procure chocolate cups, whether coarse or fine, to be made higher and narrower than what have usually been bought – that the more of them may stand upon a salver.' Chocolate and coffee were extremely popular drinks, before 1710 probably more popular than tea, and certainly such cups were very extensively featured in the Company's orders and imports. As early as 1681 cups were especially singled out to purchase: '…that which will turn us best to account are cups of all kinds…' a fact reflected in nearly all subsequent instructions.

By about 1710 teawares began to be featured – not as sets but each article individually. The teapot, sugar-bowl, jug, etc, was ordered separately in quantity by the Company. One set of instructions given to the departing Supra-cargoes of the *Rochester* in January 1710 specified:

5,000 teapots with straight spouts
5,000 small deep plates [stands] for the teapots
8,000 milk-pots
2,000 small tea canisters
3,000 sugar dishes
3,000 bowls about three-pint size
12,000 boats for the teaspoons
50,000 cups and saucers of the several patterns

A half or more of these quantities were decorated in underglaze blue. The amounts listed appear rather strange, for we assume that 5,000 sets were required (5,000 being the number of the teapots) then we have a surplus of milk pots and spoon-trays, and a deficit of tea canisters, sugar-bowls and tea cups and saucers to each set. We should also note that no plates were ordered, although tea-sets made in the second half of the eighteenth century had two plates included.

Since the tea itself was expensive teapots were small. The charming example shown in Plate 23 is

22 A large Chinese porcelain covered vase, one of a pair in the Victoria and Albert Museum. The central panels exhibit Continental influence. 29 inches high, c. 1720.
Victoria and Albert Museum (Crown Copyright)

only four and a half inches high and holds only slightly more than a modern cup-full. However, measuring its contents against a tea-bowl of the same period, the liquid capacity is four tea-bowls. The spout does not have the now normal strainer holes; the silver mounts were added in this country (or in Holland), and the chained cover represents a quite common practice of the period (see also Colour Plate 2). In common with other Oriental pots the glaze has been trimmed away from the foot, also from the top edge and from the inside of the cover-flange, so that the cover could be fired on its pot without risk of sticking. Small blue and white teapots of the 1720–40 period are rare and are out-numbered by the enamelled examples.

You will note that this teapot is faceted. Six- or eight-sided pots are nearly always of an early-eighteenth-century date. The cups or tea-bowls and their saucers tend to follow this non-circular outline and of course these early receptacles are also of small size.

The teawares sold at the Company sales held before 1706 did not include milk-jugs, at least the available catalogues did not list such articles by name, nor are slop-bowls named (although any of the bowls could have been so used), and it appears likely that the tea was usually drunk without the addition of milk. A letter dated 1698 refers to 'little bottles to pour milk out for tea' but we have no way of knowing if these were of Chinese porcelain. The 1706 and 1707 sales include milk pots (one lot of fifty-eight white milk pots and one lot of thirty-one), but these milk jugs were the exception rather than the rule.

Apart from teawares, large numbers of chocolate cups and saucers were included. The first March 1705 sale featured:

930 blue and white chocolate cups and
475 saucers

The blue and white porcelains

23 A most attractive six-sided small teapot. The silver-mounts were added in Europe. 4½ inches high, *c.* 1730–40.

Godden of Worthing Ltd

24 A rare European form of silver-shape candlestick in Chinese porcelain decorated in underglaze blue. 6 inches high, c. 1710–30.
J. Waring, Brighton

780 chocolate cups blue and white, 2 sorts with
600 ditto saucers [sold for 6d each]

Chocolate pots were not featured in the available catalogues and I assume that silver pots were normally used.

Coffee cups were also imported in quantity, the second March 1705 sale included '5,600 coffee cups, blue and white'. These were sold in four lots, at an average of $2\frac{1}{2}d$ each. Saucers were not listed. In the same sale the *Fleet* had credited to her 19,890 blue and white coffee cups without saucers. These sold for between $3d$ and $3\frac{1}{4}d$ each, a total of some £300. Coffee-pots were not featured in the early catalogues.

Another type of cup imported in vast quantity was the custard cup. The *Fleet* was credited with 14,225 blue and white examples in the 28 March 1705 sale, and these sold for $4\frac{3}{4}d$ each.

Although dinner-services as such were not listed, many plates were imported. The *Dashwood* carried home, to be included in the first March 1705 sale, 15,979 blue and white plates. The Company's valuation was a shilling each but the price they fetched was approximately 1s 6d per piece. There is a note against one lot 'English fashion'. This probably relates to the shape rather than the pattern and indicates that the edges had a condiment flange and that the plates were not of the Chinese curved saucer-like shape. Where dishes occur, and they were rarely featured in the catalogues, they were of circular form – enlarged editions of the plates – and in this regard they were similar to the standard pewter chargers of the period. Tureens and other dinner-service units were not catalogued.

Other blue-painted articles included in the 1705–8 sales were bowls with plates or under-dishes, salts, rose-water bottles, candlesticks, garden-pots, scalloped dishes, covered mugs, porringers, patch-boxes, chamberpots, large blue and white jars, vases, 'fountains' and bottles, but some of these

The blue and white porcelains

25 A detail from an oil-painting by J. Highmore of a family at tea in the 1740–50 period. It shows standard Chinese teawares of the period, with the teapot stand, sugar-bowl, slop-bowl on its under dish, spoontray, and tea-bowls and saucers.
Sotheby & Co., London

26 Two circular patty-pans painted in underglaze blue. Thousands of these small shallow bowls were imported in various sizes. 1¾ inches deep, c. 1740–50. *Godden of Worthing Ltd*

were probably of Japanese origin. The candlesticks are rare, and were of the European form with a nozzle to hold the candle. These and other Chinese export market porcelains were often modelled on European metal examples. A good early candlestick is shown in Plate 24. The Oriental specimens for their own home market were of the pricket-type with a spike, on which the candle was impaled. The cargo of the *Dashwood* sold in March 1708 included '248 candlesticks, blue and white', valued at two shillings each.

In the large auction sale which commenced on 6 March 1722 there were, in addition to the thousands of tea, coffee and chocolate cups, further items of tea equipage, articles not included in the earlier available catalogues. Apart from the teapots there were:

2,878 blue and white milk pots
[These sold for an average of 1s 2d]
1,761 blue and white canisters
[These were tea-canisters, or tea-vases as they are sometimes called. The tea-leaves were dropped into the pot or into the cup from these canisters, the average price of which was 9¼d]
2,075 blue and white slop basins
[These sold on average for 4¼d]
2,819 blue and white sugar dishes, covers and plates
[These sold for various prices according to the pattern, from 8d to nearly 2s. It is interesting to note that these covered sugar-bowls were sold with an under-plate]
24 blue and white boats for spoons
[These were what we now call spoon-trays, see p. 119. They seem to have been a recent innovation, for their use is explained to trade buyers. These spoon-trays sold for about 1s]

Such Chinese teawares are shown in a detail of a contemporary oil painting (Plate 25).

Also included with the teawares – by design or accident, we do not know – were large numbers of patty pans, or small shallow bowls (see Plate 26),

The blue and white porcelains

for example '1,527 blue and white patty pans', which sold on average for $11\tfrac{3}{4}d$ each.

Regarding blue and white dinner-wares in the late 1722 sale, in addition to the plates we find: '1,053 blue and white boats, 5 sorts'. These could have been sauce-boats but they are not so described and the price given was low for such pieces at $8\tfrac{1}{4}d$ each. We do, however, find catalogued: '2 blue and white soup dishes', '1 blue and white soup dish'. The precise shape of these soup dishes is not given (they were probably large deep circular dishes), but they are unlikely to be covered tureens as we know them today and the normal soup-tureen stand is not listed. We do, however, find many sets of dishes and, as no comment is made as to the shape, we can assume that they were still the standard circular form: '24 blue and white dishes, 6 sizes' which sold for $2s\ 1d$ each.

The table now began to be more fully furnished with the imported Oriental porcelain. We find, for example, '573 blue and white scallop shells' valued at $1s$ each (see Plate 27), also eleven blue and white knife-handles in two sizes, blue and white baskets in three sizes, six blue and white casters (Plate 28), and eleven blue and white fruit dishes. There were also thousands of porringers.

Two groups are listed under names which are today not clear, these are sneakers (which appear to be small bowls, rather larger than the tea-bowls – Samuel Johnson gives under 'sneaker': a small vessel of drink) and voiders: '4,970 blue and white sneakers, more or less in 12 lots, to be taken as they rise from the pile.' (The average price was $1s\ 2\tfrac{1}{2}d$.) '870 sneakers and plates, blue and white, in 2 lots. (The price here was $1s\ 6\tfrac{1}{2}d$ each.) In regard to voiders we have references such as: '3 blue and white voiders, 3 sizes.'

Apart from bowls and mugs, there were catalogued in 1722 twenty-eight coffee-pots and covers and utilitarian objects such as the strangely expen-

27 The obverse and reverse of two Chinese blue and white 'scollopt-shell' dishes. 4¼ × 5 inches, c. 1740.
Godden of Worthing Ltd

The blue and white porcelains

28 A rare and attractive Chinese blue and white two-piece caster. 6½ inches high, c. 1720–30.   *Phillips, London*

sive '133 blue and white chamber-pots' which sold for nearly six shillings each.

The preceding accounts have been concerned with the blue-painted Chinese porcelains sold in London, but similar wares were imported by other European countries and some of these bear special motifs, although the vast majority of the pieces were of stock designs. The covered cup and stand shown in Plate 8 is one of a pair in an English private collection and is believed to represent a historical scene, Louis IX with his mother. A French inscription runs round the top of the cup 'L'Empire de la vertu est establi jusqu'au bout de l'univers'. A further pair is in the Victoria and Albert Museum. The large plate or dish shown in Plate 21 has a French market appearance and both this and the covered cup pre-date 1750 by several years.

Unfortunately there are now no records of English East India Company porcelain sales after 1722. There is more than a thirty-year gap before we have records of goods ordered for the *Prince George* in September 1755. Of the 120 cases ordered for this East Indiaman in 1755 over ninety per cent of the goods were blue and white porcelains. Orders from one Chinese merchant, Suqua, comprised:

10,236 single blue and white plates	[costing £112]
4,188 half-pint basins	[costing £19]
742 coffee cups [no saucers are listed]	[costing £2 10s]
200 table sets [dinner-services]	[costing £69]

From Sweetia orders comprised:

7,351 blue and white plates	[costing £95]
1,931 half-pint basins	[costing £9 15s]
884 coffee cups, blue and white, flat bottomed with handles	[costing £3]
675 sets of blue and white bowls, 5 to a set	[costing £113]
200 tea-sets, blue and white	[costing £80]
7 table-sets, blue and white, octagon	[costing £35]

Oriental export market porcelain

This last item is especially interesting, first because the new shape is described as octagonal rather than round. Secondly, a table- or dinner-service was now ordered rather than separate pieces (it should be noted however that thousands of single plates were still required). Thirdly, the make-up of these services was listed, in this case they comprised:

2 tureens, covers and stands
13 dishes in various sizes
60 dinner plates
24 soup plates
8 salad dishes
1 salad bowl
2 sauce boats
4 salts

and the price of such a set is listed as 15 tales or £5. In fact, the sum paid to the merchants in Canton was in each case slightly less than that stated, as two per cent discount was deducted 'for breakage'.

Twenty-five dinner-services of similar make-up were ordered from the Chinese merchant Footia, and these were described as 'scallop'd'. Other table-services were of more modest size and comprised only plates and dishes.

An account dated 19 February 1760 made out by John Cowper, chinaman, of Jermyn Street, London, gives an idea of the retail price of these Chinese blue and white tablewares in the mid-eighteenth century. We find listed:

3 blue and white round china dishes at 8s	£1 4s 0d
2 blue and white oblong china dishes at 16s	£1 12s 0d
2 dozen blue and white china plates at 1s	£1 4s 0d
1 dozen blue and white soup plates at 1s	12s 0d
12 blue and white handled cups and saucers at 1s 8d	£1 0s 0d
1 blue and white teapot and milk pot	3s 6d
1 blue and white sugar dish	1s 6d

Since blue and white plates were now sold retail at one shilling, whereas they were fetching some fifty per cent more wholesale in the early 1700s, we can

29 A selection of Chinese blue and white meat-dishes from dinner-services. This was a standard shape from the mid-1750s onwards, and they were made in graduated sizes, from about 20 inches down to 8 inches long. *Godden of Worthing Ltd*

The blue and white porcelains

deduce that the general price of Chinese porcelain had fallen considerably. This was probably due not to the competition of the new English porcelains but to the fact that more and more East Indiamen were bringing greater quantities of Chinese porcelains into the country. The market was feeling the effect.

In 1765 a Bath chinaman advertised circular dishes at 2s 6d each and oblong or 'long' ones at 6s, with forty-two-piece tea-sets at £3 3s. The oblong or long dishes are depicted in Plate 29, where typical landscape designs are shown, but many floral patterns also occur.

In Britain the popular Chinese blue-painted porcelains acquired the name Nankin (again various spellings were used, Nankeen or Nanking for instance) although these goods, along with the other types, were purchased at, and shipped from, Canton. It is probable, however, that the goods were transported from Ching-tê Chên down-river to Nankin and from there by sea to Canton. In this regard they would not differ from other types of porcelain except that the blue and white examples were wholly decorated at Ching-tê Chên and were not enamelled by painters at Canton. The term 'Nankin' used from here onwards relates to blue-painted Chinese export market porcelain of the eighteenth century. In the United States, however, the term has a different, more restricted meaning (see p. 296). One American author notes: '...Nankeen has a cleanly executed lozenge diaper border, with a spearhead border along the inner edge...Nankeen dates from 1790 to 1850...' This is nonsense as far as British readers are concerned. Any blue-painted Chinese export market porcelain from the middle of the eighteenth century onwards was termed Nankin in contemporary English records. A London chinaman's account as early as 1756 includes among the items sold 'Nankeen cups and saucers'.

30 A shaped-oval blue and white Chinese meat-dish of the type sold in 1766 at £1 10s for six. 12 inches long.
Godden of Worthing Ltd

The blue and white porcelains

31 Representative pieces from a complete 'Nankin' type Chinese blue and white tea-service of the 1780s. The gilt enrichments were added in England. Teaport 7½ inches high.
Godden of Worthing Ltd

The first available Christie's catalogue of 5 December 1766 includes 'Nankeen' wares without any other explanation. The point that such pieces were decorated in blue, rather than with overglaze enamels, is made by the use of the simple description 'Nankeen', hence we find:

18 Nankeen plates	£2 5s 0d
A short set of Nankeen china	£1 9s 0d
A pair of Nankeen embossed jarrs	£2 9s 0d
A fine Nankeen bason and bottle	£1 3s 0d
A sett of three Nankeen mugs	£1 4s 0d
A complete table of Nankeen china	£2 10s 0d

The term was certainly widely used in Britain in the 1770s. The advertisement of a Leeds chinaman, Leonard Hobson, in June 1779 includes the wording 'Complete sets of Nankin tea china and of coloured ditto…' which surely is evidence that Chinese blue and white porcelains were grouped together under the general designation Nankin.

In 1766 and succeeding years the term 'Nankeen' is used extensively in Christie's catalogues. These catalogue descriptions give us some idea of the make-up of standard services and occasionally of shapes and patterns, for example: '6 oval blue and white dishes, stag pattern £1 10s 0d' (5 December 1766). A stag pattern dish is shown in Plate 30. It is an article which appears to link well with the 1766 sale entry.

The Nankin tea-set comprised forty-three pieces: teapot, cover and stand, sugar-bowl, cover and plate, slop-bowl and plate, tea canister and cover, milk pot and cover, spoon-tray, twelve tea-bowls, six coffee cups, twelve saucers. The standard set could be amended to suit personal requirements or the pocket, but it should be noted that only six coffee cups were supplied, and that tea-bowl saucers were used for the coffee cups. A coffee-pot was not supplied in standard sets. The contemporary catalogue descriptions suggest that the two odd-sized saucer-like plates, which we tend to call

32 An oval Nankin tureen and cover from a large blue and white dinner-service shown with one of the oval platters and a plate, c. 1780–90.   *Godden of Worthing Ltd*

bread-and-butter plates, were in fact used as underdishes to the slop-bowl and the sugar-bowl.

Although we are apt to regard eighteenth-century porcelain teacups as being handleless tea-bowls, handled teacups were apparently made, for Christie's sale catalogue of 8 July 1767 includes '12 fine Nankin teacups and saucers, with handles'. Nevertheless, the handleless tea-bowl remained in general favour for many years. This is most surprising because, if used on the saucer, and we are led to believe that they were, only the top inch or so can be sipped since one cannot tilt the shallow saucer without the tea-bowl sliding off. If the tea-bowl was held as contemporary paintings show, its thinness assured that one would hurt one's fingers if the tea was hot. Various methods of holding the tea-bowl are shown in Plates 4 and 25. The addition of a handle presented difficulties as regards manufacture and transportation, but if coffee cups could be handled so could teacups, yet English manufacturers as a general rule copied the Chinese fashion for handleless tea-bowls. Part of a Nankin tea-set of about 1780 is shown in Plate 31; a tea-bowl is shown beside the taller handled coffee cup.

The dinner-services or 'table-services' varied in composition. A modest one sold by Christie's in July 1767 comprised: a tureen, cover and stand, two smaller ditto, 16 oblong dishes, 8 various dishes, 74

The blue and white porcelains

33 A superb Chinese covered cistern decorated in underglaze blue with slight gold enrichments. 27½ inches high, c. 1780.
The Art Exchange, New York

plates, 12 soup plates, 4 sauce boats, 4 salts. Other sets included two tureens, rather more plates, and often the sauce-boats had under-dishes.

There are several complete lists detailing the china-ware ordered by the Honourable East India Company's Supra-cargoes in Canton from 1768 into the 1780s. These goods were ordered in the autumn of one year for delivery in time for the next season's vessels. On 25 October 1768 the Council of Supra-cargoes reported:

In order to have a sufficient quantity of good blue and white china ware for next season we have agreed with Linqua for two musters [sets of samples] for eight ships, of the following assortments.
100 blue and white Table sets
round dishes, 2 × 21 inches, 2 × 18 inches
2 × 16 inches, 2 × 14 inches, 4 × 12 inches
4 × 11 inches, and 4 × 10 inches
80 plates
1 tureen to 4 setts, 2 patterns
    15 Tales per set [£5]
50 blue and white Table sets, long dishes
14 dishes in 5 sizes
56 dinner plates
15 soup plates
 1 tureen to 2 setts
   at 12 Tales (£4)

100 sets salad dishes, 9, 10, 11 and 12 inches	·600
15 2 gallon bowls	1·000
15 1½ gallon do.	·800
35 1 gallon do.	·300
100 3 quart do.	·250
300 2 quart do.	·150
550 3 pint do.	·120
850 1 quart do.	·090
1,050 1½ pint do.	·070
7,000 single plates, 2 patterns	·033
2,700 water plates, deep	·026
600 sugar dishes	·070
2,500 coffee cans	·014
350 teapots, 2 sizes	·100
250 milk ewers	·100

34 An ornately moulded Chinese blue and white tureen, the basic form copied from Continental faience. 9 inches high, c. 1750.   *The Art Exchange, New York*

35 A rare covered tureen and stand of leaf-form decorated in underglaze blue. 6½ inches high, c. 1780.
The Art Exchange, New York

600 setts of long dishes	·380
250 setts of patty pans	·100
400 round dishes, 11 inches	·110
400 do., 10 inches	·100
120 tea sets of 43 pieces, 2 patterns	1·000
5,500 half pint sneakers, 2 patterns	·034
4,750 pint do., 2 patterns	·040
4,250 chocolate cups and saucers with handles, 2 patterns	·052
4,250 handled cups and saucers, 2 patterns	·058
4,250 breakfast cups and saucers, 2 patterns	·075
13,000 tea cups and saucers, large, 3 patterns	·043
29,000 do., small	·026

Here we see again that the Company's orders were restricted to useful tablewares and that only two patterns were ordered for each article, except for the cups and saucers, which were to be in three patterns. Even the 7,000 plates were apparently only decorated with two designs. Not every dinner service had its own tureen, only one to every fourth set in one case, or every second set in the other. We can also note that the early type of circular dish (and presumably circular tureen) was included in most sets ordered in 1768 for delivery in 1769. These goods would not have reached the London market until 1770. Pieces from a rather later dinner-service are shown in Plate 32.

One set of notes made by the Council of Supracargoes in 1777 is of particular interest, and we learn among other things that at this date the English Company's china was still being packed in sago: 'Examined a muster [sample] of sago sent in by Exchin and finding it to be of good quality agreed to purchase the quantity wanted for the package of the *Earl of Sandwich*'s china ware.' This vessel took ninety-eight chests and sixty-four half-chests of china-ware, costing 4,775·369 tales or approximately £1,592. On 1 October 1777 the Supracargoes reported:

Exchin having for two years performed his engagements

The blue and white porcelains

36 A rare Chinese blue and white covered vase, one of a pair. 12½ inches high, *c.* 1760.   *Godden of Worthing Ltd*

very punctually with regard to the china ware, we have resolved to continue to make our contracts for this part of the Hon'ble Company's Investments with him, accordingly we sent for him and contracted for sufficient to supply 8 ships at the following prices—

To have six patterns blue and white and six coloured and gilt.

The milk pots and sugar basons to be glazed round the edges, patterns 4 and 5 to have brown edges and patterns 6 and 12 to be ribbed.

The sauceboats to have hollow feet like bowls and the breakfast sets and tea to be different patterns from the rest of the china ware.

	Blue and White	Blue and White Ribbed	Coloured and Gilt	Coloured and Gilt Ribbed
Tea cups and saucers	·033	·035	·042	·044
Tea cups and saucers large	·043	·045	·052	·054
Breakfast c/s.	·072	·077	·090	·094
Chocolate cups and saucers	·052	·055	·060	·063
Teapots, 3 one set	·240	·260	·390	·410
Milk pots, 3 one set	·150	·170	·210	·230
Sugar basons	·110	·130	·130	·150
Coffee cups	·025	·027	·026	·028
Custard cups	·023	·025	·027	·029
Sauce boats, 3 one set	·300	·320	·360	·370
Patty pans, 3 one set	·160	·180	·200	·220
Fruit dishes, 3 one set	·360	·380	·400	·420
Mugs, 4 one set	·420	·440	·480	·500
Water plates	·032	—	·036	—
Plates	·055	—	·080	—
Soup plates	·065	—	·095	—
Half-pint basons	·032	·035	·035	·038
Pint sneakers, 8 one set	·042	·044	·055	·057
Bowls, 8 one set	1·250	1·350	1·500	1·600

37 A large Chinese blue and white mantel vase (missing its cover) decorated in a typical style. 15¼ inches high, c. 1780.
Godden of Worthing Ltd

38 A typical Chinese export market vase from a mantel garniture of five, two of which were of this form. The 'chicken-skin' effect between the panels is characteristic of the 1780–1800 period. 11½ inches high.
Godden of Worthing Ltd

The blue and white porcelains

39 A fine Chinese punch-bowl decorated with a mottled powder-blue ground with gold pattern over. Diameter 10 inches, c. 1740–50. *Godden of Worthing Ltd*

40 A selection of Chinese blue and white plates with European condiment flange. Such well-potted plates were imported in their tens of thousands, c. 1750–60. *Godden of Worthing Ltd*

Table sets	19·000	–	30·000	–
Breakfast sets	1·100	1·200	1·200	1·300
Tea sets	1·500	1·600	1·800	1·900

The contract for this 1778 order was signed on 14 October 1777 and although we do not have records of the individual sums the total cost was 41,804·991 tales or approximately £13,934, paid in two instalments.

In one season six patterns of blue and white china were ordered, two of these with the brown-line edge – so popular as a finish on Oriental blue and white dishes especially – and for the first time both plain and the rather more expensive ribbed or moulded shapes were specified for teawares.

Research on the sale catalogues of the period 1766–85 brings to light some useful facts. Sets of oblong Nankin dishes (Plate 29) such as one would find included in a dinner-service were sometimes sold on their own as 'supper-sets'. Nankin knife and fork handles were featured in a 1767 sale, as were Nankin punch-bowls. In a 1768 sale 'a noble large blue and white cistern for gold fish' was listed; it fetched £5. Wash-stand ewers and basins occur, listed in many catalogues with 'Lizard handle'. Chamber-pots sometimes had covers.

Breakfast sets were a feature of the imports and the auction sales. One lot read: 'A remarkable fine Nankeen breakfast set, containing a large teapot, 6 basons and plates, a sugar bowl, cover and plate, a bason and cream ewer.' Other lots comprised only sets of Nankeen breakfast basins and plates. Unlike the shallow cereal bowls of today, these old breakfast basins are deep, in fact they are identical with slop-bowls, and they are normally mistaken for these when found singly.

The staple Nankeen porcelains were still teawares and dinner-services, while the basic shapes were fairly standard. Certain ornate objects were made in small numbers, mainly for the Continental

The blue and white porcelains

41 A typical eight-sided Chinese blue and white plate from a large dinner-service of the 1780–90 period. Diameter 8¾ inches.
Godden of Worthing Ltd

42 A standard form of Chinese tureen popular in most export markets from the 1760s to the 1780s. The sauce-tureens were scaled-down versions of this basic form. 13½ inches high.
Godden of Worthing Ltd

The blue and white porcelains

43 A detail of the bottom of a typical Chinese porcelain meat-dish, such as that shown in Plate 44. Note the flat unglazed base with a dusting of parting material – perhaps flint chippings.

44 A typical Chinese export market octagonal meat-dish or platter such as those supplied in graduated sizes in the large dinner-services of the 1765–85 period. $8 \times 5\frac{3}{4}$ inches.
Godden of Worthing Ltd

45 An English porcelain meat-dish from the Caughley factory with the same basic design as that shown in the Chinese dish Plate 44, but the English example is a blue-*printed* design, *c.* 1785. *H. L. Lloyd, Esq.*

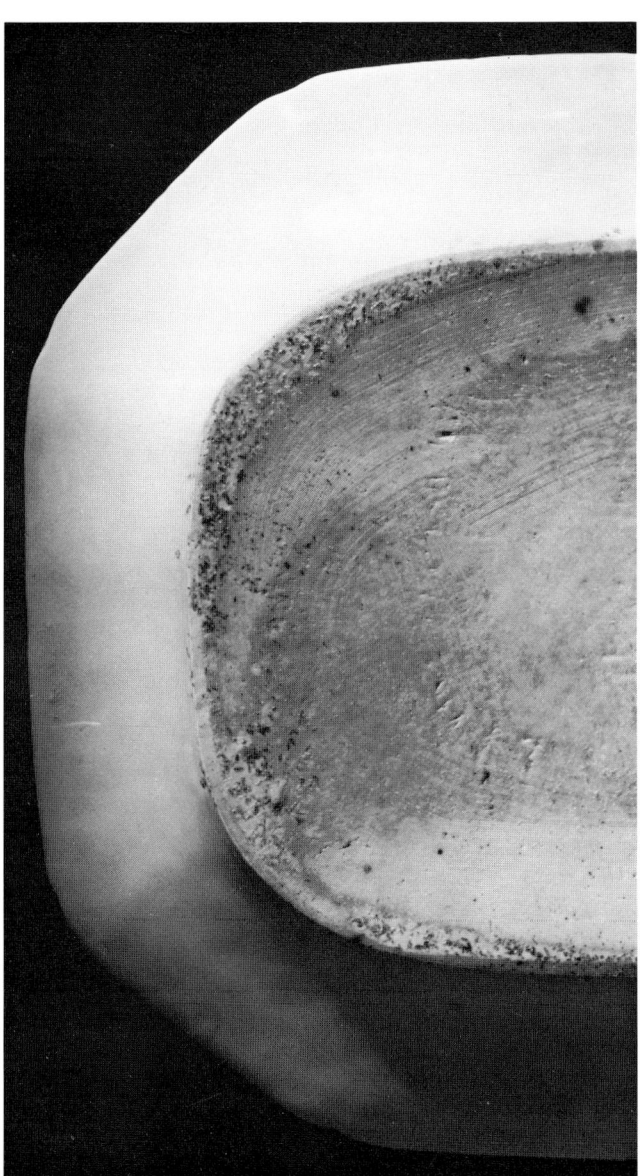

markets. A cistern over two feet high is shown in Plate 33. An ornate rococo-shaped covered tureen is featured in Plate 34, while Plate 35 depicts a leaf-shaped tureen.

Blue and white Nankeen vases occur in many shapes and in differing sizes. A rare example of about 1760 is seen in Plate 36. A large but later example is shown in Plate 37 and the standard garniture shape is featured in Plate 38. This later example is of the 1780s, and the 'chicken-skin' effect much used in the 1780s and 1790s is seen in the ground between the panels, the description 'chicken-skin' is self explanatory. These vases were made in sets, or garnitures, of five or seven but complete sets are rarely found today.

A further class of underglaze blue was decorated in powder-blue; the blue pigment was sprayed on to the ware, resulting in a mottled or speckled effect. The bowl shown in Plate 39 was decorated in this manner and then, after glazing and firing, the overglaze gilt design was added. In other cases panels were left clear of the powder-blue ground, the resisting panels being subsequently decorated in various styles. This type of panelled powder-blue was much copied by the English porcelain manufacturers of the 1760–80 period.

In dinner-services the octagonal shape first mentioned in the 1755 order (p. 127) continued to be the standard plate form up to about 1785. Formerly the plates were mainly circular (some early six-sided plates occur) with a wide, flat, condiment rim. Typical plates of the 1750–60 period are shown in Plate 40. The subsequent octagonal form is shown in Plate 41. Hundreds of different patterns were painted, mainly in scenic designs, and as a general rule they have the appearance of being rather hastily painted, having been mass-produced in quantity.

The octagonal tureens were at first of equal diameter, in other words a square octagon. These

46 A selection of Chinese blue and white salts originally included in large dinner sets. The two-piece example, top right, is a rare form; the footed example, lower right, is an attractive design of *c.* 1740–50 modelled on a silver shape.

Godden of Worthing Ltd

The blue and white porcelains

are rather rare and soon gave way to an oblong octagonal shape, as shown in Plate 42. This shape, with variations in the knob and handle form, was standard from about 1760 to circa 1785. The smaller sauce-tureens follow the shape of the larger soup-tureen. Other tureen shapes are shown in Plates 7, 34, 35, 83, 85, 86, 87, 115 and 132. These basic forms also appear with underglaze blue patterns.

The dinner-services of octagonal form contained sets of dishes, or platters, in graduated sizes. A detail photograph of a characteristic Chinese meat-dish base is shown as Plate 43. The base is flat, without a foot-rim (the similar but deeper tureen-stand often has a foot rim). This base is unglazed and sharp fragments of a flint-like substance are often to be seen sticking to some parts, like a sprinkling of desiccated coconut. These fragments were used as a bedding in the saggar or kiln and are to be found on various pieces of eighteenth-century Chinese porcelain, mainly the larger pieces.

While discussing these dinner-service dishes I shall briefly switch to a subject discussed at length in Chapter 11: the interplay and copying between the Chinese and English porcelain manufacturers. Plate 44 shows a typical Chinese Nankin dish, while a blue-*printed* English porcelain example made at the Caughley factory in about 1780 is shown in Plate 45. It is a matter of wonder that a hand-painted Chinese dish shipped across the world should undersell in England a mass-produced printed example made within two hundred miles of London, yet this was the case.

The Nankin dinner services of the 1760–85 period very often included salt troughs (but not other condiments); some typical examples are shown in Plate 46. The two forms shown on the right are very rare shapes.

From about 1785 both tureen forms and dishes were often oval, although the old octagonal shapes were occasionally favoured. The representative

47 A fine hot-water dish with hollow interior decorated with a basic Fitzhugh design in underglaze blue with the owner's crest added. 15½ inches long, c. 1790.   *Godden of Worthing Ltd*

pieces shown in Plate 32, with the rather prominent central willow tree, link well with a service which formed part of the cargo of the French vessel *La Constitution* which was captured by HMS *Leopard* in 1794. The French cargo was sold in London in July 1794 and the catalogue includes: 'A fine oval Nankin table service of the fine willow landscape, and dagger border, containing 18 long dishes in 6 sizes, 72 table plates, 24 soup plates, 24 dessert plates, 2 large tureens and dishes [stands], 2 small ditto, 4 sauce boats, 4 stands, 2 large salad vessels and 6 pudding dishes.' This lot sold for 32 guineas and, as stated, this 1794 reference matches very well the dinner wares shown in Plate 32.

The dinner-plate shapes return to the circular, but they tend to be thinner in the potting, and the condiment flange is dished or concave. The base again often lacks the normal European type of projecting foot-rim. This standard Chinese plate foot has been seen in Plate 18.

The later dinner-services of the 1780s and 1790s sometimes had hot-water plates. These are deep and very heavy, being double-walled and hollow. These hollow plates were filled with hot water, so helping to keep the plate hot. Covered oval dishes were made in this style; also similar meat platters, but these are rare. A crested hot-water dish can be seen in Plate 47. The basic blue design is known as Fitzhugh. It was very popular, especially in North America, and the pattern can be found in several different colours, but underglaze blue is the most usual. The traditional name for this design may be associated with Thomas Fitzhugh who was President of the Select Committee of Supra-cargoes at Canton in the 1780s, but he had a son of the same name and there was also a Supra-cargo named William Fitzhugh, so between them the Fitzhughs must have been responsible for the shipment of a vast quantity of Chinese porcelain to England. Other wares decorated with the Fitzhugh design are shown in Plate 213.

After about 1800 very few Chinese blue and white dinner-services were sent to England. British potters had largely captured the home market and had built up their own export trade to the Continent and to North America. The clean-looking, often sparsely decorated English creamwares were novel and enjoyed the same reception that Chinese porcelains had enjoyed a hundred years or so previously, although the Chinese influence long retained its hold on certain types of English wares – to the present day in the case of the famous Willow pattern.

There are very few special Oriental dessert porcelains, while the Continental and English porcelain manufacturers made many fine and elaborate

The blue and white porcelains

48 Two Chinese blue and white oval centre-dishes of the type found in dessert-services of the 1780–1800 period. The basic shape occurs in Caughley porcelain and also in French hard-paste porcelain. 12¾ inches long, 3½ inches high, c. 1790.
Godden of Worthing Ltd

49 A teapot and covered sugar-bowl painted in underglaze blue with one of the many 'Willow pattern'-type designs. The gilding was added in England (see p. 148). Teapot 6¼ inches high, c. 1785.
Godden of Worthing Ltd

50 Representative parts of a blue and white 'Nankin'-type Chinese teaset, embellished with English gilding (see p. 148). Teapot 5 inches high, c. 1790–95.
Godden of Worthing Ltd

The blue and white porcelains

51 An unusual Chinese barrel-shaped teapot with fancy handle and spout painted with formal floral designs in underglaze blue. 5½ inches high, c. 1780.   *Godden of Worthing Ltd*

52 A ribbed Chinese barrel-shaped teapot with a European-style intertwined-ribbon handle. 5 inches high, c. 1790.
Godden of Worthing Ltd

53 A very rare oval Chinese blue and white teapot almost certainly modelled on a European silver design. The slight gilding was added in England. 5½ inches long, c. 1795–1800.
Godden of Worthing Ltd

54 A rare variation on a standard Chinese teapot shape of the 1775–90 period with moulded handle and spout form, found also on English Caughley wares (see also Plate 55). 5 inches high.
Godden of Worthing Ltd

55 Representative pieces from a Chinese blue and white teaset, with characteristic moulded handle-forms to the teapot, jug and coffee cup. This handle-form also occurs on Caughley porcelains of the same period (see p. 359). Slight gilt enrichments added in England. Teapot $5\frac{3}{4}$ inches high, c. 1780–85.

Godden of Worthing Ltd

sets, with a variety of shaped dishes and centre-pieces for fruit. Until about 1780 the Chinese tended to neglect this type of table-set. After about 1780 some of the dinner-services – mostly the enamelled ones – incorporated European-style dessert ware, ice-pails, shaped dishes, fruit-baskets, etc. These are very rarely found in the Nankin blue and white style. Plate 48 shows a rare example: a deep oval dessert centre-dish. The basic shape is a standard one employed by the English Caughley factory (see my book *Caughley and Worcester Porcelains 1775–1800*, London, 1969) and it also occurs in French porcelain.

Teawares were often sold, as we know, not in usable sets but in large lots of teapots, bowls and cups and saucers, and the European 'chinamen' had to make up their own sets. This practice had largely ceased by the 1750s and tea-sets began to be imported as complete sets of forty-three pieces, as listed on p. 131. In general the blue and white tea-sets of the 1740–70 period are rare and are outnumbered by the enamelled examples discussed in subsequent chapters, but from the 1770s to about 1795 they again became exceedingly popular, only to go out of favour in the nineteenth century.

The tea-sets of the 1770s and 1780s were in the main painted in underglaze blue with landscape subjects which are often loosely called 'Willow'. Representative parts of such services are featured in Plates 31, 49, and 50, with rarer teapot forms shown in Plates 51–54. Turning to a more common shape of the 1770s, as illustrated in Plate 55, it is interesting to see the same relief-moulded spout and handle appearing on English examples made at the Caughley factory during the 1775–85 period. Not only were the Chinese shapes and patterns copied in Europe but the gilding on these post-1775 Chinese blue and white pots was usually added in England. The gilding on the Chinese porcelains shown in Plates 49–50 and 53–58 is in every case

The blue and white porcelains

56 A Chinese blue and white covered creamer of the 1790 period, embellished with gilding added in England. 5 inches high.
Godden of Worthing Ltd

English and contemporary with the date of importation.

This English embellishment of Chinese blue and white was standard practice and while some authorities have suggested that it was carried out in London at Thomas Baxter's London decorating studio[1] this is by no means the whole story. It appears likely that several English factories and London decorators and dealers added gilding to enhance the plain blue and white Nankin sets. Even William Duesbury of the Derby porcelain factory was interested in Chinese blue-painted tea-sets, for we have details of a letter written to him on 26 September 1789 from Robert Fogg, the well known chinaman of the period:

Sir
You receive with these as follows some patterns of Nankeen china tea-sets. The prices of the tea-sets are as follows, each cup is numbered at bottom.

The quantity is as your sets with addition of tea-jarr and spoon-boat.
No. 1. £6 10s 0d
 2. £6
 3. £5 10s 0d
 4. £5
 5. £4
 6. £3 13s 6d
 7. and 8. £3 3s 0d
The price I charge you is a wholesale price.

We can thus see that the wholesale cost for Nankin tea-sets was within the £3 3s to £6 10s range, to which we should perhaps add a third for the retailer's profit. Robert Fogg had correctly observed that the Derby tea-sets did not normally include the covered tea-caddy and the spoon-tray, both of which were still standard to the Chinese sets. While we do not know if these samples were

[1] There is as yet no record of the Baxter decorating studio in London before 1797, and most English gilding on Chinese porcelain was carried out before this date.

Oriental export market porcelain

57 A Chinese blue and white teapot and cover with gilt edges. The border motifs were added in England. 5¼ inches high, *c.* 1790. *Godden of Worthing Ltd*

58 A Chinese blue and white plate with gilt inner border added in England. See Plate 59 for reverse with gilder's number, *c.* 1790. *Godden of Worthing Ltd*

Colour Plate 8 A finely painted and well-potted Chinese plate from a dinner-service of the 1800 period, with a characteristic slightly dished concave condiment flange. *Godden of Worthing Ltd*

59 Detail of reverse of plate shown in Plate 58, showing the English gilder's personal tally mark near the foot-rim.

60 An oval Chinese porcelain dish with pierced border. The underglaze blue floral painting is a copy of a French design, and the dish bears a copy of the French mark—the hunting horn of the Chantilly factory. 11½ × 9 inches, *c.* 1790–95. *Godden of Worthing Ltd*

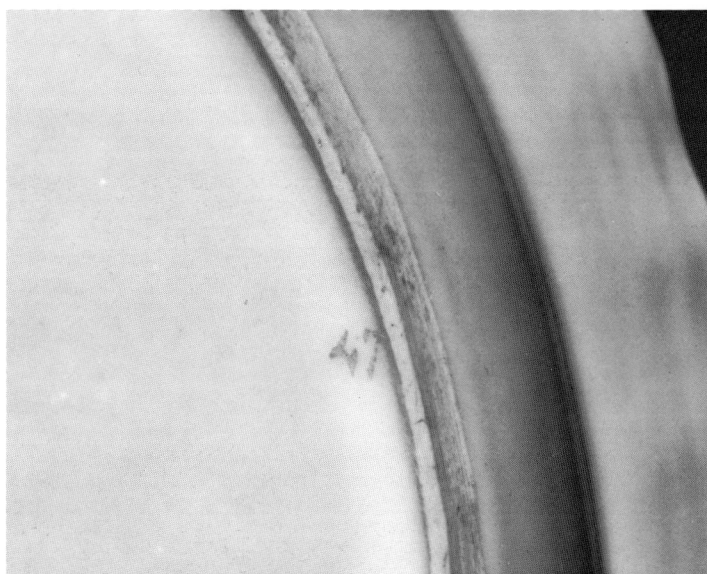

61 Two relief-moulded salad-bowls painted in underglaze blue. Right, a crescent-marked example from the Worcester factory and, left, a Chinese hard-paste copy, complete with a faked mark. Diameter 9¾ inches, c. 1770–80. *Godden of Worthing Ltd*

The blue and white porcelains

62 A Chinese hard-paste porcelain copy of a Worcester blue and white pierced cress dish and stand. Diameter of stand $8\frac{3}{4}$ inches, c. 1775–80. *Godden of Worthing Ltd*

63 A Chinese hard-paste porcelain creamer decorated in underglaze blue. This basic shape was produced at several English factories under the name 'Chelsea ewer'. $3\frac{1}{2}$ inches high, c. 1790. *Godden of Worthing Ltd*

already gilt, or if Duesbury wanted to gild them himself before re-sale, the letter obviously is in answer to an earlier request for samples and prices of the popular Nankin tea-sets.

There is further evidence, in the form of a letter to Duesbury from his London manager, Lygo, that the Derby factory was interested in blue-painted Nankin teawares. The letter dated 24 December 1792 reads: '...In this box have sent 12 Nankin tea-cups and saucers and a bason with the bill and receipt...I shall see some new Nankin teasets in a few days then will purchase the other four sets...' It should be borne in mind that Derby was one of the few late-eighteenth-century English porcelain factories not to have produced blue and white wares on a large scale and Duesbury probably found it convenient to purchase ready-made Nankin tea-sets, to which he probably added gilt borders and other embellishments. As the Chinese sets were purchased in London we can assume also that Duesbury's London retail shop also stocked such wares.

The records of the Chamberlain factory at Worcester show that on at least one occasion this important concern was asked to gild Chinese sets in the current fashion; the firm quoted gold edging at five pence per piece. Rather surprisingly we also find records of the Chamberlain management at Worcester selling English gilt Chinese wares early in the nineteenth century:

1 complete long set real Nankeen,
English gilt, £5 5s 0d   [29 September 1801]
Gilding part of a set Nankeen, £1 6s 0d   [31 July 1802]

Unfortunately we do not have records for the other possible gilding concerns, except for some accounts of the 1790s for goods supplied by a London firm of chinamen to a retailer at Bath. The firm is the well known one of Turner, Abbott & Newbury of 82, Fleet Street, a concern which, under differing

64 A Chinese hard-paste porcelain chocolate cup and stand decorated in underglaze blue. The basic shape occurs also in English Caughley and Worcester porcelains. Cup $3\frac{1}{4}$ inches high, c. 1785–90. *Godden of Worthing Ltd*

The blue and white porcelains

65 A Chinese blue and white oval platter, the feather border being copied from a standard English creamware motif. 17 × 13 inches, c. 1790–1800.   *Godden of Worthing Ltd*

66 A Chinese blue and white chocolate cup and stand modelled after a European design. Cup 3¾ inches high, *c.* 1780–90.
Godden of Worthing Ltd

partnerships,[1] sold a vast amount of Staffordshire earthenware and porcelain, glass-ware and Chinese porcelain. Like other large London chinamen this partnership engaged in embellishing the standard ceramics with their customer's crest, initials or other personal device, and the bill-heads included the following:

Their manufacture [the Staffordshire wares mainly produced by Turner] is sold at their warehouse No. 82, Fleet Street, together with all sorts of china and glass [those wares not made by Turner, including the imported Chinese wares], on the lowest terms for ready money only; where they have also a manufactory for enamelling and gilding their ware with coats of arms, crests, cyphers, borders or any other device.

Amongst the invoiced wares, Chinese dinner-services etc, we find listed, in November 1792:

1 Plain landscape Nan[kin] tea set, 8 coffee cups. Gilt chain and leaf [these wholesalers suggested to the newly established Bath retailer the selling price of £6 6s 0d]	£4 14s 6d
1 Plain landscape tea set, gilt edge, only six coffee-cups [recommended selling price £5 5s 0d]	£4 4s 0d
1 Fluted tea set small fire[d] gilt chain border, with 12 coffee-cups [Recommended retail price £7 7s 0d]	£5 15s 10
12 Nan[kin] L[arge] cups [?] and saucers, gilt edge and ring	£1 10s 0d
Gilding do.	12s 0d

This firm of London chinamen purchased Chinese goods at the 'India House', the English East India Company auction sales, together with the normal related goods such as sets of mother-of-pearl 'fish and counters'. Bevis Hillier in his *Master Potters of the Industrial Revolution: The Turners of Lane End* (London, 1965) informed us that Messrs Turner & Abbott had bound to them various crew members of East Indiamen. For example, Charles Stone, Second Officer of the East Indiaman *Princess Royal*, was bound to these Fleet Street chinamen in the sum of £227 9s 0d and we can assume that this officer purchased in China Private Trade wares for the London partnership.

It is likely that other firms of London china dealers also gilded Nankin teawares but we do not have proof of the firms concerned in this trade. Future research may increase our meagre knowledge. Signed examples apparently exist, for a leading London dealer has told me that he once had, and sold to an American, a Nankin tea-set bearing the name and address of the English gilder inside the teapot cover. I would be pleased to hear of the whereabouts of this set or of other signed pieces.

Many examples are signed, or rather marked, in another way, which proclaims the European source of the gilding if this is not already apparent to the collector. I refer to the gilder's personal tally-mark, a letter or more usually a number, added in gold inside (or near) the foot-rim or inside the cover. The foot of the Chinese plate shown in Plate 58 is detailed in Plate 59, revealing the English gilder's number 47. This rather high number points to the extent of the gilding business, and one can picture large teams of British gilders embellishing these blue and white Chinese porcelains. I have also seen a Chinese blue and white teapot with English gilt embellishments bearing the gilder's initials 'I.H.'.

There is a further class of blue and white porcelain that is connected with the British porcelain trade. I refer to the almost exact copies of European shapes and patterns. It is obvious that European samples were sent out to China to be

---

[1] In 1782 Messrs Turner & Abbott moved from Old Fish Street to 81, Fleet Street. In the following year they took over Number 82. J. Benjamin Newbury joined Turner & Abbott in the late 1780s, certainly before 1793.

67 Right, a Chinese blue and white covered custard cup with, left, a blue-printed example from the English Caughley factory. 3 inches high, c. 1775–85. *Godden of Worthing Ltd*

Colour Plate 9 A large Chinese vase in the 'Canton' or 'Rose Medallion' style of decoration. 25¼ inches high, c. 1830–40. *Godden of Worthing Ltd.*

copied, especially as the Chinese copies sometimes include a representation of the European mark. Here the story has turned full circle, first English porcelain manufacturers copied Chinese styles but from about 1770 onwards the Chinese themselves copied English wares. We can establish the basic point by reference to the oval open-work bordered dish shown in Plate 60. This is painted in underglaze blue with a simple French floral design, and the Chinese dish bears a copy of the hunting horn mark employed by the French Chantilly factory. The Chinese therefore clearly set out to copy a French original.

The two relief-moulded salad dishes shown in Plate 61 illustrate the point well. The specimen on the right is a crescent-marked Worcester example; the dish on the left is a straightforward Chinese hardpaste copy, marks and all. The pierced cress-dish and stand shown in Plate 62 is another direct copy of a Worcester original. The Chinese creamer and chocolate cup shown in Plates 63–64 are also copies. The English originals of these and other shapes are to be seen depicted in my book *Caughley and Worcester Porcelains 1775–1800*. Other examples could be cited but the point has been made that Chinese Potters directly copied European porcelains in the 1770s and 1780s. In the 1790s English creamwares were also being copied, as may be seen

68 A heavily potted and broadly painted Chinese blue and white 'guglet' or water-bottle, typical of the more utilitarian export market wares. 9 inches high, c. 1770.
Godden of Worthing Ltd

from the oval platter (Plate 65) with a Chinese version of the standard English creamware feather border.

European china-dealers placed orders for Chinese porcelain copies of wares that were readily available from the Worcester or Caughley factories purely for economic reasons. They did not find the Chinese copies more saleable, otherwise there would have been no point in adding an English mark. We have firm evidence that the Chinese imports undersold the Worcester and Caughley English wares, for in August 1790 J. Lygo, the London agent to the Derby factory, wrote to William Duesbury at Derby: '...I have been to the Salopian [Caughley] warehouse...Chamber pots they have none, they have not made any for some time and the reason is foreign Nankeen ones are so much cheaper...' We can reasonably expect that the Worcester ones were as expensive as the Caughley examples, if not more so, therefore the Chinese Nankin pots undersold the two major English producers of underglaze blue decorated porcelain.

In the 1790s, the Turner, Abbott & Newbury accounts for wares supplied to the Bath retailer, Richard Egan, included much blue and white Nankin porcelain: six blue and white dinner-services, listed as purchased at the India House auctions, sauceboats and stands, salts and salad-bowls as well as the standard items. The plates were of the octagonal and of the circular shape. Sets of dishes were still being sold in their own right in threes or fives. We find also listed gallon and two-quart blue and white bowls priced at 12s, 3s and 1s and 9d each to sell retail at 18s, 4s 6d and 2s 6d respectively, also Nankin chocolate cups and saucers at 2s 10d, probably after a European pattern such as Plates 64 and 66, and custard cups and covers at 1s each. A typical example of a custard cup is shown in Plate 67, but several different basic

The blue and white porcelains

69 A blue and white Chinese punch-bowl with overglaze enamelled motto and crest motif added in Canton to fill a special export order. Diameter 9 inches, c. 1790–1800.
Godden of Worthing Ltd

70 A Chinese porcelain teapot decorated only with the underglaze blue parts of the decoration, which was to be completed in Canton with overglaze enamel decoration, c. 1770.
British Museum

shapes are to be found.

The November 1792 accounts also include:

1 set Nankin barrel [shaped] mugs	8s
2 blue basons Nankeen scalloped	4s
4 Nankeen B & B [bread and butter] plates	£1 0s
1 Nankeen teapot	4s
12 Nankeen fluted breakfast [cups] and saucers	£1 14s
12 Nankeen plain [shape] breakfasts and saucers	£1 10s

as well as the teasets mentioned on p. 153 in connection with the added English gilding.

Apart from these well potted and neatly decorated Nankin-type porcelains, there is a class of heavily potted useful wares rather broadly painted in a slap-dash manner. The water bottle or 'guglet' shown in Plate 68 is typical of this class – made to a price for daily use.

Most Chinese export market porcelains were of standard types, perhaps combining European ideas with the Oriental style; hence we find covered 'cider jugs' with the overlapping ribbon-handle found on English creamwares, with the kylin knob retaining the Oriental influence. Plate 69 shows a Nankin scenic-pattern bowl on to which the enamellers at Canton have painted the arms of a European customer. Some underglaze blue decoration was confined to simple border designs, the rest of the piece being left to be embellished with overglaze enamels by the Canton enamellers. The teapot shown in Plate 70 illustrates this type to perfection.

In the nineteenth century when the English tax on imported wares had become prohibitive and when British wares had begun to satisfy the home market there was a marked decrease in imports of Chinese porcelains into Britain. The East India Company no longer included it in their cargo. However, other countries, notably the United States of America, were still actively engaged in

71 A page from Liberty & Co.'s 1898 catalogue showing their newly imported Chinese blue and white porcelains.

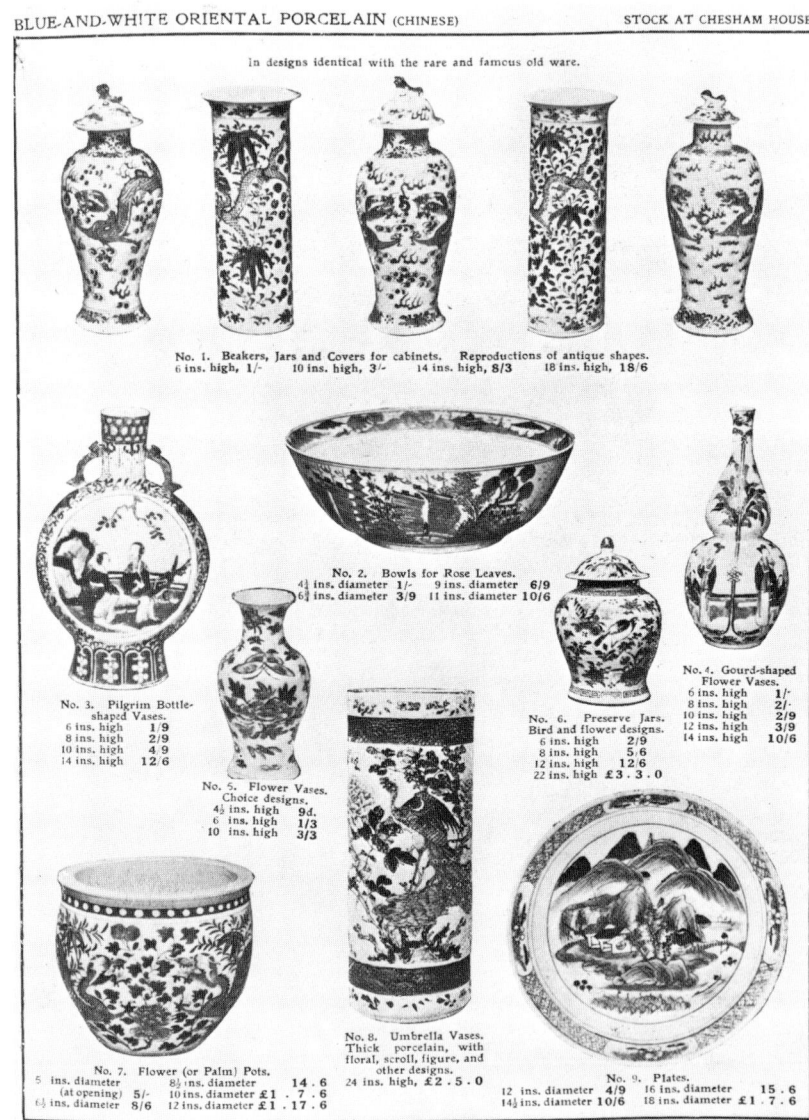

The blue and white porcelains

72 A page from a Liberty & Co. catalogue of the 1910 period showing typical new Chinese blue and white porcelains.

— Oriental Blue and White Porcelain (Modern). —

ghly finished and important Decorative Art Objects, suitable for placing in Halls, Galleries, Conservatories, Staircase Recesses, Drawing Rooms, Libraries, Studios, Smoking Rooms, &c., on large Cabinets, Brackets, or beneath Console Tables, &c., &c.

No. 1.

No. 3.
Chinese Blue and White Umbrella Spills.
Floral, scroll, figure, and other designs. 24 inches high.
Prices—27/6 and 31/- each.
Japanese ditto.
Prices— 7/6, 10/6, 12/6, and 15/6 each.

No. 4.
Chinese Blue and White Jars and Covers.
Decorated with figure and floral designs.
6½ inches high... ... 5/6 each
8 ,, ,, ... 7/6 ,,
11 ,, ,, ... 25/- ,,
12 ,, ,, ... 35/- ,,

No. 5.
Chinese Blue and White Toilet Jars and Covers.
In varied designs.
Prices—3d., 4½d., 9d., 1/3 and 2/3 each.

No. 2.
Nos. 1 and 2.
Nankin Blue and White Gold Fish Cisterns.
Can be utilized for holding tropical plants, ferns, or orange trees. Bold and rich scroll decoration.

5 inches high by 6 inches diameter, price 7/6 each.
8 ,, ,, 9 ,, ,, 10/6 ,,
9 ,, ,, 10 ,, ,, 14/6 ,,
10 ,, ,, 12 ,, ,, 25/- ,,
12 ,, ,, 14 ,, ,, 37/6 ,,
15 ,, ,, 16 ,, ,, 57/6 ,,
17 ,, ,, 18 ,, ,, 84/- ,,
18 ,, ,, 20 ,, ,, 126/- ,,

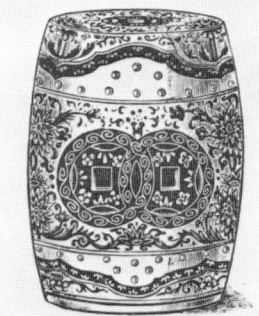

No. 6.
Nankin Blue and White Garden or Verandah Seats.
Sexagon or round. About 18 inches high.
Price 42/- each.

No. 7.
Nankin Blue and White Jars and Covers and Beaker Vases.
Reproductions of Antique Chinese shapes.
In landscape, scroll and other designs.

6 inches high, price 1/- each.	13 inches high, price 7/6 each.
8 ,, ,, 1/6 ,,	14 ,, ,, 10/6 ,,
10 ,, ,, 3/- ,,	18 ,, ,, 15/6 ,,
12 ,, ,, 4/6 ,,	24 ,, ,, 25/- ,,

LIBERTY & Co. LTD.] [LONDON & PARIS.

73 A Chinese blue and white salad bowl of the type imported into North America in the early years of the nineteenth century and there called 'Canton'. Diameter 9½ inches, c. 1820.
The Art Exchange, New York

the trade as they had few home products and certainly none to compete with the Chinese potters.

The salad bowl shown in Plate 73 is typical of the class of early-nineteenth-century Chinese porcelain imported into North America, although it was by no means restricted to that market. In America these late Nankin porcelains are usually called 'Canton' (a description given to a totally different class by British collectors, see p. 296). According to an American author 'Canton shows a simple band of blue wash over which broad criss-crosses are painted in a heavier blue…Canton was made between 1790 and 1840…Canton and Nankeen rank as Americana. It was these wares that filled the deepest holds of the clipper ships and served in the dining rooms of the old New England Inn' (*Chinese Blue and White* by Ann Frank, English edition London, 1970). Certainly in comparison with eighteenth-century porcelains these nineteenth-century wares are heavy and rather crude, lacking in charm and design, but they filled a need – a robust porcelain for the New World.

Eighteenth-century blue and white porcelains were mainly intended for the vast British middle-class market. In Britain these unpretentious wares were rightly appreciated and the British manufacturers sought to emulate these saleable porcelains on a scale unrivalled by the Continental potters. Today collectors tend to enthuse over the British copies, neglecting as they do so, the original.

Not all Chinese blue and white porcelain is of the period covered in this book. Great quantities were shipped from China right through the nineteenth century and indeed into the present century and such later wares, very often copies of earlier shapes and patterns, abound in Europe and America. To illustrate this fact I have singled out just two pages from Liberty & Co.'s catalogues of 1898 and 1910 (Plates 71–72).

5 The enamelled wares

In this chapter we consider the wares decorated with various basic types of enamelled decoration, that is, coloured patterns applied over the glaze. However, special designs – porcelains decorated with armorial bearings or with patterns showing European-style figures – are featured in Chapters 6 and 7.

The early-eighteenth-century reports from Father d'Entrecolles in Ching-tê Chên seem to have been wide of the mark when, in September 1712, he noted: 'In Europe people hardly see anything else but a vivid blue on a white ground, though I believe our merchants have also imported some of the other kinds...' There is abundant proof that coloured or enamelled Chinese porcelains were shipped into Europe in the previous century. Indeed, this Jesuit Father gives details of some of the colours used by Chinese potters.

Orders given to the Supra-cargoes of the four vessels destined for the Chinese port of Amoy in 1681 request particularly 'cups of all kinds – sizes and colours'. In 1682 we find noted in reference to an earlier voyage of the *London*: 'There are a sort of china sawcere and thea dishes bought home by the *London* which cost at Batavia but $2\frac{1}{2}d$ each, procure as many of them as you can, they being painted with redd, green and yellow.'

Orders given for the china-ware cargo of the *Wentworth* bound for Canton in 1700 include: '20 Tons of the very finest and most fancifull china ware that is to be had, with variety of fine large pieces and the neatest colours.'

In January 1701 (1702 by our modern calendar) the orders to the Supra-cargoes of the *Fleet* bound for Canton contain the following surprising statement: '...the painted china ware heretofore much sett by, yet now by reason of the great quantityes imported, sold extreamly cheap...' Nevertheless the 1712 orders given to the Supra-cargoes of the *Loyal Bliss* detail painted patterns:

Oriental export market porcelain

74 An early-eighteenth-century Chinese teapot-stand decorated in underglaze blue with added overglaze red and green enamels. Perhaps relating to the 1712 orders for 'deep square dishes...for the teapots to stand on and to be painted and coloured as the teapots...2000 in colours'. 5¼ inches across 1 inch deep, c. 1710–1702. *Godden of Worthing Ltd*

76 An important large Chinese porcelain dish painted in the *famille verte* palette and with a typical central motif. Diameter 15 inches, c. 1720–30. *Private collection*

75 A fine over-handled Chinese porcelain tea (or wine) pot decorated in pleasingly translucent *famille verte* colours (see Colour Plate 4). 6½ inches high, c. 1710. *Private collection*

The enamelled wares

77 A typical 'Chinese Imari'-style plate painted with a combination of underglaze blue and overglaze red and green enamels, with some gilding. Diameter 6½ inches, c. 1740.
Godden of Worthing Ltd

4,000 boats, three in a nest, the pattern to be the least but variety of paints and sprigs or running work instead of blue stripes in the border, with a pretty deal of scarlet, 2,000 coloured; 2,000 blue.

400 nests dishes, five in a nest, the pattern the least to be painted of variety of colours and paints.

4,000 deep square small dishes...for the teapots to stand on and to be painted and coloured as the teapots. 2,000 blue and white, 2,000 in colours.
[Perhaps these would have been similar to the example shown in Plate 74.]

20,000 handled chocolate cups in colours and gold. 10,000 with a border inside and gold edges and variety of patterns, 10,000 of ditto, lesser sort.

The available sale records also afford evidence of the importation into London of enamelled Oriental porcelain, some of which may have been of Japanese origin (see Chapter 10). For example, in December 1696 the Company sold china-ware from the *Sarah* and the *Dorothy*. This sale included:

    2 jars small in colours
    10 painted basons
    800 green and red painted cups
    7 large Bottles in colours

Many other later sale records could be quoted, but before 1700 we find listed not only crackle ware, '4 bottles as if cracked all over', but many flowered articles: '472 Brown cups with red flowers inside'; '78 Large Dishes set flowers'; '35 bowles large with set flowers'; '199 coloured painted plates'; '893 cups coloured and flowered'; or general descriptions such as '1,062 saucers finely painted'.

Chinese standard enamelled designs fall into two main categories, the floral patterns and the figure subjects. Although there is some overlap, since a few floral designs may include a figure or two and each different type can occur painted on the same basic shape, it is convenient for the purposes of this book to discuss them separately. I first consider the floral patterns.

My term 'floral pattern' is very general; it includes formal styles of landscape compositions as well as the many differing types of flower-painting, and designs based on nature. Many of the formal patterns come under the internationally accepted French terms *famille verte*, if green is the prominent colour, or *famille rose* if a particular red is the main colour. These European terms were introduced by the French authority, Jacquemart, in or before 1862.

We shall start our consideration of eighteenth- and nineteenth-century Chinese enamelled porcelain by referring to the Journal of the Supra-cargo of the *Macclesfield*. As explained on p. 34, the *Macclesfield* arrived at Whampoa in October 1699, and in December the Supra-cargo Robert Douglas and his two assistants were engaged in purchasing china-ware (and other goods) newly arrived at Canton. Unfortunately these porcelains are very briefly described with no mention of the pattern, but teawares were often listed as being painted in red and green and two types are mentioned: '23 teapots with top handles, 27 teapots side handles'. The *famille verte* teapot shown in Plate 75 is a typical example of the 'top [or "over"] handle' pot of this period, but this form went out of favour in about 1710, as the position of the handle does not lend itself to the preparation of tea, or the subsequent cleansing of used tea leaves. The basic shape was derived from Chinese winepots and as a winepot it would not have presented the difficulties encountered when used for tea. The side-handled pot listed in the 1699 purchases was far more useful. This basic form cannot be bettered, allowing as it does countless minor variations in detail and decoration.

From the records of the auctioned lots of imported Oriental porcelains it appears that some pieces

The enamelled wares

78 A superb quality Chinese coffee cup and saucer painted in the *famille rose* palette. Diameter of saucer 4½ inches, c. 1740–50.
Godden of Worthing Ltd

79 A small Chinese teapot broadly painted in the *famille rose* style. 4½ inches high, *c.* 1740–50.   *Godden of Worthing Ltd*

The enamelled wares

80 A small Chinese teapot with applied leaves and flowers painted in the *famille rose* style. 4½ inches high, c. 1740–50.
Godden of Worthing Ltd

81 A typical 'Batavia-ware' Chinese teapot, the body of which is characteristically covered with a coffee-coloured glaze or 'slip'. 3½ inches high, without cover, c. 1750. *D. Cowell, Brighton*

were decorated with all-over colours or coloured glazes, rather than with various enamelled motifs. The contemporary records include lots such as:

12 Bowls green
 6 do. murre coloured
60 do. yellow
 9 do. olive coloured
   [Sale of cargo from the *Wentworth*, 27 November 1701.]
61 large green tea cups, 2 sorts
77 do. purple
90 do. yellow   [Sale, 27 May 1705.]

Unfortunately these sale-records are very brief and are in the main concerned with the form or use of the object, rather than with the added decoration. However, in some instances we find rather fuller descriptions:

740 Landskip teacups
740 saucers   [Sale, 23 March 1703.]

12 tea cups, with butterflies   [Sale, 6 April 1704.]

If these rare designs were in overglaze enamels rather than in underglaze blue, the predominate colour-scheme would have been, at this period, that which we now term *famille verte*.

The early *famille verte* colours have a beautiful liquid, semi-translucent appearance, rather similar to the Whieldon-type colours on Staffordshire earthenwares. These enamel or glaze colours are often thickly applied so that they lie well above the surface of the glaze and consequently are rather prone to flake away. Yet, when fired to perfection, these warm-looking, semi-translucent colours are delightful. The covered bowl shown in Colour Plate 4 shows the general style and tints to perfection. Alas, they were soon replaced by *famille rose* and other later styles. In general terms the *famille verte* style is restricted to the approximate period 1700–1730. Most falls within the K'ang Hsi period which ended in 1722. A fine, large, deep dish of a typical design is shown in Plate 76. Early and rather later armorial plates are illustrated in Plates 124–125.

Another early type of enamelled decoration found mainly on export market useful porcelains is sometimes called Chinese Imari because the basic style was taken from the Japanese Imari-type porcelains with underglaze blue designs, completed and enhanced with red and green enamels, often with some thin, watery-looking gilding. A simple but typical plate is shown in Plate 77, and a rare armorial example is illustrated in Plate 123. In general, these simple Imari-style designs on Chinese porcelain belong to the 1695–1730 period.

The *famille rose* porcelains are decorated with opaque or nearly opaque enamels in contrast to the earlier *famille verte* pieces with translucent colours, and in general the quality of painting is much finer on these later pieces. The *rose* colour is not scarlet or bright red – a colour used from the seventeeth

The enamelled wares

82 A very fine Chinese punch-bowl and under-dish in the *famille rose* manner decorated with the favourite overlapping lotus-leaf design. Diameter of bowl 15 inches, c. 1750–60.
The Art Exchange, New York

83 Representative pieces from a large Chinese dinner-service decorated in the *famille rose* style. Diameter of large dish 15 inches, *c.* 1750–60.
Christies, London

The enamelled wares

84 A fine and typical Chinese export market punch-bowl decorated with a version of the popular tobacco-leaf pattern. Diameter 17½ inches, c. 1770.   *The Art Exchange, New York*

century onwards – but rather a carmine or plum-colour. This is the predominate colour, but practically all other enamels were employed as the design demanded, an opaque white enamel being noteworthy. The rather squat mug illustrated in Colour Plate 5 shows the style to good effect, and the colours have also been seen in the Frontispiece.

David Howard, by his study of armorial porcelains, has dated the introduction of the *famille rose* colours to the 1720–22 period. This general type of enamel decoration remained in favour for at least fifty years, although other types of enamelling were also employed. The early essays in the *rose* tint were not entirely successful and the colour is variable in the early or mid-1720s owing to difficulties in firing the colour correctly.

The *famille rose* class of colours were referred to by Chinese writers as 'foreign colours'. It appears that they were introduced into the Orient by Europeans, perhaps when the Jesuits and others were endeavouring to teach various crafts, such as enamelling on copper, to the Chinese. The introduction of the characteristic *rose* or pinkish colour seems to have been shortly after Brother Gravereau went to China in 1719 to assist in the manufacture of enamel on copper. An interesting Paper, 'The Origins of *Famille Rose*' by Sir Harry Garner, is published in the *Transactions of the Oriental Ceramic Society* (1967–8).

Some of the delicate *famille rose*-type teawares of the 1730s or 1740s are delightfully enamelled and gilt. The almost eggshell-thin teabowls and saucers can hardly be surpassed. Look again at Colour Plate 1, and at the little teabowl shown in Colour Plate 6, at the cup and saucer (Plate 78), and at Colour Plate 15. It should be noted that the handled coffee cups in Plate 78 and Colour Plate 15 are much thicker in the potting than the thin teabowls. Some authorities have even suggested that the cups were not made at the same place as the saucers or bowls. The answer is obvious to a practical potter – the cup walls have to be thick to support the handle in the firing. Try to fix the handle to an unfired thin teabowl and the delicate bowl will be pulled out of shape before it meets the stresses of the kiln.

Not all Chinese enamelled porcelain reached this standard. Much was rather broadly painted; the little teapot of about 1740 shown in Plate 79 is typical of the general run of *famille rose* porcelains made for Europeans. The quality of the painting is coarse, although the overall effect is good, especially on this very small pot. The equally minute teapot shown in Plate 80 is of rather better quality, and the applied leaves and flowers occur on some attractive Oriental porcelains from early in the eighteenth century.

There is a class of porcelain variously known as Batavia ware or *café au lait*. The last name arises

176   **Oriental export market porcelain**

85 Representative pieces from a large Chinese dinner-service decorated with a popular tobacco-leaf design. Tureens 11 inches long, *c.* 1770.   *Christies, London*

The enamelled wares

86 A soup-tureen and pair of sauce-tureens decorated in the *famille rose* manner with a very popular pheasant design, several versions of which occur. Tureen 12½ inches long, *c.* 1770.
Earle D. Vandekar, London

87 Representative pieces from a large Chinese dinner-service painted with a standard formal floral and rock design. Tureens 11½ inches long, *c.* 1775–80. *Earle D. Vandekar, London*

88 A Chinese teapot enamelled with a typical formal floral design. This example bears the name and address of a Bristol china-mender on the base with the date 1779. 5¾ inches high, c. 1775–7.
Godden of Worthing Ltd

89 A Chinese slop-bowl from a tea-service painted in the typical style of the 1770–85 period. Diameter 5½ inches
Godden of Worthing Ltd

from the fact that the surface of the porcelain or most of it is covered with a thick overlay of coffee-coloured glaze. Sometimes this coloured glaze, or slip, is left undecorated; at other times it may be embellished with thin watery gilding, but more often there are reserve panels showing the underlying white porcelain body. These panels were embellished with rather slap-dash enamelled floral designs. The Dutch East India Company seems to have brought home quantities of these wares from their settlement and trading-post of Batavia, and the name 'Batavia ware' was used for this reason. No doubt it was a standard commodity there, being shipped to most of the South Sea islands or countries.

Much of this class found its way to Britain, although we cannot be sure if it was purchased with other export market porcelains at Canton, or if it was purchased from the Dutch at Batavia. A typical teapot is shown in Plate 81.

A typical bowl and underdish in the *famille rose* palette, with a wide border of overlapping lotus leaves, is shown in Plate 82. Teawares and other articles were embellished with similar lotus leaf designs in the mid-eighteenth century, and the above-average quality of these porcelains suggests that they were Private Trade goods. Porcelains bearing this popular form of decoration were captured from the Spanish galleon *Santissima Trinidad* with other *famille rose* porcelains in 1762, showing the wide distribution of the type (see 'The Prize of Captain Hyde Parker' by David Howard in *The National Trust Year Book 1975–6*).

In general, floral designs before about 1760 are boldly painted (Plate 83), and into this class we can place the popular 'tobacco-leaf' designs, although in some cases the colours are not characteristic of the true *famille rose* porcelains. The fine punch-bowl shown in Plate 84 is a convenient example linking both styles, while the dinner-service shown

The enamelled wares

90 A Chinese tea-bowl and saucer painted with a typical floral pattern. These popular designs were much copied by English manufacturers, including those at Lowestoft, New Hall and Worcester. Diameter of saucer 5½ inches, c. 1775–85.
Godden of Worthing Ltd

91 A Chinese saucer-shaped bread and butter plate from a typical teaset of the mid-1770s. Such wares were inexpensive and extremely popular in the British Isles. Diameter 8 inches.
Godden of Worthing Ltd

93 A small Chinese punch-bowl decorated in a typical manner with enamelled vases of flowers etc, within underglaze blue borders. Diameter 7¾ inches. *Godden of Worthing Ltd*

92 A Chinese punch-bowl enamelled with formal sprays of European flowers within underglaze blue bordered panels. The base inscribed 'William Shaw. No 166 Aldersgate Street. 1777'. Diameter 9 inches, 1777. *Godden of Worthing Ltd*

94 An attractive and well painted Chinese punch-bowl decorated with blue enamels and gilt. Such overglaze blue decoration normally indicates a post-1790 date. Diameter 11½ inches, c. 1790–95. *Godden of Worthing Ltd*

The enamelled wares

95 A rare form of double-handled Chinese broth-bowl and stand, and an egg-cup, from a breakfast or supper set, decorated in overglaze blue and gold. Egg-cup 2¾ inches high, *c.* 1795–1800.
Godden of Worthing Ltd

96 An 'over-handle' Chinese tea or wine pot, decorated with a typical figure design in *famille verte* enamels (see Colour Plate 4). $6\frac{7}{8}$ inches high, c. 1710. *Sotheby & Co., London*

in Plate 85 shows the rich overall 'tobacco-leaf' design.

Among the popular *famille rose* dinner-service designs the pheasant pattern seems to have continued in production for a very long time. The examples shown in Plate 86 date from about 1770 and the same design represents a popular line made by the English Spode firm from about 1815 and continued by the succeeding Stoke partnerships throughout the nineteenth century. The representative pieces of a dinner-service featured in Plate 87 show one of many floral patterns of the 1760–80 period made-up of variations of rocks and flowers on a green washed foreground.

By at least the mid-1770s the enamelled flower-designs had become more European in conception. The general style, hard to explain but readily seen, is illustrated in Plates 88–93 and in Colour Plate 7 which features a particularly fine large teapot or punch-pot. The capacity of this pot is fully five and a half pints.

The standard size floral painted teapot shown in Plate 88 while not a work of art is nevertheless a most interesting documentary example. Its handle was repaired by Coombes in Bristol in 1779, and its base bears a fired-in inscription to this effect. Coombes was a china-mender who specialised in bonding together Oriental and other porcelains with a kind of heavily fluxed glaze which he fired to set at a low temperature as cement. His name and address marks are to be found on various types of Chinese porcelains, the dated pieces being particularly helpful in proving that they were in England then and must have been made at least a year before.

Many enamelled floral sprays were framed within underglaze blue panels. One particularly interesting inscribed and dated bowl of this general type is shown in Plate 92, but an inscription of this kind is the exception and denotes a Private Trade

The enamelled wares

97 A large, superb Chinese *famille verte* figure subject vase with inscription and date corresponding to the Western year 1724. 18 inches high, 1724. *Sotheby & Co., London*

importation. William Shaw of the inscription was a chinaman at 166, Aldergate Street, London in the period 1775–88, and subsequently at Red Lion Street.

These European-style floral designs were extremely popular, especially for teawares, from about 1775 to at least 1790. Hundreds of variations occur, and some are extremely well painted and most attractive. The style of painting is also found on several types of English porcelain of approximately the same period, notably on Worcester, Lowestoft and New Hall porcelains. Some English examples are discussed in Chapter 11. It is particularly difficult to know who was copying whom. It is generally thought that the English manufacturers were copying the popular Chinese imports, but a letter in the Dutch archives at The Hague reads in effect that the directors especially request that dragons and other animals should not be sent to Europe, but instead small flowers in the taste of Lowestoft ware.

From about 1790 the painting on some specimens becomes more detailed but rather restrained, with a blue *overglaze* enamel much in favour. Typical examples are seen in Plates 94–95 and again in Plates 118, 121, 122, 131, 132, 151, 152, 159, 206 and 209. After about 1820 the wares became much coarser, both in the thick, heavy body and in the thickly applied all-over designs, see Plates 109–111 and Colour Plates 9 and 10.

The mass of figure patterns (or 'Image' patterns, as they were originally called) enamelled on Chinese export market porcelain demonstrate the same basic chronological progression of styles as do the floral designs.

At the end of the seventeenth century there was the *famille verte* type of translucent enamels. A typical early 'over-handle' teapot is shown in Plate 96. As I have explained on p. 168 this type of pot had been superseded by the normal side-handled teapot by about 1710. Certainly figure-painted

98 A superbly painted Chinese porcelain vase decorated in the *famille rose* palette, bearing an inscription relating to the mid-autumn festival of 1730. 8½ inches high. *Sotheby & Co., London*

99 An attractive Chinese vase (one of a pair) painted with typical figure and garden design in the *famille rose* palette 8 inches high, c. 1750–60. *Godden of Worthing Ltd*

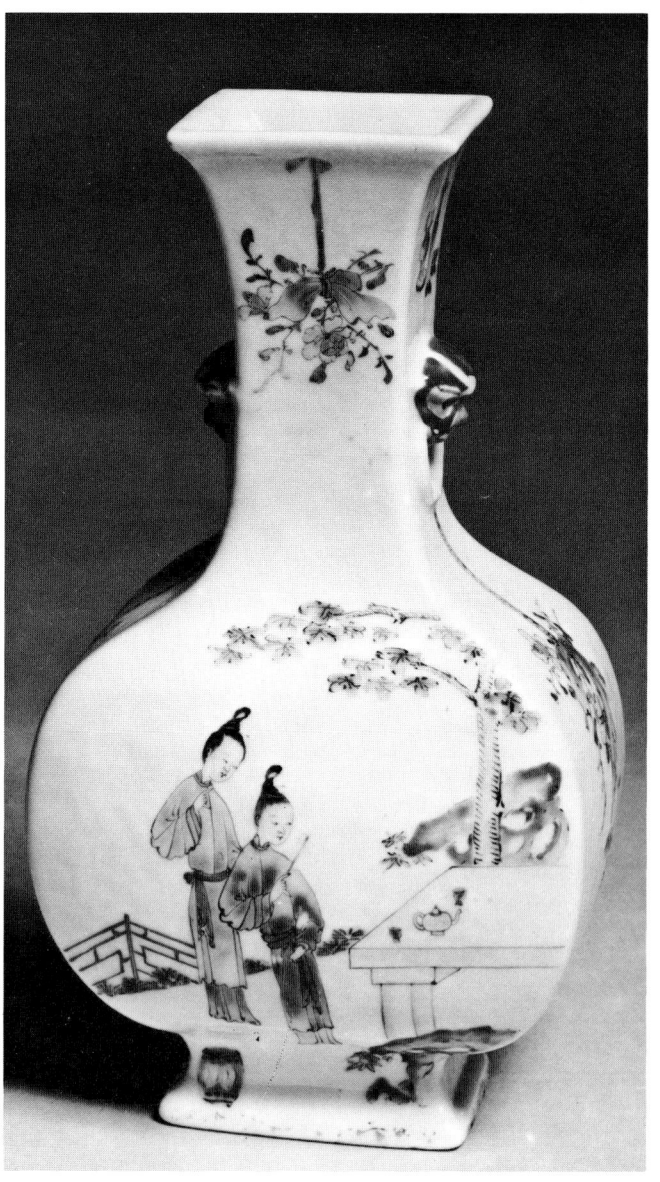

Oriental export market porcelain

100 An oil-painting by Benjamin Wilson (1721–88) depicting a hostess posed behind her prized Chinese porcelain teawares, typical of the late 1760s and 1770s. *Maple & Co., London*

porcelains were coming into England before 1700. The cargo of the *Trumball*, sold in July 1699, included '230 cups and saucers with images'. Three years later the *Dorrill*'s cargo included '9 Jarrs with images' valued at 2s each.

The superb vase shown in Plate 97 is important as it bears an inscription and date corresponding to the Western year 1724. It is noteworthy that the enamels are still in the *famille verte* palette rather than the subsequent *famille rose* style with opaque colours. The fine vase shown in Plate 98 is painted in the new 'foreign' range of colours containing some tin-oxide. This example is in the pure Chinese taste rather than in the European style and it bears a Chinese inscription and date which may be freely translated as 'a picture of wishing long life, the white cloud Hermit made this in mid autumn festival 1730 at Linman in the Pearl River district'.

However, figure decoration on the standard imports from China before about 1750 is uncommon, although European and other figures are depicted on the rather finer objects purchased as Private Trade (discussed in Chapters 6 and 7). The *famille rose* class lent itself so well to floral motifs that, except where figures are incorporated as a secondary feature, figure patterns rarely occur.

By the 1760s, however, many figure designs are found, although generally these figure designs are set in a reserve panel and do not fill the entire surface area as a floral or landscape pattern might have done. There are as always exceptions. Some objects, such as vases, lend themselves to all-over decoration and a particularly attractive example is seen in Plate 99.

If we examine the sale records concerning some of the cargo of china-ware brought home on the *Osterly* and sold in April 1769 we find the following items, which were probably typical of the imports of the period, although these particular items represent Private Trade.

101 A typical Chinese figure-panelled teapot of the mid-1770s, representing the more ordinary commercial quality export wares (compare with Plates 102–105). 6¼ inches high.
Godden of Worthing Ltd

102 A large, fine punch-bowl painted with Chinese figure-subject panels set in a complicated diaper-patterned ground. Diameter 15¾ inches, *c*. 1775. *Godden of Worthing Ltd*

A complete tea and coffee equipage of the fine imaged china, containing forty-three pieces.
A rich imaged wash-hand bason and bottle.
Two rich octagonal imaged jars [vases?].
Two rich imaged bowls.
A very fine large imaged punch bowl.
A fine square imaged teapot, and six basons and plates ditto.
A pair of fine octagonal mosaic imaged jars and covers.
A rich imaged gallon bowl.
Two fine leaf shaped tureens and covers of the imaged china.
A set of three imaged jars and covers and two beakers.
A pair of mosaic and imaged row waggons [*rouleau* vases].
Two imaged mosaic bowls.

The reproduction of an oil painting by Benjamin Wilson (1721–88) shows a fashionable lady with her fine imaged tea and coffee 'equipage' set out in the foreground. The period is approximately contemporary with the 1769 sale catalogue just quoted. The tea-set depicted in this painting seems to have been particularly well painted on a par with the magnificent specimens shown in Plates 102 and 103. Some figure-panelled teawares were, however, of a much less expensive nature, the teapot shown in Plate 101 being of average quality.

The 1769 sale catalogue of Private Trade from the *Osterly* contained several items variously described as 'mosaic' and 'imaged'. These references no doubt refer to the rich red and other backgrounds which were painstakingly over-painted or gilt and so broken up into a repetitive mosaic design. Some particularly rich examples of this type are illustrated in Plates 102–104. Another standard background is seen on the covered sauce tureen from a dinner-service of the 1770–80 period, illustrated as Plate 105. In contrast to these large pieces I show in Plate 106 some smaller, more personal objects, patch-boxes and snuff bottles.

Oriental export market porcelain

103 A magnificent large covered vase (one of a pair) typically painted with Chinese figure panels. 23½ inches high, c. 1775.
Sotheby & Co., London

104 A vase showing the type of Chinese figure decoration sometimes called 'Mandarin' which was often copied on English porcelains of the period. 11½ inches high, c. 1775.
Godden of Worthing Ltd

105 A covered tureen from an export market dinner-service painted with Chinese figure subjects against a typical diaper background. 7½ inches long, c. 1775.   *Godden of Worthing Ltd*

The enamelled wares

106 A selection of small Private Trade Chinese porcelains – covered boxes and snuff-bottles, decorated in the fashionable style of the 1770s. Bottles 2¼ inches high.

Earle D. Vandekar, London

107 A Chinese dessert dish, a mug and a helmet-shaped creamer, all decorated in the well-painted style popular in the 1800–1810 period. Dish 10½ inches long. *The Art Exchange, New York*

108 A superb Chinese fruit-cooler, a hot-water plate and a soup plate, from a finely painted service of the early 1800s. The fruit-cooler, in particular, is based on a European model.
Sotheby & Co., London

The enamelled wares

109 An important pair of large 'Canton' vases painstakingly enamelled with ornate figure-subject panels. 50½ inches high, nineteenth century.
Christies, London

Variations of the so-called mandarin figure designs remained popular for the rest of the eighteenth century, and similarly styled porcelains were produced by most English porcelain factories of the period. In the late 1790s or early 1800s a class of rare, fine quality porcelain was made, and typical specimens are shown in Colour Plate 8 and Plates 107–108. The dinner-service plates are noteworthy for having a slightly concave or dished condiment flange, and European shapes such as ice-pails were copied. These pre-1810 porcelains are thinly potted, especially the plates.

From about 1820 a complete change comes over the potting, which is thick, and the body appears coarse in comparison with the earlier wares. The glazed surface is often uneven and the decoration is laid on extremely freely, as if to cover the poorer body. In England such wares are referred to as 'Canton', but in North America the term 'Rose Medallion' is favoured. The overall effect is certainly rich. It is admired by many, and some of the finer examples are costly. Particularly rich are the superb, often inscribed, bowls and dishes made in the nineteenth century for the Persian market and other Near Eastern countries. Typical specimens of 'Canton' are shown in Colour Plates 9 and 10 and Plates 109–111 and 218–220; these wares can be very large. This type of heavy Chinese export market porcelain remained in production through the nineteenth century and into the twentieth, and on some of the later examples the tell-tale inscription 'Made in China' can be found. This was required by the import regulations of various European and North American countries. A good selection of these later export market porcelains is shown in *Chinese Export Porcelains: standard patterns and forms, 1780 to 1880* by Herbert, Peter and Nancy Schiffer (Schiffer Publishing Ltd, Exton, USA, 1975).

110 A Canton 'Rose Medallion' cup and saucer. The cup is also decorated with armorial bearings – an unusual feature on these nineteenth-century wares, c. 1840+. *Godden of Worthing Ltd*

The enamelled wares

111 A typical 'Canton' figure panelled vase, and a covered ewer and bowl of the type popular in Europe and North America from c. 1820 onwards. Vase 16¾ inches high.

Sotheby's, Belgravia, London

6 The armorial, crested and initialled wares

Probably the best known type of Chinese export market porcelain consists of those pieces which display the armorial bearing of European families, companies or societies. Yet almost without exception these wares were not imported by the English East India Company. They were Private Trade goods, usually ordered through ships' captains or Supra-cargoes. This is why we know so little about them, although of course we can often trace the families for whom such services were made.

Fortunately, this research has, in most cases, been carried out for us by David Howard, the author of the monumental and justifiably expensive standard book *Chinese Armorial Porcelain* (London, 1974). For those who seek to trace the armorial bearings found on Chinese porcelains this book is indispensable. Rather than seek to emulate the author's research on the individual arms I have in this chapter dealt with the broader picture of armorial porcelains and the related initialled and monogrammed wares.

In considering the Private Trade aspect of these armorial porcelains we recall that, in the few accounts that have been preserved, the Company is not mentioned (save for its charges). The goods are personally consigned. Two of the four accounts known to me concern the Peers family, who had important links with the Company. One service was finely enamelled with a full coat of arms and crest (see Plate 112) and this was invoiced in the following, perhaps standard, manner:

Canton, the 10th December, 1731
Invoice of two chests of China Ware laden on board the ship *Harrison*, Capt. Samuel Martin Commander, bound to the port of London and consigned to Charles Peers Esq. on his proper account and risque, being marked as in the margin (C^WP).
Chinaware painted with Coat of Arms, viz.

Colour Plate 10 A superb quality Chinese dish made for the Persian market and bearing an inscription to Zill al-Sultan Mas-un Minza, governor of Isfahan; dated AH 1297 (AD 1882). Diameter $15\frac{1}{2}$ inches. *Godden of Worthing Ltd*

112 A soup-plate from the Peers' service consigned from Canton in December 1731. A hundred such plates originally cost approximately £13. Diameter 8⅔ inches. *Sotheby & Co., London*
113 A wide, shallow sauce-boat from the Peers' service with one of the twelve trencher salts. The crested sauce-boats, originally 'boats', cost approximately 2s 6d each. 7⅝ inches long, 1731. *J. R. Peers collection*

Dishes of the 1st size	4 at 1 tale 3 mace		
2nd ,,	4 at 1·2		
3rd ,,	12 at ·9		
4th ,,	16 at ·6		
5th ,,	20 at ·5	Tales	40·4
Plates	200 at 3·3 mace		66
Soup dishes 1st size	6 at 3		
2nd ,,	6 at 2·5		33
Soup plates	100	at ·4 mace	40·0
Sauce boats	12	at ·4 ,,	4·8
Salts	12	at ·2 ,,	2·4
Teasets	2	at 7·2 ,,	14·4
Quart mugs	6	at ·5 ,,	3·0
Pint ,,	6	at ·4 ,,	2·4
Ewers and salvers	4 pair	at 3·5 ,,	14·0
Bowles, 5 in a sett	2 setts	at 3·8 ,,	7·6
		Tales	228·0

Errors excepted
pr. Chr Greenwood

The total cost in China of this magnificent and lengthy service was £76 sterling. The three hundred plates (Plate 112) and ranges of large dishes

The armorial crested and initialled wares

114 A superbly painted Chinese porcelain circular dish, the design copied from one by the English artist, Devis, and with the armorial bearings of Leake Okeover. The accounts for this service are dated 1740 and 1743. Diameter 15½ inches.
Christies, London

115 Representative pieces from the large dinner-service made for Captain John Eastabrook of the East Indiaman, *London*, enamelled with anchor, crest and initials within underglaze blue borders, c. 1785–90.
Christies, London

must have presented a magnificent sight although some of the lesser pieces such as the sauceboats and the salts bore the Peers crest (Plate 113) rather than the full arms. Some of these rare pieces are on loan to the Victoria and Albert Museum and are here illustrated by kind permission of the family. Other pieces have recently come on the market and whilst much gilding was employed in this 1731 service, it is extremely thin and has largely worn away in use. This porcelain set may have been cleared from the *Harrison* as part of Captain Samuel Martin's goods which were valued at £1,706 1s 5d in June 1733.

It seems that the enamelled service was made for Sir Charles Peers, as the arms include his Knight's helm. He was Lord Mayor of London in 1715, a commissioner of Customs, a director of the East India Company and for many years a member of the important and secret 'Committee of Seven'. It appears he was not above trading in India through his second son, who bore his name. A lesser service, decorated in underglaze blue, was in all probability made for Charles Peers Jnr (1703–81). Charles Peers

116 A superbly potted and finely painted Chinese Private Trade saucer painted in the *famille rose* palette with European crest motif. Diameter 5¼ inches, c. 1730–35. *Private collection*

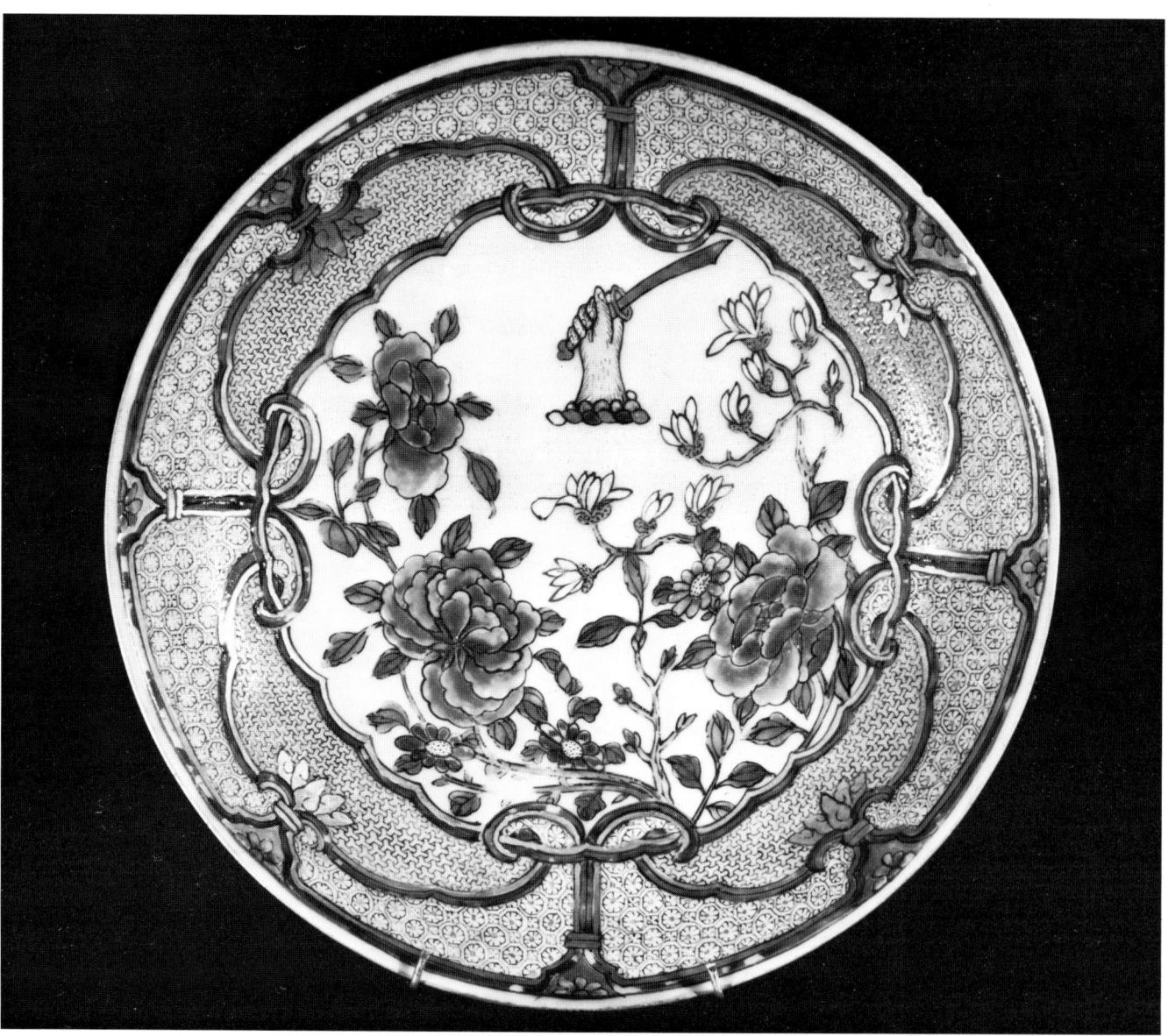

The armorial crested and initialled wares

Colour Plate 11 A magnificent Chinese Private Trade marriage-plate incorporating the couple's initials and dates of birth, together with the date of the union, 20 December 1750. Diameter 8¾ inches. *Godden of Worthing Ltd*

117 A fine quality Chinese Private Trade saucer painted in the *famille rose* palette, and incorporating panels of European initials. Diameter 5¼ inches, c. 1730–35.   *British Museum*

Jnr had served the company in Madras since 1720, where his father sent him large amounts of money each year, presumably to trade with on their joint account. The Company minutes abound with references to these shipments of internationally accepted currency. One typical entry reads: 'Ordered that Sir Charles Peers be permitted according to his request to send to his son Charles Peers, writer, at Fort St George, 2,000 ounces of foreign silver [sometimes listed as "pieces of eight"] on the usual terms.' (26 September 1722) The next year 4,000 ounces were sent; in 1730 8,000 ounces; and in 1732 a John Green Esq. sent 8,500 pieces of eight to the young Charles Peers at Fort St George.

The records also show that Sir Charles Peers was receiving back goods; on 1 September 1733 we find minuted: 'Ordered that the goods undermentioned be delivered to the persons following they paying into the Treasury what [is] due thereon – viz… Goods value £39 17s 9d. To Sir Charles Peers he paying £21 17s 9d.'

Charles Peers had gone out to India as a 'writer' (the lowest form of employee, a kind of apprentice-clerk) in 1720, having served in the accountant's office in London from December 1718. He was permitted to take to India 'one thousand ounces of foreign bullion on the usual terms'. He was promoted Factor in a Minute dated 28 December 1722: 'Ordered that Mr Charles Peers son of Sir Charles Peers who has been a writer at Fort St George, three years do commence Factor when he is of age. To commence Factor from January 31st.' In November 1729 Charles Peers was elected to the Council at Fort St George and was instrumental in the dismissal of Governor Macrae of Bengal. However, Charles himself was soon in trouble and was suspended, only to be re-elected to the Council. However, he had little time to enjoy the use of his service (consigned from Canton in November 1731) in India, for in January 1735 he was back in London under somewhat of a cloud. The following instructions were minuted: 'Ordered that the bonds entered into by Messrs Peers and Parks for their return to England be delivered up to them in Court and that the Chairman acquaint them that as there are several complaints of their behaviour and particularly of their carrying on a Trade to Europe on Danish ships the Court will in time examine into the same.'

The Peers family illustrate the way that the directors of the East India Company traded and ordered services for their own use. David Howard has traced eighty-seven armorial services made for directors of the East India Company, with many more that probably relate to such persons. The Peers story also illustrates that the Company's

118 An attractive Chinese Private Trade saucer bearing two sets of monograms with hearts and crossed arrows above and doves below. What a charming wedding present such a tea-service must have made! Diameter 5½ inches, c. 1785–90.

Godden of Worthing Ltd

officers in India commissioned many similar services, and that these were later shipped home to England.

The blue and white service made for the young Charles Peers is illustrated by the single plate now in the British Museum (see Plate 10). Again, the account, or rather the owner's duplicate copy, has been preserved and this too is of considerable interest:

Canton the 19th November 1731
Invoice of two chests of chinaware laden aboard the ship *Canton Merchant*, Capt. Timothy Tullie, Commander, bound to the Port of Madras and consigned to Nicholas Morris [? this name is not clear] Merchant there on account and risque of Charles Peers Esq., being marked as per margin (C P).

Chinaware blue and white painted with a crest, viz.

Dishes of the 1st size	4	at 1 tale	
2nd ,,	5	at 7 mace	
3rd ,,	9	at 5 mace	
4th ,,	13	at 3 mace	
5th ,,	14	at 1·5 mace	18·0 Tale
Plates	100	at 7 candareen	7·0 ,,
Soup dishes	6	at 9 mace	5·4 ,,
Soup plates	60	at 7·3 candareen	4·4 ,,
Bowles	4 setts		3·0 ,,
Sauceboats	12	at 1·5 mace	1·8 ,,
Salts	12		0·4 ,,
			Tales 40·0

Errors excepted
per Chr Greenwood

We see that this set was delivered to Charles Peers at Fort St George. The set was probably sent home to England in 1733, see p. 200. These two accounts, dated within a month of each other, and being readily related to surviving specimens, permit us to compare prime costs of the two basic forms of decoration – overglaze enamelled designs and patterns painted entirely in unglazed blue, although the enamelled arms and the whole design made for Sir Charles is somewhat more complicated than the blue set made for his son in India.

If, for convenience, we convert the prices into candareen (10 candareen = 1 mace, 10 mace = 1 tale), we can then make some interesting comparisons.

	Enamelled	Blue and White
Dishes large or 1st size	130	100
Dishes small or 5th size	50	15
Plates	33	7
Soup plates	40	7·3
Sauceboats	40	15

This table is rather bewildering at first sight. If we compare the plates, the enamelled ones cost nearly

119 A charming Chinese Private Trade saucer depicting a cobbler, or leather-worker, with his wares and the motto, 'I must Work for Leathers dear'. The initials RP most probably relate to Richard Phillcox, the name on a similar mug in the Franks collection at the British Museum. Diameter 5⅛ inches, c. 1770–75.
Godden of Worthing Ltd

The armorial crested and initialled wares

five times more than the blue examples, or even more in the case of the soup plates. The enamelled sauceboats are little more than three times the price of the blue examples, but in Plate 113 we see the reason for this – they do not bear the full arms, only the crest. However, the pricing of the dishes which head each list is perplexing. The price difference between the two styles on the largest size is extremely small, but when we get to the fifth or smallest size, the enamelled variety costs over three times as much as the blue. The cost of manufacture, discounting the decoration, would have been similar in both cases, so the difference in price should be related to the decoration. Perhaps, however, when we come to the troublesome large dishes the high price and the little difference in cost are accounted for in manufacturing difficulties and the high cost of the blanks before they were decorated.

As I have explained in Chapter 4, the underglaze decoration was added during the basic manufacturing process, which was almost certainly carried out at the great inland porcelain centre, Ching-tê Chên. However, it is believed that much of the enamelled decoration applied over the glaze was added by special decorators in Canton. Indeed, there are first-hand accounts from later in the century of such a practice. Here is the comment of an American writer: 'The chinaware is brought from the country [Ching-tê Chên] plain, and painted according to fancy in the city [Canton]; they make us pay double price when they put a cypher on it, because they say it must go again into the kiln. They are great copyists and we have several sets of china to order with the family coat of arms.'

The name of one Canton enameller, Fungmante, is recorded on a bowl given to the City of New York in 1802. This scenic-painted bowl is now in the Metropolitan Museum of Art, New York.

Unfortunately we do not have any evidence to show when the practice of enamelling in Canton was introduced and on what scale it was practised. My own belief is that large and elaborately decorated sets such as the one made for Sir Charles Peers (Plate 112) were both made and decorated inland at Ching-tê Chên and that the market in such personalised wares was not, at this pre-1750 date, large enough to warrant on-the-spot enamelling of blanks at Canton – at least not of large services.

It seems reasonable to assume that in the second half of the eighteenth century, when the Whampoa anchorage was crowded with European shipping, there was a great demand for special presents or mementoes to be purchased and taken home on the same voyage. No doubt the Canton enamellers kept a stock of standard articles suitable for this purpose, items such as bowls, mugs or teapots. Such available blanks could be decorated to order in a few days and fired in a low temperature muffle-kiln, but it would be a different matter to decorate a large service with an elaborate design even if a stock of the required undecorated dinner-service blanks were kept.

The blanks available to the enamellers at Canton were not necessarily completely undecorated. In some cases it appears that a stock design was taken and slightly embellished with the owner's arms, crest or initials. The bowl shown in Plate 69 seems to represent such a piece, for the arms have been applied over the glaze, cramping an otherwise completely decorated underglaze blue bowl. Other blanks may have been sent from Ching-tê Chên with conventional and standard underglaze blue borders, to be finished with overglaze colours at Canton.

The third and fourth contemporary account known to me relate to an armorial service made in 1742-3 for Leake Okeover, who had been a shareholder in the Company since at least 1727. The account is preserved at Okeover Hall and so is the

120 A Chinese two-handled bowl enamelled with a crest and motto motif, almost certainly copied from Robert Ouchterlony's printed book-plate which is also shown, c. 1780–85.
Ashmolean Museum, Oxford

original painted design which was sent to China to be copied on to the porcelains. This is inscribed: 'The arms of Leak Oakover [sic] Esqr of Oakover...a pattern for china plates, pattern to be returned.' Further, there is an account from the artist, Devis, 'for finishing a pattern of a plate £1 1s 0d'. This magnificent pattern is illustrated in colour (item 413A) in the David Howard and John Ayers book *China for the West*. Small wonder that the set is one of the most magnificent to have been made in China; a single plate is shown in Plate 114. The superbly painted 'pattern' was an exception; most arms or crests seem to have been copied from printed book plates or suchlike available material, sent out to the Chinese enamellers (Plate 120).

The 1743 account for this service brought home by Captain Ralph Congreve, Commander of the *Onslow*, is invoiced as from 'ye Jerusalem Coffee House, Change Alley, a consignment of four large dishes and fifty plates with your arms'. The Jerusalem was a famous London Coffee House, much frequented by the East India captains, and a great deal of Private Trade business must have been conducted here. Letters addressed to the captains of East Indiamen were normally sent 'care of the Jerusalem Coffee House'.

When the major part of this magnificent service was sold at Christie's early in 1975, a photocopy of an interesting original account was exhibited. It differed in its date and make-up from the bill which had been quoted in earlier books or articles. This previously unrecorded account was dated 16 January 1739–40 (1740 by our present calendar). It reads:

Leake Oakover Esq.
Account of china with arms
King & Company's duties for 69 plates
£11 11s 10d

Oriental export market porcelain

121 Two Chinese Private Trade pattern plates showing various numbered standard border motifs and cartouche designs for the owner's initials (see Plate 122). These bear on the reverse the name of the Canton merchant, Synchong.
Victoria and Albert Museum (Crown Copyright)

My own cost and charges for 70 plates and 30 dishes
£84
Rec'd January 18th, 1739–1740 the contents in full of all amounts

Pr Ralph Congreve

In this account we see the separate charge for the customs duty and the Company's charges, but strangely this was levied on only part of the consignment – perhaps the other plate and the thirty large dishes were smuggled ashore or were the subject of a separate account.

It appears that this was only part of the order, or that more was at once ordered, for Ralph Congreve brought home a further fifty plates and four large dishes in 1743. The pieces sold at Christie's in 1975 comprised seventeen circular dishes, with diameters ranging from $16\frac{1}{2}$ inches to 11 inches, and eighty-four plates. Many pieces were damaged, but the total commanded the considerable sum of £68,400; but it is generally conceded that this is the finest armorial service ever to have been made in China.

The Private Trade armorial wares are hardly mentioned in the Company's records. There are, however, some important exceptions that underline the private aspect of the trade. The records show that these Private Trade goods had to be submitted to sale by the candle and advertised in the normal

The armorial crested and initialled wares

Colour Plate 12 A very attractive and well-painted Chinese soup plate, the centre bearing the arms of John Fleming of Brompton Park (d. 1763), with those of his wife, Jane Coleman. Diameter 9 inches. *Private collection*

way. This was presumably so that the Customs duty could be charged and the Company's dues calculated. The price of the articles in China as shown on the surviving bills has little relation to the cost of the goods to the purchaser, especially as at least one middle-man wanted his commission in addition to other charges.

The first reference I have traced to armorial porcelain in the Company's records concerns a public sale and occurs under the date 12 November 1731:

Report of the Committee of Warehouses, dated this day being read –
Ordered that the chinaware with Coats of Arms etc. and some white goods for presents be put up to sale on Tuesday the 23rd instant and that notice thereof be given accordingly.

One presumes that the owner or the captain or Supra-cargo charged with ordering the service and bringing it home had to bid for the porcelains in order to establish a price on which dues were to be paid.

Another reference to Private Trade armorial porcelain appears in the Minutes under the date 16 December 1733: 'Request of Mr Thomas Fytche being read praying leave to remit the sum of £95 in foreign silver by the *Harrison* to Cuiqua in Canton for a parcel of china he had bespoke with Coats of Arms. Ordered that his request be granted.' Thomas Fytche was at this time second Supra-cargo of the *Harrison*, having been the fifth in line in the 1731–2 seasons, when the *Harrison*, *Hartford*, *Caesar* and *Macclesfield* had been to China. It must have been on this previous trip that the armorial china was ordered from Cuiqua (who may have been the merchant commonly known as Kingqua).

A plate bearing the Fytche arms is illustrated by David Howard in his *Chinese Armorial Porcelain* (p. 168), but we have no means of knowing if this was the service bespoke in 1731–2. The minuted request – the only one of its kind that I can trace – shows that the service could not be completed before the vessel left for Europe. This may be due to the fact that the Canton enamellers had not as yet established their local workshops to cater for this trade (see p. 203), or it could be simply that Thomas Fytche did not have the money to pay for it until the next trip.

We have read through over forty years of the Company's available records before we come across a further reference to armorial porcelain. It occurs under the date 10 January 1778 and relates to the Private Trade goods on board the *Alfred* on the account of the captain, James Williamson:

75 half chests china ware
60 tubs   ,,
3 boxes   ,,
2 boxes, china ware, arms Colonel S. Champion
10   ,,   paper hangings,
6   ,,   fans

Other available records list only the number of chests, tubs or boxes of china carried – not their contents. Full records were kept originally but these have been destroyed over the years as being of no interest or consequence.

Again, the private aspect of armorial porcelains, and the frequent link with Europeans in India, is witnessed by the following letter of 1789 from Joseph Lygo in London to William Duesbury:

I have had a Gentleman here in the name of Sir John Day which is lately come from India, and has got a very elegant set of Table china with the Duke of York and Clarences arms on it, done by mistake instead of his own, it has cost him £297 1s neat money and he would be glad of the same sum for it again – now what he wants me to do is to try to sell it to either of the Dukes.
...He informed me that when he was coming away he gave a particular friend of his a commission to get him a complete service of china made with his arms on it, and

The armorial crested and initialled wares

122 A Chinese Private Trade waste-bowl from a tea-service decorated in Canton with overglaze blue and gold, the fanciful cartouche motif appears on the Synchong pattern plate shown in Plate 121, right. Diameter 4¾ inches, c. 1795.
Godden of Worthing Ltd

Oriental export market porcelain

123 A Chinese plate decorated in the 'Imari' style with underglaze blue in conjunction with overglaze colours. The centre and border incorporates the arms of Horsemonden. A John Horsemonden was Supra-cargo on the *Marlborough*. Diameter 9 inches, c. 1715–20. *Christies, London*

124 A rare armorial dish decorated in the semi-translucent *famille verte* palette (see Colour Plate 4) and incorporating the date 1702. Diameter 11¾ inches. *Sotheby & Co., London*

he at the same time informed his friend that he thought he should send him a further commission for a set with Royal Arms on it, for the Duchess of Cumberland, therefore this set was made first in mistake.

The above letter refers to a complete service. We have seen in the account for Sir Charles Peers's service that even the early orders included not only dinner-sets but also matching teasets, mugs, ewers and bowls, and the completeness of the services in their original make-up is shown again in the following quotation from a Christies' sale catalogue. The prices, of course, do not relate to present-day values, but it should be remembered that odd plates found today would originally have formed part of a large service.

An extensive Table service enamelled with Coats of Arms, consisting of 3 terrines [tureens] covers and dishes, 4 sauce ditto, covers and dishes, 2 fish dishes with strainers, 33 oblong dishes, in sizes, 106 flat plates, 26 soup ditto, 10 pudding dishes, 12 water plates, 4 sauce boats, and stands, 36 cheese or fruit plates, 3 ale jugs, a beer mug, 2 salad bowls, and 4 salts, in all 265 pieces.
£22 1s 0d

6 elegant openwork fruit baskets and stands and 3 bowls to correspond.
£2 10s 0d

A pair of hand basons, with bottles and covers to match.
11s 0d

Forty-one pieces of breakfast and tea china to match.
£1 15s 0d

These goods were catalogued in November 1804 as part of the 'Elegant Household Furniture...the property of Captain John Eastabrook, Deceased, late Commander of the *London* East Indiaman'. While the original catalogue describes the set as enamelled with Coat of Arms it appears to be only crested and initialled within the standard shield-shaped cartouche of the 1785–95 period. The crest, well suited to a sea-captain, is an anchor and chain with the initials 'J E' below.

The armorial crested and initialled wares

125 A fine quality Chinese armorial plate decorated in the *famille verte* palette. The arms are those of Frederick with Marescoe, and can be dated to the early 1720s.
The Art Exchange, New York

126 A Chinese Private Trade armorial plate, the border panels depicting East and West as represented by Plymouth and Macao. This border design, with slight variations, was a popular one in the 1740s. *Sotheby & Co., London*

I write 'appears to be', for by a remarkable coincidence John Eastabrook's service seems to have passed through the same sale-room in November 1951, 147 years after Mr Christie first sold it. The make-up has changed slightly but the total number of pieces remains constant at 265 pieces. The price has increased from £22 1s 0d in 1804 to £1,470 in 1951. A tureen, a large oval dish and two plates from this interesting but standard pattern service are shown in Plate 115.

Only a small percentage of the population could boast full armorial bearings (although some undoubtedly invented them) and not all armigerous families required their arms to be blazoned across their tablewares. Many sets incorporated only a tasteful crest. A delightful and quite early saucer from a teaset is shown in Plate 116. The potting is thin in the extreme – of 'egg-shell' type – and the enamelling is in the *famille rose* style. David Howard, in *Chinese Armorial Porcelain*, has shown from the dating of arms that these European *famille rose* colours date from c.1720–22. This example is of the 1730–35 period.

Many other services and individual pieces bear only the owner's initials, or sometimes the initials with a crest above. After about 1770 the initialled wares outnumber the armorial pieces, for the simple reason that everybody had initials and relatively few possessed armorial bearings. Some initialled wares are of an early date. The superb quality *famille rose* saucer shown in Plate 117 is an example of about 1730. The early manner of painting the initials is noteworthy and is to be seen again in the later, dated example shown in Colour Plate 11. However, these intertwined initials are extremely difficult to decipher.

The various treatments that intertwined initials afford lend themselves to marriage services and to individual commemorative pieces. It seems very doubtful if the large plate (Colour Plate 11) with its

212   **Oriental export market porcelain**

127 A Chinese Private Trade plate enamelled with a popular type of floral design and a European crest and Latin motto (of Lauder) worked into the border. Diameter 6¼ inches, *c.* 1755–60.
Godden of Worthing Ltd

The armorial crested and initialled wares

128 An elegant Chinese Private Trade armorial mug enamelled with European-style floral sprays and festoons. 5½ inches high, c. 1780–85.
Godden of Worthing Ltd

elaborate gilt centre can have been part of a large service. Each of the initial panels incorporates the date of birth of one of the partners, 4 February 1719 and 15 December 1726, with in the centre the date of the marriage: 20 December 1750. Of a more homely nature there are the charming teasets represented here by a saucer (Plate 118) incorporating the two sets of initials under crossed arrows and hearts and above a pair of doves, all arranged within a tasteful border.

Initials were very often included in other elaborate designs that are properly considered under other headings (see Plates 117 and 129). Often these initials were added to personalise a stock pattern, but in rare cases the initials were used with special individual designs. The charming saucer shown in Plate 119 is such an example. Here there are the initials 'R P' above the wording: 'I must work for Leathers dear'. The cobbler and his assistant are seated below, and various devices of his trade are arranged in the elaborate cartouche, which might be likened to a Chinese-Chippendale mirror-frame.

Several of the fanciful armorial, initial or crest designs found on these special Private Trade orders were no doubt copied from the owner's printed book-plate, or trade-card in the case of the saucer shown in Plate 119. What easier than to supply the dealer, ship's captain, or Supra-cargo with your book-plate to serve as a guide to the enamellers in Canton. Their rendering could be amusingly naive but the source is evident, as you can see from Plate 120.

Most initialled pieces are of a more ordinary nature. Many such sets were ordered in England with the help of pattern plates with a variety of standard borders and cartouche devices. Two such plates of the 1790s are shown in Plate 121. The basic draped-shield cartouche of the right-hand plate has been used on the bowl shown in Plate 122, with its dark blue border enamelled over the glaze

129 A Chinese Private Trade saucer painted with fruit and flowers incorporating European initial motifs. Diameter 5½ inches, c. 1780.   *Godden of Worthing Ltd*

130 A finely enamelled Chinese covered sugar-bowl. The armorial bearings were added at Canton to a standard 'blank' with only the underglazed blue border. 5¼ inches high, c. 1780.   *Godden of Worthing Ltd*

and gold stars added – a very popular border in the 1790s.

While we may fancy that all armorial, crested or initialled porcelain found in Britain was made for British citizens, this is not necessarily the case. As I have stated in the first chapter, much Chinese porcelain was taken as a prize in time of war. Evidence is provided by lots from the catalogue of 'An extensive and valuable assortment of India China, being part of the cargoes of the *Zuyderberg*, *Schelde* and *Delft*, Dutch East-Indiamen.' This sale of Dutch prizes conducted by Harry Phillips, the Bond Street auctioneer, in December 1797 included:

A breakfast service enamelled gilt and cyphered V.P. contents 12 basons and saucers, teapot and stand, sugar pot and cover, milk pot, bowl and 2 plates   £1 19s 0d

A coffee set cyphered I.H.   £1 10s 0d
Twelve coffee cups and saucers, a slop bason and a gallon bowl, cyphered I.S.T.   £1 8s 0d
An elegant gilt and cyphered A.D., coffee set, contents 12 cups and saucers, pot and cover, sugar bason and cover, milk ewer, bowl and plate   £1 9s 0d
A tea and coffee service painted in arms   £2
A tea and coffee set cyphered T.Q.   £1 11s 6d
A coffee service cyphered J.J.C.H.   £1 3s 0d
A tea set cyphered T.M.   £1 19s 0d
A ditto cyphered M.E.O.   £1 19s 0d
A tea set cyphered I.C.O.   £2 0s 0d
A tea and coffee set cyphered A.V.O.   £2 15s 0d
A tea and coffee set cyphered I.D.   £2 0s 0d
A ditto cyphered ISL and dove crest   £2 5s 0d
A tea and coffee set cyphered R.E.B.   £2 3s 0d
A ditto Dutch arms and cyphers, containing 10 tea cups and saucers, 6 coffee cups, teapot and stand, milk pot, a

The armorial crested and initialled wares

131 A Chinese Private Trade initialled tea-bowl and saucer incorporating the date 1793. The gold star motifs over a blue enamel border represent a standard design of the 1790s. Diameter of saucer 5½ inches. *Godden of Worthing Ltd*

132 Representative pieces from a large armorial and initialled dinner-service made for the Marquess of Townsend, *c.* 1798. The overglaze blue and gold border should be noted, the shield-shaped cartouche occurs on the Synchong sample plate shown in Plate 121, right. *The Art Exchange, New York*

sugar dish and cover, canister and spoontray, bowl and 2 plates £1 11s 6d

You will observe that most of these lots were of initialled tea and coffee services. Only two lots represent armorial services, which were becoming rare in the 1790s. Some of these rather late initialled sets can be charming and elegant. Of course the sale, and the Dutch ships' cargoes, included a mass of more usual porcelain, Nankin blue and white dinner services and the like.

A representative selection of armorial, crested and initialled porcelains is shown in Plates 124–134. These are arranged in chronological order with the inclusion of some interesting dated, or datable, pieces. All these wares, as we know, represent Private Trade orders and, while they are in many cases individual, a definite pattern or progressive style of decoration remained in favour at various periods – so that in most cases the date can be estimated with some confidence.

We do not as yet know the precise details of how these armorial, crested or initialled porcelains were ordered, but it seems likely that in most cases (except when a ship's captain or Supra-cargo was directly placing an order) the would-be-purchaser approached a chinaman, or dealer in the standard Chinese porcelains. Here the buyer may have been shown a set of sample plates displaying numbered border designs, etc, such as the plates illustrated in Plate 121. Alternatively, he might merely have seen a standard pattern of the period and ordered that, with various personal features added. These later initialled pieces were almost certainly enamelled at Canton, on blanks representing standard international shapes of the period. It is noteworthy that while the bulk of the Company's imports comprised standard blue and white wares, which presumably sold well, very few armorial sets are decorated in underglaze blue. Many services, however, had standard underglaze blue borders, particularly those of the Fitzhugh type (Plate 130 and Colour Plate 13), and these blanks would have been embellished with arms or initials by the Canton enamellers. For this service, and presumably for the cost of keeping a large stock of blanks, the enamellers charged highly, knowing that visiting Europeans could not go elsewhere for their specially ordered personal porcelains. The Chinese, the Company's servants, the Company and the British revenue, all took their percentage, ensuring that those rich enough to order armorial porcelains paid for their vanity. David Howard has stated that Chinese armorial porcelain was as much as ten times as costly as other services. While this may be difficult to substantiate one wonders why more families did not order their porcelains from British factories – some delightful Worcester armorial teasets are known with a few other armorial articles, but the number of eighteenth-century armorial English services cannot be one per cent of those that were shipped from China; perhaps British manufacturers did not welcome such special orders. The situation changed early in the nineteenth century when comparatively little Chinese porcelain was imported, while British manufacturers stepped in belatedly to supply the still strong market for magnificent armorial or crested services.

David Howard has divided the styles of such porcelains into twenty-four groups with over two hundred sub-divisions. My own classification of the main styles is shown below. These categories relate not merely to armorial porcelains but also to the simpler crested or initialled wares, and indeed to the other types of Chinese export market porcelain. There is, of course, some overlap of dates, and at any period the buyer would have had a choice – dictated perhaps by his pocket.

First, let us exclude the porcelains painted *entirely* in underglaze blue. Such armorial sets are

133 An elegant early-nineteenth century Chinese Private Trade armorial plate bearing the arms of Hay, and showing the dished or concave condiment flange. Diameter 10 inches, c. 1815.
Godden of Worthing Ltd

very rare, but they can be of any period, from about 1700 into the nineteenth century.

1. Imari style, normally with formal floral all-over designs in underglaze blue, with overglaze red, green and some gilding (Plate 123). Mainly c. 1700–30. (These sets can be of Japanese origin, but most are Chinese.)

2. *Famille verte* designs in semi-translucent colours, green predominating. Normally more sparsely decorated than the Imari pattern (see Plates 124–125, c. 1700–30.

3. Border panelled designs, of which perhaps the most ambitious is the Lee service (see Frontispiece) showing London and Oriental views. Other pieces of this type are illustrated in Plate 126 and Colour Plate 12. Such attractive wares are normally of the 1735–55 period. The arms are often in the centre (as they were on most early examples), but they can occur in the border.

4. Centre decoration, here of necessity the arms or crest are on the border (see Plate 127). Such designs are normally of post-1745 date.

5. European-style borders, such as shell, leaf or scroll motifs, gilt spear-head border or edge and gilt chain, contrasting with the earlier Oriental-style designs amended only by the inclusion of European arms. These border motifs are mainly of the 1745–75 period.

6. European flower-sprays, festoons, etc. While flowers may be international, the way in which they are painted or arranged can be decidedly European (see Plates 128–129). These designs are mainly of the post-1765 period.

7. Underglaze blue border designs, such as that known as Fitzhugh (see p. 295). These designs are in the main of the 1775–1810 period (see Plate 130 and Colour Plate 13).

8. Narrow border designs in overglaze enamel, often with gilding. The gold stars on a dark blue band are typical of these late porcelains of the 1790–1810 period (see Plates 131–132).

9. Nineteenth-century Oriental designs. Here is a complete change from styles 7 and 8, with colourful and finely painted Chinese figures or dragon patterns (Plates 133–134). These late services are rare, and the wide, slightly concave condiment flange should be noted (see Plate 133).

NB The reader should be warned that many Continental (mainly French) copies of Chinese armorial porcelain have been made in the past hundred years. These reproductions sometimes bear a mock-Oriental seal-mark, not found on original specimens.

The armorial crested and initialled wares

134 A finely enamelled and gilt Chinese waste-bowl, similar to the wares shown in Plates 107–108 but incorporating the initial 'B' of the European owner. Diameter 6 inches, c. 1815–25.

Godden of Worthing Ltd

135 A small Chinese bowl painted in underglaze blue with the crucifixion of our Lord. Such pieces were perhaps first ordered for the Jesuits in China. 3¼ inches high, c. 1720.
Victoria and Albert Museum (Crown Copyright)

7 The special designs and the figure and animal models

The special designs found on export market Chinese porcelains are extremely varied, and in all cases such articles were imported as Private Trade.

I will discuss first the so-called 'Jesuit' china, a rather loose term that now seems to be applied not only to religious designs but to some mythological and other figure patterns. Some of these are far from religious, but they are often painted in the same style, with a thin black enamel. Such decoration is sometimes called 'pencilling' partly on account of the sombre black or grey colour tone but also because the work was carried out with a very fine brush called a pencil.

The Jesuits were firmly established in China; indeed they were the only Europeans permitted in inland China and in Peking, where they were employed teaching various Western skills. I have already related how Father d'Entrecolles passed the secrets of porcelain-making and decoration from Ching-tê Chên to France in two of his many letters. I also mentioned that when the *Macclesfield*, the first British vessel to trade at Canton, arrived there in 1699, the captain was welcomed by the Jesuit, Father Bassett.

The Company's records give some interesting references to the Jesuits. For example, the Court Minutes on 5 December 1705 record: 'Mons. Gerard Denie, lately returned from China in the *Kent*, coming into Court gave them his hearty thanks for the kindness received in the voyage and desired leave to send a small box of painting materials to the Jesuits at Pekin in China, where he had been employed by the Emperor and also by them in painting their Church which was not finished.' The Court agreed to this request. A similar reference to the passage of these Jesuits to and from China reads:

> Request of M. Baldassare Miller, Jesuit, being presented to the Court wrote in Italian, and he being called in, did by Mr du Bois who interpreted for him –

136 A detail of a Chinese saucer from a tea-service, the subjects being meticulously copied in black enamel from a Dutch medical text-book. Diameter 4¼ inches. One piece from this set bears the date 1761. *Godden collection*
137 A Chinese tea-canister (without cover) well-painted in the black Jesuit style with a rendering of the crucifixion. 3¾ inches high, *c.* 1750. *Ashmolean Museum, Oxford*

representing that he came to England in the *Townsend* and was speedily to go to Germany and expecting to return back sometime requesting leave to take passage to China on one of the outward bound ships from hence. It appearing that the Super-cargoes had given a good character as to his willingness to serve the Company and he assuring them that he would readily assist the English in whatever he was able, as well at Canton as at the Emperor's Court as he had done formerly.

Resolved that he be permitted to take passage on one of the next ships for China. (Minute of 21 June 1727.)

A third minuted request shows that, apart from the co-operation given and received by these Christian missionaries in China, some at least returned to Europe with porcelains. This record is dated 4 September 1724:

Mr Godfrey one of the China Council lately returned on the *Princess Anne*, acquainted the Court that there were two Italian missionarys without, returned from China...and they being called in, returned their humble thanks to the Company for the great civiletys showed them and to others of their character in China and then added that they had some china ware and silks on board which they prayed might be delivered.

They were there upon acquainted that the Court would be ready to gratify their request, but they must first obtain leave from the Commissioners of the Customs.

Ordered that it be left to the Committee of warehouses to give such directions in this affair as they judge proper in the same manner as was lately done with relation to Padre Goville's goods.

It is worth noting not only the Italian missionaries' link with the English Company, but also that the first European painter at the Imperial Court of K'ang Hsi was the Italian Jesuit, Christopher Fiori (see Paper by G. Loehr, 'Missionary Artists at the Manchu Court' in *Transactions of the Oriental Ceramic Society*, 1962–3).

The undecorated white porcelains from Fukien province, a class that we group together under the French term *Blanc de Chine*, were probably the

The special designs

138 A typical black-pencilled Jesuit-style Chinese plate depicting the Nativity. Diameter 9¼ inches, c. 1750.
The Art Exchange, New York

139 A Chinese black-pencilled tea-canister in the Jesuit style. The naive Chinese rendering of European figures is very typical. 4¼ inches high.   *The Art Exchange, New York*

earliest imports of religious porcelain articles into Europe from China. This trade may perhaps have originated with the Jesuits. We find imports such as '65 pulpits with Paderies' from the *Union* being sold in March 1704. Such articles were being imported in the seventeenth century. If we can read 'English Padyes' for Padres, then such goods were included among the *Blanc de Chine* porcelains sold in London in November 1699. This same sale (like many others at later dates) included 'Sancta Maria's, large and small white and painted'. These figures were almost certainly the Chinese Goddess of Mercy, Kuan-yin, given a European title to make her more saleable. These white *Blanc de Chine* wares are fully discussed in Chapter 8.

There are some rare porcelains depicting the crucifixion painted in underglaze blue. A small bowl thus decorated from the Victoria and Albert Museum collection is shown here (Plate 135). Father d'Entrecolles mentions a similar design in his 1712 letter where he states: 'I have had brought to me from the debris of a large shop [this was probably a decorating shop or workshop] a small plate that I value more highly than the finest porcelain pieces made a thousand years ago. On the bottom of the plate is painted a crucifix between the Holy Virgin and St John.'

Obviously these Christian designs were being made at Ching-tê Chên early in the eighteenth century, but Father d'Entrecolles proceeds to cloud our picture, stating: 'I believe that this porcelain used to be sent to Japan, but that it has not been made here now for sixteen or seventeen years. Apparently the Christians in Japan bought these pieces during the persecutions and, since they were well hidden in the packing-cases, they were able to escape the enemies of religion. This pious trick was later discovered and more thorough searches made, which is why such work was discontinued at Ching-tê Chên.' I find it difficult to accept this statement,

The special designs

140 A Chinese black-pencilled plate in the Jesuit style, made for the Dutch market and dated 1752. Diameter 9 inches.
Sotheby & Co., London

141 A rare Chinese Private Trade black-pencilled tea-bowl and saucer with panel of initials above the date 1756. Diameter of saucer 4¾ inches. *Victoria and Albert Museum* (*Crown Copyright*)

The special designs

but one must acknowledge that it was contemporary. Other related blue and white porcelains are decorated with scenes from the Bible. A large circular charger of this kind is seen in Colour Plate 14.

Most of the so-called Jesuit china is painted over the glaze in a black or blackish monochrome, sometimes heightened with gilding. One does not know now if such sombre colours suited the subjects depicted and the Jesuits' taste or if the style was started by the desire of the Chinese enamellers to copy accurately European prints sent for this purpose. This possibility is strengthened when we look at pieces such as the saucer in Plate 136, the unlikely tea-table subject being copied from an engraving in a Dutch medical text book, one piece from this strange set – mostly now in American collections – is dated 1761. Some pieces from this perhaps unique service are illustrated in the David Howard and John Ayers book *China for the West* (London and New York, 1978) Plates 346 and A.

The quality of painting varies greatly. Some examples are delicately rendered and the tea-canister shown in Plate 137 without its cover is of this desirable class, but some (often later) Chinese religious porcelains are of poor commercial quality. The plate shown in Plate 138 is perhaps of average quality in finish, while the rendering of Adam and Eve on the tea-canister (Plate 139) is all too candid if the piece was to grace a rectory tea-table.

Unfortunately we have no records of the importation of these porcelains as they were purely Private Trade articles, but the traditional dating of such pieces – loosely 1740–60 – is confirmed by some rare dated pieces decorated in a similar style and colour. I illustrate a Dutch market plate dated 1752 (Plate 140), and an initialled tea-bowl and saucer painted with the year 1756 (Plate 141).

Many other 'pencilled' Jesuit-type pieces bear

142 A typical black-pencilled Jesuit-style plate decorated with European mythological subject, almost certainly taken from a print. Diameter 8¾ inches, c. 1750–60. *Godden of Worthing Ltd*
143 A Chinese coffee cup and saucer painted in the black-pencilled style, and here showing the variation in intensity that can occur. Diameter of saucer 4¾ inches, c. 1755–60.
Godden of Worthing Ltd.

144 A good and typical Chinese plate enamelled in full colours with the popular 'Judgement of Paris' design. Diameter 9 inches, c. 1750–55. *Godden of Worthing Ltd*

229 **The special designs**

145 A superb quality Chinese tea-service painted and gilt in the style of Meissen porcelain of the 1730s and 1740s. Teapot 5 inches high, c. 1750. *Christies, London*

146 A Chinese teapot painted in the style of Meissen porcelain of the 1730s and 1740s, but this later example is only of average export quality; compare with the pieces shown in Plate 145. $3\frac{3}{4}$ inches high, *c.* 1760.   *E. H. Chandler collection*

The special designs

147 A rare Chinese mug depicting the Duke of Cumberland and inscribed 'In remembrance of the Glorious Victory at Culloden, April 16th 1746'. 6 inches high, c. 1750.   *Private collection*

148 A rare Chinese mug made for the Scottish market depicting the Young Pretender, Prince Charles Edward Stuart. 6 inches high, c. 1750.   *Private collection*

149 An amusing Chinese 'Arms of Liberty' teapot, depicting John Wilkes 'Always eeady in a good cause' and Lord Chief Justice Mansfield 'Uustice sans Pitie'. Note the Chinese misspelling, or incorrect copying, of the mottos. 5¼ inches high, c. 1765.　　　　　　　　　　　　　　　　*Private collection*

The special designs

150 A superb quality Chinese punch-bowl finely painted with a view of the London Hospital, c. 1750. *The Art Exchange, New York*

151 A magnificent Chinese punch-bowl meticulously painted with a view of the Mansion House, London (see also Plate 152). Diameter 15½ inches, c. 1798. *Christies, London*

152 Another view of the punch-bowl shown in Plate 151. This panel depicts the Ironmongers' Company Hall and the bowl was probably made for Sir Charles Price, master of the Ironmongers' Company in 1798. *Christies, London*

153 A magnificent Chinese Private Trade punch-bowl painted with a shipping scene. Diameter 11¾ inches, c. 1755–60.
Ionides Bequest, Victoria and Albert Museum (Crown Copyright)

154 A superb Chinese Private Trade punch-bowl, the exterior painted with European figures and children in landscape. The interior is here illustrated and is dated 1759. Diameter 15 inches.
Earle D. Vandekar, London

155 A typical Chinese export market punch-bowl painted with Masonic motifs, the base inscribed 'Brother Joseph Elliott'. Diameter 14¾ inches, *c.* 1770.   *Sotheby & Co., London*

mythological subjects (Plate 142), the original designs being no doubt copied from European prints, although much of the original effect is missing from later examples. Other 'pencilled' designs are difficult to attribute, if indeed they had any definite source. Yet all these examples have a certain charm, as is evidenced by the cup and saucer shown in Plate 143. These two related pieces from the same tea-service also serve to illustrate a slight defect of these porcelains – the colour can be of uneven intensity, as is shown here by the dark saucer and the lighter coloured designs on the cup.

These sombre porcelains were certainly popular. Even now they are not particularly rare and, more important, the style was copied by English porcelain manufactories, notably by the Worcester factory. Of course the emulation of line-engraving on ceramics of various types has long been popular and is by no means confined to the Chinese export market porcelains discussed in this work.

Many of the mythological designs were painted in full colour, instead of in the black Jesuit manner. A typical Judgement of Paris plate is shown in Plate 144. The shell and scroll motif can be approximately dated to the 1750–55 period by reference to datable armorial examples bearing a similar border design. This plate moves our study forward from the black-pencilled porcelains to a great variety of special designs – unique patterns, sometimes made to the special order of Europeans, and shipped home as permitted Private Trade (see Chapter 2).

One of the earliest and finest quality designs showing European figures is shown in Colour Plate 15. The tea-bowl and saucer are of almost egg-shell thinness, while the cup is thickly potted – a common occurrence with such 'trios' (I have explained the reason for this on p. 175). These delightful and finely painted teawares depicting European figures (probably Dutch or Portuguese) with elephants certainly pre-date 1750.

The special designs

156 A very fine Chinese punch-bowl painted with a European hunting scene. Diameter 19¾ inches, c. 1770.
Sotheby & Co., London

The special designs

157 A well-painted Chinese punch-bowl painted with panels of European hunting scenes. An erotic painting appears under the base. Diameter 11 inches, c. 1770.   *Sotheby & Co., London*

The special designs

158 The exterior and interior enamelled decoration on a typical Chinese export market hunting subject punch-bowl. Diameter 16 inches, c. 1770. *Earle D. Vandekar, London*

A further class of early Chinese export market porcelain is decorated in the style of the German Meissen factory depicting harbour scenes in a shaped-edged panel. This style appears to have remained in favour for some twenty-five years, from about 1740. The quality of the painting varies from the superb to the hasty. Typical specimens are shown in Plates 145–146.

There are some rare portrait pieces with a political significance and presumably only saleable for a limited period during the popularity of the cause, or while the event was still topical. Such a piece, a fine tankard, is shown in Plate 147. It was obviously made after the Battle of Culloden (16 April 1746) but it surely cannot be dated long after 1750. The tankard shown in Plate 148 is also of the same period, but made for the other side. It depicts the Young Pretender, Prince Charles Edward Stuart, who was defeated at Culloden. This Scottish market piece reminds us that much armorial and other Private Trade Chinese porcelain was ordered by Scottish families.

I find it remarkable that such pieces had to be made in China and that British porcelain manufacturers did not, or could not, make such commemorative wares. In this trade the first to get his wares on the market would capture it, and the placing of the order in China must have involved a wait of three or more years after the design was shipped out. Another rather more common political design is represented by the 'Wilkes and Liberty' teapot (Plate 149).

There is almost no end to the different types of decoration to be found painted on Chinese export market porcelain. It is impossible to illustrate or list all the diverse Private Trade special decorations, although many of the designs are illustrated in this book. While the designs were painted on standard forms, and on some very rare shapes, most will be found on articles suitable to be

Oriental export market porcelain

159 A very finely enamelled and attractive Chinese punch-bowl. The borders are painted in the overglaze blue and gold associated with the 1790s. Diameter 16 inches.
The Art Exchange, New York

160 A fine Chinese Private Trade punch bowl decorated with the arms of Moffat. This bowl was probably made for Captain Moffat of the East Indiaman, *Latham*. His father was a director of the East India Company. Diameter 15⅜ inches, *c.* 1765.
Sotheby & Co., London

161 A fine Chinese shipping punch-bowl depicting the East Indiaman, *Latham*, and inscribed 'Ship Latham bound to Bombay and China', 'Ship Latham at Whampoe', 'Ship Latham towards old England'. Diameter 15¼ inches, *c.* 1765.
Sotheby Parke Bernet Inc., New York

The special designs

162 A Chinese biscuit (unglazed) figure of the Goddess Kuan-yin seated on an ornate base and decorated in *famille verte* type semi-translucent coloured glazes. 11¼ inches high, *c.* 1710.
Sotheby & Co., London

163 A pair of Chinese biscuit figures of the twins – Mirth and Harmony – decorated in semi-translucent coloured glazes in the general *famille verte* manner. 8½ inches high, *c.* 1720
Sotheby & Co., London

164 A pair of early-eighteenth-century Chinese porcelain models of Jesters adapted for use as joss-stick holders. Perhaps such figures are the 'men on horses' listed in the London sale catalogues of newly-imported porcelains. $9\frac{1}{4}$ inches high, c. 1700–1740. *Sotheby & Co., London*

The special designs

165 A fine Chinese figure traditionally known as Louis XIV, decorated in *famille verte*-style semi-translucent coloured glazes. Although such models were originally made for the Continental market many were also imported by the English East India Company – mostly as Private Trade. 8⅞ inches high, c. 1700–1720.
Sotheby & Co., London

166 A fine model of the Taoist Goddess Tou Mu, here seen decorated in *famille rose*-type enamel colours but also found in *Blanc de Chine*. In this example several of the loose arms are missing. 13¾ inches high, c. 1740–50. *Godden of Worthing Ltd*

167 A fine and rare pair of flat-backed Chinese wall-figures, the vases hollowed to hold candles or joss-sticks. Many other similar Chinese figure models were made. 14 inches high, c. 1760.
Sotheby & Co., London

Colour Plate 13 An attractive Chinese mug with standard underglaze blue Fitzhugh-type borders (see p. 294). The overglaze enamelled crest would have been added at Canton to fulfil a Private Trade order. 8 inches high, c. 1785–95.
Godden of Worthing Ltd

168 A curious and extremely rare Chinese export market copy of a Chelsea or Derby scent-bottle. 3¾ inches high, c. 1760.
Sotheby & Co., London

169 A superb large Chinese model of an elephant with hollow body and an aperture in the back, perhaps for use as a flower-holder. 22¾ inches high, c. 1740–60. *Sotheby & Co., London*

brought home from China as presents. Mugs or tankards are likely gifts for a man, or a teapot or tea-service might be commissioned for a lady. But of all the single objects made for Private Trade buyers, none was as popular as the bowl. We tend to call any bowl with a diameter in excess of ten inches a punch-bowl, but from the ornate decoration to be found inside many of these magnificent articles it is likely that they often had a purely decorative use.

The large exterior surface area permitted the artist great scope and the following small selection of illustrations shows how well the artists used their curved 'canvas'. First there is the 15¾-inch bowl depicting the 'London Hospital' (Plate 150) and the later bowl showing superb views of the Mansion House and Ironmongers' Hall (Plates 151–152). Then the magnificent shipping bowl (Plate 153) from the Ionides collection, now on public display at the Victoria and Albert Museum. The bowl shown in Plate 154 illustrates my point that the internal decoration suggests a decorative rather than a utilitarian use for these bowls. The bowl illustrated as Plate 155 represents the many examples made with Masonic decoration.

As a class the bowls painted with European hunting scenes are outstanding and were made over a long period, from about 1750 onwards. In quality, and in the subject matter or the source of the design, they vary considerably but all are very collectable, and these at least were probably made as punch-bowls. I show a selection in Plates 156–159, ending with a handsome and unusual example which could be dated to the mid-1790s.

I have already pointed out that the punch-bowls painted with ships represent the ultimate in Private Trade special designs. I have previously shown an interesting dated shipping bowl in Plate 14, and here I illustrate two more good examples. First, in Plate 160, a rare bowl with the addition of the

245 The special designs

170 A fine pair of Chinese monkeys with brown bodies. The London sale records include very many references to monkey models in various sizes. $9\frac{1}{4}$ inches high, c. 1720–40.
Sotheby & Co., London

171 A fine Chinese model of a rabbit. 12 inches long, c. 1750–60.
The Art Exchange, New York

Colour Plate 14 A large Chinese dish painted in underglaze blue with biblical scene 'Mat 3.16'. A similar example is in the Victoria and Albert Museum. Diameter $17\frac{7}{8}$ inches, c. 1740.
D. Cowell, Brighton

172 An attractive pair of spaniels enamelled in a shade of red. Many different breeds of dogs were depicted in Chinese porcelain and these were made in various sizes, from some three inches high upwards. 6½ inches high, c. 1750–60.
Sotheby & Co., London

armorial bearings of Moffat. This bowl, with a diameter of 15¼ inches, was probably made for Captain James Moffat of the *Latham* in the 1763–7 period. The second bowl (Plate 161) depicts the same vessel and has inscribed above each of three scenes 'Ship Latham bound to Bombay and China', 'Ship Latham at Whampoe' and 'Ship Latham towards old England'. The interior of this fine bowl is painted with Neptune and Amphitrite in a chariot drawn by sea-horses. Not all shipping bowls were of this quality. Others were of a very commercial type painted with standard representations of unnamed vessels. Such examples were probably readily available in Canton and were sold to the crew members. They were not specially commissioned 'ship's portraits' for the captain's glorification.

Many other types of special designs found on Chinese export market porcelains are to be found elsewhere in this book. These were variously painted with European scenes, devices or figure subjects. The mention of figures brings me to consider, and illustrate, typical examples of an interesting class of Chinese porcelain figures, or 'images', as well as animals and bird models. These were almost certainly imported as Private Trade and can conveniently be discussed here, although the white undecorated examples in the *Blanc de Chine* manner are dealt with in the following chapter.

So private was the Private Trade in these models that there are few contemporary records concerning them. They are mentioned in the Company's buying orders only in a negative manner: 'buy no large pieces as jars, beakers or images etc, nor any such china ware, as it is not heavy enough for Kentlege.' (Instructions dated 18 December 1706.) However, many are mentioned in the auction sale records which, of course, included the Private Trade imports. Unfortunately, the records are so brief that it is extremely difficult to link the sale

The special designs

descriptions with surviving specimens with any degree of certainty. However, the auction sale records do enable us to gauge the general types being sold and they afford us a rough guide as to the period. Alas, we now have no positive way of telling if the models were Chinese or Japanese, or if they were of pottery, stoneware or porcelain. We may safely assume that most examples I have quoted are of porcelain, especially as on several occasions the orders stated that no stonewares were to be purchased since they did not sell to advantage.

The earliest Chinese ceramic figures to be considered here are those decorated in semi-translucent *famille verte* colours (see p. 172) on a biscuit (unglazed) body, although the colours themselves tend to form a glossy, glaze-like surface. The figure on an ornamental plinth illustrated in Plate 162 shows this type to good effect, and the unglazed, biscuit face is evident. The twins Mirth and Harmony (Plate 163) are of the same general type and period, *c.* 1700–20.

Chinese figures or 'Images' were certainly imported before this period. A sale held in June 1696 included '8 figures with riders; 40 Images largest; 60 do. middle size; 56 do. smallest', but we have no means of telling if these were white *Blanc de Chine* models (see Chapter 8) or coloured examples.

However, the sale records relating to the mass of Chinese and Japanese porcelains brought home from Amoy on the *Nassau* and sold in November 1699 do include references to *painted* animal and figure models:

24 Lyons painted
32 large Lyons gilded and painted
56 small Women painted
37 large Children do.
32 Sancta Maria's painted
21 Tartarian Women painted
 8 large Lions painted

173 A fine Chinese porcelain horse with a pink and white body. 10 inches long, *c.* 1740–50. *Christies, London*

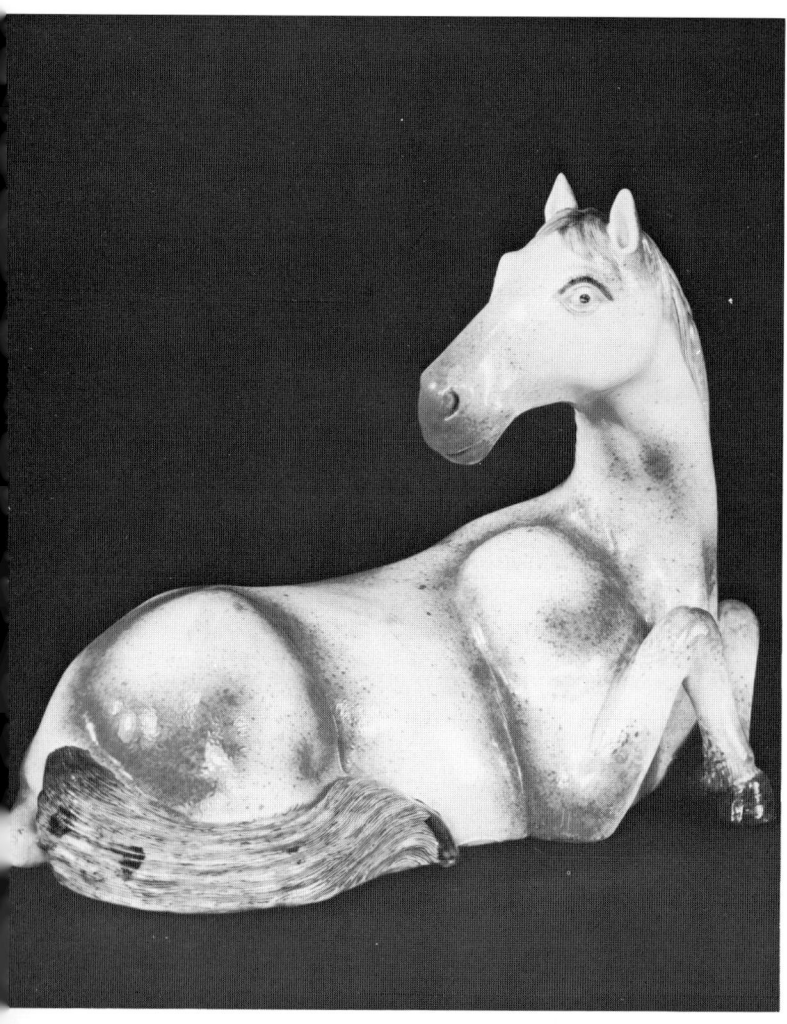

174 A rare pair of Chinese camels. The cargo of the *Fleet* sold in London in April 1704 included forty camels. 5½ inches high, *c.* 1705–20. *Earle D. Vandekar, London*

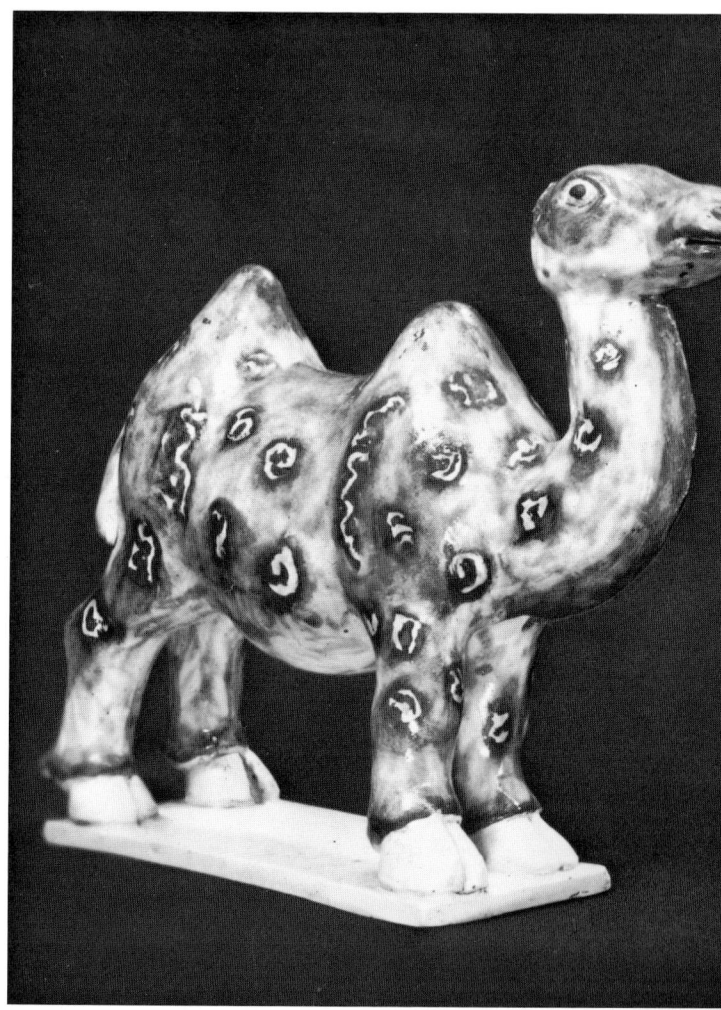

The special designs

175 A Chinese porcelain parrot with red markings, on a green rocky base. Hundreds of similar birds were imported into the British Isles in the eighteenth century but many later copies exist (see Plate 182). 8 inches high, c. 1750–60.

Godden of Worthing Ltd

176 A colourful pair of Chinese Cocks on rocky bases. This popular model was imported into Europe throughout the eighteenth century, and later reproductions abound. 9¾ inches high, c. 1740–60. *Sotheby & Co., London*

The special designs

177 A magnificent large two-piece Chinese goose tureen of the type originally made in pairs. 13½ inches high, mid-eighteenth century. *Sotheby & Co., London*

178 A rare Chinese two-piece tureen. Several different kinds of animal-head tureen forms were made as table novelties. 16½ inches high, mid-eighteenth century. *Sotheby & Co., London*

179 A pair of Chinese two-piece bird tureens of the type made in various novel forms. 8½ inches long, mid-eighteenth century. *Sotheby & Co., London*

180 A rare form of Chinese two-piece tureen. 5¾ inches high, c. 1750–60.   *Christies, London*
181 A Chinese two-piece tureen or covered box. Pairs of similar table novelties were much favoured by the English porcelain manufacturers, such as the Chelsea and Derby factories. 5¾ inches high, c. 1760.   *British Museum*

Could the 'Women with pedestalls' of the April 1702 sale catalogue be the model shown in Plate 162? This same 1702 sale included also 'Double Images' (or 'Men Double', to quote from an April 1703 sale catalogue). Can these be the twins depicted in Plate 163?

Many of these represented Oriental sages, gods or traditional Eastern figure models, and the many early-eighteenth-century sale records of 'Men on lions', 'Men on dragons', 'Men on stags', 'Men on monsters', 'Men on antelopes', 'Men on elephants' or 'Men on horses' would have been of the type shown in Plate 164.

Other rare figures depict various European figures such as the very good example shown in Plate 165. This model is traditionally known as Louis XIV but its identity is by no means certain. It nevertheless serves to make the point that many of these figure models were made originally for the Continental market rather than for English merchants – a point underlined by many of the English sale records which use descriptions such as 'Dutch men sitting', 'Dutch troopers' or 'Dutch families', but many of these are *Blanc de Chine* articles rather than painted porcelain.

In the East India Company sales between 1704 and 1707 we find lots such as:

2 large painted lions on stands [sold for £3 11s each]
648 monkeys, brown
755   ,,   smaller
191 parrots, green
 1 large bleu cat
15 smaller bleu cats
17 painted rocks with cocks
179 painted parrots
 8 large painted lions
 5 large painted women with odd hands
 2 large painted images
 1 painted women and children

However, in the absence of later sale catalogues we

The special designs

Colour Plate 15 A superbly potted and painted Chinese tea-bowl and saucer with handled coffee cup (see p. 175) depicting European figures with elephant. Diameter of saucer 4½ inches, c. 1745. *Godden of Worthing Ltd*

182 Early-twentieth-century Chinese porcelain figures and other wares as shown in a Liberty & Co. catalogue of the 1912 period. Such reproductions were often decorated in a *famille verte* palette of semi-translucent coloured glazes.

have no evidence of subsequent imports which, in view of the larger number of vessels engaged in the trade, should have been greater than these scanty early records suggest.

In the absence of later records I can illustrate only a short representative selection (Plates 166–176) of Chinese porcelain figure and animal models. In general these are of the period c. 1740–70. Perhaps the most curious is the little seated figure scent-bottle in the style of the Chelsea porcelain examples of the 1760s (Plate 168).

Apart from the numerous straightforward animal models, many forms were adapted into porcelain tureens or covered boxes for various uses. I illustrate in Plates 177–181 a small selection of these which were surely Private Trade imports. These novelties were seemingly very popular with Continental buyers.

Reproductions of the more popular traditional Chinese figure and animal models were made throughout the nineteenth century and even up to the present day. The Cocks (Plate 176) often date from late in period. By no means all articles of the type shown in Plates 162–176 are of eighteenth-century date. To underline the point I reproduce a sample page from a Liberty & Co. catalogue of c. 1912 (Plate 182). Moreover, Continental manufacturers such as Samson of Paris produced some excellent reproductions in the nineteenth century.

8 Blanc de Chine

To many collectors the most beautiful and satisfactory type of porcelain is the totally undecorated class which we call *Blanc de Chine*, borrowing the French nomenclature.

Blanc de Chine porcelains have been the subject of an excellent reference book, *Blanc de Chine* by P. J. Donnelly (London, 1969), and I do not propose here to retread the ground so well tilled by Mr Donnelly. Rather I wish to add to his researches by quoting interesting contemporary references from the English East India Company sale records of the early eighteenth century, source material which abounds with references to the standard types of *Blanc de Chine* figures and other wares imported into Europe at this period.

Blanc de Chine porcelains were not made at the ceramic centre of Ching-tê Chên, but at, or near, Tê-hua in the Province of Fukien. These Fukien porcelains are of variable quality and were produced over a long period. Many objects are superb in design, modelling and texture, depending for their beauty entirely on the undecorated porcelain body and glaze. The figure shown in Colour Plate 16, is, I suggest, a ceramic masterpiece of this kind. Other examples, such as the figure shown in Plate 187, are of a more commercial quality, imported into Europe at relatively little cost. These wares were, however, novel and apparently highly saleable. They were widely copied in Europe early in the eighteenth century. (See Chapter 11.)

Blanc de Chine wares were undoubtedly imported before the available sale records feature them. Some examples may have come into Britain from the Continent, for the white wares were also popular with the other European trading Companies. We find recorded in the April 1697 Inventory of Queen Mary II's former possessions at Kensington House: 'Two large white fine figures being women each with child.' This was a classic Fukien *Blanc de Chine* model, indeed, several were in this Royal

183 A typical *Blanc de Chine* figure of Kuan-yin, an exceedingly popular subject that appears in many variations and in various sizes. 16¼ inches high, *c.* 1720–40.

Godden of Worthing Ltd

collection. In the same source we find listed: 'Two elephants with women on them, in gold mantles.' These too are almost certainly *Blanc de Chine* pieces, for although I have written of this class as being undecorated, some examples bore originally gilt enrichments (see p. 270). These porcelains, formerly belonging to Queen Mary (d. 1694), may have been received as Royal gifts, and certainly Augustus the Strong, Elector of Saxony and King of Poland had much porcelain of this type in his collection, which was formed mainly in the early years of the eighteenth century.

The now internationally accepted term *Blanc de Chine* is a comparatively recent one and was not used at the time of importation, at least not in contemporary English records. Available records give only a brief description of the subject offered for sale, '36 Women with children' and the like, only occasionally adding the description 'white', as this fact was abundantly clear to the buyers at the sale. Nevertheless, I think there can be no doubt that the references I shall be quoting refer to white *Blanc de Chine* porcelain made at Tê-hua in Fukien.

This centre lies some seventy miles to the north of the port of Amoy, and it is significant that most of the English vessels mentioned in this chapter traded at that port. In general the ships' logs are unhelpful (except for pinpointing the port, or ports, at which the vessel traded). They give only basic records of the cargo, such as 'This day took on board 22 chests and 2 tubs of china ware', but in one important instance we find a reference to 'white images'. This reference is to be found in the log of the *Union* which left the Thames in March 1702 for Amoy, where she arrived in November 1703. On 23 December 1703 we find recorded: 'Took in 11 chests of china ware and 50 peculls of cowrys and 22 baskets of white images.' The *Union* arrived home in November 1704 and her china-ware was

Blanc de Chine

184 A typical *Blanc de Chine* figure of Kuan-yin, a popular model which often occurs in the British sale records early in the eighteenth century as 'Women with child' or 'Sancta Marias'. 18 inches high, *c.* 1700–1740. *Godden of Worthing Ltd*

sold by auction in March 1705 (see p. 276).

The Company's sale records, however, included figures of this type at an earlier date, in the last years of the seventeenth century. When referring to sale dates remember that the objects would have been made and shipped from China some two years before they were offered for sale in London. I must regretfully start on a hesitant note, for the early records comprise the briefest of descriptions. On 24 March 1692 the Company sold the following items from the *Rochester*: '14 images of lyons, 2 smaller, 1 women, 2 men, large', and in December 1696 (slightly before the 1697 Kensington House Inventory of Queen Mary's collection was made) the cargo of the *Dorothy* was offered for sale by the Company at its London House. The following were included: '194 images [valued at 2*s* 6*d* each], 40 images, largest, 60 images, middle size, 56 images, smallest, 8 figures with riders'. We can only suppose that these figures, sold in 1692 and in 1696, may have represented white *Blanc de Chine* porcelain figures, rather than stoneware or coloured porcelain types such as I have shown in Plates 162–168.

However, in a sale held on 7 and 8 November 1699 we are on firmer ground for fuller descriptions were given, and in several cases we can recognise models well known in *Blanc de Chine* porcelain. At this sale a large selection of Oriental porcelain was sold, both Chinese and Japanese specimens. These goods were from the *Nassau* and were brought home on her 1697–9 voyage to Amoy.

A general review of the china-ware cargo (over 242,000 objects) is given on p. 61. Amongst this large and varied selection imported from Amoy the following were listed. The first price given is the reserve or starting price per piece. The bracketed amount represents the selling price, so that with the first lot the buyer paid 7*s* 2*d* for each of seventy figures.

185 A rare variation of the standard version of the Chinese goddess figure here represented by Plate 184, but in this case the face, and particularly the child, exhibit European features. 15 inches high, *c*. 1700–1740. *P. J. Donnelly collection*

70 women with children valued at	5s	[Sold at 2s 2d advance]
71 ,, smaller	2s	[Sold at 2s 1d ,,]
39 large Sancta Maria's	4s	[Sold at 2s 2d ,,]
67 small ,, ,,	2s	
69 white Sancta Maria's	[no price given]	
37 large white lyons	5s ⎫	
36 middle size ,,	3s ⎬ [Sold at 1s 9d advance]
120 very small images	6d ⎭	
1,247 small white lyons	6d	
613 small white lyons or dogs	6d	
1,470 white chocolate cups	6d	
2,360 white square dram cups	1d	
477 white cans	9d	
255 white cans and mugs	9d	
497 white mugs	9d	

In addition several lots although not listed as white were undoubtedly so, since the following items are differentiated by the description 'painted', as in this case:

45 Tartarian women	2s
21 ,, ,, , painted	2s

In this class of probably white models we must include '82 English Ladyes' at 2s. Also, several seemingly *Blanc de Chine*-type figures and animals are described as gilded: '10 large lyons gilded 5s'. This gilding on *Blanc de Chine* figures was only lightly fired and was extremely prone to wear. Occasionally slight traces of old gilding, or even of paint, are found in protected crevices of figures or animals which otherwise are now white. Other entries are general and all-embracing: '760 women at 2s' or '210 images at 6d', '12 women with top-knots, 2s', 'Lyons in four sizes', 'cocks, elephants, griffins, horses with men'. I am sure these were of *Blanc de Chine* porcelain, and several similar objects occur in later sales in conjunction with known white Fukien wares.

In quoting here sample lots I have included the reserve or starting price and, in some cases, the

Blanc de Chine

186 A very rare *Blanc de Chine* version of the standard Kuan-yin model, here remodelled for the European market to depict Mary and the child Jesus. 19¼ inches high, early eighteenth century. *Victoria and Albert Museum (Crown Copyright)*

advance upon this basic price. I am unable to give the selling price in all cases as many of the items formed only part of a single mixed lot, perhaps comprising twenty figures and hundreds of plates or cups and saucers, so that the selling price of the lot bears little or no relation to the value of the figure models. However, the first quoted price – the official valuation, reserve or starting-price – gives us a guide to the size or importance of each model or object, for such valuations would have been constant, and arranged by one person, or committee, conversant with the market. These prices were probably also related to the cost price of the goods in China, plus transport, Customs duty, etc. It is unlikely that these, or any other commodity, would have been imported over a period if they were not sold at a good profit, and in October 1687 the Court of Directors had 'Resolved that ye china goods now to be sold be rated at 50 per cent upon ye invoice price'. If this resolution included all types of Chinese imports, and if the practice remained constant in later years, the original cost price would have been two-thirds of the price quoted here as the valuation or reserve.

There are many references to 'Sancta Marias', often with the description 'white' added. They were evidently the most popular model and it is reasonable to relate them to the figures which we now more correctly term Kuan-yin, the Chinese Goddess of Mercy, a selection of which is shown in Plates 183–188. It is understandable that when imported and sold in Europe they should have been given a European name adapting them to local interest. Although Father d'Entrecolles' published letters on Chinese porcelain were confined to those types made at Ching-tê Chên, Du Halde's writings, published in Paris and London in the 1730s, mention the white wares of Fukien and also the Chinese figures of Kuan-yin: '...they also make abundance of statues of Kuan-yin, a Goddess famous in China.

187 Another version of the popular Chinese goddess Kuan-yin, perhaps one of the '12 women with top-knots' valued at 2s each, and sold in London in November 1699 (see p. 260). 14¾ inches high, late seventeenth–early eighteenth century.

Godden of Worthing Ltd

She is represented holding a child in her arms...we may compare her to the antique statues of Venus and Diana, with this difference, that the statues of Kuan-yin are extremely modest.'

The Chinese potters made an abundance of Kuan-yin figures in various poses over a long period, but she was not always depicted holding a child, and in some cases the original catalogue descriptions differentiate between the two classes: '80 women, with 1 child each, 20 women, without child' (Sale, 20 October 1702).

With regard to the figures described in 1699 as 'English Ladyes', it would be safer to regard these as European-style ladies. We have no proof that they were English, although a standard model would probably be described as English in England and Dutch in Holland. What is interesting is that in the seventeenth century the Chinese potters of these *Blanc de Chine* figures were apparently making models expressly for the European market. The child in arms shown in Plate 185 is also very European in his hair style, and the whole composition of the model illustrated in Plate 186 is totally European.

Apart from three sizes of 'Sancta Marias', there were listed in this 1699 sale catalogue three sizes of 'white lyons', also 613 'small white lyons or dogs'. In the latter case we cannot be sure if the lot contained models of both lions and dogs or if the cataloguer was not sure what animals were represented. The latter is not surprising for here we almost certainly have another of the standard *Blanc de Chine* models – the lion on an oblong plinth which even today goes under various names. One can see from Plate 189 that these Chinese pieces are often so stylised as to defeat accurate description. As with other models made at Tê-hua, they relate to the Buddhist faith and are temple guardians originally made in pairs (the male has a ball by its front foot, the female a cub, although some so-called

188 Another standard version of the popular *Blanc de Chine* Kuan-yin model here adapted to form a joss-stick holder: the branch to the left of the principal figure is hollow. Such groups were much used in the Orient for private shrines and they proved very popular in Europe. Many slight variations occur and, as with all models, different qualities of finish, and of the porcelain, are to be found. 14½ inches high, c. 1720–40.
Godden of Worthing Ltd

pairs are of the same gender). Many examples have one or more hollow upright tubes, for incense or joss-sticks, added on the plinth (see Plate 189). The religious significance of these Buddhist lions was no doubt unknown to most Europeans. They were evidently very popular ornaments, the available records listing hundreds of examples in various sizes and at varying prices.

These white porcelains comprised useful, as well as purely ornamental, objects. Cups, cans (straight-sided cups) and mugs are listed in large numbers. The mugs shown in Plate 190 are of characteristic type.

Many returning East Indiamen did not include white *Blanc de Chine* porcelains in their china-ware cargo. For example, not one figure was included amongst the 321,360 items brought home on the *Wentworth* and sold in November 1701.

On the other hand, the Chinese and Japanese porcelains brought home from Amoy on the *Dorrill* – amounting to over 253,348 pieces and sold in April 1702 – did include some figures which, although not described in the brief records as white, were almost certainly of the type we now call *Blanc de Chine*. Here we find the standard 'Sancta Marias' or Kuan-yin, as well as some new models:

30 Sancta Marias	4s	Sold at 6s 3d advance
22 ,, ,,	1s	
14 women each with a child	8s	Sold at 5s advance
10 ,, ,, ,, ,, ,,	4s	
18 ,, ,, ,, ,, ,,	2s 6d	
46 buffelloes with men	2s	
34 double images	1s	
359 small images	3d	
450 lyons	4d	Sold for 1s 0¼d each
760 lyons	2d	
80 rocks	6d	
17 ,,	3d	
4,200 white chocolate cups	2d	

A series of fifty-nine women and pedestals valued at

189 A *Blanc de Chine* male lion, or temple guardian mounted on a simple plinth, with the incense tube added. Pairs of these traditional Buddhist emblems were imported into Europe in large numbers. 13½ inches high, c. 1710–20.

Godden of Worthing Ltd

the high price of £1 5s 0d each and sold at between £1 18s 6d and £1 8s 6d each may have been decorated examples rather than white.

The English East India Company also imported metal (brass or bronze) figures. Amidst the mixed cargo brought home on the *Dashwood* and sold on 23 March 1703, we find listed:

35 cranes, brass 4s	
7 cripples, ,, [undoubtedly the immortal Li T'ieh-Kuai, the lame beggar]	Sold at 8s 1d each
5 lyons, ,,	
1 hawke, ,,	

The following lot may also have been of brass although this is not stated:

29 buffeloes with riders	
16 bucks with riders	Sold at 9s 1d each
1 toad with rider	

This sale, which commenced 23 March 1703, included an assortment of china-ware credited to the *Dashwood*. The *Dashwood* sailed for Amoy under Captain Marmaduke Rawdon in 1700. Captain Rawdon acted as second Supra-cargo under George Pettry, with Abraham Wilmer acting as third Supra-cargo. This vessel arrived home in September 1702. By February 1703 the owners of the *Dashwood*, the Supra-cargoes and the crew were requesting delivery of their own china-ware and on 12 March 1703 the directors minuted the following resolution: 'Resolved that none of the china ware by the *Northumberland* and *Dashwood* be put up at the next sale, except only the Private Trade.'

If this resolution was acted upon, and if it meant what it appears to mean, then the goods sold from the *Dashwood* in the sale which commenced on 23 March and continued until 2 April 1703 comprised Private Trade goods only – not the Company's

Blanc de Chine

190 Three typical *Blanc de Chine* mugs of the type that were imported into Europe in quantity early in the eighteenth century. 5½ and 4¾ inches high. *British Museum*

191 A selection of *Blanc de Chine* handleless cups showing some of the basic types that were imported into Europe in vast quantities in the first quarter of the eighteenth century. They remained popular over a long period and were copied at several European factories, including Chelsea and Bow. 2¾ to 3 inches high, c. 1700–1725. *P. J. Donnelly collection*

Oriental export market porcelain

192 A typical *Blanc de Chine* group depicting European figures. Such models are listed in the British sale records from 1703 as 'Dutch Families' and then valued at 3s, 2s 6d or 1s 6d each. 6¼ inches high, c. 1700–1710.
Sotheby & Co., London

193 A slightly different version of the standard Dutch Family group seen with portions of the seemingly unfired painting which sometimes adorned (or spoilt) these *Blanc de Chine* models (see p. 270). 6¼ inches high, c. 1700–1710.
Sotheby & Co., London

standard imports (see p. 66). The china-ware figures and animals credited to this one vessel, which would have been loaded at Amoy in the winter of 1701, included:

Women with children, several valued from 2s 6d to 3d each.

7 Rocks with men and beasts	3s
4 Dutch familyes	3s
41 Dutch familyes	1s 6d
14 Dutch tropers	2s 6d
110 Dutch men	2d
7 Pulpits and padries	1s 6d
258 Pulpits with padries	1s
5 Women on fountains	1s
76 Wrestlers	8d
160 Wrestlers	6d
94 Wrestlers	3d
100 Whistlers	3d
37 Sancta Marias	6d
140 Sancta Marias	4d
200 Devils	2d
230 White women	2d
70 Men, double	[no value given]
11 Soldiers	4d
2 Men on monsters	2s 6d
2 Men on horses	2s
30 Men on antelopes	1s 6d
20 Men on dolphins	1s
36 Men on lyons	6d
230 Men on goats	[no value given]
22 Men on dragons	3d
10 Men on birds	3d
50 Images with cocks	3d
2,240 Men on lyons	[no value given]
780 Men on dogs	2d
60 Men on dogs	1½d
36 Men on horses	1½d
200 Men on beasts	1d
113 Men with whistles	[no value given]
13 Men on stags	[no value given]

Not all the figures listed for sale from the *Dashwood* were in undecorated white porcelain, for

194 A *Blanc de Chine* European figure, one perhaps related to the 1703 sale description 'Dutch Troper' and then valued at 2s 6d each. 12½ inches high, c. 1700–1710. *British Museum*

we find lots such as:

21 Dutch familyes	2s 6d
29 White ,,	—

We can therefore deduce that these well-known *Blanc de Chine* groups (Plates 192–193) were also imported in the painted state.

An amazing range of animal models was imported on this vessel from Amoy and at generally low valuations, or starting prices:

144 Parrots	2s
2 Pheasants	2s
20 Parrots	3d
18 Crabs	1s
8 Partridges	1s
8 Cranes with candlesticks	1s
340 Rabbits on stands	[no value given]
140 Goats	[no value given]
20 Geese	8d
40 Griffins	8d
12 Horses	8d
33 Lyons	8d
9 Lyons in their dens	[no value given]
2 Bulls	6d
5 Dogs	6d
43 Swans	6d
20 Tigers	6d
5 Toads	4d
60 Cocks	4d
7 Rabbits	4d
90 Buffeloes	4d
20 Dragons	3d
8 Fishes	3d
20 Eagles	3d
113 Parrots	3d
556 White dogs	2d
63 Fishes	2d
490 Dogs	1d
250 White birds	1d
780 White lions	1d

195 An enamelled version of the 'Dutch Troper' seen in its white state in Plate 194, and seemingly produced from the same mould. 12½ inches high, c. 1700–1710.
Victoria and Albert Museum (Crown Copyright)

2,300 White dogs	1d
1,786 Beasts	1d
160 Crabs	1d
116 Camells	[no value given]
290 Sea dragons	[no value given]

Also listed are:

1 Junk	2s
52 White rocks	3d
3,693 Pipes	2d
40 Pipes	1d
140 White salts	2d
7 White bottles	$\frac{1}{2}d$
5,400 Toyes	$\frac{1}{2}d$
10,800 Square toys	$\frac{1}{2}d$

as well as many 'Images', 'White josses', 'White cans', 'White mugs', and a mystery item which appears to read '2,150 Shocks crouching' (perhaps crouching cocks?). We also find included with other typical *Blanc de Chine* items such articles as 10,510 cups valued at 1d each. These could well be undecorated Fukien examples, such as those shown in Plate 191. These are to be found in a great variety of forms and were obviously imported in large quantities.

I have extracted from the sale records of the *Dashwood*'s cargo sample items which seem to relate to the subject of this section. Many items were duplicated many times, and most objects here listed separately formed part of large lots. I quote below, however, two complete lots – as offered:

300 Horsemen	2d	⎫
1,000 Women	–	⎬ Sold at 1$\frac{3}{8}d$ advance each
3,550 Dogs	–	
40 Horses	–	⎭

Blanc de Chine

8 Partridges	1s	
12 Horses	8d	
4 Cocks	6d	
179 Parrots	4d	
34 Dogs	4d	
324 Lyons	3d	
20 Parrots	3d	
32 Josses	3d	Sold at 3d advance each
100 Whistlers	3d	
63 Fishes	2d	
94 Horsemen	2d	
280 Men	2d	
307 Images	–	
75 Wrestlers	–	

The dashes given against several lots were probably intended as ditto marks but this intention is not crystal clear, although obviously the items had a value to which the bid advance had to be added. Much of the other china-ware credited to the *Dashwood*'s 1700–2 voyage to Amoy is listed as of Japanese origin.

While it must be admitted that few of the figures, groups and animals listed have the prefix 'white', I think readers familiar with the *Blanc de Chine* porcelains, or with P. J. Donnelly's book, will recognise many of the models and concede that most if not all the models I have listed belonged to this class.

In some cases there can be little or no doubt, and in examples such as the 'Dutch Familyes' we can gauge the basis of the contemporary valuation; obviously models listed at four pence or less must have been very small objects – little more than miniatures or 'toys'. The Dutch Family group is a well-known *Blanc de Chine* model. Donnelly describes it as the most widely distributed of the European figure models. A typical example is shown in Plate 192, but many minor variations occur. These groups are sometimes called 'Governor Duff', apparently because some writers

196 An ornate *Blanc de Chine* hunting group, perhaps linked with the 'Rocks with men and beasts' valued at 3s each in the English sale catalogue of April 1703 relating to articles loaded at Amoy in 1701. 7 inches high, c. 1700–1710.
Sotheby & Co., London

197 A *Blanc de Chine* pulpit linking with the many early-eighteenth-century sale records of 'Pulpits and Padries' or 'Pulpits with Padries' variously valued at 1s 6d or 1s each. $4\frac{3}{4}$ inches high, c. 1700–1710. *P. J. Donnelly collection*

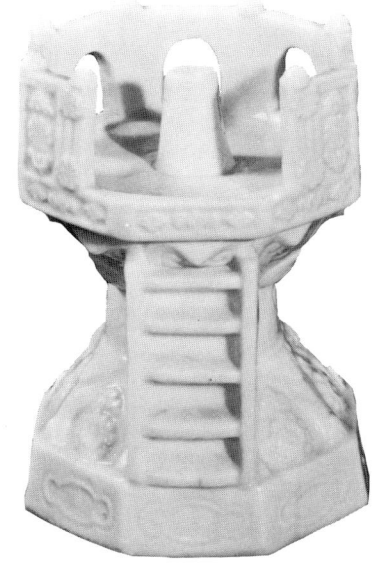

Oriental export market porcelain

198 Two *Blanc de Chine* figures perhaps linking with the 'men on horses' and 'men on monsters' at 2s and 2s 6d each as recorded in the English sale records. 11¼ inches high, c. 1700–1710.
Sotheby & Co., London

thought that they represented Governor 'Duff', as the Chinese called Diederik Duivver (or Duvivier), Governor of the Dutch East India Company during the 1729–31 period, but these sale records show clearly that the British were buying examples in Amoy in 1701 and that they were on sale in London in the spring of 1703. It is unlikely that they were portrait groups depicting any special individuals.

This one sale included 'Dutch Familyes' valued at three differing amounts, 3s, 2s 6d and 1s 6d. If we can deduce correctly from the two consecutive entries '21 Dutch Familyes 2s 6d, 29 white do.' that the first twenty-one were decorated, then we reopen the troublesome question of the source of the unfired colouring found on many figures and other wares of *Blanc de Chine* type. Today such colouring has become dull and dark and often remains only as patches in protected crevices (Plate 193). Donnelly writes of a Dutch family group 'treated in a range of garish colours resembling nothing that ever came out of China'. This may be true of the specimen which he had in mind, but the English East India Company was almost certainly selling coloured versions of this (and other 'painted' models) in the early 1700s. The Company would not have troubled to decorate these pieces before offering them to the trade, and certainly the trade buyers had not had the chance to embellish them. As the pigments are normally unfired it is unlikely that the original manufacturers of these figures decorated them. It is more likely that the colours were added at Amoy by (or for) the Chinese china-ware dealers while they were awaiting the seasonal arrival of European vessels. There is a slight possibility that the white figures could have been embellished by the ship's crew on the homeward voyage. However, most (but not necessarily all) of the stowed china would have been inaccessible below the upper main cargo. The catalogue entries seem to indicate strongly that the painted figures were so

decorated before they reached Europe – a statement which conflicts with the opinion of some earlier writers.

These groups of Europeans were called by the English Company 'Dutch Familyes' because the cataloguer was no doubt following the invoice description or the description given by the Supra-cargoes, the captain or other persons who had purchased the wares from the Chinese traders at Amoy. Such descriptions indicate that these models had been made for the Dutch at a period prior to the purchase by the English Supra-cargoes and ship's officers of the *Dashwood* in 1701. The fact that the goods made for one Company were readily purchased and sold by another underlines the point I made on p. 50, that the trade was international, and that the goods were so novel and saleable that foreign-market items were purchased without question.

The model described in the 1703 sale record as 'Dutch Troper' may be the one shown in Plate 194. This model certainly occurs in an enamelled version (Plate 195), but here the colours have been fired on and the decoration was evidently done at the place and time of manufacture. Two types of decoration therefore occur on Chinese Fukien porcelains: the fired enamels and the unfired painting. The '110 Dutch men' valued at 2*d* each were obviously not directly related to the big Troopers, for at this price they can only have been small, toy-like figures. Perhaps they were of the type which P. J. Donnelly calls Halberdier and illustrates as his Plate 117C.

The objects given the highest value by the London cataloguer, who perhaps had details of the original cost price, were the most expensive version of the 'Dutch Family' and the '7 Rocks with men and beasts' which were each valued at 3*s*. These rocks can almost certainly be linked with the elaborate hunting designs found in Fukien *Blanc de*

199 Two small *Blanc de Chine* figures perhaps of the type mentioned in the English sale records as 'men on beasts' and valued at a mere penny each. 4 and 3½ inches high, c. 1700–1710.
Blenheim Palace collection

200 A selection of small *Blanc de Chine* animal models such as were imported in large quantities and valued at prices down to a penny each. Maximum height 4¼ inches, c. 1700–1720.
P. J. Donnelly collection

Chine porcelain. A good example is shown in Plate 196, and another can be seen at Goodwood House in Sussex. Related articles but with the simple description 'Rocks' were valued at 2s 6d. Also on a lesser scale we find listed '52 white rocks' valued at 3d each.

Another interesting and identifiable item comprises the 'Pulpits and Padries' or 'Pulpits with Padries' valued at 1s 6d and 1s each. These have hitherto given much trouble, for only the bases – the pulpits – seem to be known today (Plate 197). While, as Donnelly states, 'its real purpose remains shrouded in mystery', these original catalogue entries show that a Padre or preacher originally accompanied the known bases (although the March 1705 sale includes examples both with and without the Padre). These figures had a hollow base to fit over the dowel-like projection in the centre of the pulpit. I regard these objects purely as novel curiosities of the period without any set purpose, although small hollow-based figures such as these were made in England in the nineteenth century to serve as candle-snuffers. Perhaps here we have the prototype. Two examples of the Pulpits are to be seen in the Salting collection at the Victoria and Albert Museum.

The cargo of the *Dashwood* included numerous men on various animals ranging in their valuation from '2 men on monsters' at 2s 6d and '2 men on horses' at 2s, down to '200 men on beasts', at 1d each. Obviously we are dealing here with different size models. The more expensive models were probably similar to those shown in Plate 198. Two smaller examples, some four inches high, are shown in Plate 199. Other little toy figures or whistles can be under two inches high.

The selection of animal models sold in this 1703 sale likewise varies in price, and presumably in size, from 2s to 1d a piece. Many of the listed models are featured by Donnelly, and some repre-

Blanc de Chine

201 A larger *Blanc de Chine* animal or fowl model of the type valued up to 2s in the English sale records or, in this case, 'White Cocks' at 1s 6d. Many different subjects were depicted and at that time they were both novel and inexpensive. 8 inches high, c. 1700–1725.
Private collection

sentative examples are shown here in Plates 200–201.

Donnelly also illustrates examples of pipes – perhaps similar to those offered as '3,693 pipes' at 2d. Also listed were white bottles valued at a mere halfpenny. At this low valuation we also find listed in 1703, '10,800 square toys'. These were probably the square-based *Blanc de Chine* seals, normally found surmounted by an animal figure. The 5,400 toys also valued at a halfpenny each were doubtless very small white porcelain animals and figure models, of the type shown by Donnelly in his Plates 62C, 68C and 120C. I have included in my list a 'Junk' valued at two shillings because such a model (in this cargo) would be likely to be in white Fukien porcelain. Donnelly illustrates as Plate 105A a boating party, and the intricate model shown in his Plate 118B could also depict a ceremonial junk carrying figures and horses, although it is described as a carriage.

A further selection from the *Dashwood* was sold in a sale commencing on 28 September. The selection appears to be only a clearing-up assortment but it includes:

130	Devils	2s
490	Small white dogs	1d
240	White cans	2d
2,335	White cups	1½d
1,902	,, saucers	1d
540	,, tea cups	1d
940	,, dram cups	½d

The 'Devils' have been listed in earlier sales and some *Blanc de Chine* models of Buddhist divinities, such as Ta-ko, could be so described by a European.

A sale which commenced on 6 April 1704 included goods from the *Hampshire* and the *Fleet*. The *Hampshire*'s assortment included:

1 Large rock at	10s
21 do. smaller at	2s

Sold at 2s 6d advance

202. A *Blanc de Chine* figure of the Taoist immortal Li T'ieh-kuai, probably one of the models simply described as 'cripples' in the November 1704 and June 1707 sale catalogues, and valued at 1s each. 7½ inches high, c. 1700–1720. *Mr and Mrs Cheng Te K'un*

and

123	Parrots at	½d
630	Dogs	–
13	Tygers	–
44	Elephants	–
290	Horses and cows	–

The large rock can be related to the '7 Rocks with men and beasts at 3s' in the March 1703 sale, but this one at ten shillings must have been a very grand affair – or perhaps even a coloured version of that shown in Plate 196. Nevertheless, we now have records of these at three valuations: 10s, 3s and 2s, plus the ones valued only in pence (p. 263).

From the *Fleet* we find offered for sale in April 1704 a selection including the following items of *Blanc de Chine* type. One single lot comprised:

1,146	Buffelloes	½d
1,350	Does	–
1,240	Birds	–
410	Fishes	–
140	Tortiose	–
460	Goats	–
40	Men	–
180	Rabbits	–
13	Boys on toads	–
120	Boys	–
100	Cats	–
200	Tygers	–
200	Monkeys	–
40	Camels	–

This one lot of 5,639 items was sold at 1¼d advance on the valuation or starting price of a halfpenny each. The price may seem extremely low. One could argue that, if the valuation were only the cost price (and it most probably included also a profit margin), then the selling price of 1¾d showed a very good percentage of profit since the complete lot cost the buyer £41 2s 4¾d against the Company's valuation of £11 14s 11½d.

The large number of items included in this one

Blanc de Chine

203 A *Blanc de Chine* figure of Hui-nêng perhaps one of the models simply described as 'old men' and valued at 1*d* each in the June 1707 sale. 4 inches high, *c.* 1705–10. *P. J. Donnelly collection*

lot reminds us that the sales were held mainly for the benefit of china dealers and that the selling prices quoted are the dealers' cost price; the items, before being sold individually or in small numbers to the public, may have passed through several hands before the final retail sale at an enhanced price.

Apart from the previously quoted large lot from the *Fleet*, there was:

2 China junks at	8*s*
38 Images	3*s* 6*d*
88 Parrots	2*s* 6*d*
20 Monkeys	2*s*
43 Lyons with men	2*s*
4 Ducks	6*d*
10 Men on lyons	4*d*
10 Men on elephants	4*d*
493 Buffelloes with boys	4*d*
729 Toyes	1*d*
28 Spoons	1*d*
1,360 Men with bottles	1*d*
376 Cammells with monkey	1*d*
610 Little old men	1*d*
200 Birds and beasts	$\frac{1}{2}d$
20 Lyons with men	[no value given]
1,110 Elephants	[,, ,, ,,]

Not all animal models were necessarily white, for in this sale there were 628 small brown monkeys at 6*d*, 179 Painted parrots at 2*s*, 10 large painted lyons at 15*s*, and 26 similar at 10*s*.

Most of the objects listed above from the *Fleet* on her 1702–1704 voyage are items which appear in earlier sales, but here china junks are valued at 8*s* rather than at 2*s* in the 1703 sale. Obviously these objects too were made in several sizes or styles. Spoons, here valued at a penny each, are one of the many *Blanc de Chine* articles illustrated in Donnelly's book, Plates 67B and 69D. Several *Blanc de Chine* figures would fit the description 'Little old men' although, at the value of one penny, the emphasis must surely be placed on the word 'little'. Apart from the 'toyes' valued at 1d each, other objects of this nature were imported in the *Fleet*. A Court Order of 17 March 1704 directed that thirty boxes of toys from this vessel should not be put up to sale but set aside till further order of the Court.

The china-ware from the East Indiaman *Union* was offered for sale in a series of auctions commencing on 27 March 1705. This vessel is of especial interest for its log contains an apparently unique reference to 'white images'. The *Union* left the Thames in March 1702, arriving at the Chinese Port of Amoy in November 1703. Under the date 23 December 1703 we find logged: 'Took in 11 chests of china ware and 50 peculls of cowrys and 22 baskets of white images.' The log – like others – also includes references to other goods, but they are described in the most general terms, normally as so many chests, baskets, tubs or bundles of china-ware. The *Union* arrived home in November 1704 and among the mixed selection of 199,987 pieces of Chinese or Japanese china-ware, the following were offered for sale:

2 Dutch Familyes	2s 6d
2 Dutch men	2s 6d
2 St Marias	4s 0d
26 ,, ,,	2s 0d
70 Dutch men siting	6d
65 Pulpits with Paderies	1s 0d
3 ,, without Paderies	6d
12 Men on monsters	2s 0d
2 Images	£1 5s 0d
12 ,,	3s 0d
60 ,,	1s 0d
53 ,,	6d
10 Figures on stands	2s 6d
7 ,, ,, ,,	2s 0d
3 ,, ,, ,,	1s 6d
21 Images	2d
250 ,,	1d
6 Rocks	5s 0d
14 Lyons	8s 0d
12 Birds	5d
2 Horses	6d
4,735 Small beasts	$\frac{1}{4}d$
4,260 Essence bottles	$\frac{1}{4}d$
1 Chest toyes	£1 [the chest sold for £1 6s 0d]
12 Incense pots	5s 0d

While we cannot be sure that all the items I have selected to list were of white *Blanc de Chine*, we do know from the log that the *Union* carried 'white images', and many of the objects have been previously listed, sometimes with the prefix or description 'white'. The 4,735 small beasts valued at $\frac{1}{4}d$ each must at this low value have been the small white toylike models, and the chests of toys probably held similar items. I have included the 4,260 essence bottles because their low valuation points strongly to their being undecorated white porcelain. I have also introduced at the end of the list one simple entry relating to incense-pots or censers, because these are often of Fukien white porcelain and they are listed in this sale in association with *Blanc de Chine* figure models. Donnelly illustrates several censers and devotes his Chapter 4 to a discussion of these Chinese religious vessels.

The March 1705 sale also includes a few items of *Blanc de Chine* type credited to various vessels. These items appear in very mixed lots and seem to be Private Trade goods. No new models are mentioned.

In the September 1705 sale we find one odd lot credited to the *Fleet*:

2,240 Lyons	$\frac{1}{2}d$	
118 Double josses	–	Sold at $\frac{5}{8}d$ advance,
310 Birds	–	or $1\frac{1}{8}d$ per piece.
35 Elephants	–	

also 4 Sancta Marias valued at 2s 6d each credited to the *Regard*.

The April 1706 sale included several lots comprising Private Trade. From the *Tavestock* we find listed:

4 Sancta Marias, white	1s 6d
6 Small white women	3d
4 White cocks	1s 6d (see Plate 201)
4 White josses	1s 0d
4 Birds with rocks	9d
2 White griffins	5s 0d
2 Horsemen	4s 0d
4 Small lyons	6d
6 White chocolate cups	4d
243 Toys	$\frac{1}{2}d$

In the September 1706 sale the following items of white useful wares were listed from the cargo of the *Chamber*.

13 White bottles	1s
100 White milk pots	9d
40 White can mugs	4d
17 White mugs	4d

In the same sale we find also, credited to the *Sidney*, 400 white milk pots valued at 9d and 177 white mugs valued at 4d each.

In the sale held in June 1707 there was one lot of seemingly Private Trade goods which included several figure models but it is not clear if these were white or all painted. Certainly the description 'painted' occurs against some models but even accepting this point we cannot now be sure if the decoration was unfired paint or whether the wares were decorated with fired enamels. These lots, from the *Somers*, were:

2 Large painted lyons	7s 0d
1 ,, ,, lyon, smaller	4s 0d
6 ,, ,, lyons ,,	1s 0d
4 Painted images	2s 0d
4 ,, ,, , smaller	1s 0d
2 ,, ,, ,,	6d
2 Women with children	1s 0d
3 Women with children, smaller	6d
3 Sancta Marias	1s 6d
2 Women sitting	6d
2 Josses	6d
2 Images on stands-broke	6d
2 Men on horses	1d
2 Cocks	4d
8 White toys	$\frac{1}{4}d$

In the same sale, but credited to the *Toddington*, further painted figures were catalogued:

2 Large painted images	16s 0d
1 Painted woman with children	2s 6d
2 Painted women with children, smaller	1s 0d

In the two lots, totalling 3,206 items, from the *Herne*, we find an interesting selection – again almost certainly Private Trade. The first lot is worthy of recording in full:

6 Large painted images	£1
16 Smaller painted images with children	7s
(9 do. broke)	
25 White and gold images with children	1s
17 Smaller white and gold images with children	1s
89 Women sitting	1s
14 Josses	1s
6 ,, , smaller	6d
18 Images on stands	2d
480 Toys, 4 sorts	$\frac{1}{2}d$
110 ,, , broken	—
1,840 China seals various sorts	$\frac{1}{8}d$

This lot was sold at $\frac{5}{8}d$ advance per piece.

The 1706 reference to white and gold images with children is interesting: for a long time controversy has surrounded the Kuan-yin type figures bearing now dark, unfired gilding (see p. 270). The china seals valued at a mere eighth of a penny were almost certainly of the kind illustrated by Donnelly in his Plate 67C.

204 A *Blanc de Chine* nest of three boxes probably linking with the November 1704 English sale record 'nests of white salt boxes, 3 in a nest'. 3¾ inches high, *c.* 1700–1720.

P. J. Donnelly collection

This June 1707 sale also included a small selection of seemingly Private Trade goods from the *Montague*, amounting to only 1,477 items, a very high proportion of which are extremely interesting articles of *Blanc de Chine* type:

2 Large white and gold images	£1 5s 0d	
1 Large white and gold image	£1 0s 0d	
13 Smaller white and gold images	6s 0d	
9 ,, ,, ,, ,, ,,	2s 6d	
16 ,, ,, ,, ,, ,,	1s 6d	
4 Sancta Marias	7s 0d	
8 ,, ,, , smaller	6s 0d	
31 White and gold Sancta Marias	2s 6d	
2 ,, ,, ,, ,, ,, , smaller	2s 0d	
17 Smaller white Sancta Marias	1s 0d	
26 Painted images	2s 0d	
70 Dutch familys	1s 0d	
2 Paderies and pulpits	1s 0d	
26 Images on stands	1s 0d	
2 Double images on pedestals	[no value given]	
2 Single ,, ,, ,,	2d	
9 Women and children	2s 6d	
8 ,, , smaller without children	2s 0d	
8 Harlots	2s 6d	
2 Cripples	1s 0d	
4 Old men	1s 0d	
2 ,, ,, , smaller	6d	
2 Women on lyons	2s 6d	
2 ,, ,, elephants	2s 6d	
4 ,, with rabbits	6d	
3 ,, smaller	3d	
4 Sancta Marias	7s 0d	
14 White and gold Sancta Marias, smaller	2s 6d	
17 White Sancta Marias, smaller	1s 0d	
4 Lyons on pedestals	6s 0d	
2 ,, , smaller	1s 0d	
3 Monsters – 2 sorts	2s 6d	
2 Parrots	2s 6d	
3 Parrots	2s 0d	
2 Lyons crouching	2s 0d	
1 Monster without a stand	1s 0d	
62 Lyons on pedestals	6d	
59 Horses	9d	
2 Buffeloes	6d	
4 Crabs	1s 0d	
2 Cranes with candlesticks	6d	
2 Cocks	[no value given]	
2 Toys	½d	
2 Cocks with whistles	¼d	

and in useful wares:

2 Incense pots	6s 0d
12 Nests white salt boxes, 3 in a nest	9d
1 White can	3d

Some of the very few non-*Blanc de Chine* articles that were included in this sale serve to relate the prices of white goods to presumably enamelled useful wares. We find Japanese teapots valued at

7s, seven times the value given to the Dutch Family group (Plate 192). Large teacups were valued at 7d more than the 'cranes with candlesticks' or the 'Lyons on pedestals' valued at 6d each.

In the selection of models from the *Montague*, loaded at Amoy in November 1704, there was an unusually large number of figures described as white and gold. There are some new models, or rather fresh descriptions: Harlots, a cripple (Plate 202), women with rabbits, cocks with whistles and the 'nests of white salt boxes, 3 in a nest' (Plate 204).

In the sale which commenced on 25 September 1707, we find credited to the *Loyal Cooke* some *Blanc de Chine* type goods amidst her mixed cargo of china-ware loaded at Amoy in January 1705:

3 Painted images	6d
30 White ,,	6d
36 ,, ,, , smaller	3d
1 Harlot	2s 6d
4 Large images	3s 0d
21 Images with children	2s 0d
12 ,, , smaller	1s 0d
15 White lyons	1s 0d

Also listed are several 'very small teapots' valued at 3d each which could have been of white Fukien porcelain. There were 80 small ink-bottles at $\frac{1}{4}d$ each and 460 smaller ink-bottles at $\frac{1}{8}d$ each, which on the evidence of the low price were almost certainly white. There is also a strange listing: '2 funnels' valued at 4d each. These may have been of *Blanc de Chine* porcelain.

Other small objects given very low valuations were sold in June 1708 and credited to the *Loyal Bliss*. The following items may have been in white Fukien porcelain:

4 Bird bottles	$\frac{1}{4}d$
1,277 Toys	$\frac{1}{4}d$
6,239 Essence bottles	$\frac{1}{8}d$

205 A small *Blanc de Chine* footed cup with relief floral design of a general type which, seemingly, was imported in large numbers, and which remained popular over a long period. The metal mounts on this example were added in Europe. $2\frac{3}{4}$ inches high, c. 1705–20.   *Godden of Worthing Ltd*

The available records are unhelpful in regard to what are perhaps the most plentiful examples of *Blanc de Chine* porcelain – the objects which are sometimes incorrectly called Libation cups, exemplified by the small cup of shaped oval form in Plate 205.

The records include items such as:

1,470 White chocolate cups	6d
4,200 White chocolate cups	2d
2,335 White cups	$1\frac{1}{2}d$
2,360 White square dram cups	1d
540 White teacups	1d
940 White dram cups	$\frac{1}{2}d$

but not in the quantity one would expect. Perhaps, as with some patently *Blanc de Chine* figure models, the obvious description 'white' was not written or printed in the official sale record and most white cups are hidden in the thousands of cups listed only as 'cups'. The 'boat cup with feet' offered in June 1707 seems to fit the general form of some *Blanc de Chine* cups, but the contemporary valuation of 9*d* each would have been extremely high for white cups, especially when we recall that the Dutch Family groups were valued at a mere 1*s* each. However, the available records do not list 'Libation cups' or any special cups such as wine cups. The tens of thousands of cups are described only as tea, chocolate, or coffee cups, or just as 'cups' with, in some cases, reference to shape, decoration or size. Certainly these white cups were imported over a long period – one is depicted in a Dutch oil painting of 1681.

Unfortunately the available auction sale records cease in 1708, except for catalogues of sales in 1722, but the later catalogues do not appear to include *Blanc de Chine* type porcelains. The *available* sale records relating to *Blanc de Chine* porcelains span approximately a ten-year period from the late 1690s. These porcelains were imported mainly from Amoy, with much Japanese porcelain (see Chapter 10), and it seems that the majority of the figure and animal models were imported as Private Trade. However, it appears, from one set of instructions given to the Supra-cargoes of the *Neptune* in December 1700, that not only did the Company wish figures to be purchased but they sent out on this vessel samples of 'Images'. The relevant instruction reads: '...when you have made what you think fitt of the samples of Flower potts, Images, etc, which you carry with you, leave them with or send them, to our Factory at Lingpo [Chusan] or Canton, or with any of our Factors where they are settled.'

The samples sent out on the *Neptune* were probably goods brought home by earlier vessels, perhaps as Private Trade, but they were articles which the directors regarded as profitable and worthy of import on the Company's account.

However, this 1700 instruction is somewhat of a freak. Most instructions refer only to tablewares, mainly cups and saucers, plates and dishes. Instructions given in 1705 and 1706 are quite definite and suggest that the Company was not at all interested in figures or ornamental wares of this kind: 'China ware, ten tons to consist of the ordinary cups and Table Plates and no other sort whatsoever.' (Supra-cargoes' instructions dated 28 November 1705.) '...buy no large pieces as Jars, beakers, Images etc. nor any such china ware, as it is not heavy enough for Kintlage.' (Supra-cargoes' instructions dated 18 December 1706.)

The available later instructions concerning the import of porcelain on the Company's account do not mention figures or ornamental wares. The *Blanc de Chine* porcelains were nevertheless imported over a lengthy period, although the more interesting figure models mostly seem to be confined to the 1690–1710 period, and I consider that they were mostly items of Private Trade. The popularity of the white Chinese figures is evidenced by the fact that in the 1750s the English porcelain factories were copying these wares, even white cups, into the 1760s.

9 The American market wares

Accounts of the North American trade with China usually start with the voyage of the first vessel from the newly formed United States to complete the round journey from America to Canton and back, the *Empress of China*, which left New York on 22 February 1784 but, of course, Chinese and other porcelains had been shipped into North America ports ever since it was first settled by the white man, or at least sizeable shipments were arriving from England throughout the eighteenth century and no doubt the Dutch East India Company shipped some to New Amsterdam. Pieces of late Ming blue and white porcelain have been found on the Pacific coast of the United States. These pieces may have originated from the Spanish galleon *San Agustín* wrecked in 1595, certainly they pre-date the settlement of this area.

In more recent times, when the English East India Company was shipping home great quantities of Chinese (and Japanese) porcelains and selling these in huge wholesale lots in their auction sales, much of this porcelain was resold in Britain but the few surviving records show that large amounts were exported, some to Holland, some to Ireland and much to the North American colonies. The will of a Long Island widow includes as early as 1696: 'Three East India cups, three East India dishes, three Cheenie pots, one Cheenie pot bound in silver and thirty nine pieces odd small china ware.' Several early-eighteenth-century American records also include mention of Chinese porcelain. Isaac Caillowell's 1718 effects included: 'Five china dishes, twelve china plates, 2 china muggs, a china teapott, two china bowls, 4 china cups and saucers and one china spoon dish' – articles which at this date can only have been of Chinese origin imported from Europe.

At later dates we find various newspaper advertisements relating to the sale of this Chinese or 'India' or 'Indian China Ware', as it was termed.

These references relate as we might expect, to imports from London. A typical example runs:

China Ware Sold

Lately imported for sale by Rebecca Kearny, in Front Street, [Philadelphia]...complete and neat table [dinner] and tea-table set of India China Ware, with other large assortments of said ware consisting of burnt, enamelled and blue and white long table and pudding dishes of different sizes; table, soup, butter and bread and butter plates; sauce boats and tea pots, sugar dishes with covers; custard cups; tea cups and saucers; breakfast cups and saucers, chocolate cups and saucers, with or without handles; quart, three pint, two and three quart and gallon bowls...

Pennsylvania Packet, 3 August 1772

These goods may have been imported from London on the *Phoebe*, for the same paper of 18 May 1772 carries an advertisement of Joseph Stansbury: '...a large and general assortment of India china is by him daily expected in the *Phoebe*, from London. A small parcel of ornamental china for chimney pieces...' This last item reminds us that not only utilitarian objects were sent to the Colonies.

In July 1776 this same Philadelphia china dealer was 'selling off his large and elegant stock of china...' and if all these following goods were of Chinese origin, as well they might have been (certainly the 'Nanquin' or Nankin goods were Chinese), then his stock must have equalled in scope many a London china shop. The china goods included:

Nanquin and common dining table sets, complete
Rich enamelled tea table sets complete
Blue and white and rich enamelled bowls
Nanquin and common table and dessert plates
Rich enamelled table plates
Blue and white soup Turennes, two sizes
Blue and white and enamelled sauce Turennes, two sizes
Nanquin bottles and basins and chamberpots
Blue and white round dishes, very large
Blue and white oblong dishes in sizes
Enamelled round soup dishes, large
Blue and white pieces for desserts, in sets
Enamelled pickle shells and mustard pots
Blue and white and enamelled sauce boats in sizes
Blue and white butter tubs and mustard pots
Blue and white artichoke cups and spitting pots
Blue and white oval baking dishes and patty pans
Blue and white and enamelled mugs and jugs, several sizes
Blue and white and enamelled jars and beakers of all sizes

with several other articles which were probably of English manufacture.

Other American papers were regularly carrying reports of imports of presumably Chinese 'chinaware' via London. The *New York Gazette and Weekly Mercury* of 14 July 1777 printed the following: 'Chinaware just imported in the *Hannah* from London, a large and very general assortment among which are six complete blue and white table sets; bowls of all sizes, breakfast bowls and saucers, cups and saucers of different sizes and patterns.'

On 16 May 1785 the *Pennsylvania Packet* carried a report on the successful arrival of the American vessel *Empress of China* from Canton, a report which includes the following historic passage: 'As the ship has returned with a full cargo and of such articles as we generally import from Europe, a correspondent observes, that it presages a future happy period of our being able to dispense with that burdensome and unnecessary traffick, which heretofore we have carried on with Europe.'

At last the Americans were dispensing with the middle-men, and were seeking to trade directly with the Chinese, instead of with the dealers, wholesalers and shippers in London. However, prior to this period in the mid-1780s all Chinese porcelain had entered North America via Europe and mainly

The American market wares

from London and consequently the vast majority of the wares featured earlier in this book as the East India Company's imports were just as much 'American market' as 'English market'. This does not apply to most of the Private Trade porcelains, which were of a more individual nature, although there was nothing to stop an American order being transmitted to a ship's captain and shipped as Private Trade.

The American War of Independence was sparked off by the English Company's importation of Chinese teas, or rather by the English Government's tax on this commodity, which came from China on its 'flooring' of china-ware. American readers will be quite familiar with the Boston Tea Party and the events that preceded and succeeded the Party, but their knowledge was no doubt gleaned from their history books written from American source material. The records of the English East India Company contain some very interesting correspondence relating to this historic occasion and, as far as I have been able to ascertain, these English records have not previously been quoted. I propose therefore to take this opportunity to illustrate the events leading up to the Boston Tea Party as seen by the directors of the English Company.

The story starts in the late 1760s. The Company found itself in grave financial difficulties. They owed millions of pounds to the Government for duty on imported tea and other goods and, worse still, they had vast and costly cargoes of tea which they could not sell; they had glutted the market.

Not unreasonably, they sought to find new markets in an effort to turn surplus stock into much needed cash. This was not easy, for Europe was also well stocked with teas imported by the Dutch, the French and the Swedish East India Companies – teas which were cheaper than British imports, as their governments were not so tax-greedy.

The North American Colonies were deemed to be the market ripe for development by the Company, which now sought to export their tea direct, bypassing the middle-men. On 6 December 1769 the first tentative plans were laid. The official Minutes state: 'The following proposals on the part of the Company be offered to the consideration of the Lords of the Treasury...That the three pence in the pound duty laid upon tea in America be taken off without which the Company see no probability of finding a market for teas in America...'

The Government of the day, aided by the tea-dealers (the middle-men), did not support the request, and the duty remained.

The Minutes of 12 December 1770 record the arrival of a letter which in its modest way foresaw the troubles to come. The records state: 'Letter signed "A Briton" dated at Charlestown, South Carolina, the 25th October last [1770] representing the great detriment that will accrue to the Company unless the Duties laid on the importation of tea in America are taken off.' The situation was in fact well known to the Company, and on 14 January 1773 they once again solicited the Government to repeal the Townsend Act of 1767. This levied a mere three pence in the pound on teas imported into North America – against the shilling levied on the British tea drinker. On 18 January 1774 the Chairman and Deputy Chairman of the East India Company waited on Lord North regarding this tax but 'His Lordship did not give hopes that the three pence per pound duty on tea in America could be taken off.'

The Company in London was thus seeking to lift the taxes, although the Americans, not the Company, would have to pay it. In fact, the collection of the three pence tax was a question of principle only for George III and Lord North. The income was so small as to be laughable; most of the tea in America was smuggled in by the Dutch and other European maritime powers, and of course no tax was paid on this. In April 1773 the Government relented to some degree by allowing a full 'drawback' (or tax relief) of British import duty on teas re-exported to America, as previously the drawback had been three-fifths. This concession was, however, to result in the first of a series of misunderstandings for it was widely believed, even by the Company, that all tax on teas shipped to America had been lifted. In May 1773 the London tea-merchants asked the Company for clarification of the position before they bid for the teas offered at auction; the merchants wanted to know if the Company was about to ship tea in bulk to America on its own account. The Company gave the following non-committal reply: '...The Parliament having given liberty to the East India Company to export teas to the British plantations in America or to foreign parts free of all duties, the Court do not know how soon they may avail themselves of such permission.'

The next move came in June 1773 when various letters were received from tea merchants in America offering themselves as the Company's agents at the various ports. These agents even offered their own vessels to carry the tea. In August 1773 it was

resolved that the terms offered by the several merchants mentioned in the report be accepted and that the quantity of tea to be exported to equal the weight of 1,700 large chests of Bohea [black tea].

To Boston	300 chests
New York	600 chests
Philadelphia	600 chests
South Carolina	200 chests

The Committee had to refer the matter back to the Government but apparently they were enabled to go ahead for on 15 September 1773 the following fateful resolution was made: 'that the tea to be exported to America be shipped for the different colonies in the several proportions and consigned to the persons mentioned...' The three hundred cases for Boston were shipped in the *Beaver*, the *Dartmouth* and the *Eleanor*.

Nothing further is recorded in the Company records about this shipment for over three months and then, on 7 January 1774 we read:

The Deputy Chairman acquainted the Court that some alarming advices having been received from North America which gave room to apprehend that the landing and sales of tea which the Court had lately exported thither would be prevented...in such case it had appeared most expedient to order the teas which had been consigned to Boston, New York, Philadelphia and South Carolina to be sent to Halifax in Nova Scotia as the properest place for the sale and disposal thereof throughout America.

Resolved that – if the said teas shall be rejected in the several provinces to which they have been consigned...the same be ordered to Halifax. The secretary to sign the orders in the Court's name and to transmit the same forthwith to be dispatched according to Lord Dartmouth's permission by packet boat now under detention awaiting the orders from the Company...

Lord Dartmouth was Secretary of State for the American colonies, and by his orders the packet boat for America had been held back to take the Company's orders for withdrawing the tea vessels from the American ports to Canada. Neither the British Government nor the East India Company was seeking a conflict with the Americans. Unhappily red-tape in Boston complicated matters. The citizens of Boston, or at least the committee of patriots, had at first merely required that the teas be shipped back to England without any duty being payable, and this is what happened at the other ports, but at Boston the Customs forbade the ship to leave until the duty had been paid. From the Customs point of view the tea had arrived in the

The American market wares

206 A selection of late-eighteenth-century Chinese porcelain painted with vessels displaying the American flag. Blue enamel borders with gilt dots or stars. Helmet creamer 4½ inches high, c. 1795. *Reeves collection, Washington and Lee University*

harbour and the duty was due. It was stalemate.

By the time the orders were written to divert the cargo the Boston Tea Party had already occurred – three weeks previously. The directors in London did not hear of the event until 28 January 1774. On that day they received three letters from their agents in Boston – letters dated 2, 9 and 17 December; the last one, written the day after the Party, was the vital one. Here lies the crux of the problem – communications. Letters had to await the sailing of a boat, and the crossing took three weeks at least.

The teas sent to New York, Philadelphia and South Carolina caused relatively little trouble. The Americans refused to pay the British tax as they had no representation in the British Parliament and the vessels simply brought the teas back to this country.

Up to this point the damage was not irretrievable, that is, the East India Company and the British Government had not attempted to force the issue but now things went from bad to worse. The Company wanted redress for their loss at Boston and turned to the Government. The Minutes for 5 February 1774 state:

The Chairman acquainted the Court that he had waited on the Lords North and Dartmouth to the losses and disappointments which had attended the late exportation of teas to America and to request reparation for the damages which had been sustained by the Company...and finding their Lordships well inclined to give the Company every assistance that the nature of the case required they had there upon directed Mr Nuthall to prepare draughts of the proper memorials to the Lords of the Treasury and the Secretary of State for the American colonies...

The case was duly prepared and the Company's losses were calculated at £7,532 9*s* 3*d*. The efforts to recoup this modest loss must be the most expensive exercise in history.

First, the citizens of Boston were formally requested to repay the loss. On 21 July the agents in Boston wrote 'that the inhabitants did not at that time appear disposed to pay for the tea which was destroyed'. The Government's reply to this was to close the important port of Boston, paralysing the trade of the city. They sent men-of-war to ensure that no vessels entered or left the harbour. They also ordered the trial in England of American agitators. These were the sparks that set America alight, as other American ports and cities rallied to support Boston. They, in turn, replied by banning trade with England or sales of British goods. Feeling spread until the Declaration of War in 1775. The conflict ended with the Treaty of Paris in 1783 and the birth of a new nation – the United States of America.

In the following year, just a month after the Treaty was ratified, the first American vessel went to trade at Canton. The Americans went as individual trade adventurers, not as a unit of a great and cumbersome company, and in this way they reaped many of the benefits of free enterprise, although their vessels were far smaller (but also swifter) than those of European nations.

As I have previously stated, American writers tend to commence their story of the American–China trade with the voyage of the *Empress of China* (of only 360 tons burthen) which brought home 137 chests of china-ware (reported also as six tons of china-ware), mainly purchased from the Canton merchants, Synchong and Exchin, from whom the English Supra-cargoes had purchased most of their porcelains for many years, so that the main selection purchased by the Americans probably differed very little from that shipped to Europe, although some goods appear to have been decorated to the special orders of American families. The *Empress of China* sailed from New York on 22 February 1784 and arrived at Whampoa in

The American market wares

207 A rather coarsely painted Chinese mug enamelled with a representation of an American vessel. 5 inches high, *c*. 1790–1800. *Reeves collection, Washington and Lee University*
208 A Chinese bowl painted with a representation of the first New England vessel to trade with China, inscribed 'Ship Grand Turk at Canton, 1786'. *Courtesy Peabody Museum of Salem*

August 1784, arriving before most of the European vessels of that season. She also left earlier, having had a quick turn-round, for the log of the English East Indiaman, the *Ponsborne*, records 'American ship at 2nd bar on start of voyage home.' The *Empress of China* arrived back at New York on 11 May 1785 after a successful trip which prompted the quotation given on p. 282. A seemingly unique bowl marks this – or a later – trip of the *Empress of China*. The exterior bears simple conventional floral sprays and swags, but the interior is painted with an American vessel and is inscribed 'John Green, Empress of China, Commander'. This piece is in the New Jersey State Museum and is illustrated in *Antiques*, February 1975.

The English records suggest that the 'Country' ships from India also took advantage of the new trade with the now independent nation. The records include an extract from a letter from the Council in London to their President and Supra-cargoes in Canton. The letter is dated 24 February 1786: '...In your letter by the *Ponsborne* you acquainted us of a report that the *Pallas* country ship commanded by Captain John O'Donnel is to carry a cargo from Canton to America. The report was well founded as that vessel has since arrived in Maryland.' The *Pallas* arrived at Baltimore in August 1785, being reputedly the second vessel to arrive in America direct from Canton – slightly beaten into second place by the *Empress of China*. Yet this Indo-English 'Country' vessel carried among her china-ware a service decorated with the emblems of the Society of Cincinnati. This or a similar set has since become known as the George Washington service, the major part of it being displayed in the Capitol. The *Pallas* was chartered by the Supra-cargo of the small *Empress of China* to carry surplus cargo back to the new United States of America. This cargo included much utilitarian blue and white porcelain.

As the American trade became established the number of her vessels at Canton increased with, in July and August 1795, the arrival of the *Pigou*, the *Delaware* and the *Atlantic* from Philadelphia, the *Sampson* and the *William Howell* from New York, the *John Jay* from Rhode Island, and the *Harris* from Boston. Some instructions relating to the china-ware cargo of the *John Jay* from Providence, Rhode Island, have survived. She was to bring home: 'Dining setts of common blue and white china, setts of rather better quality, coffee cups and saucers, Tea setts, Pint and Quart bowls, Nankeen blue cups and saucers.'

Indeed, at this rather late period from the mid-1780s we have much more information about American purchases in Canton than about British buys. As I have shown on p. 48 the English East India Company decided to cease their bulk purchases of china-ware in December 1791 so that, after this period, we have no records from the English Company. In contrast, several letters or instructions addressed to or from American captains have been preserved and are quoted in American books such as Jean McClure Mudge's *Chinese Export Porcelain for the American Trade, 1785–1835* (University of Delaware Press, 1962). Some reports are of a very general nature, such as that of the captain of the *Grand Turk* from Salem reporting back in 1786: 'We are now taking a cargo for America on your account consisting of the following articles. China ware – table sets, tea and coffee ditto and cups and saucers the whole amounting to about $2,000...' This selection would have been of the ordinary standard types of Chinese export market porcelain available to all buyers in Canton, probably mostly blue and white.

Several lists of prices for standard goods at Canton in the mid-1790s are quoted. Table sets (dinner-services) of 172 pieces, ordinary blue and white, cost then a mere $22. 'First quality Nankeen stone' sets ranged from $80 to $100 (enamelled sets were from $150 to $200). There are many references in American records to sets of 'Nankeen stone', or to 'Nankin stone china'. In 1826 the *General Hamilton* carried home to America five boxes, each containing a dinner-service of 'Nankin stone china' of 209 pieces at $72 per set and one hundred boxes, each containing a set of 'blue and white china' of 157 pieces at $15·25 per set. As we know, the description 'Nankin' traditionally refers in Europe to Chinese blue and white porcelain shipped to Canton by way of Nankin, not made there, and in view of these American references it appears that the Nankin stone sets were somewhat superior in body or make, for they were more costly and warranted separate listing.

These standard Chinese porcelains must have flooded into North America. Jean McClure Mudge quotes a letter written in February 1820 which states: '...the porcelain of China, displaced the English ware hitherto in use and became exclusively employed by the higher and middle ranks; even the poorest families could boast at least a limited proportion of china ware...few young girls at the present day, enter into the marriage state without contributing their respective china ware tea setts...' However, this author states that the trade steadily declined in the 1830s, and that by 1841 it had been fairly well superseded by European wares. This is not surprising. The importation of Chinese porcelains into Europe had also decreased radically, and the European porcelains far exceeded in quality the heavy, coarsely decorated Chinese export wares. Fashionable and gay French and German porcelains ruled supreme, with fine quality English wares now being made at the Worcester factories, by Minton and Spode at Stoke and by a host of lesser-known manufacturers. America and other markets were now buying good quality light-weight English earthenwares with

The American market wares

209 A selection of Chinese porcelains enamelled with the Great Seal of the United States adopted in 1782. Blue enamel border with gold stars. Coffee pot 10 inches high.
Reeves collection, Washington and Lee University

Oriental export market porcelain

Colour Plate 16 A fine quality Fukien white porcelain figure in the *Blanc de Chine* style, depending for its beauty solely on the pleasing tone of the pure porcelain and the tranquil flowing lines of the model. These white wares were much copied by European porcelain manufacturers. $15\tfrac{3}{4}$ inches high, mid-eighteenth century.
Godden of Worthing Ltd

210 A selection of American market Chinese porcelains embellished with the American eagle device, a now rare but originally standard basic design often, as in these examples, incorporating the owner's initials, *c.* 1790–1800.
The Art Exchange, New York

211 A fine American-market dish from a Chinese porcelain dessert-service painted with the American Great Seal device and the standard Fitzhugh-type border design (see p. 294) here painted in orange. 11 × 8 inches, c. 1800.
Reeves collection, Washington and Lee University

212 A well-potted Chinese pierced covered bowl and stand painted in underglaze blue with the four floral groupings associated with the popular Fitzhugh design. Compare with Plate 211. Diameter of stand 10¼ inches, c. 1790.
Godden of Worthing Ltd

decorative and well-engraved designs in underglaze blue – often bearing special designs of American views.

By far the most important and interesting aspect of the American china trade in the 1780s and 1790s was the Private Trade requirements – the special orders. In 1786 the Philadelphia merchant, Benjamin Fuller, ordered the following goods to be brought home on the *Canton* for his wife: '...this china of the most fashionable kind and must have my coat armorial on each piece. The best Nankin china light blue and white except the coat of arms which must be of the colours here pictur'd – the crest and field to be a silver colour.'

Such an order would have been completed by the Canton merchants and decorators adding the Fuller arms to standard blanks with blue borders, perhaps 'Fitzhugh' (Plate 211) or other typical underglaze blue designs, added during manufacture at Ching-tê Chên. In 1790 an American noted, obviously referring to such a special order, 'If this article is to be ship'd orders ought to be given the first thing after your business with the Hong merchant is fixed – as the patterns are all painted after order and require three to four weeks to complete.' This must refer to the decoration of ready-made and available blanks; the time-factor rules out manufacture of the basic porcelain. Indeed a further American report makes the point clearly: 'The China ware is brought from the country plain and painted according to fancy in the city [Canton]; they make us pay double price when they [the Canton enamellers] put a cypher on it because they say it must go again into the kiln. They are great copyists and we have several sets of China to order with the family coat-of-arms.' So wrote Thomas Trowbridge of the *Neptune* from New Haven on her 1796 voyage to Canton; this vessel brought home 545 boxes of china-ware. Not all added Canton decoration was confined to armorial bearings;

The American market wares

213 A detail of an American-market Chinese porcelain saucer, the basic design taken from the New York State Arms, but the central cartouche containing only the owner's initials, c. 1800.
The Art Exchange, New York

214 A rare American-market Chinese porcelain tea-bowl and saucer decorated in sepia and gold. The central panel depicts a view of Mount Vernon, c. 1805–10. *The Art Exchange, New York*

much had merely a simple, and often mock, crest or initials (see p. 211), and others orders were individual in different respects. The following order placed by Samuel Fleming with the Captain of the *Jay* in 1788 appears to relate to Chinese porcelains decorated to match exactly existing curtains or perhaps chair coverings: 'purchase for me at Canton a complete set of table china with the dessert [service], white ground and violet coloured border, as per the small specimen of silk affixed with ware to border…' (*Antiques in Miniature* by Katherine Morrison McClinton, New York and London, 1970).

In June 1804 one of the leading Canton merchants advertised his services, especially directing himself to American buyers: 'Yam Shinqua, China ware merchant Canton, begs leave respectfully to inform American merchants, super cargoes and Captains, that he promises to be manufactured in the best possible manner all sorts of china ware with arms, cyphers and other decorations (if required) on the most reasonable terms.' However, some designs which we may consider special were apparently available in mass, for among the standard wares listed in the 'Price Current' notes of an anonymous American trader in 1797 we find 'Masonic bowls 1 to 1½ gallons $2 to $3, do. mugs, 3 in a set $1·75, do. pint mugs $20 per 100'. (Yes, they were quoted by the hundred!)

The main types of American Private Trade special commissions include porcelains bearing representations of American vessels, or at least of vessels flying the American flag for these seem to be standard designs adapted by the flag to suit the seamen of many nations. A selection of these designs on typical forms of the 1780s and 1790s are shown in Plates 206–207. The bowl (Plate 208) is particularly noteworthy for it bears a 'portrait' of an individual vessel and is inscribed inside 'Ship Grand Turk at Canton 1786', so marking the arrival

215 A nineteenth-century Chinese cup and saucer painted with an amusing representation of the signing of the Declaration of Independence. *The Art Exchange, New York*

of one of the earliest American traders.

A highly valued class of American trade Chinese porcelain bears the American eagle device (derived from the Great Seal of the United States, adopted in 1782) in various forms. A selection of these rare articles is shown in Plates 209–210. Obviously such wares postdate the mid-1780s. The European-shape dessert-service dish (Plate 211) bears a version of the popular American market Fitzhugh design in iron-red. This basic pattern occurs in underglaze blue and in other colours, sometimes without the usual ornate border (see Plate 212).

I have mentioned in Chapter 1 how this design, complete with the American eagle crest, can be found in Britain, as can many pieces of the standard Fitzhugh patterns. I have also mentioned how the Supporters of the Arms of New York State were adapted to uphold a cartouche of initials (Plate 213) or a spray of flowers.

Other rare porcelains bear full and detailed State and other arms, notably those of the Society of Cincinnati, which occur with the initials of individuals. One such set was ordered by Samuel Shaw, Supra-cargo of the *Empress of China*, who wrote from Canton on 20 December 1790: 'Accept, my dear friend, as a mark of my esteem and affec-

The American market wares

216 A rare nineteenth-century Chinese punch-bowl painted for the American market, showing 'The Surrender of Burgoyne', with the Great Seal of the United States above.
Herbert Schiffer Antiques Inc.

217 A typical nineteenth-century Chinese blue and white pitcher of the type called in America 'Canton'. The border is characteristic. 6¾ inches high, c. 1820. *Godden of Worthing Ltd*

tion, a tea set of porcelain, ornamented with the Cincinnati and your cypher…' This set contained two teapots and stands, a sugar bowl (with cover) and stand, waste-bowl and dish, milk-jug, six breakfast cups and saucers, also twelve afternoon teacups and saucers. Samuel Shaw himself ordered a dinner-service and one or more punch-bowls with the same complicated insignia, and with his own initials, 'S.S.' Such a bowl is in the Metropolitan Museum of Art, New York. Many excellent and typical examples of American market Chinese porcelains are included in the Reeves collection at Washington and Lee University, Lexington, Virginia. A good illustrated catalogue is available. Over three hundred specimens of American market Chinese porcelains are in the Diplomatic Reception Rooms of the Department of State in Washington, while there is the specialist Museum of the American China Trade at Milton, Massachusetts. For information on the Washington china-ware and the Milton Museum see *Arts of Asia*, May/June 1976.

Some tasteful American market porcelains bear simple scenes, such as the cup and saucer shown in Plate 214, with views of Mount Vernon painted in sepia and gold. Other rather late and coarsely painted wares bear representations of American historical events, such as the signing of the Declaration of Independence (Plate 215).

These are of course rare historical pieces whereas the great mass of Chinese porcelains imported into North America as well as into Europe were of an ordinary nature. First, we should consider the formal Fitzhugh designs which seem to have come into favour in the late 1780s or early 1790s, and continued into the early 1800s. The basic design, of which several variations occur, was normally painted in underglaze blue. The stand to the rare open-work covered bowl shown in Plate 212 illustrates the style well, but it is to be found on a host

218 A fine quality covered vase richly enamelled in the style called 'Canton' in Great Britain and 'Rose Medallion' in North America. The scenic panels are quite unusual in this class of floral or figure patterned wares. 15 inches high, c. 1805–15.
Godden of Worthing Ltd

of more ordinary objects. It can more rarely be found painted in other colours, such as green, iron-red or yellow. The design is seen again with a wider ornate border in the American market dish shown in Plate 211. Several services incorporate armorial bearings with this design, or within the ornate border so often associated with it. This border design was copied on much blue-printed English pottery and porcelain of the 1790–1810 period, a fact which underlines the general popularity of the style.

While the description 'Fitzhugh' (see p. 294) is known and understood by collectors and dealers on both sides of the Atlantic, other terms can cause confusion. I have already explained that in Europe 'Nankin' was used to describe any type of Chinese blue and white porcelain, as here used in a 1755 auction advertisment in the *Norwich Mercury* of 6 September 1755 '…Drinking mugs in sizes, both imaged, enamell'e and Nankeen…Row Waggons, imaged, enamell'd and Nankeen…' But in the United States the term is normally applied to a special class of late-eighteenth-century or early-nineteenth-century blue and white normally superior in quality to the Canton wares or pattern.

The wares described by North American collectors as 'Canton' are well described and illustrated by Hiram Tindall in the article 'The Canton Pattern' published in *Antiques*, August 1975. The mode of painting the outer border is characteristic of this class. After the white undecorated extreme edge there is a wide diapered band, followed by a series of short diagonal lines or dashes inside a scalloped line (Plate 217). There is sometimes an inner border before the main scenic design.

The principal 'Canton' pattern features a broadly painted willow pattern type design with a bridge in the foreground and an island to the left. No figures appear on the bridge.

The potting of these pieces is thick and often

The American market wares

219 A Chinese pillar candlestick, a covered box and a chamber candlestick with snuffer, decorated in the popular nineteenth-century style called 'Rose Medallion' by American collectors. 3½ inches high, c. 1840–50. *The Art Exchange, New York*

220 A very rare form of Chinese urn-shaped vase decorated in a very typical nineteenth-century style with a colourful 'Mandarin'-type figure design. 16 inches high, c. 1820–40.

Sotheby's, Belgravia

Colour Plate 17 A colourful Japanese covered vase decorated in underglaze blue and with overglaze enamels and gold and of the type called 'Imari'. 24 inches high, c. 1710–30.

Godden of Worthing Ltd

clumsy. These wares were no doubt made to a price, but they undoubtedly met a widespread need in America for durable useful porcelains. In period they range from about 1790 well into the nineteenth century. I have not observed this type of border on English blue and white porcelains and it seems likely that it was introduced after the English Company ceased its own bulk importation of Chinese blue and white, so that blue 'Canton' is mainly (but not exclusively) an American market class.

The colourful type of enamelled decoration which we in Europe call 'Canton', because it is associated with the enamellers working in Canton, is often termed in America 'Rose Medallion' or 'Mandarin' and, as I have just shown, the term 'Canton' is linked in America with a class of underglaze blue decoration. The colourful wares with enamel colours thickly applied over most of the surface are of nineteenth-century date. Some can be of the 1810–1820 period but much is later, approximating to our Victorian era. These once-despised wares are coming into favour; they are certainly gay, and several novel forms can be found in these late 'Canton' decorated porcelains. The fine urn-shaped vase shown in Plate 218 is of very good quality. A later article is the chamber candlestick and snuffer (Plate 219) decorated in typical style; other pieces are shown in Plates 109–111. The 'Rose' in the term 'Rose Medallion' relates more to the use of a rose-pink enamel than to the flower.

The very similar porcelains featuring panels or a background of figures are often called 'Mandarin'. A typical but rare urn-shaped vase is shown in Plate 220. Other examples have been illustrated as Plates 110–111. Some magnificent large punch-bowls bear these mandarin or Rose Medallion styles of decoration, also gay dessert and dinner-services and even toilet articles. The general style was made for over a hundred years, into the present

century, and some examples that bear red stencilled country-of-origin markings proclaim their late date. An article by Carl L. Crossman on these nineteenth-century American trade porcelains is contained in the October 1967 issue of *Antiques*. (This excellent American magazine has over the years published several important articles on this aspect of Chinese export market porcelain, and the names of the leading American dealers in these wares are to be found in its advertisements.)

10 The Japanese porcelains

Compared with our knowledge of Chinese porcelains very little is known about Japanese wares. Many collectors do not realise that the English East India Companies imported large quantities of Japanese porcelains, especially in the early part of the eighteenth century. The situation is not helped by unqualified statements even in recent books to the effect that, two years after the 1637 massacre of the Christians in Japan, the Dutch East India Company negotiated an agreement with the Japanese giving the Dutch exclusive trading-rights. These authors neglect to mention that the Dutch agreement was by no means water-tight. Indeed, the contemporary sale records of the original London East India Company show clearly the extent of British imports of Japanese porcelains. In the early eighteenth century some English vessels seem to have brought home more Japanese wares than Chinese.

In 1620 there were at Hirado, the main European trading base in Japan, no less than twelve English or Dutch trading vessels, that is to say more than were at Chinese ports in most years in the first half of the eighteenth century. English and Dutch trade with Japan had been preceded by Portuguese trade, and as early as 1583 the Portuguese had shipped Chinese porcelains from Macao to Japan.

Compared with the Chinese the Japanese were late in the field of porcelain manufacture. Authorities differ on the exact date of commencement of manufacture but in general they opt for a period within twenty years of 1600, one leading modern Japanese authority giving the date 1616. The various opinions, and a discussion of them, is contained in Soame Jenyns's scholarly book *Japanese Porcelain* (London, 1965). Decoration in overglaze enamel colours is believed to have been introduced in the early 1640s, and the earliest Japanese export porcelains to be recorded were gallipots made for the Dutch East India Company

Colour Plate 18   A typical Japanese large covered vase decorated in the 'Imari' palette with underglaze blue used in conjunction with overglaze enamel colours. The knob perhaps relates to the 'spire-head' examples sold in March 1705 (see p. 328). 29¼ inches high, *c*. 1710–30.

Godden of Worthing Ltd

for their Apothecary's shop in Batavia.

The English had established a Factory or trading station in Japan well before they began trading with the Chinese, but then abandoned it. A good contemporary account of the establishment of the British Factory in Japan is contained in *The Voyage of Captain John Saris to Japan 1613* (edited by Sir Ernest Satow, London, 1900). An English captain even claimed to have been instrumental in gaining access for the Dutch to Japan in 1609. Captain William Adams wrote in 1612: 'Could our English Merchants after settling in Japan, procure trade with the Chinese, then shall our Country not have need to send money out of England; for in Japan there is gold and silver in abundance. The Hollanders are now settled in Japan and I have got them that privelege which the Spaniards could never obtain in the fifty or sixty years since they first visited Japan.' It is interesting to note that the first recorded reference to the drink, tea, occurs in correspondence dated January 1615 between the English Company's agent in Hirado and his colleague in Macao requesting that a 'pot of the best chaw' be sent to Japan.

The link between Japan and China was a point of great interest to the British. The Company's records relate: 'In August 1614, the Company's factors in Japan commenced a negotiation for opening a trade into China, in which they employed as Agents two Chinese Merchants usually resident in Japan but trading periodically to their own Country…In this attempt the Japanese Factory expended large sums of the Company's money and presents to persons in power at the Chinese Court and in cash supplied to the intermediate Envoys…'

Although a previous report, dated 14 December 1614, had stated 'Japan itself affords no profitable exports except silver. All vendible commodities come out of China', the return cargo requested in 1615 included Japanese lacquer-ware such as 'rich escritoires and trunks'. The European goods wanted in Japan were reported as 'Drinking glasses of all sorts, bottles, cans, cups, trenchers, platters, beer glasses, salts, wine glasses, beakers gilt and looking glasses.' To this list we can add earthenware gallipots and other earthenwares. In September 1616 the British gave various gifts to the Emperor of Japan and to Court officials. Apart from looking-glasses we find listed: '6 Gallipots (2 flat, 6 bl pots, 2 high do., and 2 flat 2 bl pots). 2 Green jugs, 2 white jugs, 1 posset pot and 2 green porringers.'

These goods were shipped to Japan on the Company's vessel *Advice*; we can now only ponder or the source of these gallipots and other wares which could well have been English tin-glazed earthenware, or perhaps Dutch wares or even Rhineland stoneware. In 1616 two ship-loads of European gallipots had flooded the Japanese market, and Richard Cocks reported back to London that there were more than he could sell if he lived to be a hundred. In his diary, under the date 2 July 1616, he noted that he had unsuccessfully tried to sell twenty porringers at 6 mace each.

English stonewares were also in demand in Japan. The Minute of 14 November 1614 in the Company's records is of interest: 'and hearinge by Captaine Sairys [Saris] that stone potts are much requested there, it was held fitt to send some for a tryall, and therefore entreated Mr Middleton to take Captaine Sayris with him to the house in Southwarke[1] where they bee made or any other place where they can find them, to make choise of the fashions, and lett a chestfull be packt very saflie to be sent.'

[1] This Southwark potter could well have been Christian Wilhelm, see p. 339, one should note the wording 'in Southwarke where they bee made…', so we are not concerned with imported Continental goods.

Humble as these English stoneware pots and the earthenware gallipots may have been, these references show that the Anglo-Japanese trade was very much a two-way one.

Captain Saris, the agent in Hirado, reported at this early period: '…in the moneths of February and March, heere commeth three or foure Junckes from China, very richly ladden with silkes, raw and wrought, China casles, Purseline…as followeth – Purseline basons the peeces…very broad and fine…coarse Purseline…'

Our contemporary review of life and trade in Japan after Captain Saris had returned to London is continued by Richard Cocks. Richard Cocks's diary (edited by Edward Maunde Thompson and published in two volumes by the Hakluyt Society, London, in 1883) gives a very good account of his adventures as the Company's agent in Japan between 1615 and 1622. Although no mention is made at this early date of Japanese porcelain, only of lacquer-ware, we do find mention of seemingly Chinese porcelains being presented by the Dutch and English merchants to the Japanese. For example in 1621 the following were given as presents:

1 china bason, full ginger conserve
1 china bason, full nutmeg conserve
1 china bason, with pepper

Other presents included English or Dutch earthenware such as 'greate gallipottes', 'small gally pottes' and 'Dutch jugges' presented to the King's brother in August 1618.

These diary entries show the great concern and expense involved in trying to enter into trade with China by way of Japan. We learn also that prior to 1617 Japanese nationals had been to England. The troubles with the Dutch are continually mentioned and entries such as the following one of 24 February 1618 show that Japan at that early period was a centre of trade with both the Chinese and the Europeans: 'Many Chinas, Japons and Portingals and Spaniards came to visit me, knowing of my arrivall. It is said the Carrick [see p. 19] will not goe out this year for fear of the Hollanders.'

Unfortunately the English Company and its agents at Bantam did not then press the Japanese trade. The reports state that little profit was earned, British exports did not sell well and there were few goods to ship home. No vessel was sent to the British Factory at Hirado (or Firando as it appears in the old records) in the 1616–19 period, and in 1623 the Company's agents at Bantam sent the *Bull* to bring home the British personnel from their Japanese Factory. The letter to their chief Factor at Hirado, dated 22 May 1623, instructed him to deliver the Company's House into the King of Hirado's hands that he may appoint a person to keep it for the Company until they send to repossess the same. In the letter to the King the chief reason given for the withdrawal of the British was 'The small hope we have of procuring Trade into China to which our Honourable Company have directed their endeavours of great charge.'

Some forty years later, when the Japanese were producing their own porcelain, the agent at Bantam endeavoured to re-open the trade. In a letter dated 31 December 1664, he explained to the directors in London that rich presents would be needed to establish a trading-post in Japan: 'As for the presents they must be rich, as finest scarlets and other sorts of cloth, rich saddles and bridles – gilded or silvered, Barber's cases with instruments tipt with silver and some with tortoiseshell, fair large looking-glasses, gold lace…rich amber hafted knives large and small with other rich knives, branches of coral tipt and spangled with gold, rich sattins, some rich muskets and bandoleers, some fowling and birding pieces of the best, fine coat cloth and what else you shall please to think fit…'

However, these gifts were not sent or, if they

The Japanese porcelains

221 A typical early-eighteenth-century Japanese export market jug decorated in underglaze blue, in style and form very similar to some Continental and British tin-glazed earthenwares. 10½ inches high, c. 1700–1710.   *Godden of Worthing Ltd*

were, they did not succeed in opening the trade. The following account is extracted from the letter of the Company's agent in Bantam to the directors in London, dated 5 October 1674:

…Your ship…got safe to Japan, but were not admitted trade there, all the reason they gave was because the Queen of England is a Portuguese and a Roman Catholick. The people of Japan were very fond of our nation at their arrival wishing and hoping the Emperor would grant a settlement but the Dutch wrought so with the Chief Mandareen, that from Jeddo the chief place of the Emperor's abode it was concluded in the negative and being there refused they went with their ship and cargo to Macarow in China…

…Concerning the Dutch trade at Japan they are every year brought to stricter terms than other, the Japanners prohibited them [to bring or ship] goods thither which the Chinese may carry and they do not allow them near the same price for goods as they do the Chinese, which is thought to be done to weary them out of the Trade by degrees and not to forbid them at once. They have an old Prophecy that red-haired men – which they call all that have not black hair – will one time or other do their land an injury, and from thence also some think we were not admitted trade at Japan…

Various accounts apparently addressed to the Company's directors in London list articles wanted by the Japanese and those commodities available for export. These reports probably originated from a Dutch source or from persons having knowledge of the items in which the Dutch traded, and it is interesting to note that one undated seventeenth-century list includes, among the items required, 'Hollands earthenware'. Japanese porcelains often display a similarity to Dutch tin-glazed Delft wares and it was generally believed that Dutch potters were copying the imported Japanese porcelain. It now seems, however, that the Japanese were in some cases copying Dutch originals, or rather Dutch copies of earlier Japanese or Chinese designs. The Japanese blue and white porcelain jug shown in Plate 221 exhibits similarity with some Delft earthenware.

Under the heading 'Japan affords' the same undated seventeenth-century list includes: 'Uncoined or Schuyt silver in abundance, gold, divers sorts of curious wax work; curious refined copper, camphire, purceyleyn or china ware, yet not so good as that of China; curious silk coats, cotton and silk cushings or conssen of all colours, divers sorts of silk stuffs, wheat, rice.'

Just as the early British trade to Japan was carried out by way of Bantam, so the Dutch settlement at Batavia was their centre of the trade. The Dutch vessels from Holland did not themselves sail to Japan, only to the staging-post of Batavia. Batavia was a most important post, being 'Capital of all the Dutch factories and settlements in the East Indies'. The Chinese and Japanese junks delivered their china-wares direct to Batavia which served as a clearing-house and as the international market-place of the South Seas. This system suited the Dutch East India Company, which did not need to trade directly with Japan or China since the goods were brought to them.

In the seventeenth century most of the Japanese porcelains to reach Europe came via the Dutch station of Batavia. Many were regular trade shipments but other wares represented Private Trade of the Company and ships' officers, who purchased the Japanese porcelain in Batavia. The Dutch Company charged 50 per cent (or 40 per cent after 1718) on Private Trade, including porcelain shipped back to Holland from Batavia.

The Dutch Company also sent much Japanese and Chinese porcelain from Batavia to India and Ceylon as well as to Persia. Unless the British happened to be at war with Holland the English East Indiamen made good use of the Batavia facilities to repair storm damage and take in fresh water and food. Here, too, Japanese porcelains were available although, as we shall see, this was not the main source of supply. The Dutch at Batavia seem to have had some idea of the cargo carried by the various vessels which called there. Dr T. Volker, our authority on the Dutch records, notes: 'From the Batavia register itself it seems that the English did not favour porcelains very much [before 1682] for their return freights and when they took home porcelain from Bantam, it was usually in the shape of well-filled ginger jars and as private goods.'

The early Dutch trade in *Chinese* porcelain was by way of Formosa but in the 1655–6 season no porcelain was available there and in 1658 the Formosa trade ceased. The Dutch then turned to Japan to meet the deficit although these porcelains were dearer than those from China. The first important shipment of Japanese porcelain to the Dutch at Batavia arrived in December 1659, and it included wares painted in red and green for Arabia. Almost at once the Dutch were seeking special shapes and objects to suit the European market. In 1661 the Court of Directors in Amsterdam ordered models to be made and sent out to make the Japanese porcelain best desired and most in demand in Holland. However, Dr Volker shows that comparatively little Japanese porcelain was shipped to Holland by the Dutch Company in the twenty-three years, 1659–82. He estimates the total as some 190,000 pieces against some three million pieces of Chinese porcelain shipped home between 1602 and 1657.

While the Dutch were undoubtedly the main importers of Japanese porcelain (and probably the related earthenwares) into Europe in the seventeenth century, some of this found its way into Britain. The Japanese wares subsequently established a reputation that occasioned the English East India Company to seek its own share of the market by importing Japanese porcelains on its own account.

The Japanese porcelains

Apart from Batavia (a port not always open to the British vessels) Britain's main source of Japanese porcelain was China. From quite early in the history of Japanese porcelain a trade in ceramics as well as in other goods had been established between these two Oriental countries. The Dutch records give under 5 and 8 November 1658 the information that seven Chinese junks had sailed out of Nagasaki Bay for Amoy with 'much coarse Japanese porcelain in various assortments', to quote again from Volker, who adds: 'the odds are that this Japanese porcelain was intended for the overseas trade of the Chinese merchants...and not for the Chinese home trade', a view confirmed by the British records. Apart from the Japanese porcelains purchased by the British in China, some came via Formosa. The Dutch records quoted by Volker show that in 1676 the English vessel *Eagle* brought to Bantam Japanese porcelain from Formosa.

The directors of the Company appear to have had knowledge that Japanese goods were available in Chinese ports. In August 1677 they recorded, '...upon ye whole debate we do offer it as our opinion, that the trade of Amoy be settled as being very hopeful for obtaining Japan and other goods at the best rates...' Three years later, in August 1681, the directors gave definite instructions concerning the trade in Japanese goods from China. In a letter to their agents at Bantam they stated: 'The last ship you are to dispatch for this years business is the *Amoy Merchant*, Captain Nicholson, who by contract is to stay at Amoy until the return of the Junks from Japan, wherein we promise ourselves...we may have the opportunity and choice of all sorts of fresh goods from Japan to complete his loading.' The wording 'the return of the Junks from Japan' suggests that they were Chinese junks from Amoy, junks voyaging to Japan, rather than Japanese vessels bringing their goods to China, and the fact that the British directors were content to let their vessel await the arrival of these junks in order to get a good choice of merchandise, suggests that there was competition for these Japanese goods. The British here endeavoured to have first choice.

The April 1697 inventory of William III's and more especially the late Queen Mary's, collection of porcelains and other furnishings at Kensington House includes many objects that were almost certainly of Japanese origin and clearly shipped into England before the date of the inventory, although some pieces may have been brought over from Holland. These articles include several described variously as 'six squares' or 'eight square' – puzzling terms we shall read of again shortly when discussing the original sale records. However, after Queen Mary's death all the porcelains listed in the 1697 inventory were given to the Earl of Albemarle. The 1700 inventory therefore contains notes such as 'all this china delivered to ye Earl of Albemarles lodgeings by his Majesties command November ye 24th 1699'. The porcelains now in Kensington Palace should not be linked with the original 1697 inventory, although this dated document does show what was in the Royal Collection at that period.

I have previously referred to the trade of the original London Company, but the 'New' Company was also endeavouring to open up a trade direct with Japan. Their 'President' in China, Allen Catchpole (see p. 30), in a letter to his directors in London, dated Chusan, 19 November 1701, made the following observation, giving his sentiments on their intended trade with, or settlement in, Japan. He declares that 'he has no expectation that so cunning a people as the Chinese will assist them in effecting it – for the Chinese traders make great profits on the Japan goods which they sell to the English.'

222 The reverse of a typical eighteenth-century Japanese porcelain circular dish showing the marks caused by the small stilts on which it was supported during firing – marks also found on English porcelains from the Chelsea factory – c. 1720.
Godden of Worthing Ltd

Japanese porcelains were purchased (or bartered) at Canton as well as Amoy. The Journals of Edward Barlow list the cargo of his vessel in 1703: '...On Monday the first day of February we set sail from a place called Whampow in the river of Canton praying to God for a good passage to England, being a full ship and laden with goods, namely – 205 chests of China and Japan ware porcelain...and a great deal rare loose china and Japan earthenware...' This was no odd shipment, for the Supra-cargo of the *Kent* at Canton in the winter of 1704 recorded: 'Bought of the Chusan merchant and Leanqua Japan ware to the amount of 3,272 tale, 8 mace in truck for cloth at 1 tale per yard...Delivered in payment of Japan ware, cloth $3,272\frac{8}{10}$th yards at 1 tale – 3,272 tale, 8 mace' [approximately £1,091].

Some contemporary accounts show that Japanese porcelains were available and being sold in London early in the eighteenth century. The April 1709 account from Henry Tombes, the great London china dealer, lists goods supplied to the Duke of Bedford:

1 pair Japan jars	£4 0s 0d
1 Japan jar	£2 10s 0d
1 Japan jar	£2 10s 0d
12 white dishes	18s 0d
3 baskets	12s 0d
1 blue and white dish	6s 0d
2 Japan soup dishes	£2 3s 0d
2 bottles arrack and bottles	13s 6d
4 Japan basins and covers	£2 0s 0d
3 large Japan plates	13s 6d

The existence of at least six Japanese porcelain services decorated with armorial bearings points to the possibility that the Japanese potters were in contact with European agents, and that they would produce articles to special order – a fact also evidenced by the inscribed apothecary bottles etc, which must have been made and decorated to a set pattern.

Although there were several individual centres of porcelain manufacture in the Japanese islands the late-seventeenth- and early-eighteenth-century export market porcelains are very much of one type. In general, they are, in comparison with the Chinese examples, thickly potted and heavy and the body tends to be slightly grey. The underglaze blue is greyish or slaty in comparison with the rich, purer, Chinese blue, and the Japanese colour has a tendency to appear slightly granular. Plates and other flat objects, especially the large dishes, show the traces of the stilts on which the object was supported in the kiln; a typical example of this characteristic is shown in Plate 222. These stilt-marks, which also occur on English Chelsea porcelains, are not present under Chinese plates.

Seal marks in underglaze blue are not uncommon, especially on the blue decorated wares. A

The Japanese porcelains

223 An eight-sided Japanese porcelain bowl painted in underglaze blue, tilted to show the typical seal-mark quite commonly found on these export market porcelains. Diameter $4\frac{1}{4}$ inches, c. 1720+. *Godden of Worthing Ltd*

typical example is shown in Plate 223. The faceted shape of the bowl is more likely to be found in Japanese than Chinese porcelain and this basic form is also found in plates, dishes, teapots and other objects. Other typical Japanese shapes are shown in Plates 224–226, 228–229, 233–237. Most of the useful wares were decorated in underglaze blue, rather than with enamelled and gilt decoration.

Much Japanese porcelain is finished with a simple brown line edging the plate or other object (Plate 224). Chinese blue and white and other export market wares frequently display a lighter, often green, edging or finish, and the English copies of Japanese porcelains have the brown edge of the original.

Among the more colourful decorative pieces is the class known in Europe as 'Imari'. This is the name of the port from which the wares were believed to have been shipped, although Europeans did not trade directly from there. Porcelains purchased by the English were in the main transported by junks to the Chinese trading ports. The wares loosely called 'Imari' were chiefly made in or near the town of Arita, in the province of Hizen. The description 'Imari' has come to refer to a special style of decoration, in which underglaze blue (of the typical slaty hue) is used in conjunction with overglaze iron-red and green enamels and gilding. The overall effect is rich, although the painting is broad and normally only of a commercial quality, indeed they were probably made only for the export trade, not for the Japanese home market. However, these gay Imari designs must have had a great impact when they reached Europe in the late seventeenth century, particularly the great covered jars and beakers which were featured again and again in the sale records. Typical examples of these Imari-style jars are shown in Colour Plates 17 and 18 and in Plate 231.

The popularity of the Imari styles is evidenced by the fact that the Chinese potters made very close imitations, presumably to meet the growing demand of the European East India Companies. The designs were also copied by English porcelain manufacturers in the mid-eighteenth century and one typical design, the flower-pot pattern (see Plate 225 and p. 323), was a standard popular design of British manufacturers in the nineteenth century. Late in the nineteenth century, and in the present century, modern Japanese Imari-ware was flooding into Europe once again and in Plate 244 I reproduce wares as featured in one of Liberty's advertisements of the 1910 period. In England these colourful red, blue, green and gold designs are also called 'Japan' patterns. The Derby porcelains have featured these Japan patterns for nearly two hundred years, in fact to many collectors Japan patterns are synonymous with Derby.

224 A Japanese plate painted in underglaze blue showing the brown-line edge seen on so much Japanese export market porcelain. Diameter 9¾ inches, c. 1720–40.
Godden of Worthing Ltd

225 A typical Japanese export market barber's or shaving-bowl decorated in the Imari palette (see Colour Plates 17 and 18) with a rather rare version of the standard flower-pot design with face-handles (see p. 309). Diameter 10¾ inches, c. 1710–30.
Godden of Worthing Ltd

In complete contrast to the rather over-burdened export-market Imari style there is the restrained and often charming enamel patterns normally associated with the Kakiemon family of potters or porcelain painters, although there seems to be a lack of proof to support this attribution. Here we have pieces made to Japanese taste largely for the home market; typical examples are shown in Plates 226–227. Generally they are very similar to the Chinese *famille verte* porcelains and some of the typical Kakiemon designs were popular with English porcelain manufacturers (and presumably with the buying public) in the early 1750s. The dating of the Japanese originals is open to question, and my personal opinion is that most of these Japanese porcelains in the Kakiemon style do *not* pre-date 1700.

The sparsely decorated Kakiemon-type porcelains – I use the word 'type' as I do not consider that all such pieces were from the hand of one decorator, or even of one family – are rare in Europe, being vastly outnumbered by the gay, richly decorated Imari-style porcelains, where the pattern covers the greater part of the object. One can assume that most of the original purchasers of Japanese porcelain – the ships' captains or crew buying their Private Trade – preferred the decorative Imari designs to the barely decorated Kakiemon-style porcelains. Today, the collector or the student of ceramics tends to prefer the tasteful, simple pieces which show to such effect the white porcelain body that was the despair of the European potters who were striving to emulate it, or at least to dress their earthenware in a white coat to pass off as porcelain. I am writing of pieces such as the modest little saucer-dish or plate shown in Plate 226.

Just as the commercially-minded ships' captains and the Company's Supra-cargoes were concerned mainly with the richly decorated Imari-type

226 A Japanese porcelain saucer-dish enamelled in the typically restrained style associated with the Kakiemon family of potters and painters. Note typical brown-line edge (p. 309). Diameter 5½ inches, c. 1710–30. *Godden of Worthing Ltd*
227 A Japanese porcelain plate enamelled with a typical Kakiemon-style design. Such patterns were much copied in Europe, and English manufacturers were prone to add a more ornate border design. Diameter 10 inches, c. 1710–30.
Sotheby & Co., London

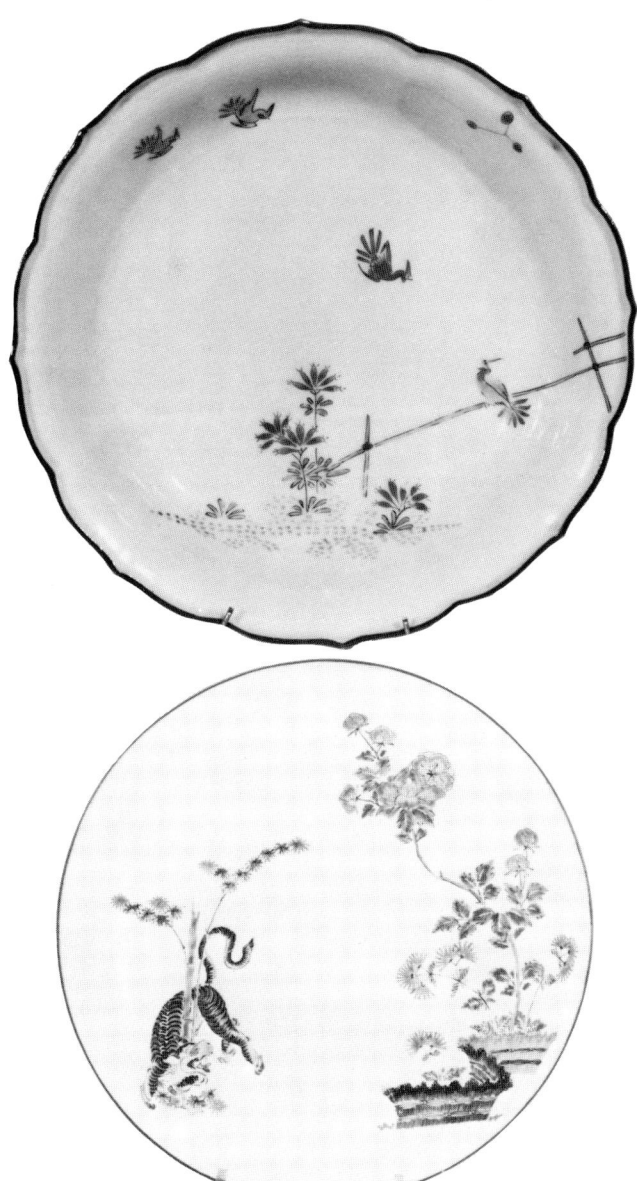

porcelains (wares that were made for the export market) rather than with the more refined Kakiemon-type designs, so there are other types of Japanese porcelains which are rarely seen in Europe, and which seem not to have been exported in the seventeenth and eighteenth centuries. Among these are the Nabeshima and the Ko-Kutani wares which are featured in Soame Jenyns's *Japanese Porcelain*, also in an article by Sir John Figgess in *Arts of Asia*, September–October 1975. The stonewares and porcelains made at Hasami are discussed in an article by O. R. Impey in *Oriental Art*, vol. XXI, no. 4, winter 1975.

Most of the Japanese export market porcelain featured in this book was made at Arita in Hizen, or at the nearby kilns of Koshida at Mikawachi, Okawachi, Shida and Yoshida. There was no great ceramic centre like Ching-tê Chên. The Japanese potters were in the main independent individuals with small kilns, seemingly lacking in organisation and selling their wares through middle-men, having themselves no direct contact with the European market. This was no doubt the fault of the social organisation of eighteenth-century Japan but it was responsible to a great degree for the failure of Japanese potters to match the vast trade carried on by the better organised Chinese merchants and potters.

Japanese porcelains of the eighteenth century and earlier are quite scarce in Europe today; even the flasks which were sold in London in thousands are rarely found. At the time of writing in the late 1970s these Japanese porcelains are little understood, and are probably under-priced in comparison with some fashionable ceramics. However, in the interval between writing these words and checking the material for publication the market has strengthened appreciably due, to a great degree, to the presence in Europe of Japanese buyers. The wheel has turned full circle. Originally Europeans

Oriental export market porcelain

228 A superbly potted Japanese Arita bottle painted in underglaze blue. Such delightful bottles, often with longer necks, were exported in large quantities early in the eighteenth century, 10½ inches high, c. 1700–1720.   *Private collection*

journeyed to the East to purchase fine Oriental porcelains for their pleasure and use. Now Oriental buyers fly to London to buy back these self-same porcelains and other Oriental products.

Descriptions of Japanese porcelain often include terms such as 'early Edo period' or 'middle Edo period'. Such dating is unhelpful as the period covers more than three hundred years, from 1615; in fact it covers the whole period during which Japanese porcelain was made. There are, however, subdivisions and I list these for the convenience of readers who may come across these terms and be bewildered by them. I do not use these descriptions in this book, preferring to give conventional dating, even where this is very approximate, such as 'c 1700' or '1700–1720'.

EDO PERIOD
Seventeenth century or 'early' period

Genwa	1615–1623
Kanei	1624–1643
Shoho	1644–1647
Keian	1648–1651
Shoo	1652–1654
Meireki	1655–1657
Manji	1658–1660
Kambun	1661–1672
Empo	1673–1680
Tenwa	1681–1683
Jokyo	1684–1687
Genroku	1688–1703

(The reader is unlikely to find Japanese porcelain made before this period.)

Eighteenth century or 'middle' period

Hoei	1704–1710
Shotoku	1711–1715
Kyoho	1716–1735
Gembun	1736–1740
Kampo	1741–1743

The Japanese porcelains

229 An elegant Japanese Arita bottle painted in underglaze blue. 12½ inches high, c. 1700–1720.   *Godden of Worthing Ltd*

Enkyo	1744–1747
Kanen	1748–1750
Horeki	1751–1763
Meiwa	1764–1771
Anei	1772–1780
Temmei	1781–1788
Kansei	1789–1800

Nineteenth century or 'late' period

Kyowa	1801–1803
Burka	1804–1817
Bunsei	1818–1829
Tempo	1830–1843
Koka	1844–1847
Kaei	1848–1853
Ansei	1854–1859
Manen	1860
Bankyu	1861–1863
Genji	1864
Keio	1865–1867
Meiji	1868–1911
Taisho	1912–1925
Showa	1926+

The sale records prove the extent of the British Company's trade in Japanese wares, although we must again bear in mind that not all the goods were on the Company's accounts, much was Private Trade. We must also bear in mind that the official buying instructions given to the Supra-cargoes invited them to purchase Japanese goods if they were available. Typical instructions list the porcelains required and end with the following note: 'If any Japan Junks are at Canton while you are there, which have Japan earthenware, you may buy some of the above sorts or pretty near them, but buy none that are large pieces such as jars, beakers, or great dishes or bowles.' (Instructions given to the Supra-cargoes of the *Loyal Bliss* and *Hester* in December 1712.) Earlier imports were from the Chinese ports of Amoy and Chusan, rather than from Canton.

The use – as in the above quotation – of the term 'Japan earthenware' or 'Japan ware' needs explanation. Japanese potters made both porcelain and earthenwares and at first I took the Company's description at face-value but when one examines the goods listed they are in most cases objects known only in Japanese porcelain, not in earthenware. The contemporary records, even when listing Chinese porcelains, do not use the word 'porcelain', only 'China-ware', meaning ware from China. They could not very well, especially in the brief sale listings, use the term 'Japan China ware', which would be a contradiction, so they used the term 'Japan earthenware' or 'Japan ware'. (The 1704 Customs Act also used this description: 'all porcelain commonly called China or Japan Ware'.) On other occasions this was abbreviated simply to 'Japan beakers' or 'Japan plates' under sale headings which covered both types, i.e. 'China and Japan ware'.

Unfortunately, many sale records do not identify the source of the goods listed – perhaps because the cataloguer in London did not know the source, or was unable to distinguish between Japanese and Chinese porcelains. The goods from the *Dorothy*, sold in December 1696, include many objects which we might reasonably regard as of Japanese origin – 'flasks', 'large bottles with soy', 'long-neck bottles' and the like. Such bottles can be extremely graceful, and are probably not as appreciated as they should be. I show in Plates 228–229 two blue and white Japanese bottles of the 1700 period.

One of the complications is that in general only very brief sale records as recorded in the Court Minutes have survived, not the fuller descriptions as printed in the official catalogues. When we have both records available for comparison we can see why some objects, which we can now only surmise

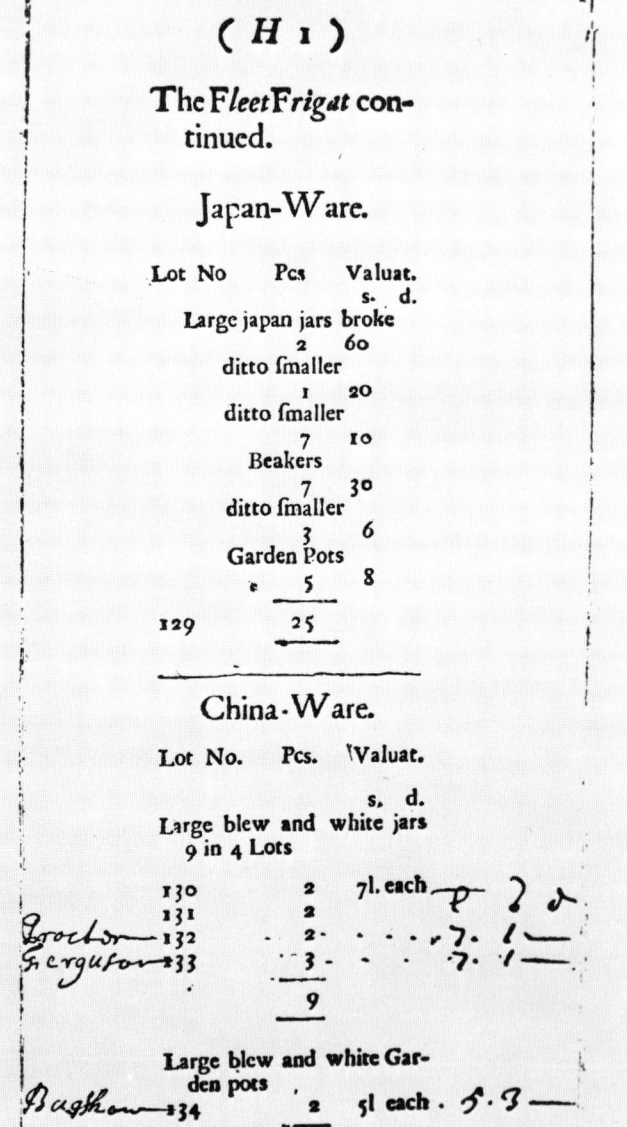

230 A page from the English East India Company's sale held on 26 September 1704, involving Japanese and Chinese porcelains imported by the *Fleet*. This vessel brought home over 11,000 articles described as of Japanese origin (see p. 317).

India Office Records, London

were of Japanese origin, were not so designated in the Court Minutes. The reason was because the catalogue had all-embracing sub-headings – 'Japan Ware' or 'China Ware' – whereas the brief handwritten Court Minutes do not contain these sub-headings. To illustrate this point I show in Plate 230 a page from a printed catalogue of a sale held in September 1704, showing the sub-headings not given in the hand-written brief Minutes. We should here recall the wording of the 1704 Act, which imposed a $12\frac{1}{2}$ per cent tax on all porcelain 'commonly called China or Japan ware…'

Frustrating though it is, I will confine my listing of imported Japanese porcelains to those objects or lots which include the prefix 'Japanese' or 'Japan', although many other articles almost certainly were of Japanese origin.

The first instance of the description 'Japan' being used occurs in the sale of the *Trumball*'s cargo held in July 1699. This is not to say that Japanese goods were not imported and sold earlier; they almost certainly were, but they do not appear to be so described in the all-too-brief sale records. Indeed Soame Jenyns, in *Japanese Porcelain*, records that Queen Sophie Charlotte of Prussia received Japanese porcelains from the British Company as early as 1688. However, Soame Jenyns did not apparently research the available Company records. I will proceed to quote from these. The original valuation or starting price quoted is, unless otherwise stated, the price *per piece*.

Sale, July 1699
Goods ex. *Trumball*, 1697–9 voyage:

400 Saucers Japan painted
395 Cups do.

These were valued at 1s each and sold for 1s $7\frac{1}{2}d$.

Sale, November 1699
Goods ex. *Nassau*, 1697–9 voyage to Amoy:

	Valued at
1 very fine Japan bason	12s
1 do. very fine	£1
150 Japan scol. [scalloped] bowls	5d
4 Japan dishes	5s
6 Japan plates	7s
1 Japan bason	10s
6 Japan bowls	6s
8 do.	5s

Also included were many objects, such as essence bottles, which were probably Japanese, but the records give only the briefest of descriptions, sometimes a single word: 'Jars', 'bowles', etc.

Sale, April 1702
Goods ex. *Dorrill*, 1699–1701 voyage to Amoy:

	Valued at
58 Nests Jappan bowls	15s 0d each
6 do.	8s 0d ,,
2,500 Jappan tea cups	6d ,,
2,690 do. saucers	
814 Jappan tea cups	1s 6d ,,
330 Jappan tea cups	5d ,,
340 do. saucers	

Sale, March–April 1703
Goods ex. *Dashwood*, 1700–1702 voyage:

	Valued at
2 Japan basons	10s 0d
2 Japan dishes	5s 0d
152 Japan plates	3s 0d
802 Japan plates	2s 0d
20 Jappan dishes	8s 0d
70 do.	6s 0d
3 Japan bowls	4s 0d
2 Japan basons	£3 0s 0d
5 Japan cups	1s 0d

2 Japan bowls	£1 0s 0d	
1 Nest Japan bowles [no value given]		
2 Japan dishes	4s 0d	
4 Japan fruit dishes	5s 0d	
6 Japan dishes	5s 0d	
2 Japan bowls	3s 0d	
81 Japan cups	6d	
4 Japan bowles	£1 5s 0d	
4 do.	12s 0d	
8 do.	10s 0d	
27 do.	4s 0d	
3 do.	7s 0d	
13 do.	13s 0d	
1 Japan teapot	£1 0s 0d	
6 Japan sugar cups	3s 0d	
12 Japan tea cups	10d	
6 Japan sugar cups	4s 0d	
1 Japan bowl	6s 0d	
6 Japan chocolate cups	3s 0d	
107 Jappan sugar dishes	4s 0d	
107 do.	3s 0d	
4 Jappan dishes	12s 0d	
10 do.	10s 0d	
9 Jappan dishes	6s 0d	
5 do.	15s 0d	
4 Nests Jappan plates [no value given]		
10 Jappan plates	4s 0d	
4 Nests Japan marmolet pots	12s 0d	
28 Japan cups	3s 0d	
3 do.	2s 6d	
18 Jappan bottles	1s 0d	
16 Jappan bowles	15s 0d	
24 Jappan cups	10d	
4 Jappan jars	£5 [Sold for £9 11s each]	
360 Japan chocolate cups	1s 0d	

Sale, September 1703
Goods ex. *Northumberland*, 1701–1703 voyage to Canton:

	Valued at
10 Large Japan dishes	12s 0d
10 do. smaller	10s 0d
10 do. smaller	8s 0d
38 do. smaller	6s 0d
6 Japan scollopt dishes	10s 0d
6 do.	8s 0d
6 do.	6s 0d
9 Japan bowles scollopt	14s 0d
9 do. quartered with blew	10s 0d
318 Japan tea cups	7d
308 do. saucers	7d
74 Japan tea cups scollopt	7d
73 do. saucers	7d
25 Japan tea cups	1s 6d
3 Japan tea pots	6s 0d
3 do.	5s 0d
110 Japan mustard pots	1s 0d
2 Large Japan punch bowls	£4 0s 0d
2 do.	£3 0s 0d
1 do.	£2 0s 0d
1 do.	10s 0d
245 Japan custard cups	4d
2 Japan bowles	3s 0d
81 Japan tea cups	6d
18 Nests Japan bowles	15s 0d

Goods ex. *Fleet* 1702–1704 voyage to Canton:

	Valued at
30 Japan sugar dishes	15s 0d
118 Japan bowles	3s 0d
3 Japan tea pots [no value given]	
12 do. [no value given]	
11 do.	2s 6d
2 Japan jars	£12 each, sold for £14 10s
35 Japan barbers basons	10s 0d
10 Japan sugar dishes	10s 0d

The Japanese porcelains

Item	Price
2 Japan jars	12s 0d [an error in writing perhaps, for £12 as they were sold for £12 5s]
69 Japan bowls	3s 0d
10 Nests Japan dishes	£1 5s 0d
5 do.	10s 0d
6 Japan bowls	£1 0s 0d
10 Covers	1s 0d
1 Japan bowl	£2 0s 0d
8 do.	£1 15s 0d
44 Japan bowls	£1 0s 0d
79 Japan sugar dishes	10s 0d
6 do.	7s 0d
70 do. [no value given]	
4 do.	4s 0d
8 Japan sugar dishes	15s 0d
21 Japan bowles	5s 0d
19 Nests Japan plates	15s 0d
3 Japan bowles	£1 15s 0d
13 do.	£1 0s 0d
19 do. [no value given]	
35 Japan sugar dishes	15s 0d
32 do. [no value given]	
15 Nests Japan plates	15s 0d
5 Nests Japan bowles	£2 0s 0d
25 Nests Japan plates	15s 0d
3 Nests Japan plates	10s 0d
40 Japan sugar dishes	15s 0d
60 do.	7s 0d
67 do.	4s 0d
7 Large Japan bowles	£1 15s 0d
13 do.	£1 0s 0d
28 do. [no value given]	
5 Nests Japan bowles	£2 0s 0d
20 Japan bowles	15s 0d
38 Nests Japan plates [no value given]	
1 do.	10s 0d
3 Japan tea pots	7s 0d
11 do.	3s 0d
124 Japan bowles	3s 0d
84 Japan sugar dishes	15s 0d
4 do.	10s 0d
1 Japan barbers basons [no value given]	
1 Japan bowl	3s 0d
4 Japan flasks	3s 0d
1 Japan sugar dish	3s 0d
12 Japan tea cups and saucers	10d
2 Japan Punch bowls	£10 [Sold for £11 each]
3 Japan Jars	£8 0s 0d
2 Japan beakers	£6 0s 0d
2 Japan Jars	£1 0s 0d
1 Japan beaker	£1 0s 0d
2 Japan sugar dishes, covered	10s 0d
2 do.	7s 0d
2 Japan tea pots	3s 0d
12 Japan tea cups and saucers	10d
1 Japan bowl	10s 0d
6 Japan flasks	5s 0d
1 Nest Japan bowls	£2 0s 0d
2 Japan bowls	10s 0d
2 Japan flasks	5s 0d
6 Japan sugar dishes	7s 0d
12 Japan chocolat cups	3s 0d

Further items from the *Fleet* were sold in the next china-ware sale, held in September 1704. For this sale we have, fortunately, a copy of the original catalogue, a page of which I reproduced as Plate 230. Under the heading 'Japan Ware' we find:

Item	Valued at
1,800 brown tea cups, 2 sorts	3d
1,000 do. saucers	
1,260 brown tea cups [no value given]	
1,060 do. saucers, 2 sorts	
40 nests of Japan bowles, covers and dishes, scollopt, 3 in each nest, 2 sorts	£2 a nest
100 Japan sugar dishes, covers and plates	15s 0d
399 Japan flasks with stoppers	6s 0d
106 Japan barbers basons	10s 0d
214 Japan flasks with stopper	6s 0d
615 Japan tea cups and saucers	10d
570 Japan chocolate cups	3s 0d

231 A set of Japanese covered jars and beakers of the type originally sold in sets of five, in various sizes and styles of decoration. Jars 15 inches high, c. 1710–20.

Sotheby & Co., London

20 Japan Garden pots	£3 0s 0d
89 Japan bowles	8s 0d
11 do.	6s 0d
320 small Japan bowles	4s 0d
33 Japan bowles	£1 0s 0d
5 do.	15s 0d
23 Japan Garden pots	£3 0s 0d
22 nests Japan bowles	£2 0s 0d
29 Japan sugar dishes	15s 0d
332 Japan chocolat cups	1s 0d
328 do. saucers	1s 0d
716 Japan tea cups	1s 0d
708 do. saucers	1s 0d
12 Japan jars and covers	15s 0d
25 large Japan sugar dishes etc.	17s 0d
296 smaller do.	2s 0d
11 Japan Jars and covers	£1 0s 0d
7 Japan jars	15s 0d
13 do. beakers	15s 0d
1 do.	10s 0d
10 Japan Jars	£1 0s 0d
20 do. beakers	£1 0s 0d
9 Japan jars	15s 0d
18 do. beakers	15s 0d
6 Japan Jars	£1 0s 0d
12 do. beakers	£1 0s 0d
18 Japan Jars	15s 0d
16 do.	£1 0s 0d
91 Japan garden pots	£3 0s 0d
12 Japan jars	15s 0d
8 Japan Jars with covers	£8 0s 0d
6 do.	£6 0s 0d
12 Japan beakers	£3 0s 0d
16 Japan garden pots	£3 0s 0d

Comparison between the Court Minutes and the catalogue shows that the Minutes record only the sold lots. Even though the Minutes I have quoted do not include the unsold items we still find that this one vessel, the *Fleet*, had at least 11,739 items of Japanese porcelain aboard from her 1702–1704 voyage.

Later sale records abound with references to

319 The Japanese porcelains

Japanese porcelains, but as, in general, the lots are of standard wares such as previously quoted from the *Fleet*, I will now confine my attention to those lots which are described in some detail.

Sale, March 1705
This sale included porcelains from the *Union*, in all 192 chests or tubs of 'China and Japan Ware' and 44 'open lots'. The *Union* sailed from Amoy in March 1702, where she loaded during December 1703 and January 1704. On 17 January 1704 the log recorded: '…this day took on board 110 basketts of Jarrs and beakers and 14 chests of China ware and 13 tubbs.' These jars and beakers were almost certainly of Japanese make, and probably were the items sold in a single lot on 6 March 1704 and catalogued as: '19 sets of Japan jars and beakers, 3 jars and 2 beakers in a set.' These ninety-five vases were 'putt up at £200' and sold to Captain Bromwell for £203. A typical set or garniture of Japanese jars and beakers, missing the fifth centre vase, is shown in Plate 231.

Apart from standard Japanese wares we find credited to the *Union* also:

	Valued at
27 Japan case bottles	12s
43 do. smaller	10s
21 Japan case [square] bottles, smaller	8s
5 do.	6s
104 Japan caudle cups covers and plates	

This sale also included Japanese and Chinese porcelains from the East Indiaman *Aurengzeb*. Of special interest is one lot with a vague description of the design: '4 Japan dishes, in quarters', valued at 4s. There are also consecutive lots which help to illustrate the point that Japanese porcelains were in general more expensive than Chinese wares – a fact which the Dutch had cause to complain about on numerous occasions. Here were:

232 Sample page from the English East India Company's written notes on the results of its London auction sales, in this case concerning goods from the *Kent* sold on 7 November 1706. This sale included many Japanese items.

India Office Records, London

	Valued at
6 Japan teapots, valued at	7s
4 China do. ,, ,,	4s

although, of course, we now have no way of telling the relative size or decoration of these two types. A further point arises from a following lot; some of the Japanese cups had covers: '976 Japan cups with covers, two sorts' valued at 1s each.

Now, for the first time, we find figure decoration recorded:

	Valued at
6 Japan dishes, with figures	8s
1 do. with flowers	7s
4 do. smaller	6s

Sale, April 1706

Private Trade goods ex. *Tavestock*, *Duchess* and *Kent*. This selection of goods includes:

	Valued at
20 Japan plates	2s 6d
2 large deep Japan dishes	15s 0d
12 Japan chocolat cups, covers and saucers	3s 0d
1 large Japan jar and cover	£4
2 do. with raised work	£3
1 Japan dish with flower pot	6s 0d

and an assortment of Japan jars and beakers, also '3 setts Japan Rowl Waggons' valued at £3 each.

Sale, September 1706

Goods ex. *Chamber* from Amoy. The assortment includes hundreds of Japanese covered cups and saucers (valued at 3s 6d), also flasks and lots such as:

	Valued at
27 large Japan dishes	8s
20 do. smaller	6s
3 Jappan dish scollopt edges	6s
49 do. plain	2s
75 Japan scollop'd bowles	10s
88 Nests Japan scollop't plates	8s
65 Japan bowles, scollop'd	4s
90 do. smaller, rubb'd	3s
7 Japan basons	£2
6 large Japan dishes	15s
36 Japan Jars	£3

The *Sidney* which sailed to Canton also brought home some Japanese porcelains but not as much as came from Amoy on the *Chamber*. We find the now normal assortment of cups and saucers, dishes and bowls and 'Japan Barbers Basons' valued at 4s each (see Plate 225). An interesting item was 'Japan Garden pots' valued at £1 5s each. Many previous sales had included Garden Pots but without the prefix 'Japan'.

The *Dashwood*'s cargo, some of which was sold in September 1706, also includes some Japanese wares.

Sale, November 1706

Goods ex. *Kent*, from Canton. This vessel carried

The Japanese porcelains

home a large selection of wares listed as of Japanese origin. In the main we find the standard wares, including barber's basins in two sizes, also:

	Valued at
17 Japan canisters with covers	4s
88 Small Japan dishes, 2 sorts	3s
31 Jappan bowls with flat bottoms	5s
3 Japan bowles and covers, with handles	£2

Amidst goods described as 'Japan' there were the following wares which could well be of Japanese origin:

489 Tea cups and saucers, oval red and gold
865 Tea cups and saucers, red and gold 6 square
657 Tea cups and saucers red and gold 4 square
436 Tea cups and saucers oval with squares
855 Tea cups and saucers quartered with gold

certainly Japanese teacups were purchased for also listed were '823 Japan tea cups, 4 sorts' valued at 9d each.

Some of the original hand-written results of this sale, listing Japanese wares, are shown in Plate 232.

Sale, June 1707

Goods ex. *Somers, Toddington, Seaford*. This sale appears to have been of Private Trade imports. The items included the normal selection of Japanese covered sugar dishes and stands in various sizes, also Japanese jars and beakers valued at £4 or £3 each.

Reference has previously been made to objects described as '6 square' or '4 square', normally without the prefix 'Japan'. We now have a linked description '10 Jappan dishes 12 square', valued at 5s. It is difficult to know exactly what was intended. Did the pieces have in the decoration four, six or twelve squares, a supposition supported by the description 'teacups...oval with squares'? In most cases I believe the description referred to the out-

line shape, i.e. the dishes mentioned above were twelve-sided.

Also of interest from the *Toddington*'s cargo are '4 Jap. Caudle cups with dishes and covers, raised work', valued at 10s; '2 do. with broken ears'. Some of the jars must have been of large size for we find featured '2 Jap. Jars with odd covers, one packed with china' (valued at £12, the two).

These items were probably Private Trade purchases. If we refer to the directors' instructions given to the Supra-cargoes of the *Toddington* in November 1704 we discover that they did not require Japanese wares, in fact they did not favour *any* porcelains. This vessel was to take in cargo both at Batavia and at Amoy. The instructions for Batavia read in part: '...you must by no means bring any sugar or sugar candy and if possible no China or Jappan ware.' And regarding Amoy: '...we would have you provide china ware as far as twenty tons in useful sorts, which stow close, but no Jappan ware it being more for our advantage that you come home with ten or twenty tons of dead freight than stay another year...' In other words they were not to wait for the next shipment of Japanese porcelain to arrive at Amoy.

The *Seaford* also carried a selection of Japanese wares and some of this was carried over to the September 1707 sale. In this sale the following items were credited to the *Sidney*:

	Valued at
30 High Japan cups	15s
32 do.	12s
5 do	10s

If these were indeed cups, rather than a form of vase, they must at this valuation have been quite special.

Sale, March 1708

Goods ex. *Somers, Fleet, Chamber, Sidney* and *Dashwood*. The sale of the porcelains from these vessels, sold on 16 and 17 March 1708, included a great quantity of ware described as Japanese. The complete selection of Japanese goods listed for this two-day sale is given below. First, the *Fleet* carried:

	Valued at
106 Japan barbers basons, 3 sorts	4s 0d
214 Japan flasks, with stoppers	2s 6d
294 Japan flasks	2s 6d
1,016 Japan tea cups	8d
1,314 do. saucers	8d
160 Japan sugar dishes	6s 0d
185 Japan sugar dishes	5s 0d
163 do.	4s 0d
4 Japan cups	1s 6d
295 Japan bowles	3s 0d
8 Japan beakers	£1 5s 0d
16 Japan garden pots	£1 12s 0d
60 Japan bowles	12s 0d
3 do.	14s 0d
17 Japan bowles	£1 0s 0d
221 do.	16s 0d
160 do.	12s 0d
66 do.	10s 0d
219 do.	8s 0d
234 do.	7s 0d
6 do.	6s 0d
7 do.	5s 0d
79 Japan dishes	12s 0d
85 Japan dishes	10s 0d
55 Japan bowls	4d
197 Japan sugar dishes	6s 6d
63 Japan barbers basons	4s 0d
1,918 Japan tea cups	9d
20 Japan jars	10s 0d
38 Beakers	10s 0d
42 Japan jars and beakers	10s 0d
12 Japan jars	£3 0s 0d
2 do.	£1 10s 0d
7 do.	4s 0d
7 Beakers	12s 0d
3 do.	2s 6d

and from the *Chamber*:

136 Japan bowls and plates	8s 0d
447 Japan flasks	2s 6d
2 Japan basons	£1 12s 0d
24 Japan tea cups	6d

(Also other items such as 1,330 essence bottles which were probably of Japanese origin but which were not so designated.)

From the *Sidney*, there were:

	Valued at
118 Japan plates	1s 8d
381 Japan flasks	2s 6d
13 Japan garden pots	£1 5s 0d

and from the *Dashwood*:

	Valued at
47 Japan spitting pots	2s 0d
25 Japan sugar dishes	3s 0d
445 Japan tea cups	1s 6d
115 Japan cups	8d
361 Japan tea cups and saucers	2s 0d
1,439 do.	6d
605 Japan flasks	2s 6d
540 Japan sugar dishes	3s 6d
10 Japan bowles	15s 0d
16 do.	10s 0d
11 do.	10s 0d
29 do.	8s 0d
42 do.	7s 0d
36 do.	6s 0d
171 do.	5s 0d
586 do.	3s 0d
428 Japan chocolate cups	2s 6d
20 do.	1s 0d
20 saucers	1s 0d
13 Nests Japan bowls	12s 0d
18 Nests Japan plates [no value given]	
674 Japan cups [no value given]	
84 Japan sugar dishes	3s 6d
4 Japan fruit dishes	10s 0d
96 Japan plates	3s 0d
6 Japan dishes	15s 0d

The Japanese porcelains

233 A typical Japanese porcelain 'four square' stoppered flask of the type sold in large quantities in London early in the eighteenth century. Imari style of decoration. $9\frac{1}{4}$ inches high, c. 1710–20. *Victoria and Albert Museum (Crown Copyright)*

23 do.	12s 0d
92 do.	8s 0d
2 do.	4s 0d
32 Japan basons	£1 12s 0d
17 Japan dishes	3s 0d
16 Japan bowles	2s 6d
3 Nests Japan bowls	10s 0d
2 Nests Japan plates	8s 0d
3 Japan sugar dishes	3s 0d
3 do.	2s 6d
20 Japan tea cups	1s 0d
2 do.	8d
2 Japan spitting pots	2s 0d

These items have been extracted from the brief hand-written Court Minutes, but the available printed catalogue provides a few fuller descriptions, some of which may permit us to identify the wares being sold in 1708. For example:

  9 Large Japan teacups, gr [green] squ. and 8 saucers
 13 Japan teacups, red and gold
 12 Japan bowls quart [quartered?] with blue
  4 Japan fruit dishes ringed
  3 Large Japan dishes
  5 Odd ditto, lesser, quartered with red
  4 ditto with flower pots
  3 Japan dishes with gold
173 Large Japan teacups and saucers with a rim flowered
115 Small Japan cups with covers, blue rings
 96 Japan plates, small, flow. [flower?] pot
 50 Japan bowls, cheq. brims
 77 ditto with stars
 42 Japan bowls with covers, red
 42 ditto with sprigs
 15 Large Japan teacups, red squ.
  4 ditto with balls

The Japanese porcelains carried by the *Dashwood* and sold in the 1708 sale were much better described than the earlier goods. The '96 Japan plates, small, flow pot' and the four dishes decorated with flower pots surely relate to a standard Imari-type design combining underglaze blue with

234 A fine covered bowl in the Imari style (see Colour Plates 17 and 18), perhaps similar to those valued at £1 5s each in 1708. 14½ inches high, c. 1710. *Sotheby & Co., London*

overglaze enamels and thin gilding. A dish of this kind is shown in Plate 225. Circular dishes bearing this flower pot design occur in various sizes, some over two feet in diameter. With further research some of the other articles can probably be matched with the sale descriptions – the large cups with red squares, the cups with green squares, or the dishes quartered with red. The flasks with stoppers, sometimes further described as 'four square', were probably similar to the one shown in Plate 233.

On 24 March 1708 other porcelains were offered for sale at the Company's auction. From the *Loyal Cooke* we find catalogued the normal range of useful wares such as I have listed; also expensive objects such as:

	Valued at
1 Large Japan jar	£4
2 Large Japan bowles	£4
1 do.	£5

and once again consecutive lots show that the Japanese goods were much more expensive than the Chinese:

4 Japan sugar dishes valued at	8s 0d
2 China do. ,, ,,	1s 6d

Sale, May 1708

Goods ex. *Loyall Merchant*, *Dashwood* and *Fleet*. In this sale relatively little Japanese porcelain is credited to the *Loyall Merchant*, except teacups and saucers and 'Japan jars', but a further selection from the *Dashwood* (see March 1708 sale) and from the *Fleet* was catalogued:

	Valued at
6,350 Japan tea cups	3d each
723 Japan cups	2s 9d and 9d
510 Japan cups	5d
21 Japan dishes	15s 0d

30 do.	10s 0d
215 Japan sugar dishes	3s 0d
430 do.	2s 0d
1 Japan Jar	£4 0s 0d
6 do.	£2 5s 0d
32 Japan bowls	13s 0d
11 Japan dishes	12s 0d
19 Japan dishes	8s 0d
19 do.	7s 0d
134 do.	6s 0d
6 do.	5s 0d
11 do.	4s 0d
7 do.	3s 0d
30 Japan beakers	£1 10s 0d
24 do.	£1 3s 0d
23 do.	8s 0d
2 do.	4s 0d
31 Japan jars	£2 5s 0d
55 do.	£2 0s 0d
7 do.	£1 10s 0d

Sale, June 1708

First, a mere 230 items were listed from the *Hallifax*. This small selection must have been Private Trade goods, but it includes:

3 Jappan bowls, covers and dishes
11 Chocolate cups and covers
30 Jappan saucers
56 Small Jappan tea cups

There were also small selections from the *Loyal Bliss*, including:

	Valued at
2 Jappan jars	£2 10s 0d
3 Large Jap. bowles and covers	8s 0d
5 Japan dishes	7s 0d
5 do. smaller	6s 0d
7 do. smaller	5s 0d
4 do. smaller	3s 0d
9 do. smaller	2s 6d
3 do. smaller	1s 6d

49 Japan saucers	1s 0d
23 do. sugar dishes	2s 0d
9 do. ,, ,,	1s 6d
48 Japan bowls	8s 0d
67 do. plates	2s 0d
16 do. bowles	3s 0d
16 do. deep dishes	6s 0d
117 do. dishes	5s 0d
33 do. smaller	3s 0d
65 do. plates	2s 0d
76 Japan dishes	6s 0d
80 do. smaller	5s 0d
63 do. smaller	2s 6d

Sale, November 1708

A small selection of porcelains, most probably Private Trade, from the *Katherine*, was sold on 3 November 1708. Only two articles have the prefix 'Jap', but the fact that this vessel traded only to the Dutch station of Batavia serves to remind us of this source of Japanese goods: '2 Jap. Punch bowles and covers valued at £1 5s 0d.' These were perhaps similar to the colourful Imari-style example shown in Plate 234. Other covered bowls were, perhaps, used as tureens on the dinner table (Plate 235).

Sale, February 1709

In this sale held on 25 February 1709, several clearing-up lots or small selections of Private Trade goods were offered, from the *Chamber*, *Dashwood*, and *Fleet*. The Japanese goods included:

	Valued at
6 Japan jars	£2 each
2 Japan bowls	2s 6d
81 Japan tea cups	5d

At this point the Court Minutes cease recording the result of sales. We can be thankful that, from this source, we have been able to glean records of the importation of Japanese porcelains over some eleven years, from the sale of July 1699 to that of February 1709.

We can, however, deduce that the importation of Japanese porcelains into England continued for a number of years after 1709. First, we find that the director's purchasing instructions of 1712 period include the following paragraph: 'If any Japan junks are at Canton while you are there, which have Japan earthenware, you may buy some of the above sorts or pretty near them, but buy none that are large pieces, such as Jars, beakers or great dishes or bowles.'

In fact, these large items were the standard Japanese export wares. They were extremely colourful (see Colour Plates 17 and 18) and must have been very popular articles of Private Trade. They feature often in the sale catalogues, although as early as 1706 the Company's orders stated '…buy no large pieces as Jars, beakers, images…', the apparent reason being that these fancy goods did not stow closely and lacked the bulk weight required for the kentledge.

Secondly, we have a few records of the re-export of porcelains sold by the Company in London. One such entry dated February 1719 relates to the shipping of 30 Jappan milk pots at 13s 1d each, being part of the cargo of the *Loyal Bliss*. These goods were probably sold with the main cargo late in 1718, but we do not have any records of this sale, or of any from 1709 onwards. We do, however, have available the catalogue of the cargo of the *Carnarvon* sold in March 1722. This catalogue includes the following goods described as being of Japanese origin:

3 Japan jars
2 Japan beakers
29 Japan cups and saucers, 2 sorts
2 Japan plates, 2 sorts
50 Japan cups and 50 saucers

but the quantity of Japanese porcelain was relatively small in comparison with Chinese wares, and one has the impression that the trade in Japanese porcelain was declining. There is, however, some evidence that captains, and presumably other ships' officers and Supra-cargoes, were bringing in some Japanese wares as part of their Private Trade allowance. A Court Minute of 9 February 1726 states: 'Request of Captain Charles Boddam and Captain John Gordon dated the 9th February was read complaining that several lots of tea, fans, China and Japan ware belonging to them sold in the March sale last [1725] remain yet uncleared and desire leave to sue the buyers in order to clear the same.'

Japanese wares were of course also available to buyers from other nations trading with China. The French Company was apparently still importing some Japanese porcelains in the late 1730s and early 1740s, for in instructions written in 1738 or 1739 the directors ordered five to six thousand enamelled cups, preferably from Japan rather than China, and it was suggested that covered jars and pots should be purchased ready-made, either from Japan or China.

We do not know if the English East India Company continued to import Japanese porcelains in the mid-eighteenth century. The Dutch apparently did not import any between 1757 and 1795, but while the Japanese shut themselves away from foreign influences and trade, they probably continued the trade to and from China, and this trade could well have included porcelains that subsequently found their way to Europe. However, the available English records do not suggest the importation of Japanese wares, although the list of permitted Private Trade imports, as revised in 1753, included mention of both 'China Ware' and 'Japan Ware'. If imported in the mid-eighteenth century it was almost certainly as Private Trade. An interesting, perhaps unique, Japanese porcelain watch

235 A typical Japanese covered bowl painted in underglaze blue. Such examples were perhaps used as tureens on European dinner tables. $10\frac{1}{4}$ inches high, c. 1710–20. *Phillips, London*

holder in the Mottahedeh collection is copied from an English metal design of about 1760 and shows that at this late period the Japanese were still catering for the European trade. Chinese porcelains were, however, in the mid-eighteenth century, readily available at a cheaper price than the Japanese. The Chinese workmanship was also better, as early as 1713 the English Company was ordering Chinese porcelains in the Japanese style, for example:

2,000 cups in colours, to be painted after the Japanese pattern   [1713 order]
15,000 cups and saucers in colours to be painted after the Japanese patterns   [1719 order]

The general dearth of contemporary information

236 A rare Japanese teapot painted in underglaze blue with overglaze colours. The bottle depicted in the foreground by the handle bears European initials. $4\frac{1}{4}$ inches high, c. 1720.

Godden of Worthing Ltd

on Japanese porcelain, and the subsequent value of the few available sale records, prompts me to return to this source material and to list some of the objects that we can fairly regard as being of Japanese origin, although the catalogues do not in these cases include this designation.

In the sale of March 1705 we find '7,595 essence bottles, various sorts' and '15 blue and white garden pots'. The latter link with several blue and white garden pots which had the prefix 'Japan'. Also the '6 dishes painted and quartered in red' were almost certainly Japanese, and it is likely that the blue and gold jars, bottles and 'Rowl waggons' were also from Japan. There are many references to 'Rowl waggons', various spellings occurring. These were straight-sided vases called by the Dutch Rolwagen. The 'large blue and white jars' which sold for £7 1s each must have been truly large, and were probably of Japanese origin, being listed with other known types such as 'large blue and white garden pots' (sold for £5 3s).

Other Japanese-type porcelains in the March 1705 sale, mainly from the *Fleet* and the *Union*, were:

  200 blue and white essence bottles
2,900 blew ditto
  360 light blue ditto
  600 Virgo colour'd
1,000 cream colour'd
  200 smaller
1,500 red and gold teacups and
1,500 ditto saucers [3,000 pieces at $6\frac{1}{4}d$]
    13 bottles with brown figures
    84 rib'd bowls with flower pots
    42 smaller [see Plate 225 for this standard flower pot design]
  720 painted teacups, red and gold, 850 saucers
1,390 smaller teacups red and gold, 2 sorts
  798 ditto saucers
1,050 teacups red and gold and 1050 saucers [2,100 pieces at $5\frac{1}{4}d$]
1,600 teacups red and gold, 2 sorts [at $9\frac{1}{4}d$]
    13 jars with spire-heads
     2 ditto, flat heads

(The 'jars with spire-heads' could relate to large covered vases, such as is here seen in Colour Plate 18, the unusual knob being perhaps best likened to a spire.)

  342 large black and gold teacups, 190 saucers
  540 scollop'd teacups, red and gold and 648 saucers [1,188 pieces at $6\frac{1}{2}d$]
     7 Beakers checq. blew and gold
     6 Rowl wag. red, gold and white
     6 Beakers ditto
  130 white red and gold bowls and 130 ditto plates
     6 white and gold jars with beakers and covers [valued at £6 each, but fetched £7 each]
     6 white and gold Rowl wag.

The Japanese porcelains

275 rib'd teacups with figures, and 290 ditto saucers
  [these were valued at 8d each and they may have
  been enamelled cups and saucers of Kakiemon type]
76 hubblebubble bottles, 2 sorts (valued at 2s 6d each)

Four lots are particularly interesting as the description relates to the inclusion of silver, rather than gold, in the decoration:

16 nests sugar dishes, blue and silver, 3 in each
  2 ditto smaller, 2 in each
1,360 brown and silver teacups, 1,360 ditto saucers
  200 brown and silver teacups, 200 saucers

The sale of September 1705 included 850 red and gold teacups and saucers, 40 long-necked bottles (See Plate 229), 7 Rowl waggons, 110 red and gold bowls, 15 blue and gold bowls, 20 similar dishes, 29 large red and gold beakers, 27 ditto with narrow necks, 10 large painted beakers and 10 large hubblebubbles fine (41s each), all of which could have been of Japanese origin.

The 1707 sale featured other articles which again could have been of Japanese origin and, as with the earlier sales, these undesignated goods occur with others marked 'Japan'. The cargoes were therefore clearly mixed ones containing both Chinese and Japanese goods. The *Somers* had:

207 large blue and white bottles
980 large painted teacups [other large teacups in the
  same sale had the prefix 'Japan']
195 blue and gold bowls
282 blue and gold dishes
  60 small blue and white jars with covers
140 hubblebubble bottles
  30 painted hubblebubbles

Other typical early-eighteenth-century Japanese porcelains are shown in Plates 235–240. Some of the figure and animal models mentioned in the sale records listed in Chapter 7 could have been of Japanese rather than Chinese origin; see Plates 239–240.

237 A typical and pleasing Japanese covered bowl decorated in underglaze blue with overglaze red and green. Perhaps a sugar dish, as mentioned so often in the sale records. $3\tfrac{3}{4}$ inches high, c. 1720–30.   *Godden of Worthing Ltd*

Numbers of white, undecorated Japanese bottles, vases, flasks and similar objects were imported into Holland, where they were enamelled by European painters. A selection of these from the British Museum collection is illustrated in Soame Jenyns's *Japanese Porcelain*, Plate 77c, and it is interesting to note that many lots of white porcelain were included in the English East India Company sales, although we cannot be sure if these were of Chinese or Japanese manufacture.

Most British collectors know of Japanese ceramic designs only from European soft-paste porcelain copies. These designs were popular on Chelsea and Bow porcelains in the 1750s. The English copies feature two very different Japanese styles: on the one hand the simple so-called Kakiemon designs with, typically, a minimum of

238 A fine and typical six-sided Japanese export-market blue and white covered jar. 14¼ inches high, c. 1720.

Godden of Worthing Ltd

decoration enhancing rather than covering the white porcelain body (see Plate 226), and on the other the all-over 'brocade' or Imari designs, similar in general effect to the new traditional Derby 'Japan patterns'. In May 1756 the management of the English Bow factory acquired Japanese porcelains: 'Patterns received from Lady Cavendish, a Japan octogon cup and saucer, lady pattern, a ribbed and scollop'd cup and saucer, Image pattern, a basket-bordered dessert plate; a Japan bread and butter plate.'

One wonders if the English porcelain manufacturers in the 1750s were copying contemporary Japanese Kakiemon porcelains or if they were emulating designs imported forty years or so previously. This question is of importance in deciding the date of these elegant Japanese porcelains but the available pre-1709 sale records are unhelpful. Perhaps British manufacturers were only copying Meissen essays in the Japanese taste. Far from providing details of the design or even simple descriptions such as 'Lady' or 'Image' pattern, the only reference in the sale records to figure decoration is the '6 Japan dishes with figures' included in the cargo of *Aurengzeb*, sold in March 1705. The Japanese Kakiemon designs are often attributed to the seventeenth century, but I think they are later. I am, admittedly, unable to offer evidence to support this belief.

In the 1760s the fashionable London auctions held by Mr Christie and others included Japanese porcelains, but in these cases the porcelains appear to have been old, or at least second-hand goods from established households. Taking into account the ruling prices, and the high value of money compared with ours today, these 'old' Japanese goods fetched good prices, a fact that accounts for the favour these designs found with contemporary British porcelain manufacturers. Typical sale lots include:

The Japanese porcelains

239 A rare and important Japanese porcelain figure decorated in enamel colours in a typical style and palette. 15¾ inches high, c. 1700. *Sotheby & Co., London*

A remove of 12 dishes of the old Japan	£4 15s 0d [Dec. 1766]
A set of three fine old Japan jars and 2 beakers	£12 10s 0d [Feb. 1767]
A set of three fine large magnificent jars and covers and two beakers of the rare old Japan	£11 11s 0d [Nov. 1767]
A set of three octagon jars and covers and two beakers of the blue Japan (faulty)	£12 17s 0d [Feb. 1769]
Two fine Japan dishes of the flower-pot pattern	16s 0d [Feb. 1769]

Dishes of this pattern were featured in the 1707 East India Company sale, and a barber's bowl of this standard pattern is shown in Plate 225.

The English East India Company directors seem to have continued their endeavours to open, or re-open, the trade to Japan. On 20 November 1774, the Supra-cargoes in Canton wrote home to the Honourable Court of Directors in London: 'Not withstanding our constant endeavours to get the clearest information of the means of opening a trade to Japan, we are sorry to acquaint your honours that it has not yet been in our power to procure such intelligence as we give any grounds to hope for success in forming an intercourse with that Country.'

Soame Jenyns, in his *Japanese Porcelain*, sums up the general view: 'Defeated in the world markets, Japan retreated into herself and from the latter half of the eighteenth century onwards concentrated on her art-loving ceramic public, until Perry's black ships arrived in Japan in 1853...' A popular belief, but is it strictly correct? Some Japanese wares, mainly lacquer, were included in the 1851 exhibition. Henry Cole was reputedly acquiring contemporary Japanese objects in 1852 for the Museum of Manufacturers; and an exhibition of Japanese Art was held in London in 1854. The 1862 exhibition is generally acknowledged to have opened British eyes to the new Japanese taste, yet such wares were already or at least soon to be on the market. The *Art Journal* of December 1862 printed a review of Messrs Rittener & Saxby's stock of porcelain in their Albemarle Street Shop. This report stated: '…at the present moment their showrooms are filled, in every available nook and corner, with all that would delight the most accomplished judge of rare Dresden, fine Sèvres and gorgeous Chinese and Japanese wares…' Unfortunately the Customs records of imports help only in a negative manner, for before 1865 imports from Japan were not separately tabulated. In 1865 only 162 cwt of Japanese pottery and porcelain was recorded as being imported into Britain. However, one of the most famous Victorian potters, R. W. Binns of 'Royal Worcester' fame, wrote in his book *Worcester China, a record of the work of forty-five years, 1852–1897* (London, 1897):

The Art of Japan has, in a remarkable manner, made for itself a home in the West. It has entered the drawing-room and the library, the boudoir and even the nursery…Japanese cabinets, screens, fans, umbrellas and china are seen on every side and the consequent influence upon Western art is very marked. This invasion of the West by the East has been accomplished by slow degrees, but there can be no doubt that it had its beginnings in the Exhibitions held in London in 1862, and in Paris in 1867.

The wonderful displays then made by the Japanese will never be forgotten by the artists and the manufacturers who had the good fortune to study them. The ideas were so original, the work so perfect and so highly finished…that everybody was captivated by their beauty…

While Binns was writing of Japanese imports generally, these wares most certainly had their effect on European fashion and on ceramic design.

The opposite view is expressed by Soame Jenyns: 'For the greater part of the porcelain produced in

240 A rare pair of Japanese porcelain dogs enamelled in the Kakiemon style. Some of the models listed in Chapter 7 could well have been of Japanese origin and sold in London by the English East India Company. 5¾ inches high, *c.* 1700.

Sotheby & Co., London

The Japanese porcelains

Japan in the latter half of the nineteenth century and onwards is, in my experience, aesthetically worthless, and quite profitless to study.' Which authority are we to follow? We can best use our own discrimination for, as with most things, there are good and bad sides. But the good is worth seeking and can profitably be studied. Unfortunately, very little has been written about even the later Japanese wares, which are in fact outside the scope of this book. I have, however, included in my illustrations a selection showing typical Japanese wares of the type imported in the latter part of the nineteenth century and in the opening years of the present century. These wares are of a commercial type, imported into most European countries and into North America in quantity, and sold at modest prices. These and similar wares are not rare museum pieces, certainly not approaching in quality the superb Satsuma wares which at their best are probably unequalled for their minute quality decoration. These Satsuma wares are now finding respect after years of neglect by most collectors.

Satsuma earthenware lies outside the scope of the present book but since much Satsuma has a porcelain-like quality, and since it is rightly coming back into favour, I have included a few illustrations of typical specimens of what we now generally call Satsuma. However, the term has for long been misused, and the name has been applied to large and rather hideous objects. As long ago as 1890 a Japanese writer, Masayuki Kataoka, in the *Magazine of Art*, attempted to clarify the position, and in so doing he helps us to understand now the types of Japanese ware coming into Europe towards the end of the last century:

Europeans have long been accustomed to recognise as Satsuma pieces which are, in truth, mercantile products, made chiefly at Awata and Kioto. They are composed of almost as much porcelain as faience, a good deal of the porcelain clay being mixed with them. They are profusely

241 Large Japanese twentieth-century wares of the type known as 'Satsuma'. Reproduced from a Liberty & Co. catalogue of c. 1920.

242 A selection of twentieth-century Japanese 'Kaga ware' with retail prices. Reproduced from a Liberty & Co. catalogue of c. 1920.

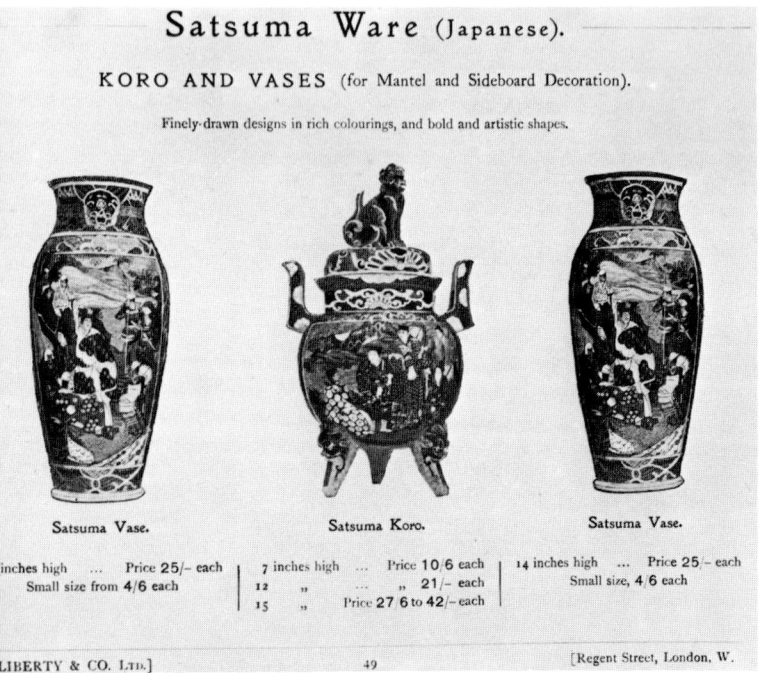

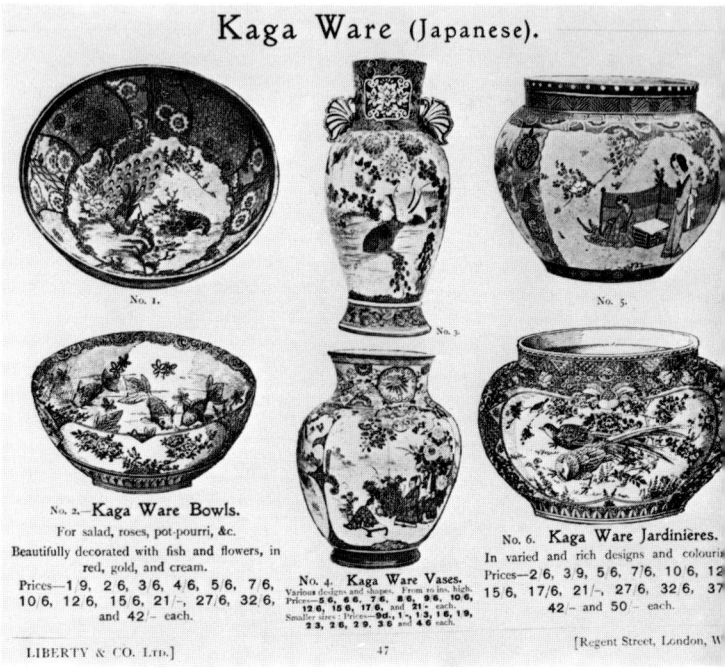

decorated with figures, commonly of Buddhist character, but often with scenes from the old history of Japan. They are richly decorated with reliefs in gold and coloured enamels. It would be quite safe to say that when you see any large specimens of jars, incense-burners, huge pots for flowers, surmounted by dragons profusely painted and heavily gilt, you may at once make up your mind that they are not old Satsuma…I hope that what I have written about old Satsuma may not have disappointed the many persons who have been accustomed to form their ideas of Satsuma by reference to the enormous flood of florid, heavily gilt, and richly painted Kioto ware which has for the last twenty years been poured into European markets and passed off as Satsuma and which has, I am afraid, often deceived collectors and been sold for very high prices, although really they are mere mercantile products which can be reproduced *ad infinitum* with great rapidity and ease, and have only the value of ordinary crockery…

This nineteenth-century authority was no doubt referring to the large coarse Japanese pottery vases and similar objects, examples perhaps similar to those shown in the contemporary advertisement reproduced in Plate 241. Other late Japanese export wares are shown in the advertisements reproduced in Plates 242–244. These wares have little relation in quality and charm to the delicate small gems, such as the box shown in Colour Plate 19 or the jar shown in Plate 245. Further information on later Japanese wares may be found in William Burton's *A General History of Porcelain* (London, 1921), or in the more recent book by Irene Stitt *Japanese*

Ceramics of the Last 100 Years (New York, 1974). See also an article by David Battie, '19th Century Japanese Earthenware' published in *Antique Collecting*, May 1978.

Not long ago I observed in an antique trade publication an advertisement for modern Japanese vases in the traditional styles. The wording is of some interest: 'Even today, in the town of Arita in the Imari district of Japan, craftsmen practise their art in much the same way as they did over three hundred years ago…Each item is hand-painted and retains the same timeless beauty and superb craftmanship which has made it a favourite with collectors and enthusiasts down the years.'

Today the Japanese ceramic industry is certainly a very powerful force, producing not so much traditional designs but rather slick porcelains in the modern manner. These wares are exported to the world's markets and in many cases they undersell the home product. After a somewhat uneven passage Japanese wares have lasted for over three hundred years and present-day retailers might re-echo the January 1701 instructions of the East India Company directors to their agents in China: 'Gett what Japan earthenware you can if you think it profitable.'

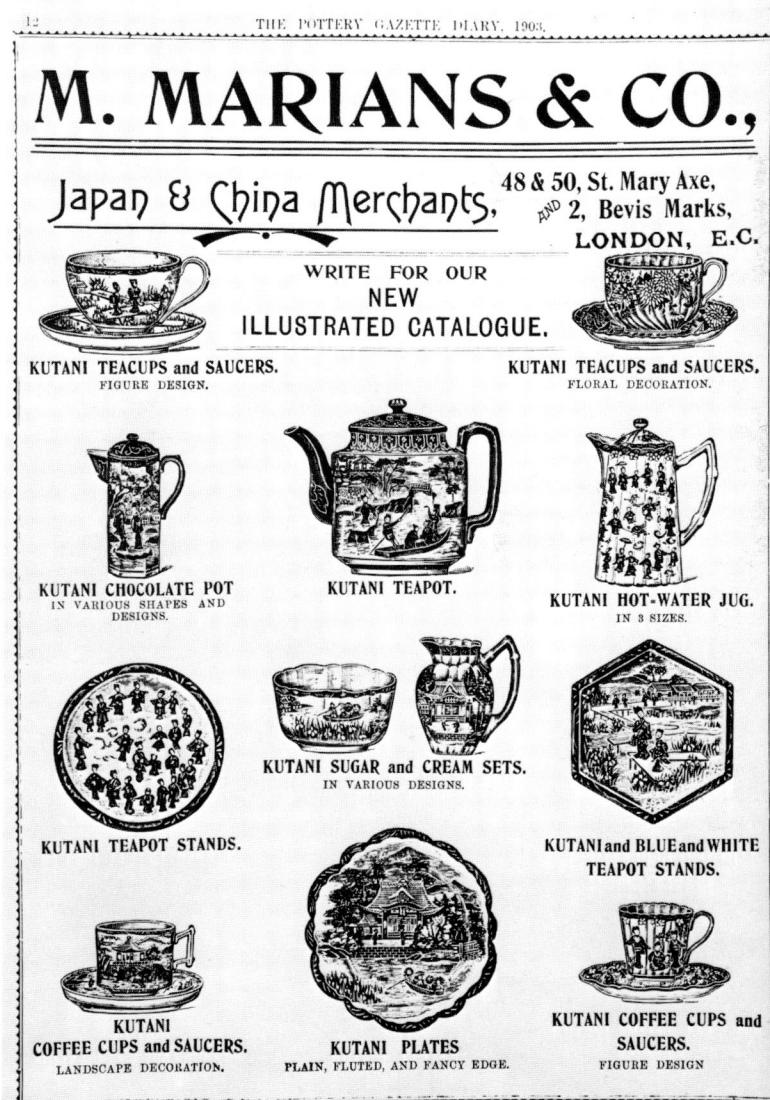

243 A selection of twentieth-century Japanese porcelains of the type exported to Europe and North America in vast quantities. Reproduced from the *Pottery Gazette Diary* of 1903.

244 A selection of twentieth-century Japanese porcelain decorated in the old Imari style. Such wares were cheap and colourful, and fulfilled a popular demand. Reproduced from a Liberty & Co. catalogue of c. 1910.

Imari Ware (Japanese).

Vases (open top and with covers), Plates, Bowls, Cups, Saucers, Teapots, Jugs, Umbrella Spills, &c., in endless variety of design. Colourings—Red, Blue, White and Gold, one or more of the colours predominating, or blending in equal proportion.

No. 1. **Imari Jars and Covers.**
(Kylin Tops.) Bold and decorative designs.
18 inches high ... Price 15/6 each.
Small sizes from 1/6 each.

No. 2.
Imari Jardinières.
Rich and bold floral and other decorations, in deep blues and reds.
Prices—1/9, 2/6, 3/9, 5/6, 7/6 and 10/6 each.
Size suitable for palm — 7 inches diameter by 8 inches high.
Price 7/6 each.

No. 3.
Imari Jardinières.
Rich and bold decoration in varied colourings.
Prices—1/9, 2/6, 3/9, 5/6, 7/6 and 10/6 each.
Size suitable for palm — 7 inches diameter by 8 inches high.
Price 7/6 each.

No. 4.
Imari Tea and Pot-Pourri Jars and Covers.
In rich red and blue colours, decorations in medallions, 8 inches high.
Prices from 1/9 each.

No. 5. **Imari Bowls.**
In varied colours and figured, floral, and conventional designs, for table decoration.
Prices—6d., 9d., 1/-, 1/6, 1/9, 2/6, 3/6, 5/6, 7/6, 10/6, 15/6, 21/- and 30/- each.

No. 6.
Imari Vases.
(Beaker shaped.) In rich floral and figure decoration and effective colourings.
In a variety of sizes.
Prices from 1/- to 63/- each.

No. 7.
Imari Vases.
(Bottle shaped.) In floral and conventional designs and bold rich colourings.
Prices from 1/- to 63/- each.

No. 8.
Imari Vases.
Richly decorated in red and blue colours and medallion designs.
In a variety of shapes and sizes.
Prices from 1/- to 63/- each.

LIBERTY & Co. LTD.] [LONDON & PARIS.

245 A superb quality Japanese 'Satsuma' ware covered hexagonal vase typical of the finer late-nineteenth-century examples. 11½ inches high, c. 1880. *Christies, London*

Colour Plate 19 A finely enamelled Japanese satsuma ware covered box – superb quality if rather fussy. 2½ inches high, c. 1880.
Godden of Worthing Ltd

11 The influence of Oriental wares on European porcelains

Countless books could be filled with illustrations of British pottery and porcelain decorated in the Oriental style, for probably over fifty per cent of the total British ceramic output shows this influence, and even today the traditional blue-printed Willow pattern can be found in most modern china shops, together with many other designs which can be traced back to Oriental prototypes.

The following discussion focuses solely on typical pieces from the major English factories, but it underlines the importance of the eighteenth-century trade in Chinese porcelains and its influence on British potters. Also, of course, Oriental porcelains served as the ideal of all British potters. As early as 1638 Christian Wilhelm, the Southwark 'Gallipot maker', claimed that he had invented the making of 'white earthenware pots glazed both within and without which show as fair as Chinese dishes'. This potter may have been the one that Captain Saris was to visit at Southwark in November 1614 to purchase stone pots for trade with Japan (see p. 302).

While this chapter covers only the major British porcelain factories it should be remembered that the late-seventeenth- and early-eighteenth-century Elers-type redware teapots were made in close imitation of the Oriental pots (Plate 5), and that these early English copies bore Chinese-style seal-marks. Also, the many potteries turning out tin-glazed Delft-type earthenwares favoured Oriental motifs. The Bristol tin-glazed earthenware plate shown in Plate 246 is dated 1679, showing Japanese or Chinese influence at an early date. Late in the eighteenth century and throughout the nineteenth century the staple blue-printed English earthenwares bore designs in the main based on Chinese designs, or rather the engraver's often naive idea of what Chinese buildings and landscapes looked like.

340 Oriental export market porcelain

246 An early Bristol tin-glazed earthenware plate painted in the fashionable Oriental style, although probably not a direct copy of any Oriental piece. Diameter 7¾ inches, dated 1679.
Sotheby & Co., London

247 A powder-blue ground Bow porcelain plate painted in underglaze blue in the popular Chinese style. The word 'Bow' has been worked into the design at the base of the vase in the central panel. Diameter 8½ inches, c. 1755–60.
Sotheby & Co., London

Bow (c. 1747–1776)

The Bow factory in London was established in the 1740s and the first recorded printed reference to it underlines the association with Chinese porcelains. This reference appeared in the fourth revised 1748 edition of Defoe's *Tour of Great Britain*: '…a large manufactory of Porcelain is lately set up. They have already made large quantities of tea-cups, saucers, etc, which by some skilful persons are said to be little inferior to those which are brought from China…'

The proprietors, then Alderman Arnold & Co., in fact traded on the popularity of the imported Chinese porcelains and chose to call their own works in London 'New Canton'. Some small inkwells bear the inscription 'Made at New Canton', with a date 1750 or 1751. The enamelled design is rather more Japanese in feeling than Chinese, but china-ware from Canton was the popular commodity. Fragments of true Chinese porcelain have been found on the Bow factory site in London, and Alderman George Arnold, a partner in the concern, had many dealings with the English East India Company.

The Chinese influence on Bow porcelain is mainly to be seen in the pieces decorated in underglaze blue. This factory produced a wide range of blue and white wares over a lengthy period – from the late 1740s to the mid-1770s. Of this, probably more than ninety per cent bears designs showing the popular Oriental influence and some pieces bear mock-Chinese character marks. The Bow management favoured copies of powder-blue ground designs, mainly found today on plates and dishes. The example shown in Plate 247 shows clearly the granular appearance of the dusted-on blue pigment and the word 'Bow' can be read at the base of the vase in the central panel. The small blue and white Bow porcelain teapot shown in Plate 248 represents a class of teawares bearing simple

The influence of Oriental wares on European porcelains

248 A small Bow porcelain globular teapot decorated in underglaze blue with a mock-Chinese landscape. The imported Chinese porcelains, and these early English wares, were in direct competition for the favours of the buying public. 5 inches high, c. 1760.   *Godden of Worthing Ltd*

249 A rare Bow porcelain presentation mug painted in underglaze blue exhibiting the preoccupation with Chinese-style designs on mid-eighteenth-century English porcelains. 5¾ inches high, dated 1770. *Victoria and Albert Museum (Crown Copyright)*

Chinese-inspired designs. Most of these wares were made in the 1760s. Such tearwares are normally unmarked, except for the presence on some pieces of the English painter's reference number.

While most Bow blue and white porcelains comprise tablewares, some special pieces were made and the presentation mug shown in Plate 249 is an example. It is dated 1770 under the base.

The enamelled Bow porcelains often show a decided Japanese influence, and some charming designs in the Kakiemon style were made. The pair of bottles shown in Plate 250 are typical and indicate a continued demand for Japanese-style porcelains in the 1750s and 1760s, although the original records usually describe these designs as after the 'old Japan' wares rather than as copies of contemporary imports. The *Public Advertiser* of 13 April 1757 contained the following report: 'We hear that this day and tomorrow will finish the sale at the new auction-room in Spring Garden of the Bow china, and that there will be exhibited large table services of the finest old Japan patterns...' and I have already related that the Bow management borrowed Japanese porcelains from Lady Cavendish to copy the designs on to English porcelains.

A *Public Advertiser* announcement of a sale of Bow porcelain in February 1758 contains the words '...some part of this Porcelain is very little inferior to the fine old brown edge Japan...', and in a report of May 1764 a standard Bow Japanese-type design is mentioned as being removed direct from the manufactory at Bow and the Bow warehouse in Cornhill, on the bankruptcy of John Crowther. This stock in trade included 'Five desserts of the fine old Partridge [or Quail] and Wheatsheaf pattern...' The Bow dish shown in Plate 251 is of this general Japanese type in the Kakiemon style. The red and gold border design is characteristic.

While most Bow porcelains reveal Oriental

The influence of Oriental wares on European porcelains

250 A fine pair of Bow porcelain bottles enamelled in the still fashionable Japanese fashion. 8 inches high, c. 1760.
Sotheby & Co., London

251 An oval shaped-edge Bow porcelain dish with Kakiemon-type decoration. It represents one of the standard and seemingly very popular Bow essays in this style. 7½ inches long, c. 1755–60. *Godden of Worthing Ltd*

253 A finely enamelled Chelsea porcelain dish depicting the 'Hob in the Well' subject from a Kakiemon original, perhaps via a Meissen copy, but showing the continued popularity of Japanese designs in the mid-eighteenth century. Diameter 12 inches, c. 1750. *Sotheby & Co., London*

252 A typical Chelsea porcelain saucer-shaped dish enamelled in the Kakiemon style but perhaps copied second-hand from Meissen porcelains. Diameter 16¾ inches, c. 1750. *David Newbon, London*

254 The front and back view of a Chelsea porcelain figure of the Chinese Goddess Kuan-yin in the style of *Blanc de Chine* porcelains. Raised-anchor mark on reverse. 4¾ inches high, c. 1749–52. *Private collection*

The influence of Oriental wares on European porcelains

255 A fine Chelsea porcelain vase of the raised-anchor period decorated with relief-moulded prunus blossom in the style of the still popular Chinese *Blanc de Chine* wares (see Chapter 8). 9 inches high, c. 1749–52.

Sotheby & Co., London

256 A marked 'Bristoll' porcelain figure in the style of Chinese *Blanc de Chine* wares (see Chapter 8) bearing also the moulded date 1750 and evidencing the continued popularity of these white porcelains. 7 inches high, moulded date 1750.

Victoria and Albert Museum (Crown Copyright)

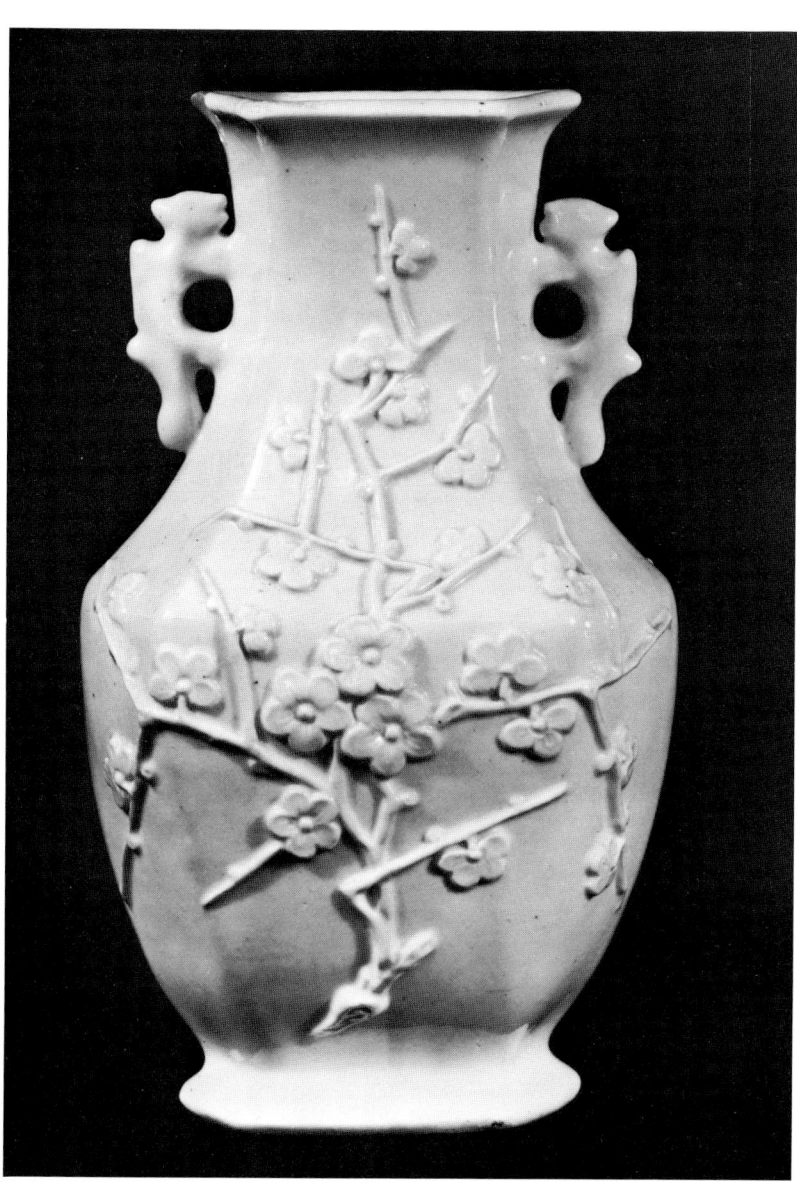

influence, the basic body from which they were formed is vastly different from the Chinese. As previously stated, the Oriental body is of true or hard-paste porcelain – cold, compact and glittery – but the Bow porcelain is relatively soft. It is almost open in texture and will stain quite easily where the protective covering of glaze is faulty. The Bow potting is often decidedly inferior to the Chinese. Like the Lowestoft body, Bow porcelain contains a relatively high proportion of bone-ash, normally about forty per cent.

Chelsea (c. 1745–1769)
The Oriental influence most notable on the fine porcelains made at this great London factory is more Japanese than Chinese, although it is by no means certain whether the designs were taken from true Japanese porcelains already in this country or if they were copied second-hand from Meissen or other Continental wares. Whichever is the case they are most attractive and typical examples are seen in Plates 252–253.

Chelsea copies of Oriental porcelains did not bear mock-Oriental marks; they bore (if marked at all) the standard Chelsea factory emblem, an anchor device. Japanese- or Chinese-style Chelsea designs occur in the earlier period, in the late 1740s and early 1750s, rather than in the more flamboyant later gold-anchor period, c. 1756–69. Most Chelsea porcelain bears enamelled decoration. The underglaze blue designs are extremely rare, and this style of decoration, standard at most other factories, seems to have been avoided by the Chelsea management. Nevertheless the few designs that are known show the prevailing Oriental taste.

The Chelsea management did, however, produce some charming porcelains in the style of the white *Blanc de Chine* Chinese porcelains (see Chapter 8). I show in Plates 254–255 two typical examples. The figure of the Goddess Kuan-yin shows, in the back view, the raised anchor mark of the approximate period 1749–52. At an earlier period these white porcelains had been made at Meissen and at the early French factories.

As I have explained in Chapter 8, the available records show that the white porcelains were imported into London in the very early years of the eighteenth century. The Chelsea essays in the same style show that the plain porcelains were still saleable, and perhaps they suggest that the Chinese white porcelains were still being imported in the middle of the century.

Bristol (c. 1749–1752)
The first known English porcelain factory in the West Country was established by Benjamin Lund and William Miller at Redcliff Backs, Bristol, in about 1749. It was taken over by the Worcester management in 1752, and transferred to that city. In these three years a charming assortment of porcelain was made. The great majority of pieces seem to have been fashioned or decorated in the Oriental style, but unfortunately few examples were marked. I show in Plates 256–257 a *Blanc de Chine* figure with the relief-moulded mark 'BRISTOLL, 1750', also a relief-moulded large sauceboat with Chinese-style landscape designs in underglaze blue.

Derby (c. 1750 into nineteenth century)
The enamelled porcelains produced at this important Midland porcelain factory seem to have been influenced by Continental rather than Oriental wares, indeed the management were moved to term their factory or products the 'second Dresden'. Nevertheless, some teawares were decorated with Chinese-style figure patterns.

However, Derby blue and white porcelains display a decided swing towards mock-Oriental landscape and figure designs – presumably broadly in competition with Chinese blue and white

The influence of Oriental wares on European porcelains

Colour Plate 20 A superb large Chinese porcelain deep serving dish painted in England by a talented ceramic painter; his hand is to be found on many other examples of once undecorated mid-eighteenth century Chinese porcelain. Diameter 15 inches, $3\frac{3}{4}$ inches deep, *c.* 1755. *Godden of Worthing Ltd*

257 A marked Bristol porcelain sauceboat, the panels painted in underglaze blue in the highly popular Chinese style of decoration. 8 inches long, c. 1750–52.
Geoffrey Godden Chinaman, reference collection

258 A fine Derby porcelain dish painted in underglaze blue in the fashionable Chinese style. 8 inches long, c. 1760.
Sotheby & Co., London

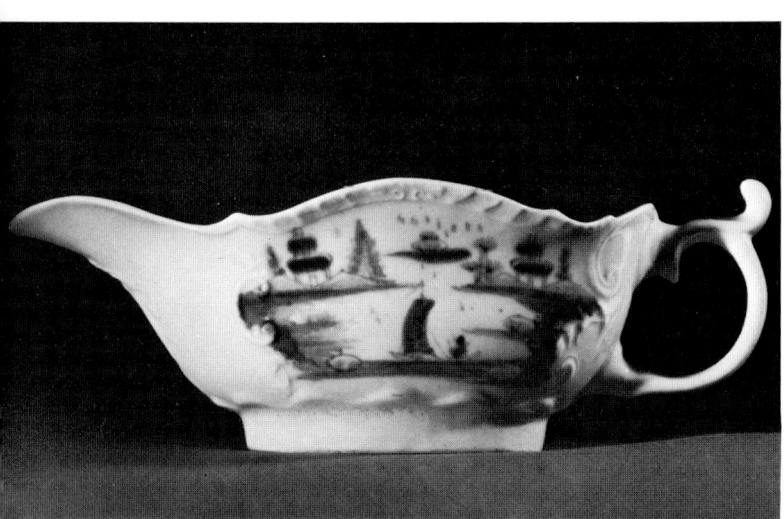

porcelains. A typical Derby example is shown in Plate 258.

In the late 1750s the Derby management's agent or factor in London was a china dealer, Thomas Williams, 'at his large Foreign China Warehouse' near the Admiralty, where he also stocked a 'great variety' of Chinese porcelains, fans and the like. Some charming early Derby figures and groups show Oriental influence although they are not direct copies of Chinese imports. Recently, however, a Derby Kuan-yin in the style of Plate 254 has been reported.

The one class of design long associated with the Derby factory are the 'Japan' patterns. These are quite different from the Chelsea essays in the Kakiemon style, such as those shown in Plates 252–253. The Derby Japan patterns are represented by very colourful formal floral designs with areas of underglaze blue and overglaze red and gilt enrichments. Early designs in this style were probably included in the Derby auction sale held in May 1783. The catalogue included lots such as: 'A pair of beautiful pint mugs enamell'd rich old Japan pattern.' 'A very elegant complete desert service enamell'd, the fine old Japan pattern.'

Most of the Derby 'Japan' patterns are of nineteenth-century date and are similar to the examples shown in Plate 259. The point must be made, however, that these English 'Japan' patterns (which were by no means confined to the Derby factory) are very far removed from true Japanese ceramics and probably no student of Japanese design would acknowledge their source.

Longton Hall (*c.* 1750–1760)
This Staffordshire porcelain manufactory produced, among its other products, a range of porcelains decorated in underglaze blue. Most of these designs display the current fashion for Oriental-style designs.

The influence of Oriental wares on European porcelains

259 A typical early-nineteenth-century Derby porcelain jug decorated in the ever-popular 'Japan' style of the earlier Imari wares. Most other English factories followed this fashion. $4\frac{1}{2}$ inches high, c. 1820. *Godden of Worthing Ltd*

Oriental export market porcelain

260 A fine early Worcester sauceboat, and a small creamboat, delicately enamelled with mock-Chinese figures in landscapes in a style popular in the mid-eighteenth century. Sauceboat 7 inches long, c. 1755.

Geoffrey Godden Chinaman, reference collection

Worcester (c. 1751 into the nineteenth century and, by various changes in management, up to the present day)

I have already explained that the Worcester partners bought the secrets and working materials of the first Bristol porcelain manufactory, and the early Worcester porcelains, both in underglaze blue and enamelled designs, show an almost complete mock-Chinese air. I illustrate in Plate 260 two representative pieces of early Worcester porcelain in the mock-Chinese or 'Chinoiserie' style. The fine soaprock-type body was extremely compact and durable and was often compared to the Chinese. In 1765 the *Handmaid of the Arts* by Robert Dossie recorded that the Worcester pieces 'have great tenacity and bear hot-water without more hazard than the true China ware'.

Many of the Worcester enamelled floral designs reflect the influence of Chinese *famille verte* and *famille rose* porcelains. The Worcester painters also

The influence of Oriental wares on European porcelains

261 A finely 'pencilled' Worcester porcelain spoon-tray in the general style of the black-pencilled Jesuit porcelains (see Chapter 7). 6 inches long, c. 1755–60. *Godden of Worthing Ltd*

produced essays in the Jesuit style of black-pencilled decoration; witness the charming spoontray in Plate 261. They also produced armorial porcelains (Plate 262) very much in the style of Chinese export market porcelains (see Chapter 6).

The Worcester factory also produced a host of patterns which they were pleased to name 'Old Japan' and which often bore mock-Oriental marks in underglaze blue as depicted in Plate 263. A 1769 auction sale of Worcester porcelains included, for example:

A complete tea and coffee equipage of the fine old Japan star pattern.
Twelve beautiful plates, old mosaik Japan pattern.
Six breakfast basons and plates in fine old scrole Japan pattern.
A complete tea and coffee equipage with handles, fine old scarlet Japan pattern.

It would be impossible to illustrate here more

352　　　　　　　　　　　　　　　　　　　　　　　Oriental export market porcelain

262　A rare Worcester porcelain bowl in the style of the Chinese armorial porcelains (see Chapter 6). This example may well be a replacement for a broken Chinese original. Diameter 6¾ inches, c. 1775.　　　　　　　　　　　　　　　*Godden of Worthing Ltd*
263　A large Worcester porcelain teapot decorated in one of the popular 'Japan' patterns. A matching saucer is reversed to show the typical mock-Oriental mark often found on these Worcester examples. Diameter of saucer 4¾ inches, c. 1765.
Godden of Worthing Ltd

than a token selection of Worcester porcelain in the Oriental taste, but the interested reader can consult such standard books as Henry Sandon's *The Illustrated Guide to Worcester Porcelain 1751–1793* (London, 1969; second edition 1974).

Liverpool (*c.* 1754 into the nineteenth century)
The city of Liverpool housed many potteries producing tin-glazed earthenwares and several porcelain manufactories, some of which enjoyed a wide export trade. It is a difficult exercise to differentiate between the various makes of Liverpool porcelain, and this is not the place to discuss these wares at any length. Interested readers should consult Bernard Watney's *English Blue and White Porcelain of the 18th Century* (London, 1963; second edition 1973). However, I cannot resist showing one blue and white cup and saucer (Plate 264) from the Chaffers factory, dating from the late 1750s.

Lowestoft (*c.* 1757–1799)
The old authorities on English ceramics endeavoured to suggest that the hard-paste Chinese export market porcelains, such as those described in this book, were made at this very modest English porcelain factory which boasted only two kilns, the proprietors of which termed themselves 'China manufacturers and Herring curers'. This old belief was nonsense, but it is still reflected in outdated terms such as 'Chinese Lowestoft' which is sometimes used to describe true Chinese porcelain made for the European market.

　The real Lowestoft porcelains are of the soft-paste type containing a large proportion of bone-ash. In general, Lowestoft wares are very similar to Bow porcelains. The early blue and white examples often have charming, rather naive Chinese landscape designs similar to those seen in Plate 265. Other pieces, such as the rare plates and dishes, are rather closer to the Chinese in the basic shape. The

The influence of Oriental wares on European porcelains

264 A fine Liverpool blue and white cup and saucer from the Chaffers factory which, like other concerns, relied heavily on mock-Chinese designs. Note also the Oriental-type markings under the cup. Diameter of saucer 4 inches, *c.* 1758.
Sotheby & Co., London

265 A selection of typical early soft-paste Lowestoft relief-moulded porcelains decorated in underglaze blue with panels of the fashionable Chinese-style figure and landscape designs. Sauceboat 7¾ inches long, *c.* 1760–65.
Geoffrey Godden Chinaman, reference collection

greater part of the factory's output was decorated in underglaze blue, but from about 1770 we find an interesting class called 'Redgrave' patterns, which incorporate areas of underglaze blue with overglaze red, green and gold in the style of some Chinese and Japanese porcelains. The saucers shown in Plate 266 are typical, the example on the left is Lowestoft soft-paste, that on the right Oriental hard-paste.

Much of the enamelled Lowestoft porcelain made from about 1770 into the 1790s bears Chinese-style figure designs (Plate 267), while other standard enamelled patterns are very similar to the formal Chinese export market floral patterns but not all Lowestoft porcelains were decorated in the Oriental style. Lowestoft wares are in many respects the most English of all English porcelains. A full selection of the patterns and basic shapes are depicted in my *Illustrated Guide to Lowestoft Porcelain* (London, 1969).

Plymouth (*c.* 1768–1770)
At this small West Country porcelain factory the first English hard-paste porcelain was made. It was not very successful. Difficulties were experienced in firing the body and glaze correctly, so that it is also the shortest-lived of the British porcelain factories.

Many of the blue and white porcelains were painted with naive Chinese-style landscape designs (Plate 268), while some rare enamelled designs also show this influence. When marked, the Plymouth porcelains bear the factory device, the alchemical sign for tin, a 2 and 4 conjoined: ♃.

Bristol (*c.* 1770–1781)
The Plymouth concern was transferred to Bristol in about 1770 and here, first under William Cookworthy and then under Richard Champion hard-paste porcelain was produced. In quality it is superior to the earlier rather smoky-glazed Plymouth porcelains. Again the underglaze blue

266 An interesting comparison: right, a Chinese hard-paste export market saucer decorated in underglaze blue with overglaze red and green and gilding and, left, the same design in soft-paste Lowestoft porcelain, one of the popular 'Redgrave' patterns. Diameter 4¾ inches, c. 1780.　　*Godden of Worthing Ltd*

patterns were often in the Chinese style and the less expensive enamelled teawares also show this influence, while the more expensive porcelains have a decidedly Continental flavour. The latter pieces often bear a copy of the Meissen crossed-swords mark. The standard Bristol factory mark is a blue cross, often with a painter's or gilder's number added below.

Caughley (*c.* 1775–1799)
The Caughley, or 'Salopian', porcelains are in body, and often in form and decoration, very similar to the Worcester soapstone porcelains. The vast majority of the products were decorated in underglaze blue. More often than not these were printed rather than hand-painted. Most of the blue and white designs were very Chinese in feeling, and often the same design can be found hand-painted on contemporary or near-contemporary Chinese export market porcelains. Sometimes the shapes, too, are similar, as in the case of the teapot shown in Plate 269 which can be compared with the Chinese specimens shown in Plates 54 and 55. See also Plate 67.

In general, the Caughley management (that is, Thomas Turner) confined products to tea and dessert wares instead of trying to rival or undersell the Chinese dinner-services, but when dinner wares

The influence of Oriental wares on European porcelains

267 A selection of soft-paste Lowestoft porcelains enamelled in the style of the fashionable Chinese imports. Coffee-pot 8 inches high, c. 1780. *Sotheby & Co., London*

are found in Caughley porcelain they are normally decorated with the fussy, printed, 'Full Nankin' design, as contemporary accounts termed it. A large meat-dish of this kind is shown in Plate 45. Mock-Chinese marks can occur on powder-blue decorated pieces, but the more usual pieces bear the impressed name-mark 'SALOPIAN' or the blue printed initial marks 'S' or 'C'.

A full selection of Caughley shapes and patterns is illustrated in my *Caughley and Worcester Porcelains 1775–1800* (London, 1969).

New Hall (c. 1781–1835)

To most collectors of English porcelain the name New Hall is associated with simple, rather cottage, sprig-patterned teawares typified in Plate 270 by the pieces of pattern '195', a very popular design. These can be broadly linked with some Chinese export market porcelains of the 1775–90 period. Other standard New Hall useful wares were decorated with Chinese-style figure designs of the type shown in Plate 271. They were often formed by colouring printed outline-designs by hand.

The basic New Hall porcelain body is of the hard-paste type, although not so hard as that used at Bristol or Plymouth, or by the Chinese. The hard-paste body was changed to the standard English bone-china body in about 1812. The earlier New

268 A Plymouth hard-paste porcelain creamer painted in underglaze blue and a small mug (in this case the design has also been embellished with red enamel). Creamer 3¾ inches high, 1768–70. *Geoffrey Godden Chinaman, reference collection*
269 A typical blue-painted Caughley teapot. The relief-moulded handle and spout forms also occur on blue and white Chinese export market porcelains (see Plates 54 and 55). Printed 'S' mark. 5½ inches high, c. 1785. *Godden of Worthing Ltd*

270 A selection of New Hall teawares of pattern number 195, one broadly based on the popular enamelled floral motifs of Chinese export market porcelains of the 1780s. Teapot 5¾ inches high, c. 1790–95. *Godden of Worthing Ltd*

The influence of Oriental wares on European porcelains

271 A New Hall coffee-pot of pattern 425, a popular Chinese-style design printed in outline and coloured in by hand. 10¼ inches high, c. 1800. *Godden of Worthing Ltd*

Hall wares do not bear a factory mark, only painted pattern numbers, and many other firms produced very similar fashionable designs on shapes that can resemble the New Hall forms. For further details consult David Holgate's *New Hall and its Imitators* (London, 1971).

Chamberlain-Worcester (1788–1852)
Robert Chamberlain, reputedly the first apprentice taken on by the original Worcester porcelain company, established his own decorating establishment in Worcester in 1788. At first he decorated white porcelains purchased from Thomas Turner of the Caughley factory, but by about 1791 Robert and his son Humphrey were producing their own porcelains.

The early pieces, before about 1810, were mainly confined to useful wares such as tea or dessert-services, and several of the early designs show the prevailing Oriental influence. The tea-bowl, coffee cup and saucer of the early 1790s shown in Plate 272 are naively charming, but the design was probably copied from early Worcester porcelains rather than direct from a Chinese prototype. However, the plate shown in Plate 273 is an almost exact copy of Chinese export market porcelains of the 1775–80 period.

Coalport (*c.* 1796–present-day)
Before about 1815 the Coalport porcelains were of the hybrid hard-paste type, heavy and rather thickly potted. Many of the early useful wares were decorated in underglaze blue, and these were often extremely close to imported Chinese wares. The two small dinner-service tureens shown in Plate 274 illustrate this similarity. The one on the left is Chinese, the one on the right is a Coalport copy bearing an underglaze blue transfer-printed copy of the hand-painted Chinese original.

In 1799 John Rose and his Coalport partners

272 An early Chamberlain-Worcester trio of tea-bowl, coffee cup and saucer, painted with an attractive and popular Chinese-style design. Diameter of saucer $4\frac{1}{4}$ inches, c. 1795.

Godden of Worthing Ltd

The influence of Oriental wares on European porcelains

273 A Chamberlain-Worcester plate enamelled in the popular manner of *famille rose* Chinese porcelains. Diameter 8 inches, c. 1795. *Godden of Worthing Ltd*
274 Left, a Chinese tureen, hand-painted in underglaze blue, and, right, a very close copy in Coalport porcelain printed in underglaze blue. Shown with a fragment from the factory site. 5¾ inches long, c. 1800–1805.
Geoffrey Godden Chinaman, reference collection

bought up Thomas Turner's Caughley factory and continued this with their own Coalport works until 1814, when the latter premises were enlarged to form one of the largest porcelain manufactories in Britain.

The Coalport factory produced a wide and colourful range of 'Japan' patterns; indeed, it seems to have been more prolific even than the Derby factory. But after about 1820 the John Rose management turned their attention more to European or English designs.

Spode (*c.* 1797–1833)
Josiah Spode (1733–97), one of the most famous of English potters, produced a range of high quality earthenwares. It was his son, Josiah Spode II, who introduced the famous English bone-china in about 1800.

These trimly potted, early-nineteenth-century Spode porcelains were often decorated in the prevailing Oriental fashion. The 'Japan' pattern teawares shown in Plate 275 show design number 967, one of the many in this general style. These patterns may be found on a wide range of useful and ornamental objects.

The icepail, dessert centrepiece and candleholder shown in Plate 276 are of Spode's design 2083, a coloured-in printed version of a Chinese export market design popular in the 1770s which illustrates the continued popularity into the nineteenth century of then traditional Oriental designs. Of all the British essays into this style, the Spode examples are generally accepted as being of the finest quality.

In 1833 the Spode name gave way to the Copeland and Garrett partnership which continued the Spode tradition. In 1847 the firm became W. T. Copeland but in recent years the old trade name 'Spode' has been re-introduced.

275 Representative pieces from a Spode bone-china teaset painted with a popular and colourful 'Japan' pattern. Teapot $6\frac{3}{8}$ inches high, c. 1810. *Godden of Worthing Ltd*

Miles Mason (c. 1796–1813)

Miles Mason was a leading 'chinaman' in London in the latter part of the eighteenth century, but when the English East India Company ceased its bulk imports of Chinese porcelains after 1791 he formed a partnership with a Liverpool potter and porcelain manufacturer, Thomas Wolfe, seemingly in an effort to ensure a continuing supply of saleable wares for his London shop.

The Liverpool partnership of Thomas Wolfe, Miles Mason and John Luckcock (or Lucock) traded as Thomas Wolfe & Co. Recent excavations at or near their Islington Pottery site has shown that a range of blue-printed porcelains was made on the lines of the fashionable Chinese 'Nankin' wares. Enamelled porcelains were also made and decorated with formal floral designs in the New Hall manner. This Liverpool partnership was dissolved in June 1800.

Miles Mason then set up his own porcelain manufactory in Staffordshire, and in an advertisement published in October 1804 he claimed that his Staffordshire porcelain 'is now sold only at the principal shops in the city of London and in the country as British Nankin'. He also noted that the wares 'are stamped on the bottom of the larger pieces to prevent imposition'. A blue-printed teapot with the impressed mark 'M. Mason' is shown in Plate 277, and readers will see from the design how apt was the trade description 'British Nankin'. The teapot shown in Plate 278 also bears Mason's name-mark impressed into the foot-rim. This piece illustrates well the attractive New Hall-type floral sprig-patterns also to be found on so much late-eighteenth-century Chinese export-market porcelain. One of the favourite Miles Mason enamelled designs features Chinese-style figure subjects and buildings in the style of the so-called Mandarin patterns.

Miles Mason seems to have retired about 1813,

The influence of Oriental wares on European porcelains

276 A Spode bone-china ice-pail, a dessert centre-piece and a Chinese figure candlestick, each decorated in the very popular design, 2083, being a printed design coloured in. Ice-pail 11 inches high, c. 1810–15. *Godden of Worthing Ltd*

Oriental export market porcelain

277 An impress-marked 'M Mason' blue-printed teapot of the type made by this former London 'chinaman' at his Staffordshire factory. 10¼ inches long, *c.* 1805.
Geoffrey Godden Chinaman, reference collection

278 An attractive enamelled teapot, marked 'M Mason', in the general style of New Hall and Chinese porcelains of the 1780–90 period. 10¼ inches long, *c.* 1805.
Geoffrey Godden Chinaman, reference collection

when the patent for the famous 'Mason's Patent Ironstone China' was taken out in the name of Miles's third son, Charles James Mason. From this period onwards the main concern was with this durable earthenware body rather than with the more delicate porcelains.

The nineteenth century is beyond the scope of this book, but it is relevant to make the point that most of the post-1813 'Patent Ironstone' wares were decorated with colourful Oriental-style designs. In many cases the basic shapes of the objects were copied from Chinese originals or were designed to give the impression of being Oriental.

12 European decorated Oriental porcelains

Apart from Chinese porcelain wholly decorated in China and the English (and Continental) porcelains decorated in the prevailing Oriental style, there is a most interesting class of European painting applied to white Oriental porcelain. Unfortunately very little is known about the source of this added decoration as it was mostly the work of independent painters rather than the large porcelain manufactories.

From quite early in the eighteenth century white Chinese porcelain devoid of any decoration was shipped into Europe. In the china-ware purchasing orders relating to the *Townsend* bound for Canton in 1726 we find listed not only the normal 150 chests of useful porcelains 'most blue and white', but also 'some entire white china of all the before mentioned sorts'. The majority of these basic sorts were dishes, plates, bowls and teawares.

Originally this white Chinese, or Japanese, porcelain was probably imported merely to undersell the decorated varieties, or to sell on its own merits like the *Blanc de Chine* porcelains discussed in Chapter 8. In the mid-eighteenth century vast quantities of Staffordshire salt-glaze stonewares and the later creamwares were sold 'in the white', or in an undecorated state, so why not also the Chinese porcelains.

However, once this fine, unblemished white Oriental porcelain was brought to Europe the idea must have occurred to many dealers and independent decorators to have such 'blanks' dressed up to attract a higher price, or to fulfil special orders. Within three years of the placing of the order to bring home from Canton 'some entire white china' we have a strong indication that at least one china dealer was employing hands to decorate such articles. Interestingly the list of apprentices bound to Freeman of the Worshipful Company of Glass Sellers of London (this was the china dealers' company, since they did not have one of their own) is

Oriental export market porcelain

279 A Chinese waste-bowl finely enamelled and gilt by a German porcelain painter and inscribed 'Bayreith, 1744'. Diameter 4½ inches, c. 1740–44.
Victoria and Albert Museum (Crown Copyright)

281 A Chinese porcelain waste-bowl with relief-moulded floral design under the glaze, enamelled in England and inscribed round the foot 'John and Sarah Jefferyes…1756'. Diameter 6 inches, c. 1750–56.
Victoria and Albert Museum (Crown Copyright)

280 A selection of mid-eighteenth-century Chinese porcelains imported in the white state and decorated by English painters. Creamer 4 inches high, c. 1750–65. *Godden of Worthing Ltd*

preserved in the Guildhall Library (MS. 1645·1–2), and it includes the entry: 'Abraham Giles, son of James Giles of St Giles in the Fields – China Painter, bound to Philip Margas for seven years on 26th June 1729.'

At this period there was no English china in existence, and any porcelain blanks must have been Oriental, or perhaps Continental, although this latter suggestion is highly unlikely. Philip Margas, to whom Abraham Giles was bound apprentice, was a very important London 'chinaman', being a large purchaser at the East India Company's sales of Oriental porcelains. He also had trade contacts in Holland and was engaged in exporting Chinese porcelains from London. The Company's records include numerous references to Charles and William Margas in the 1740s and 1750s. While a Philip Margas appears in the Company's records as early as 1696, most records, including shipment to Holland, are in the name of Margas & Co.

It is not at present known if James Giles, Abraham's father, was himself employed by Margas as a china painter, or if he was engaged in this trade independently, but certainly we have firm evidence that the trade of 'china painter' was being practised in London in the late 1720s – if not before. We shall hear more of James Giles's younger son of the same name on subsequent pages, for he became a leading decorator of porcelains in the 1750s and into the 1770s.

Much of the early European decoration of Oriental porcelain was of Continental origin. Some was German; this is not surprising for there was a tradition there of independent painters of porcelain purchased in the white from Meissen or Vienna. This outside decoration is called *Hausmalerei*. A charming *Hausmalerei* Chinese porcelain bowl is contained in the Victoria and Albert Museum collection (reference number c98·1930) and is here shown in Plate 279. It is inscribed under the base 'Bäyreith 1744'.

Apart from the German painters using Chinese porcelain as their canvas, the Dutch decorated quantities of Japanese porcelains, often with rather broadly painted figure subjects. This seemingly mid-eighteenth-century work suggests that Japanese porcelains were imported into Europe at a rather later date than is generally believed (see Chapter 10).

However, I am concerned with English decorators of Chinese porcelains rather than with Continental additions. Strangely, while British porcelain manufacturers tended to give a Chinese flavour to their own products, when they came to decorate Chinese wares the motifs were purely European. If any passing-off was employed it was to suggest that the Oriental porcelain was of English origin. A selection of typical English-decorated Chinese porcelain is seen in Plate 280, showing the three main types: floral designs, exotic birds and figures in landscapes. Indeed, this selection could be taken as Chelsea or Bow porcelain, rather than Chinese.

An important English-decorated Chinese porcelain bowl is illustrated in Plate 281. This presentation piece is inscribed around the foot 'John and Sarah Jefferyes. 1756…' (The J's are written as I's, as was the custom of the period.) It will be seen that the Chinese porcelain bowl itself was decorated with a floral design in slight relief. This relief-decorated Chinese porcelain was widely employed by British china-painters in the mid-eighteenth century. Further typical examples are shown in Plates 282, 283 and 284. Here the relief seems to have been hand-painted with 'slip' (porcelain body diluted to the consistency of thin cream) on to the china before glazing. It is, however, noticeable that the added 'slip' appears rather whiter than the underlying porcelain. This type of decoration is sometimes referred to as

282 A Chinese cup and saucer with relief underglaze floral and fence design over-painted in England with coloured flowers and insects. Diameter of saucer $4\frac{1}{4}$ inches, c. 1755.

Geoffrey Godden Chinaman

European decorated Oriental porcelains

283 A fine Chinese porcelain mug with relief underglaze floral design over-painted in England with typical exotic birds in the Giles manner (see p. 369). 4⅞ inches high, c. 1760–65.
Sotheby & Co., London

284 A superb Chinese porcelain mug enamelled in the style of James Giles with exotic birds in a landscape (see p. 369). 5¾ inches high, c. 1760–65.
Victoria and Albert Museum (Crown Copyright)

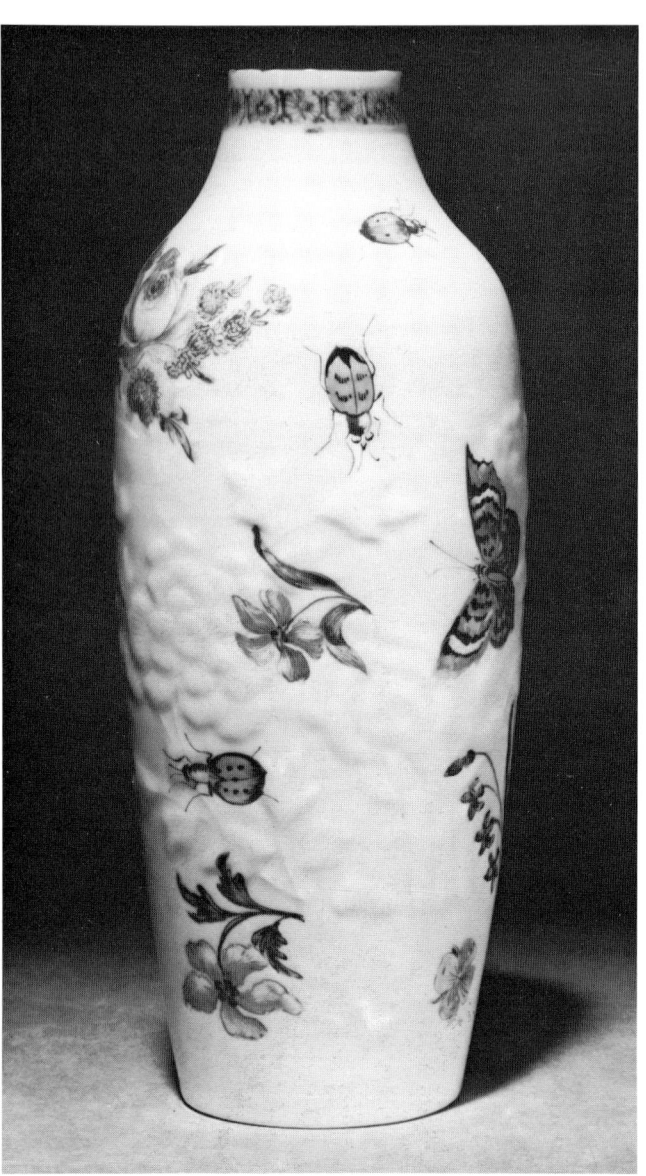

285 A Chinese bottle-vase with relief underglaze floral design, over-painted in England with typical sprays of flowers and insects. 6½ inches high, c. 1755. *Geoffrey Godden Chinaman*

bianco sopra bianco and was copied on European wares. In other examples, such as the vase shown in Plate 285, the reliefs may have been formed by moulding.

English floral painting in a similar style can also occur on Chinese figure models but it is notable that the vast majority of English decoration is to be found on teawares or on presentation objects such as bowls and mugs. It is very rarely found on dinner plates or component parts of dinner sets, and the only example of this type known to me is the large deep meat dish or charger shown in Colour Plate 20, with the owner's crest added on the brim. This piece, by its form, should be dated no later than 1755. Perhaps the reason for this dearth of English-decorated Chinese plates and dinner wares is due not so much to the few blanks imported, as to the fact that the decoration of large surfaces would have been very costly; consequently the wholly Chinese sets, which were imported in large quantities, could not be undersold or indeed bettered.

The English enamel decoration on these Chinese hard-paste porcelains has been widely attributed to James Giles and his London decorating establishment and to the hand of Jefferyes Hamett O'Neale, but clearly many other porcelain painters must have used Chinese blanks.

The name of Jefferyes Hamett O'Neale (1734–1801) is often associated with a class of decoration comprising attractive European or classical landscape and figure motifs painted with a black outline and shading, and washed over with a semi-transparent green enamel. A typical example, a Chinese saucer in the Victoria and Albert Museum (reference number c21.1969), is shown in Plate 286. The obelisk bears the name O'Neale, but unfortunately this refers not to our artist but to Owen Rowe O'Neale, the Irish General and patriot (see an article by J. V. G. Mallet in the *Burlington Magazine* of June 1971). Other pieces in this

286 A Chinese saucer from a teaset painted in England with landscape design washed over with a semi-translucent green enamel, in a typical manner. Diameter 4¾ inches, c. 1755.
Victoria and Albert Museum (Crown Copyright)

general style are shown at the foot of Plate 280, but there is no real evidence that O'Neale painted all (or any) of these green-washed designs. Moreover, the Giles workshop in London also practised this charming form of decoration on various types of English porcelains.

O'Neale was by trade a miniature painter and illustrator who turned his hand to porcelain painting. In 1765 he was to be found 'at the China Shop, Oxford Road, London', now Oxford Street, but he was living in Worcester during the 1768–70 period, before returning to London in the spring of 1770. Signed examples of his figure-painting on Worcester porcelain are in the British Museum and the Dyson Perrins Museum at Worcester, but his name is normally associated with fable subjects, such as those depicted on the Chinese teapot and stand shown in Plate 287, although some of the Worcester- and Chelsea-type exotic bird designs may have been by his hand.

While O'Neale's output of ceramic painting was probably small, that of James Giles and his employees was considerable. James Giles was born in 1718. In 1733 he was apprenticed to John Arthur, a jeweller of St Martins in the Fields. The City Westminster Poll list of voters in the November–December 1747 election includes the entry: James Gyles, chinaman at Berwick Street. In Mortimer's Directory of 1763 we find again James Giles at Berwick Street, Soho, but now described not as a dealer in china wares but as 'china and enamel painter'. I have already shown on p. 365 that James's elder brother had been bound to Philip Margas, china dealer, in 1729, and that he or his father was then a 'china painter'.

In 1763 James Giles claimed to copy 'patterns of any china with the utmost exactness, both with respect to the design and the colours, either in the European or Chinese taste…' But before this date James Giles had occupied premises at Kentish Town with a kiln for firing-on his enamel decoration and gilding. It has been suggested by Aubrey J. Toppin in the *Transactions of the English Ceramic Circle* (no. 1, 1933) that Giles had taken over the so-called Kentish Town China Manufactory run by William Kempson up to his bankruptcy in 1756, and continued it as a decorating establishment. It could also be that Giles had been employed by, and trained under, Kempson. James Giles himself went bankrupt in 1776 when some of his stock in trade was sold by Christie's (see *Transactions of the English Ceramic Circle*, vol. 6, part 3, 1967). Giles had acted as a retailer as well as a decorator; Christie's sale catalogue of March 1774 correctly describes James Giles as 'chinaman and enameller'. His account book shows sales of

287 A Chinese teapot, cover and stand painted in England with fable subjects in the manner of O'Neale (see p. 369). Teapot 7½ inches high, c. 1755–60. *Christies, London*

Chinese blue and white porcelain such as the 'Nankeen breakfast sett' sold in February 1774 for £2 5s. Giles died in 1780.

James Giles's painting can be found on many basic types of porcelain – English (mainly Worcester), Chinese and Continental – as well as on glass. The principal styles of decoration attributed to the Giles workshop are discussed by the late W. B. Honey in his Paper 'The Work of James Giles' published in the *Transactions of the English Ceramic Circle* (vol. 1, no. 5, 1937). They are here typified by the bird-painting, Plates 283 and 284, and the tea-bowl, Plate 280, top left. However, these pieces seem to be of the 1760–76 period, and the identification of any earlier Giles enamelling on Chinese porcelain presents great difficulties, especially as it was probably confined to the floral spray motifs so popular in the 1750s. Dr Bernard Watney has suggested that as early as 1754 Giles was decorating Chinese porcelain blanks as well as English porcelains with the type of floral decoration which he designates 'type B' in his Paper in the *Transactions of the English Ceramic Circle*, vol. 7, part 1, 1968. I have shown that the family association with china-painting can be dated back to the 1720s. He attributes the flower-painting on the 1756 dated bowl (Plate 281) to this class, and tentatively to Giles's hand. My Plate 282 falls into this classification, but it must be stated that these early specimens are different in style to the paintings normally attributed to Giles's workshop in the 1760s. Indeed, it is rare to find Giles-type painting on Chinese porcelain after about 1760, perhaps because he found the Worcester wares and glaze a more friendly 'canvas' and easier to re-fire in order to fix the added enamels and gilding. Worcester also provided blanks with scale-blue grounds not available from China.

There must have been several other craftsmen besides Giles engaged in decorating Chinese por-

European decorated Oriental porcelains

288 A Chinese porcelain creamer printed in England with the subject of a shepherd and sheep; the print has been washed over with semi-translucent enamels. 3¼ inches high, c. 1755.
Geoffrey Godden Chinaman

celains in the 1750–60 period. Dr Watney has suggested that the class represented by the vase shown in Plate 285 was, or could have been, painted by John Bolton of the Kentish Town manufactory which, as I have stated, was taken over by James Giles after 1756. John Bolton, an experienced hand, had earlier been employed by Messrs Crispe and Saunders at their Vauxhall China Manufactory but had been engaged by William Kempson to manage the new Kentish Town works in the 1755–6 period. Nothing is as yet known, however, of the products of these two concerns, apart from the basic facts recorded by Aubrey Toppin in the *Transactions of the English Ceramic Circle*, vol. 1, no. 1, 1933.

Another London decorator who may have painted Chinese blanks was Thomas Hughes of Pall Mall who sold Chelsea and Bow porcelains and other wares in the 1750s. Of great interest is the fact that Hughes had china painters bound to him as apprentices, showing that he was engaged in this trade. In April 1749 he had John Gabriel Jorney bound to him, and in October 1751 James Boushell was apprenticed to Thomas Hughes of St Pancras as a china painter. These details are gleaned from a Paper by the late Major W. H. Tapp published in the *Transactions of the English Ceramic Circle*, vol. 2, no. 6, 1939.

Mrs Elizabeth Adams has discovered an insurance policy relating to another London china painter who, like Giles, worked in Kentish Town. This policy was taken out in December 1767 by Robert Campman 'china painter'. His brick-built and tiled workshop was separate from his house and was then valued at £50. At present this 1767 policy is the only reference we have to this enameller who may well have continued Giles's trade, for at this period Giles was mainly concerned with dealing rather than with decorating.

In the early 1750s William Duesbury was practising the enamelling craft in London, decorating

English porcelains and saltglaze stonewares. He may have used Chinese porcelain blanks from time to time.

Decorators were probably also working in other centres. For example, we find Robinson & Rhodes issuing the following advertisement in the *Leeds Intelligencer* of 28 October 1760: 'Robinson and Rhodes, opposite the George in Briggate, enamel and burn in gold and colour foreign and English china and tea ware and make them complete to any pattern required – either Indian [meaning Chinese] or Dresden. They also enamel Coats of Arms etc., and sell a good assortment of foreign china…' In November 1764 David Rhodes wrote to Josiah Wedgwood: "I have burnt gold on china often and am certain I can do it on your ware…' and it is possible that some of his enamelling and gilding were on Chinese blanks. In 1770 Rhodes was in Chelsea advertising for enamellers to paint figure and floral subjects but he died in reduced circumstances in 1777.

Apart from the hand-enamelled English decoration to be found on Chinese porcelain, there is a further rare and surprising class, English transfer-printing. This appears to fall into two periods, some early prints of the 1750s and some later, more accomplished prints of the mid-1760s. The earlier prints include the 'Round Game', a design by Robert Hancock which occurs in an album in the British Museum with the wording 'according to Act 1754' as a form of copyright. This subject also occurs on Liverpool porcelain from William Ball's factory of the 1755–69 period, and on enamels which may be of Battersea or Birmingham make, as well as on Chinese porcelain blanks.

Another seemingly early print depicts a shepherd sitting under a tree. A Chinese porcelain saucer bearing the design is in the Franks collection in the British Museum. This example is washed over in green enamel, and in this respect is similar to Plate 286 and the two lower specimens in Plate 280. This print is here seen on a Chinese porcelain creamer formerly in my collection (Plate 288), and in this case the print has been washed over or coloured with various enamels. It is strange that the print has not yet been recorded on English porcelains – only on Chinese.

In July 1978 a hitherto unrecorded print on Chinese porcelain was featured on a plate sold at Messrs Phillips' auction rooms in London, a plate now in the Godden reference collection.

The basic Chinese plate bore only a simple narrow underglaze-blue edge, the whole inner area being embellished with a slip decoration in slight relief, similar to that on the dated 1756 bowl illustrated in Plate 281. Over the centre of this unlikely surface had been added in England a classical figure subject print after Gravelot; the subject being Venus preventing her son Aeneas from killing Helen. This print has also been recorded on an English salt-glaze plate in the Metropolitan Museum of Art, New York. The basic design and the New York plate are discussed in a paper by Dr Bernard Watney contained in the *Transactions of the English Ceramic Circle*, vol. 9, part 3, 1975.

Dr Watney suggested that the saltglaze plate and other related examples were possibly decorated at Birmingham perhaps by John Brooks who, as early as September 1751, had endeavoured to patent a method of printing on enamel and china. If, as now seems likely, some of these early prints on Chinese porcelain were added at Birmingham then it is possible that some of the more normal overglaze painting to be found on Chinese blanks were also added at that centre of the enamel trade. Future research on English enamels and English decorated Chinese porcelain of the 1750's may well show decorating similarities.

At least twelve examples of Chinese porcelain tea wares are recorded bearing versions of the well

European decorated Oriental porcelains

289 A Chinese porcelain tea-canister and cover printed in England with the 'Tea Party' print which occurs on Worcester porcelains. The two main prints are signed 'R Hancock' (see p. 374). 5½ inches high, c. 1760.
Geoffery Godden Chinaman, formerly Tuke collection

290 Part of a Chinese porcelain teaset of the late 1770s with a typical formal floral design, with replacement pieces made at the Worcester factory about 1775–80. (Coffee pot, teapot and saucer, top left, are Worcester.) Coffee pot 8¾ inches high. *Godden of Worthing Ltd*

known and popular 'tea-party' print. Some examples are coloured over while four are left in the plain, untinted state (Plate 289). The interesting point about these prints is that in most cases they bear the signature of the master engraver, Robert Hancock – 'R Hancock fecit', with in one case the date 1757, but without the place-name, Worcester, which often occurs on specimens made and decorated at the Worcester factory.

It appears that Hancock supplied copper-plates to someone who used them to decorate Chinese blanks. It has been suggested that this person was James Giles, who is thought to have coloured printed Worcester porcelains which he purchased in the uncoloured state. However, it has also been suggested that the Worcester factory may have been responsible for printing these Chinese porcelains – an idea which seems rather unlikely, but it is discussed in my Paper 'Chinese Porcelain, transfer-printed in England', published in the *Transactions of the English Ceramic Circle*, vol. 4, part 2, 1957.

In considering the sources of English decoration on Chinese porcelains we must not forget the enamel manufacturers and the decorators of these wares. Had they sought to expand their range of frail products into useful teawares they would have welcomed a supply of ready-made Chinese blanks. First, we must consider Alderman Janssen's Battersea Enamel Works. Cyril Cook, in a discussion arising from the Paper just referred to, stated that he had discovered some advertisements relating to the 1756 stock of the Battersea Works which suggested that it was a decorating establishment responsible for painting and/or printing all types of wares – enamels, earthenware tiles, salt-glaze plates and porcelains of various descriptions. Certainly when Dr Richard Pococke visited the Battersea Works in 1754 he used the description 'China and enamel manufactory'. It has, however, been suggested that the so-called Battersea Enamel Works were no more than a decorating establishment for wares made elsewhere (see 'New Light on Battersea Wares' by Cyril Cook in the *Antique Collector* of June 1953. This article reproduces newspaper advertisements relating to the auction sale of Alderman Janssen's 'entire stock' on 7, 8 and 9 June 1756).

Many enamellers of enamel blanks practised their craft in and around the city of Birmingham. These decorators, too, might well have sought out a supply of Chinese white porcelains to decorate with overglaze enamels, or to print. It is interesting to note that 'china painters' are mentioned in the following advertisements which appeared in *Aris's Birmingham Gazette*:

Abraham Seaman, enamel painter, at Mrs Weston's in Freeman St, Birmingham, makes and sells all sorts of enamelling colours, especially the ROSE colours, likewise all sorts for China Painters...

[23 September 1751]

Thomas Benton, agent for Mrs Seaman, who furnishes Enamel and China painters with fine rose colour... is removed from his house in High Street, Birmingham to Church Street, where all Enamel and China Painters may be furnished as usual, upon the lowest terms.

[2 April 1753]

These two advertisements were quoted by R. J. Charleston in a Paper (one of several linked contributions on Birmingham wares) published in the *Transactions of the English Ceramic Circle*, vol. 6, part 2, 1966.

Apart from the enamelling and printing of these white porcelain blanks several decorating establishments, and even English porcelain manufacturers, were engaged in adding gilt borders and other embellishments to Chinese porcelains painted in underglaze blue. I have already mentioned this practice in Chapter 4, and illustrated typical examples of English gilding in Plates 49–50, 53–58. This gilding of Chinese blue and white porcelains is mainly confined to the 1775–1800 period. Similar treatment was sometimes extended to Chinese enamelled porcelains, in particular the simpler floral designs where the London 'chinamen' sought to lift their own wares a little above the wares sold by their competitors, or where these dealers endeavoured to dress up or up-date stock that was proving difficult to sell.

Most English porcelain manufacturers were, from time to time, called upon to make replacements for Chinese porcelain services. Eighteenth-century Worcester porcelain replacements or additions to Chinese services are often to be found. One such Anglo-Chinese teaset of the 1775–85 period is shown in Plate 290. The teapot and coffee pot are Worcester, as is the saucer, top left, while the other pieces are Chinese hard-paste porcelain with the original Chinese enamelled decoration made expressly for the European market.

The story of Chinese export market porcelains and their influence on European wares is long and complex but at the same time, highly interesting. I hope that I have in this book exposed some of the long-standing myths and explained how these diverse Chinese and Japanese porcelains came to be imported into Europe and how they, by their excellence, spurred British manufacturers to seek and achieve a near-perfect porcelain body with a beauty and character of its own – a different but worthy offspring of its Oriental forebears.

In the summer of 1978 whilst on holiday in Devon we called at an attractive 17th century half-timber, thatched-roofed cottage for a traditional cream tea. The oak table was laid with a charming porcelain tea service decorated with an English rose design – entirely in keeping with the whole delightful old world village atmosphere. Out of habit I turned up an empty teacup, to find much to my surprise the printed legend 'Made in China'.

Today in the age of jet air travel the Oriental potters continue the tradition established in the age of sail – supplying the world's markets with fine porcelains made especially to suit various foreign tastes. Then, as now, the motive was commerce resulting in satisfaction alike for the Chinese potter and for the Western user.

Selected Bibliography

(English language books only)
including important magazine articles

Source material preserved at the India Office Records, London, being documents relating to the trade of the English East India Company in the seventeenth and eighteenth centuries

Home Miscellaneous Series. These lengthy records include the warehouse keepers' accounts of goods sold in the Company's auction sales from 1631, but there are many gaps.

Home Cash Ledgers. These include details of goods imported and their prime cost to the Company.

China Factory Records. Reports etc, relating to trade with China.

Letter-books Outwards. Copies of letters, orders etc, sent to the Company's overseas agents.

Minute Books. Records of the many meetings of the Court of Directors etc, of the East India Company containing orders and other interesting items of information on the trade at home and overseas.

Ship Logs. Logs relating to the voyages of vessels chartered to the East India Company.

General reference books, containing mainly background information

An Embassy sent by the East India Company of the United Provinces to the Grand Tartar-Cham Emperor of China – described by Jan Nieuhof (English version by John Ogilby, 1699)

A description of the Empire of China (English translation of 1735 French original). J. B. Du Halde. 2 vols. (Edward Cave, London, 1738–41)

A Voyage to China and the East Indies. Peter Osbeck. 2 vols. (B. White, London, 1771)

A General Description of China – translated from Abbé Grosier's French original (G. G. & J. Robinson, London, 1795)

An authentic account of an Embassy from the King of Great Britain to the Emperor of China. Sir George Staunton (G. Nicol, London, 1797)

Oriental Commerce. William Milburn (Black, Parry & Co., London, 1813)

Porcelain. Edward Dillon (Methuen, London, 1904)

Porcelain, a Sketch of its Nature, Art, and Manufacture. William Burton (Cassell, London, 1906)

A General History of Porcelain. William Burton (Cassell, London, 1921)

Description of Chinese Pottery and Porcelain, being a translation of the T'ao Shuo. Dr Stephen W. Bushell (Clarendon Press, Oxford, 1910)

Memoirs of William Hickey, ed. Alfred Spencer (Hurst & Blackett, London, 1913)

Transactions of the Oriental Ceramic Society (London 1921 onwards)

The East India Trade in the 17th century in its political and economic aspects. Shafaat Ahmed Khan (Oxford University Press, 1923)

The East India House, its history and associations. W. Foster (Bodley Head, London, 1924)

The Chater Collection – pictures relating to China, Hongkong, and Macao, 1655–1860. James Orange (Thornton Butterworth, London, 1924)

Handbook of the Pottery and Porcelain of the Far East in the British Museum. R. L. Hobson (London, 1st edition, 1924; last edition, 1948)

The Later Ceramic Wares of China. R. L. Hobson (Ernest Benn, London, 1925)

The Chronicles of the East India Company Trading to China, 1635–1834. Hosea Ballou Morse (Clarendon Press, Oxford. vols. 1–4, 1926; vol. 5, 1929)

Guide to the Later Chinese Porcelain. W. B. Honey (Victoria and Albert Museum, London, 1927)

The Book of Famille Rose. Dr G. C. Williamson (Methuen, London, 1927)

Transactions of the English Porcelain Circle (London, 1928–32)

Europe and China, a survey of their relations from the earliest times to 1800. G. F. Hudson (Edward

Selected Bibliography

Arnold, London, 1931; reprinted, 1961)
Transactions of the English Ceramic Circle (London, 1933 onwards)
Barlow's Journal of his life at sea in King's Ships, East and West Indiamen and other merchantmen from 1659 to 1703. Transcribed by Basil Lubbock (Hurst & Blackett, London, 1934)
Trade in the Eastern Seas 1793–1813. C. Northcote Parkinson (Cambridge University Press, 1937)
The Ceramic Art of China and other Countries of the Far East. W. B. Honey (Faber, London, 1945)
Later Chinese Porcelain. R. Soame Jenyns (Faber, London, 1951; fourth edition, 1971)
Ching-tê Chên – The Potteries of China. Translation and introduction Geoffrey R. Sayer (Routledge & Kegan Paul, London, 1951)
Two Thousand Years of Oriental Ceramics. Fujio Koyama and John Figgess (Abrams, New York, 1961)
Chinese Porcelain. Anthony Du Boulay (Weidenfeld & Nicolson, London, 1963)
A Short History of Chinese Art. Michael Sullivan (Faber, London, 1967)
Ming Porcelains, their Origins and Development. Adrian M. Joseph (Bibelot Publishers, London, 1971)
The China Trade – export paintings, furniture, silks and other objects (not porcelains). Carl L. Crossman (Pyne Press, Princeton, 1972)
The Ceramic Art of China – 1971 exhibition catalogue (Oriental Ceramic Society, London, 1972)
The Arts of China. Michael Sullivan (Thames & Hudson, London, 1973)
Chinese Ceramics. Michel and Cécile Beurdeley (English translation, Thames & Hudson, London, 1974)
Chinese Ceramics. W. B. E. Neave-Hill (J. Bartholomew & Son, Edinburgh and London, 1975)
The Chinese Potter, a Practical History of Chinese Ceramics. Margaret Medley (Phaidon Press, Oxford, 1976)
'The Dutch at the Tea-Table', article by T. H. Lunsingh Scheurleer published in *The Connoisseur*, October 1976

Export Market Wares

Oriental Commerce. William Milburn (Black, Parry & Co., London, 1813)
Letters received by the East India Company from its servants in the East. 7 vols. F. C. Danvers and W. Foster (Sampson, Low, Marston & Co., London, 1896–1904)
The Chronicles of the East India Company Trading to China 1635–1834. Hosea Ballou Morse (Clarendon Press, Oxford, vols. 1–4, 1926; vol. 5, 1929)
'Lowestoft: What is it? – centres of manufacture and classification', article by Homer E. Keyes, published in *Antiques* (New York), November 1928, pp. 422–6
'Lowestoft: What is it? (Genre Designs)', article by Homer E. Keyes, published in *Antiques* (New York), June 1929, pp. 487–92
Europe and China – a survey of their relations from the earliest times to 1800. G. F. Hudson (Edward Arnold, London, 1931; reprinted, 1961)
Oriental Lowestoft. J. A. Lloyd Hyde. (Scribner's, New York, 1936. Reprinted with additional illustrations by The Ceramic Book Co., Newport, Mon., 1954)
Chinese Export Art in the Eighteenth Century. Margaret Jourdain and R. Soame Jenyns (Country Life, London, 1950; American edition Scribner's, New York, 1950)
Porcelain and the Dutch East India Company, 1602–1682. T. Volker (Rijksmuseum voor Volkenkunde, Leiden, 1954)
China Trade Porcelain. John Goldsmith Phillips (Harvard University Press, 1956)

Chinese Porcelain for the European Market. J. A. Lloyd Hyde, R. E. S. Silva and E. Malta (Editions R. E. S., Lisbon, 1956)
'Western Ceramic Models for China-Trade porcelain', article by John Goldsmith Phillips published in *Antiques* (New York), November 1956, pp. 465–7
Porcelain of the East India Companies. Michel Beurdeley (English translation, Barrie & Rockliff, London, 1962)
'Fitzhugh and Fitzhughs in the China Trade', article by J. B. S. Holmes, published in *Antiques* (New York), January 1966, pp. 130–31
'Oriental porcelain frivolities (figure and animal models)', article by Pamela C. Copeland published in *Antiques* (New York), May 1966, pp. 709–16
'The Dutch China-cabinet – an exhibition at the Groningen Museum (Holland)', article by Elka Schrijver, published in *The Connoisseur*, May 1969, pp. 6–13
The Reeves Collection of Chinese Export Porcelain at Washington and Lee University, Lexington, Virginia. Catalogue by Callie Huger Efird and Katherine Gross Farnham (Washington and Lee University, Lexington, 1973)
Chinese Export Porcelain – Chine de Commande. D. F. Lunsingh Scheurleer (English translation, Faber, London, 1974)
China Trade Porcelain: Patterns of Exchange. Clare Le Corbeiller (Metropolitan Museum of Art, New York, 1974)
Chinese Ceramics. Michel and Cécile Beurdeley (English translation, Thames & Hudson, London, 1974)
'Crosscurrents in China Trade porcelain', article by Clare Le Corbeiller published in *Antiques* (New York), January 1974
Chinese Export Porcelain – standard patterns and forms 1780 to 1880. Herbert, Peter and Nancy Schiffer (Schiffer Publishing, Exton, 1975)
'The Prize of Captain Hyde Parker', article by David Howard in *The National Trust Year Book 1975–1976*, pp. 103–108
Collecting Chinese Export Porcelain. Elinor Gordon (Main Street Press, New York, 1977)
'The Portuguese Porcelain Trade with China', article by Jorge Graça published in *Arts of Asia* (Hong Kong), Nov.–Dec. 1977
'Chinese Ceramics Carried by the Dutch East India Company' article by Effie B. Allison published in *Arts of Asia* (Hong Kong) Nov.–Dec. 1977
Chinese Porcelain of the 19th and 20th Centuries. H. A. Van Oort (Lochem, 1977)
China for the West. David Howard and John Ayers (Sotheby Parke Bernet, London & New York, 1978)

Blue and white
Oriental Blue and White. Sir Harry Garner (Faber, London, 1954; third edition, 1970)
'The use of imported and native Cobalt in Chinese Blue and White', article by Sir Harry Garner, published in *Oriental Art* (London), summer 1956, pp. 48–50
Chinese Blue and White. Ann Frank (Studio Vista, London, 1970)
Ming Porcelains, their Origins and Development. Adrian M. Joseph (Bibelot Publishers, London, 1971)
'The Craze for Blue and White', article by Gerald Reitlinger, published in *The Connoisseur*, July 1975, pp. 216–21
'Some Unmarked Blue and White Porcelain of the Fifteenth century', article by Adrian M. Joseph, published in *The Connoisseur*, July 1975, pp. 192–197
'The Canton pattern (the later scenic designs made mainly for the American market)', article by

Selected Bibliography

Hiram Tindall published in *Antiques* (New York), August 1975, pp. 226–33

Armorial porcelains
Armorial China – a catalogue of Chinese porcelain with coats of arms. Frederick Arthur Crisp (Privately printed, 1907)
Armorial Porcelain of the Eighteenth Century. Sir Algernon Tudor-Craig (Century House, London, 1925)
'Chinese Armorial Porcelain for the British Market', article by W. Cyril Wallis, published in *Apollo* (London), April 1952, pp. 114–16
'Armorial Porcelain from China', article by James Tudor-Craig, published in *Country Life Annual*, 1967, pp. 16–21
Chinese Armorial Porcelain. David Sanctuary Howard (Faber, London, 1974)

Blanc de Chine
Blanc de Chine. P. J. Donnelly (Faber, London, 1969)

American market wares
'America's East Indiamen and the China Trade', article by Frances Little, published in *Antiques* (New York), January 1929, pp. 27–31
The Arts and Crafts in Philadelphia, Maryland and South Carolina 1721–1785. Alfred Coxe Prime (Walpole Society, 1929)
Oriental Lowestoft. J. A. Lloyd Hyde (Scribner's, New York, 1936. Reprinted with additional illustrations by The Ceramic Book Co., Newport, Mon., 1954)
American Ships in the China Trade (Catalogue of loan exhibition). Bulletin of the Art Division, Los Angeles County Museum, winter 1955.
China Trade Porcelain. John Goldsmith Phillips (Harvard University Press, 1956)
Chinese Export Porcelain for the American Trade 1785–1835. Jean McClure Mudge (University of Delaware Press, 1962)
A Design Catalog of Chinese Export Porcelain for the American Market. Carl L. Crossman (Peabody Museum, Salem, 1964)
'Fitzhugh and Fitzhughs in the China Trade', article by J. B. S. Holmes, published in *Antiques* (New York), January 1966, pp. 130–31
'The Rose Medallion and Mandarin Patterns in China Trade Porcelain', article by Carl L. Crossman published in *Antiques* (New York), October 1967, pp. 530–35
China Trade Porcelain (exhibition catalogue) published by the New Haven Colony Historical Society (New Haven, Connecticut, 1968)
The Reeves Collection of Chinese Export Porcelain at Washington and Lee University, Lexington, Virginia. Catalogue by Callie Huger Efird and Katherine Gross Farnham (Washington and Lee University, Lexington, 1973)
China Trade Porcelain: Patterns of Exchange. Clare Le Corbeiller (Metropolitan Museum of Art, New York, 1974)
'The Canton pattern (the later scenic designs made mainly for the American market)', article by Hiram Tindall published in *Antiques* (New York), August 1975, pp. 226–33.
Chinese Export Porcelain – standard patterns and forms 1780 to 1880. Herbert, Peter and Nancy Schiffer (Schiffer Publishing, Exton, 1975)
China for the West. David Howard and John Ayers (Sotheby Parke Bernet, London & New York, 1978)

Japanese Porcelains
Diary of Richard Cocks, Cape-merchant in the English Factory in Japan 1615–1622, ed. Edward Maunde Thompson. vols. 1 and 2. (Hakluyt Society, London, 1883)
The Voyage of Captain John Saris to Japan 1613,

ed. Sir Ernest M. Satow. (Hakluyt Society, London, 1900)
The Ceramic Art of Japan. Tadanari Mitsuoka (Japan Travel Bureau, Tokyo, 1949)
Porcelain and the Dutch East India Company 1602–1682. T. Volker (Rijksmuseum voor Volkenkunde, Leiden, 1954)
The Japanese Porcelain Trade of the Dutch East India Company after 1683. T. Volker (Rijksmuseum voor Volkenkunde, Leiden, 1959)
Japanese Ceramics. R. A. Miller (Charles E. Tuttle, Rutland and Tokyo, 1960)
Japanese Ceramics from Ancient to Modern Times. Fujio Koyama (Oakland Museum, California, 1961; Paragon, New York, 1961)
'Japanese Export Porcelain', article by R. G. Gerry, published in *Antiques* (New York), June 1961, pp. 548–51
The Ceramic Art of Japan. Hugo Munsterberg (Charles E. Tuttle, Vermont and Tokyo, 1964)
Japanese Porcelain. R. Soame Jenyns (Faber, London, 1965)
Two Hundred Years of Japanese Porcelain. R. S. Cleveland (City Art Museum of St Louis, 1970)
'Japanese Porcelains in American and Canadian Collections', article by Richard S. Cleveland, published in *Antiques* (New York), December 1970, pp. 927–31
Japanese Pottery. R. Soame Jenyns (Faber, London, 1971)
The Heritage of Japanese Ceramics. Fujio Koyama, translated by John Figgess (Weatherhill, New York, 1973)
Japanese Ceramics of the Last 100 Years. Irene Stitt (New York, 1974)
'An Import for Exotic Tastes – Japanese porcelain in England', article by Hiroko Nishida, published in *Country Life* 6 June 1974, pp. 1402–6
'The Charm of Japanese Trade porcelain', article by John Figgess, published in *Arts of Asia*, March–April 1975, pp. 17–25
Blue and White, Early Japanese Export Ware. M. Lerner (Metropolitan Museum of Art, New York, 1978)

British wares
Transactions of the English Ceramic Circle (London, 1933 onwards)
Old English Porcelain. W. B. Honey (Faber, London, revised ed. 1977)
English Blue and White Porcelain of the 18th century. Dr B. Watney (Faber, London, 1963; revised edition, 1973)
British Porcelain 1745–1850, ed. R. J. Charleston (Ernest Benn, London, 1965)
Caughley and Worcester Porcelains 1775–1800. Geoffrey A. Godden (Herbert Jenkins, London, 1969)
The Illustrated Guide to Lowestoft Porcelain. Geoffrey A. Godden (Herbert Jenkins, London, 1969)
The Illustrated Guide to Worcester Porcelain. H. Sandon (Barrie & Jenkins, London, 1969; revised edition, 1975)
The Illustrated Guide to Mason's Patent Ironstone China. Geoffrey A. Godden (Barrie & Jenkins, London, 1971)
New Hall and its Imitators. D. Holgate (Faber, London, 1971)
British Porcelain. Geoffrey A. Godden (Barrie & Jenkins, London, 1974)
Godden's Guide to English Porcelain. Geoffrey A. Godden (Granada Publishing, London, 1978)

Index

Adams, Mrs E.   371
Adams, W.   302
Albemarle, Earl of   307
Allot, R.   19
American Eagle motif   *Pls. 209–211, 215–216*; 50, 294
American Flag motif   *Pls. 206–208*; 293
American market   *Pls. 206–220*; 50, 281–300
American War of Independence   *Pl. 215*; 283–6
Amoy   22, 23, 24, 25, 28–30, 33, 38, 258, 270–71, 276, 280, 307, 321
Anchor mark   346
Anglo–Japanese trade   21, 22, 302–307
Animal models   *Pls. 169–82, 189, 240*; 249, 254, 256, 262, 267–8, 274
Aniseed   65
Antiques Magazine   287, 300
Arita   *Pls. 228–9*; 309, 311, 335
Armorial services   *Frontispiece, Col. Pl. 12; Pls. 20, 112–34*; 16, 17, 76, 116, 117, 195–218
    Bewicke   *Pl. 2*; 17
    Champion, S.   208
    Duke of York   208
    Eastabrook   *Pl. 115*; 210–211
    Johnson   *Pl. 20*; 116, 119
    Lee   *Frontispiece, Pls. 1a & b*; 16–17
    Okeover   *Pl. 114*; 203–206
    Peers   *Pls. 10, 112–113*; 82–4, 195–203
Arnold & Co   340
Arnold, G.   340
Art Journal Magazine   332
Arts of Asia Magazine   30, 311
Atlantic   288
Auction sale conditions   27
Auction sale records   *Pls. 9, 230, 232*; 26, 27, 61, 62, 66–8, 70, 74, 119, 120, 124, 168, 172, 186, 214, 249, 254, 259, 260, 263, 264, 266–9, 273, 274, 275, 276, 277, 278, 279, 315–318, 319, 320, 321, 322–3, 325, 326, 327, 328, 329
Auction sales – general   42, 48, 59, 60, 66
Augustus the Strong   258
Awata   333

Bagshaw, J.   43
Ball, W.   372
Ballast   38, 102
Bankshall   96, 105
Bantam   21–4, 304–306
Barber's basons   *Pl. 225*; 320, 321
Barlow, E.   41, 64, 308
Batavia   21, 23, 35, 53, 94, 178, 302, 306, 307, 321, 326
Batavia – ware   *Pl. 81*; 175–6
Battersea   372, 374

Battie, D.   335
Baxter, T.   149
Bäyreith   *Pl. 279*; 365
Bedford, Duke of   308
Beloe, W.   53
Bencoolen   91, 92, 94
Benton, T.   374
Beurdeley, M.   103
Bianco sopra bianco   368
Binns, R. W.   332
Bird models   *Pls. 175–82*; 267, 269, 275
Birmingham   372, 374
Blackwall   89, 92
Blanc de Chine (type)   *Col. Pl. 16, Pls. 183–205, 254–6*; 16, 29, 62, 67, 257–80, 346
Blanc de Chine – painted   *Pls. 193, 195*; 260, 267, 270–71, 277, 278, 279
Blue & white   *Col. Pls. 3, 13, 14, Pls. 3, 8, 10, 17–73, 135, 212, 217, 221, 223, 224, 228, 229, 235, 238, 246–9, 257–8, 264–5, 268–9, 274, 278*; 111–64
Bolton, J.   371
Bone-ash body   346, 352
Book-plates   *Pl. 120*; 205, 213
Boston Tea-Party   283–6
Boushell, J.   371
Bow   *Pls. 247–51*; 340
Brass figures   264
Breakfast services   *Pl. 95*; 138
Bristol   *Pls. 246, 256, 257*; 339, 346, 353
'British Nankin'   360
Bromefield, T.   19
Brooks, J.   372
Brown-line edging   *Pl. 224*; 135, 138, 309, 342
Burton, W.   112, 334
Bushell, Dr S. W.   116

C-mark   355
Campman, R.   371
Candlestick   *Pl. 24*; 124
Canton   11, 16, 21, 28, 33–8, 41, 96–109, 217, 280, 292–3, 308, 313
Canton type designs   *Col. Pls. 9–10, Pls. 73, 109–111, 217, 218–20*; 164, 191, 203, 296, 298
Cape of Good Hope   94
Carrack   *Pl. 3*; 19, 304
Casters   *Pl. 28*; 125
Catchpole, A.   30–31, 307
Caughley   *Pls. 45, 67, 269*; 12, 116, 143, 148, 160, 354–5
Chamber pots   127
Chamberlain-Worcester   *Pls. 272–3*; 153, 357
Chamberlain, R.   357
Champion, R.   353
Chantilly porcelain   158

Charleston, R. J.   374
Chelsea   *Pls. 252–5*; 340
Chests of China-ware   103
Chicken-skin effect   *Pl. 38*; 142
China Council   75
China-ware   11, 27, 28, 32, 35, 314–315
China-ware orders   43–4, 47–8
'Chinaman'   53, 66, 79, 86, 128, 131, 217
Chinese Emperors – periods   53
'Chinese Lowestoft'   11, 352
Ching-tê-Chên   16, 103, 111, 112, 292
Chocolate (cups)   *Pls. 64, 66*; 119, 120, 160, 168
Christie, Mr   78, 210, 330–31, 369
Chusan   28, 30–33, 40, 62, 280
Cider-jugs   161
Coalport   *Pl. 274*; 357
Cobalt, oxide of   111
Cocks, R.   302, 304
Coffee cups   *Col. Pl. 15, Pl. 78*; 122, 175
Cole, H.   331
Committee of Private Trade   70
Cook, C.   374
Cookworthy, W.   353
Coombes   *Pl. 88*; 182
Copeland & Garrett   359
'Country' vessels   23, 28, 29, 30, 34, 35, 47, 56, 81, 84, 287
Crackle-ware   168
Crew lists   92
Crispe & Saunders   371
Cuiqua   208
Custard cups   *Pl. 67*; 122, 160

Delaware   288
d'Entrecolles   112, 113, 165, 221, 224
Derby   *Pls. 258, 259*; 309, 346, 348
Devis   *Pl. 114*; 205
Diamonds   59, 60
Dillon, E.   112
Dinner services   *Pls. 32, 83, 85, 86–7*; 128, 133, 143–4, 148, 160, 210, 288
Dishes   *Pls. 29, 30, 43–5, 48, 60, 65*
Donnelly, P. J.   257, 269, 270, 271, 272, 273, 275, 276, 277
Drawback   49
Du Halde   112, 261
Duesbury, W.   149, 153, 371
Duff, Governor   269, 270
Duivver, D.   270
Dunnage *see* Palleting
Dutch decoration   329, 365
Dutch East India Company   *Col. Pl. 2*; 19, 50, 56, 178, 214, 270, 281, 301, 306, 327

'Dutch family' groups *Pls. 192–3*; 266–7, 269–71, 276
Dutch trade 19–20, 23, 50–51, 305–306

Earl of Elgin 108
East India Company's charges 64, 69
East India Company's vessels *Pl. 14*; 11, 16, 26, 41, 89–94, 98
  Advice 22, 302
  Alfred 208
  Amoy Merchant 307
  Anson 78
  Armenian Merchant 59, 64
  Aurengzeb 319, 330
  Beaufort 26, 56
  Benjamin 59
  Bull 304
  Caesar 23
  Canton Merchant 82, 201
  Carnavon 41, 326
  Carolina 25
  Chamber 277, 320
  China Merchant 28
  Clove 21, 55
  Cruttenden 78, 91
  Dashwood 66, 68, 120, 264, 266–7, 268, 271, 272, 273, 315, 323
  Dorothy 26, 28, 168, 259, 314
  Dorrill 65, 82, 185, 263, 315
  Duke of Richmond 108
  Eagle 307
  Earl of Elgin *Pl. 14*; 89–109
  Earl of Holderness 32, 91
  Earl of Sandwich 134
  Eaton 30
  Fleet *Pl. 230*; 60, 64, 122, 165, 274, 276, 316, 317, 318, 322, 325, 328
  Formosa 22, 23
  Griffin 32
  Grosvenor 46
  Hampshire 273
  Harcourt 78
  Hardwicke 30
  Harrison 197, 208
  Herne 277
  Hester 72, 313
  Houghton 29, 30
  James 21
  Katherine 326
  Kent *Pl. 232*; 65, 70, 308, 320–21
  Latham *Pls. 160–61*; 248
  Liampo 31, 69
  London 57, 165, 210
  Loyal Bliss 71, 165, 279, 313, 325, 326
  Loyal Cooke 279, 325
  Loyal Merchant 82
  Lyall 103
  Macclesfield 30, 33–4, 35–41, 42, 56, 113, 168, 221
  Monmouth 105
  Montague 29, 32, 74, 278, 279
  Nassau 42, 61–2, 249, 259, 315
  Neptune 40, 106, 280
  Northumberland 32, 66, 316
  Oley 26, 69
  Onslow 205
  Osterly 185–6
  Pitt 77
  Plassey 97, 100
  Ponsborne 287
  Prince George 127
  Princess of Denmark 59
  Princess Royal 98, 157
  Rainbow 77
  Regard 276–7
  Return 21, 23
  Rochester 27, 32, 98, 119, 259
  Rooke 30
  Royal James 25
  Sarah 31, 59, 60, 168
  Seaford 35
  Sidney 32, 70, 277, 322
  Somers 277, 329
  Stretham 32
  Stringer 27, 43, 69
  Tavestock 277, 320
  Toddington 277, 321
  Townsend 363
  Trumball 30, 31, 40, 61, 185, 315
  Tywan 23
  Union 53, 258, 276, 319, 328
  Wentworth 82, 165, 172, 263
East India House 90
Egan, R. 160
'Egg-shell' porcelain *Col. Pl. 1*; 17
Elers Brothers 38, 339
Emoy *see* Amoy
Empress of China 281, 282, 286–7, 294
English decoration *Col. Pl. 20, Pls. 279–90*; 363–375
English enamels 374
English gilding *Pls. 49, 50, 53–9*; 148–9, 157, 374–5
English Trading companies 19
Exchin 43, 47, 49, 80, 134, 286
Exports to China/Japan 22, 31, 34, 40, 42, 61, 91, 302–304

Factor 16

Factories *see* Hongs
Famille Rose *Col. Pl. 5, Pls. 78–80, 82–4, 99, 116, 117, 166*; 168, 172, 175, 185, 211
Famille Verte *Col. Pl. 4, Pls. 76, 77, 96, 97, 124, 125, 162, 163, 165*; 168, 172, 183, 218, 249
Fans 38, 41, 43
Figures – groups *Col. Pl. 16, Pls. 162–7, 183–8, 192–200, 202, 203, 239*; 61–2, 248–56, 257–80, 329
Firando *see* Hirado
Firing temperature 115
Fitzhugh designs *Pls. 47, 211, 212*; 144, 217, 218, 292, 295–6
Flasks *Pl. 233*; 311, 325, 329
Flint 91, 93, 100, 102
Flooring of chinaware 102
Flower-pot design *Pl. 225*; 309, 325
Fogg, R. 149
Footia 128
Footrim form *Pl. 18*; 114
'Foreign colours' 175, 185
Formosa 21, 23, 24, 306
Fort St George 24, 25, 26, 56, 81
French East India Company trade *Pls. 8, 21*; 34, 36, 53, 127, 327
French Island 96, 102
Fuller, B. 292
Fungmante 203

Gallipots 302, 304, 339
Garner, Sir H. 113
General Hamilton 288
George III 283
Gilder's marks *Pl. 59*; 157
Gilding 197
Giles, A. 365
Giles, J. *Pls. 283–4*; 365, 368, 369–71, 374
Glass wares 34, 40, 91
Grand Turk *Pl. 208*; 288, 293
Guglet *Pl. 68*; 161

Halifax 284
Hancock, R. *Pl. 289*; 372, 374
Hannah 282
Hard-paste porcelain *Pl. 19*; 11, 115, 346
Harris 288
Hausmalerei *Pl. 279*; 365
Hickey, W. 101, 103
Hillier, B. 157
Hirado 21, 301, 304
Honey, W. B. 115, 370
Hongs *Pl. 16*; 41, 100–102
Honourable East India Company 19
Hot-water dishes/plates *Pl. 47*; 144

Howard, D.   195, 200, 205, 208, 211, 217
Hughes, T.   371
Hunting horn mark   *Pl. 60*; 158
Hunting subjects   *Pls. 156–9*

'Imaged'   78, 183
Images *see* 'Figures–groups'
Imari-style   *Col. Pls. 17, 18, Pls. 77, 123, 231, 234, 244*; 172, 218, 309, 335
Imports discontinued   48–9
'India China'   11, 84
India Office Records   33, 89, 376
Indian imports   81–4
Indulgencies   57–9, 77
Inglaze   111
Initialled designs   *Col. Pl. 11, Pls. 117, 118, 119, 121, 122, 129, 131, 132, 134*; 211–217
International aspect of trade   50, 98

Jacquemart   168
Jakarta *see* Batavia
James II   24
Janssen   374
'Japan earthenware'   314
'Japan ware'   *Pl. 230*; 314–15
Japanese periods   312–13
Japanese-style   *Pls. 259, 263, 327, 330, 348, 359*
Japanese wares/trade   *Col. Pls. 17–19, Pls. 221–244*; 28, 29, 41, 55, 66, 69, 72, 301–338
Jenyns, S.   112, 301, 311, 315, 331, 332–3
Jerusalem Coffee House   205
Jesuits   34, 112, 175, 221–4
Jesuit-style   *Pls. 135, 136, 137, 138, 139–43, 261*; 221, 351
John Jay   288
Jorney, J. G.   371

Kaga ware   *Pl. 242*
Kakiemon-style   *Pls. 226, 227, 250, 251, 252*; 310–311, 329, 330, 342
K'ang Hsi   41, 53
Kearny, R.   282
Kempson, W.   369, 371
Kensington House/Palace   307
Kentish Town   369
Kentledge   35, 69
Kingqua   208
Kioto   333
Knife-handles   125, 138
Ko Kutani   311
Koro ware   *Pl. 241*
Kraak   *Pl. 3*; 19

Kuan-yin   *Col. Pl. 16, Pls. 183–8, 254*; 261–3, 277, 346, 348

Lacquer ware   23, 26, 28, 40, 41, 60, 302
Leanqua   308
Libation cups   279, 280
Liberty & Co   *Pls. 71, 72, 182, 241–2, 244*; 164, 309
Limpoo *see* 'Chusan'
Linqua   133
Liverpool   *Pl. 264*; 352
London East India Company   19
Longton Hall   348
Lord Dartmouth   284, 286
Lord North   283, 286
Lowestoft   *Pls. 90, 265–7*; 11, 183, 352
Luckcock (Lucock)   360
Lund, B.   346
Luzon *see* 'Chusan'
Lygo, J.   48, 153, 160, 208

Macao   21, 34, 95, 301
'Made in China'   191, 300
Madras *see* 'Fort St George'
Mandarin-style   *Pls. 101, 105, 219, 220*; 191, 298
Margas, C.   365
Margas & Co   365
Margas, P.   365
Margas, W.   365
Mason, M.   *Pls. 277, 278*; 49, 360–62
Mason's Patent Ironstone China   362
Masonic bowls   *Pl. 155*; 293
Medley, M.   116
Meissen-style   *Pls. 145, 146*; 237, 330, 365
Meissen swords mark   354
Milk jugs   120, 277, 326
Miller, W.   346
Ming porcelains   22
Musters   46

Nabeshima   311
Nankin   11, 30
Nankin stone china   288
Nankin (Nankeen) type wares   129–31, 282, 288, 296, 360
Neptune   292
'New Canton'   340
New Company   19, 27, 30, 32, 33, 307
New Hall porcelains   *Pls. 270, 271*; 355–6
New York   281
New York arms   *Pl. 213*; 50

Okeover   *Pl. 114*; 203–206
Old Company   19, 31
'Old Japan' style   351
O'Neale, J. H.   *Pl. 287*; 368–9
Ouchterlony, R.   *Pl. 120*; 16

Painter's numbers   342
Pallas   287
Palleting   59, 79
Pattern plates   *Pl. 121*; 217
Patty-pans   *Pl. 26*; 124–5
Peers, C.   82–4, 197–203
Pencilling   *Pls. 135–43*; 221, 227, 234
Pepper   94
Permission money   57, 59, 73, 74, 75, 77
Perry, M.   331
Persian-market wares   *Col. Pl. 10*; 22, 23, 53, 191
Phillcox, R.   *Pl. 119*; 213
Phillips, H.   214
Phoebe   282
Pigou   288
Plates   *Col. Pls. 3, 8, 11, 12, 14, Pls. 10, 18, 40, 41, 58, 77, 91, 112, 114, 123–7, 133, 138, 140, 142, 144, 222, 224, 238, 246, 247, 273*; 114–115, 122, 128–9, 142
Platters *see* Dishes
Plymouth   *Pl. 268*; 353
Pococke, Dr R.   374
Portuguese trade   19, 21, 34, 301, 304
Powder-blue decoration   *Pls. 39, 247*; 142, 340, 355
Presents   61, 65, 86
Prints on Chinese porcelain   *Pl. 288*; 372–4
'Private Trade' imports   19, 25, 31, 48, 55–88, 96, 103, 104, 106, 108, 195
'Private Trade' markings   *Pl. 9*; 65, 70
Profit margin   261
Pulpit models   *Pl. 197*; 272
Punch bowls   *Pls. 12, 13, 14, 16, 39, 69, 82, 84, 92–94, 102, 150–61, 208, 217*; 244, 248

Queen Mary's Collection   257–8, 259, 307

Red Wares   *Pl. 5*; 38, 339
Redgrave pattern   *Pl. 266*; 353
Rhineland stonewares   302
Rhodes, D.   372
Robinson & Rhodes   372
Rolwagen *see* 'Rouleau'
Rose, J.   357
Rose Medallion style   *Col. Pl. 9, Pls. 110, 218–20*; 191, 298

Rouleau, vase form 67, 328
Rowl waggon *see* 'Rouleau'

'S' mark *Pl. 269*; 355
Sago 36, 38, 134
Salad bowls *Pls. 61, 73*
Salopian porcelain 354–5
Salts (condiments) *Pl. 46*; 143
Sample 'images' 280
Sampson 288
San Agustin 281
'Sancta Marias' 260–63, 278
Saris, J. 302, 304, 339
Satsuma (type) *Col. Pl. 19, Pls. 241, 245*; 333–4
Seal-marks *Pl. 223*; 218, 308
Seaman, A. 374
Shaw, S. 294–5
Shaw, W. *Pl. 92*; 182–3
Shell-shape dishes *Pl. 27*; 125
Shinqua 293
Shipping subjects *Pls. 12, 14, 153, 160, 161*; 77, 84, 89
Ship's measure 97
Silk 27, 31
Smalts 91
Smuggled goods 71, 76, 78–9, 104
Sneaker 125
Soapstone porcelain 115–116, 350
Society of Cincinnati 287, 294–5
Soft-paste porcelains 115–116, 346
South Sea trade 31, 35
Southwark(e) 302, 339
Spanish trade in Japan 304
Spode, J. *Pls. 275–6*; 182, 359

Spoon-trays (boats) *Pl. 261*; 119, 124
St Helena 104, 105
Stansbury, J. 282
Steatitic porcelain 115–116
Stilt (Spur) marks *Pl. 222*; 308
Stonewares 302, 339
Supra-cargo (Super-cargo) 16–17
Suqua 127
Surat 23, 24, 25, 82
Swedish trade 47, 53, 95
Synchong *Pls. 121, 122, 132*; 49, 286

Table services *see* 'Dinner services'
Tax on porcelains 42, 48, 50, 80–81, 205, 315
Tê-hua 16, 258
Tea 24, 25, 26, 27, 28, 96, 104, 105, 283–6, 302
Tea, packing of 28
Tea canisters (vases) *Pls. 137, 139, 289*; 124
Tea party print *Pl. 289*; 374
Tea wares *Pls. 4, 25, 31, 49, 50, 55, 185*; 36, 60, 119, 131, 148, 149, 186
Teapots *Col. Pls. 2, 7; Pls. 5, 23, 51–4, 70, 75, 79–81, 88, 96, 101, 146, 149, 236, 248*; 27, 28, 38, 119–120, 168, 279
Teapot stands *Pl. 74*; 168
Tin-glazed earthenwares 302, 304, 305, 339
Tobacco-leaf design *Pls. 84, 85*; 178
Tombes (Toombes) 66, 68, 84, 308
Tonquin 23
Toppin, A. J. 369, 371
Townsend Act 283
Treaty of Paris 286
Tureens *Pls. 7, 34, 35, 42, 83, 85, 86, 87, 115, 132*; 134, 142–3

Turner, T. 354
Turner, Abbott & Newbury 153, 157, 160
Tutenage 28, 32
Tywan *see* 'Formosa'

Underglaze blue *see* 'Blue & White'
United Company of Merchants of England 19

Vases *Col. Pls. 9, 17, 18, Pls. 22, 36, 37, 38, 71, 72, 97, 98, 99, 103, 104, 109, 111, 218, 220, 231, 241, 242, 244, 255, 285*; 142, 185
Vauxhall 371
Vereenigde Oostindische Compagnie *see* 'Dutch East India Company'
Victualling list 92–3, 105
VOC *see* 'Dutch East India Company'
Voider 125
Volker, Dr T. 23, 82, 306, 307

Watney, Dr B. 370–71, 372
Whampoa *Pls. 1b, 15*; 17, 35, 41, 95–6, 100, 102
Wilhelm, C. 302, 339
Wilkes, J. *Pl. 149*; 237
William Howell 288
Williams, T. 348
Willow pattern 339
Wolfe, T. (& Co) 360
Wooden patterns 43
Worcester porcelains *Pls. 61, 260–63, 290*; 155, 158, 160, 350, 374, 375

Yi-hsing wares *Pl. 5*; 38.